This Present Triumph

WEST Theological Monograph Series

Wales Evangelical School of Theology (WEST) has produced a stream of successful PhD candidates over the years, whose work has consistently challenged the boundaries of traditional understanding in both systematic and biblical theology. Now, for the first time, this series makes significant examples of this ground-breaking research accessible to a wider readership.

This Present Triumph

An Investigation into the Significance of the Promise of a New Exodus of Israel in the Letter to the Ephesians

Richard. M. Cozart

WIPF & STOCK · Eugene, Oregon

THIS PRESENT TRIUMPH
An Investigation into the Significance of the Promise of a New Exodus of Israel in the Letter to the Ephesians

Copyright © 2013 Richard M. Cozart. All rights reserved. Except for brief quotations in critical publications or reviews, no part of this book may be reproduced in any manner without prior written permission from the publisher. Write: Permissions. Wipf and Stock Publishers, 199 W. 8th Ave., Suite 3, Eugene, OR 97401.

Unless otherwise indicated, Scripture quotations are from the New Revised Standard Version of the Bible, copyright 1989, by the Division of Christian Education of the National Council of the Churches of Christ in the United States of America. Used by permission. All rights reserved.

Wipf & Stock
An Imprint of Wipf and Stock Publishers
199 W. 8th Ave., Suite 3
Eugene, OR 97401

www.wipfandstock.com

ISBN 13: 978-1-62032-240-6

Manufactured in the U.S.A.

Contents

List of Tables and Figures / vii

Abbreviations / viii

1. Introduction / 1
2. The Formative Influence of the Exodus / 27
3. A Review of the Approaches to the Use of the OT in Ephesians and the Works That Have Recognized the Influence of the INE in the Epistle / 71
4. An Introduction to the Triumphal Aspect of the INE in Ephesians / 78
5. Co-enthronement with Christ as Present INE Triumph, Eph 1:1–23 / 95
6. Present INE Triumph Observed in Redemption, Reconciliation, and Temple Building, Eph 2:1–22 / 125
7. The Author's Explanation of Apostolic Ministry in Accordance with Present INE Triumph, Eph 3:1–21 / 145
8. The Present INE Triumph of the Ascended and Gift-Giving Christ, Eph 4:1–16 / 164
9. Manifestations of Present INE Triumph in Ethical Renewal, Eph 4:17—5:20 / 178
10. Present INE Triumph Exhibited in Household Codes, Eph 5:21—6:9 / 210

11 Reflections of INE Triumph in the Panoply Metaphor, Eph 6:10–24 / 231

12 Conclusion / 252

Bibliography / 269
Scripture Index / 303
Subject and Names Index / 321

Tables and Figures

Figure 4.1: Pauline Eschatological Development / 91

Table 12.1: Ephesians Use of Isaiah Distributed in Isaiah / 253

Table 12.2: Ephesians Use of Isaiah Distributed in Ephesians / 253

Table 12.3: New Exodus Distribution in Isaiah as Found in Ephesians / 256

Table 12.4: The Use of INE Passages in Ephesians / 258

Table 12.5: Non-Isaiah Usages Distributed in Ephesians with Comparison to Isaiah Usages / 260

Abbreviations

GENERAL

OT	Old Testament
NT	New Testament
INE	Isaianic New Exodus

BIBLE VERSIONS

LXX	Septuagint
LXX-A	Septuagint, Alexandrian Version
MT	Masoretic Text

APOCRYPHA AND SEPTUAGINT

Bar	Baruch
1–2 Esd	1–2 Esdras
Jdt	Judith
1–2 Macc	1–2 Maccabees
3–4 Macc	3–4 Maccabees
Pr Azar	Prayer of Azariah
Sir	Sirach
Tob	Tobit
Wis	Wisdom of Solomon

QUMRAN/DEAD SEA SCROLLS

1QM	*1QWar Scroll*
1QpHab.	*1QPesher to Habakkuk*
1QS	*1QSerek Hayaẏad*
4Q174	*4QFlorilegium*
4Q175	*4QTestimonia*
4Q252	*4QCommentary on Genesis A*

4Q416	*4QInstruction*
4Q418	*4QInstruction*
4Q434	*4QBarkiNafshi*^{a}
4Q436	*4QBarkhiNafshi*^{c}
4Q522	*4QProphecy of Joshua*
4Q554	*4QNew Jerusalem*
11Q13	*11QMelchizedek*

PSEUDEPIGRAPHA

2 Apoc. Bar.	*2 Apocalypse of Baruch*
As. Mos.	*Assumption of Moses*
1 En.	*1 Enoch*
Jub.	*Jubilees*
Pss. Sol.	*Psalms of Solomon*
T. Abr.	*Testament of Abraham*
T. Dan	*Testament of Dan*
T. Iss.	*Testament of Issachar*
T. Jud.	*Testament of Judah*
T. Levi	*Testament of Levi*
T. Moses	*Testament of Moses*

TARGUMIC TEXTS

Tg. Ps.	*Targum Psalms*

APOSTOLIC FATHERS

Herm. *Mand.*	Shepherd of Hermas, *Mandate*
Pol. *Phil.*	Polycarp, *To the Philippians*

JOSEPHUS

B.J.	*Bellum judaicum*, or *De Bello Judaico*

OTHER RABBINIC WORKS

Pesiq. Rab Kah.	*Pesiqta of Rab Kahana*

1

Introduction

IN 2005, MOYISE AND Menken did not include a chapter on Ephesians in their volume, *Isaiah in the New Testament*. They reason, "Ephesians might have qualified, with over a dozen or so allusions listed, but then we could easily find double or treble this number of allusions in the books represented here. The New Testament (NT) writings that have been included here are those in which Isaiah plays a major role, and so this collection gives an accurate overview of the significance of Isaiah in the New Testament."[1] Moyise and Menken's admission opens the possibility that the uninvestigated Isaiah usages in Ephesians may reveal more than previously thought. In a more recent examination, Thielman builds on Lincoln,[2] Moritz,[3] and other works, looking exclusively at the use of the Old Testament (OT) in Ephesians.[4] In contrast to Moyise and Menken, Thielman asserts that the author of Ephesians makes extensive use of the OT for specific reasons. In speaking of the author of the epistle he writes, "His interaction with the Old Testament played an important role in accomplishing his purpose. He alluded to a range of texts in Psalms and Isaiah to remind his readers that if they were 'in Christ,' they had joined God's anointed king in the victory God had given him over the enemies of his people."[5]

1. Moyise and Menken, *Isaiah*, 5.
2. Lincoln, "Use," 16–57.
3. Moritz, *Profound Mystery*, 16, 28–29, 56–86, 90, 154–55, 200–203.
4. Thielman, "Ephesians," 813–33.
5. Ibid., 813.

If an OT "victory" theme is sustainable in Ephesians, what is left undone is the question of what the cumulative use of the OT passages meant to the author as he composed his letter. It is the "dozen or so allusions" as well as several other usages of the OT victory theme in Ephesians that may make a case for the new exodus in this present thesis. In an attempt to demonstrate this proposal several introductory factors will be discussed including Paul's authorship, the occasion and destination of the epistle, a survey of approaches to the purpose of Ephesians, the OT as the basis of the Pauline thought world, the author's OT sources, and the utilization of a typological-historical hermeneutic.[6]

1.1 THE QUESTION OF PAUL'S AUTHORSHIP

It is unnecessary in this present effort to maintain an unassailable position on Paul's authorship or the epistle's solidarity with the rest of the Pauline Corpus; however, Pauline authorship will be assumed.[7] The authorship of Ephesians has been vigorously debated by many prominent scholars. Some dispute Paul's hand in the writing (such as Goodspeed,[8] Lindemann,[9] Dahl,[10] Lincoln,[11] Brown,[12] Best,[13] and Dunn[14]), while others affirm it (Percy,[15] Caird,[16] M. Barth,[17] Dodd,[18] Hoehner,[19] and O'Brien[20]), and still others are

---

6. Portions of this book utilize the author's work: Cozart, "Theological Use."

7. Both the disputed and undisputed Paulines are in view. The undisputed are commonly regarded as Romans, 1 and 2 Corinthians, Galatians, Philippians, Colossians, 1 and 2 Thessalonians, and Philemon. The disputed are Ephesians and the Pastorals (1 and 2 Timothy, and Titus).

8. Goodspeed, *Key*, vi. Mitton's view is closely aligned with Goodspeed: Mitton, *Epistle*, ii. But note Cadbury's critical review of Mitton and Goodspeed: "The Key to Ephesians," 210–12.

9. Lindemann, *Aufhebung*, 9–12.

10. Both Dahl and Lincoln's convictions concerning non-Pauline authorship came later in their careers: Dahl et al., *Studies*, 241–64.

11. Lincoln, *Ephesians*, lix–lxxii.

12. R. Brown, *Churches*, 47; R. Brown, *Introduction*, 620.

13. Best, *Critical and Exegetical*, 35–36.

14. Dunn, *Theology of Paul*, 13 n. 39.

15. Percy examines the subtler evidence for Pauline authorship: Percy, *Probleme*, 352–53.

16. Caird, *Apostolic Age*, 133; Caird, *Paul's Letters*, 11–17, 20–22.

17. M. Barth, *Ephesians, Chapters 1–3*, 36–50.

18. Dodd, *Ephesians*, 1224–25.

19. Hoehner, *Ephesians*, 60–61.

20. O'Brien, *Letter*, 45–47.

uncertain (e.g., Schnackenburg[21]). Even as the debate continues,[22] those who doubt Paul's authorship proceed in investigating the use of the OT in the epistle.[23] Although not all letters in the Pauline Corpus may be regarded as stemming from Paul, they are nevertheless regarded as Pauline in nature.[24] Those scholars who focus on the use of the OT in Ephesians do so by accepting the letter generally as it stands, with authorship remaining a relatively minor issue.

However, doubts concerning Paul's authorship should elicit caution on the part of interpreters. Although the use of the OT in Ephesians may share common themes with the disputed and undisputed Paulines, comparisons that "prove a similarity of thought on some particular point between Ephesians and Paul tells us very little."[25] When seeking to affiliate the usages of the OT in Ephesians with the Pauline Corpus, clear correlations must exist and each linkage should stand on its own merit. Dependence on common OT texts cannot be the sole proof for common authorship or connecting passages. For example, Eph 1:20–22 and 1 Cor 15:25–27 both use Pss 8:6 and 110:1.[26] Although it may be maintained that Paul wrote both Ephesians and 1 Corinthians, the apostle uses the psalms from different perspectives.[27] In 1 Cor 15 the triumph of God is future, in Ephesians it is present. This reminds the interpreter of the complexities involved in seeking to understand the use of the OT in the NT, even if the same supposed author is in view.

In summary, this work assumes Paul's authorship of Ephesians but not without reservation. Old Testament parallels between Ephesians and other portions of the Pauline Corpus cannot be mechanistically applied due merely to common authorship. All potential correspondences must be

---

21. Schnackenburg, *Ephesians*, 24–29.

22. Hoehner demonstrates (contra R. Brown and Dunn) that more scholars have embraced Paul's authorship of Ephesians than those who have not: Hoehner, *Ephesians*, 18–20. But Arnold says that "perhaps a majority of scholars today" maintain that Ephesians did not come from Paul: Arnold, "Ephesians," 240. Cf. McDonald and Porter, *Early Christianity*, 482–88.

23. Three serve as examples of this practice: Kreitzer, *Hierapolis*, 1–6; Lincoln, "Use," 36–37, 44; Yoder-Neufeld, *Put On*, 78, 94–96, 117.

24. This is the view of Dodd and Ellis: Dodd, *According*, 30 (Dodd discusses Ephesians: 33, 35, 38, 94, 121); Ellis, *Paul's Use*, 5–6. Even the long-disputed pastorals show commonality with the rest of Paul: Ellis, 7–9; Jeremias and Strathmann, *Briefe*, 4–5.

25. For a discussion of similarities and differences between Ephesians and Paul: Best, *Critical and Exegetical*, 32–33.

26. These passages are also used in other places in the NT: Matt 22:44; Mark 12:36; Luke 20:42–43; Acts 2:34–35; Heb 1:13; 2:8.

27. Wright, *Resurrection*, 236.

4   THIS PRESENT TRIUMPH

analyzed based on *prima facie* evidence, without automatically assigning parallels.[28]

1.2 OCCASION AND DESTINATION OF THE EPISTLE

Concerning the knotty textual problem, ἐν Ἐφέσῳ (Eph 1:1),[29] the destination of the epistle will be regarded as Ephesus and perhaps other cities of Asia Minor.[30] If ἐν Ἐφέσῳ was in the original composition, then the epistle may have had a single destination; if not, a stronger case might be made for its circularity,[31] with destinations that included Hierapolis and Laodicea (Col 1:13–17). Solutions to the single or multiple destination problems have been offered for centuries.[32] Bruce realizes that the evidence is inconclusive and thus proceeds on the assumption that the destinations included cities in Asia Minor other than Ephesus.[33]

The occasion and destination of the letter are closely connected with its relationship with Colossians.[34] Knight points out that there are available three biblical perspectives on the makeup of the Christian community in Ephesus: the letter to the Ephesians, 1 and 2 Timothy, and Acts 19–20.[35] In addition to these three sources, Colossians should be added, given its shared content with Ephesians. Mention should be made of 1 Corinthians, since an argument is made that Paul wrote 1 Corinthians while staying at Ephesus.[36] Revelation 2:1–7 and the address to the church at Ephesus may have merit as well. Moritz maintains that Ephesians and Colossians have synoptic-like

---

28. Sandmel, "Parallelomania," 1–13. Sandmel's oft-used pejorative refers to the careless and exaggerated use of parallels with little or no substantiation. He adopts the term from a forgotten French source, ca. 1830, 1.

29. The variant lacks the most important manuscripts: P46, ℵ and B. Hoehner's excursus on the textual variant deals with the internal, external, transcriptural, and intrinsic evidences: *Ephesians*, 144–48. Roon considers why the absence of Ἐφέσῳ may have contributed to the ecumenical validity of the epistle: *Authenticity*, 81.

30. For a recent survey of the cultural, historical, religious, and biblical background of Ephesus: McDonald, "Ephesus," 318–21.

31. Goodspeed makes the case for an encyclical missive: *Meaning*, 3.

32. For a survey of the debate up to the early twentieth century: Schmid, *Epheserbrief*, 393–408. Cited by Lincoln, *Ephesians*, l. Cf. Best, *Critical and Exegetical*, 1, 2, 6, 19.

33. Bruce, *Epistles*, 230–31.

34. Though dated, two foundational works explore the relationship between Colossians and Ephesians: Holtzmann, *Kritik*, 35–129; Percy, *Probleme*, 1–31, 137, 149, 179–252, 278–86. More recent works are discussed in the body of this present study.

35. Knight, *Pastoral Epistles*, 72.

36. Koester, "Ephesos," 119–40; Shauf, *Theology*, 97 n. 22.

affiliation.³⁷ He considers Colossians to be written first, and then rewritten as Ephesians. Both letters seem to address encroaching syncretism, but they are dissimilar in that Ephesians appears to speak to a more Jewish-minded audience. The syncretism in the case of Ephesians may have to do with elements of Judaizing. Josephus writes of a large Jewish community in Ephesus that petitioned and was granted considerable freedom in their worship and religious practices, including release from military service.³⁸ This is not to say that the OT is not used in Colossians. Recent scholarship attests to a strong internal evidence of the OT there.³⁹ Colossians refers to Sabbaths, festivals, circumcision, and food laws; but it will be found that Ephesians makes greater and more explicit use of the OT. Where Ephesians and Colossians share commonality there is not significant OT involvement. This is understandable if it is maintained that the two letters had different audiences.⁴⁰ Such distinguishing characteristics concerning the use of the OT in the two epistles introduces the possibility that Ephesians should be set apart from Colossians. The peculiar use of the OT in Ephesians will become clearer as other distinguishing marks are investigated later in this study.⁴¹

There are certain nuances to the problem of occasion and destination that warrant consideration in this present work, such as the Jewish and Gentile makeup of the intended audiences and their receptivity to an epistle such as Ephesians. Colossae may not have had a Jewish population, as did Laodicea and Ephesus.⁴² However, regardless of the situation in Colossae, Schürer and Trebilco make a strong case that a mixed audience resided in Ephesus and in other Asia Minor cities.⁴³ Although some have argued for a Gentile audience only in Ephesus,⁴⁴ the external historical evidence and the internal evidence in the epistle point to a mixed audience.⁴⁵ If it is conceded

37. Moritz, "Ephesians," 315.

38. Josephus, *Works of Josephus*, Vol. III, 315–16. Similar grants were given to Delos, Laodicea, Pergamum, Halicarnassus, and Sardis: 310–15. For the military exemption: 311–12.

39. Beale, "Colossians," 841–70.

40. Moritz, *Profound Mystery*, 8.

41. Section 2.3.6 of this present work.

42. Schürer, *History*, III: 1, 17–36; Trebilco, *Jewish Communities*, 17.

43. Schürer, *History*, III, 222, 225, 258, 263, 270, 273, 276, 282 ; Trebilco, *Jewish Communities*, 33–36, 57, 83–84, 103, 126, 142–44, 164–66, 183–90.

44. This is based primarily on Eph 2:11 and 3:1; but contra, 3:6, 8; 4:17. The "I" and "we" use "is such that it becomes impossible to apply a single rule to the epistle": Moritz, *Profound Mystery*, 24. This does not mean that a degree of certainty concerning identities cannot be attained within sections of the epistle, such as in the Jewish and Gentile discussion in Eph 2.

45. Moritz, *Profound Mystery*, 24–25 n. 3; Best, *Critical and Exegetical*, 4.

that no Jews were in the congregations, the Gentile nature of the churches would not prove insurmountable. Gentile God-fearers in the Roman Empire had a grasp of the OT, presumably enough to make an epistle such as Ephesians comprehensible. In the Jewish synagogues there was extensive use of the Septuagint (LXX),[46] and an openness to Gentiles who shared in the religious life of Jews: "Gentiles were also involved in some Jewish communities, most notably as 'God-worshippers' or as patrons, which suggests that the communities concerned had not withdrawn into themselves. There is evidence from Apamea and Smyrna that Jewish communities encouraged non-Jews to be involved in synagogue life; the existence of God-worshippers also suggests this. Jewish communities we have studied belonged to the cities in which they lived. They were a part of the social networks of the city and shared in many of the characteristics of everyday life."[47] This social interaction between Jews and Gentiles in Asia Minor, especially in synagogue life, suggests openness in the church at Ephesus and at other churches in the cities of the region. Furthermore, from the book of Acts and other places in the NT the impression is left that Gentiles were welcomed into Christian churches. Most notably is Cornelius in Acts 10 who as a Gentile God-fearer comprehends key concepts of the OT. This should be balanced with Acts 17:22–31, where Paul is said to address philosophers in Athens who likely had little understanding of the OT.[48] In this latter passage there is no evidence of OT usage, however, because the aim is one of the evangelization of outsiders rather than the nurture of those who believe. This reflects the style of speeches in the book of Acts that move from a Semitic focus to a reflection on the contemporary setting.[49]

The level of receptivity of OT concepts among the audiences of the Pauline letters is an ongoing debate. The "author-centered" argument maintains that the writer understood what he wrote but those who received his message did not share this level of understanding. This is the position of Stanley.[50] But in a recent work arguing against him, Abasciano (who builds

---

46. In this present work it is understood that the LXX is not a static, monolithic arrangement, although it may have begun from one original text. The LXX is regarded as "Septuagints" rather than in a singular fashion. The edition utilized here: Rahlfs and Hanhart, *Septuaginta*. The preferred version is Alexandrian (cf. footnote 152 in this chapter).

47. Trebilco puts forth evidence for the use of the LXX in a synagogue in Apamea which, along with Paul and other NT authors' use of the LXX, suggests a practice in that region: *Jewish Communities*, 186–90.

48. Witherington, *Acts*, 44.

49. Bock, *Acts*, 13.

50. Stanley, "Pearls," 124–44.

on Hays,[51] Beale,[52] Ciampa,[53] and others) observes, "A careful sifting of the evidence would suggest that Paul's original audiences would be better characterized as 'diamonds in the rough,' groups that might at first appear to be scripturally ignorant, but whose respective aggregate knowledge would have rendered them capable of interacting with sophisticated forms of biblical allusion, rhetoric, and argumentation."[54] Abasciano faults Stanley for not fully considering community dynamics, orality, the centrality of Scripture to early Christianity, and the contextual character of Paul's use of the OT. He summarizes, "Paul's original audiences are best taken as corporately learned in the Scriptures and his quotations interpreted accordingly."[55]

Apart from the question of reader competency of the Pauline audiences, NT authors are undaunted in their utilization of the OT. This would presuppose some level of understanding, and would appear to hold more plausibility than a strictly author-centered approach.[56] Time and again, with little explanation, authors present the OT as an assumed authoritative source that is understood by a wide spectrum of audiences.[57] It is important, therefore, not to minimize the abilities and receptivity of NT addressees in understanding the OT, despite their Hellenistic heritage. It is unlikely that NT authors would have used the OT in ways that were unintelligible to their audiences.[58]

In summary, the letter to the Ephesians reflects both Jewish readership and Gentile proselytes who could be expected to understand and recognize the authority of the OT.

1.3 SURVEY OF APPROACHES TO THE PURPOSE OF EPHESIANS

The purpose of Ephesians in large part is the principal reason for this present work. The goal here is to determine to what extent the triumphant

---

51. Hays, *Echoes*, 9.
52. Beale, *Book of Revelation*, 82–83.
53. Ciampa, *Presence and Function*, 256–70.
54. Abasciano, "Diamonds," 154.
55. Ibid., 153.
56. Meeks, *First Urban*, 146.
57. Köstenberger makes a similar point utilizing Mark: "Remarkably, this is the case despite Mark's predominantly Gentile readership": "Hearing," 270.
58. This is maintained despite remarks in 2 Pet 3:15–16 that lament Paul's letters having "some things . . . hard to understand." The author of 2 Peter decries this state of affairs because some people twisted Paul's writings. This assumes that despite the difficulty, having a comprehension of Paul's letters was entirely possible.

INE affected the composition of the letter. Later in this current study the origination (ch. 2) and triumphant nuances (chs. 3, 4) of the INE will be considered. At present a survey of scholarship's approaches to the general rationale behind Ephesians will serve to provide parameters by which to draw conclusions concerning the INE. Approaches to the purpose of Ephesians are as complex[59] as the question of authorship and have been debated for centuries.[60] Certainly these issues are intertwined.[61] The following section will consider several perspectives on the purpose of the letter.

1.3.1 Anti-Gnostic Polemic

Under the scholarship of F. C. Baur (1845) Ephesians came to be seen as a polemic against the influence of Jewish-related Gnosticism.[62] Many scholars follow Bauer, including Bultmann,[63] Schlier,[64] Käsemann,[65] Pokorný,[66] Conzelmann,[67] Lindemann,[68] Schmithals,[69] and Norden,[70] among others. It is claimed that Gnosticism is evidenced in the head-body imagery, mystery, fullness, age, ruler, the once-now concept, and spatial eschatology. The author's purpose for the epistle is to combat Gnostic inroads into the

---

59. Coleridge considered Ephesians "the divinest composition of man," but Goodspeed's warning, "Ephesians is the Waterloo of commentators," reflects the trepidation many undergo in considering the meaning of the epistle: Coleridge and Coleridge, *Specimens*, 88; Goodspeed, *Meaning*, 15. Muddiman regards Ephesians confusing in form and structure: *Epistles*, 9. Dahl sees the epistle as a "sublime yet elusive document": *Studies*, 447.

60. For surveys concerning the purpose of Ephesians that consider recent scholarship: Best, *Critical and Exegetical*, 63–74; R. Brown, *Introduction*, 620–37; Carson and Moo, *Introduction*, 309–12; Hoehner, *Ephesians*, 97–106; O'Brien, *Letter*, 51–56. Helpful is Kirby, *Ephesians*, 145–49.

61. Dahl et al., *Studies*, 257, 451–59. Dahl speaks of the "illocutionary function" of the epistle: how it is utilized for purposes focused upon the author rather than for just what it says; as well as its real versus fictional setting.

62. Baur, *Paul*, 2:7–22; Hafemann, "Paul," 666–70.

63. Bultmann, *Theology*, vol. 2, 133–35, 175–80; Bultmann, *Gospel of John*, 16–21.

64. Schlier, *Christus*, 19–21. Bruce notes that Schlier presented a more balanced approach later in his career in *Brief*, his commentary on Ephesians, accepting Paul's authorship: Bruce, *Epistles*, 236 n. 20.

65. Käsemann, "Ephesians," 288–97.

66. Pokorný, "Epheserbrief," 160–94; Pokorný, *Epheserbrief*, 21; Pokorný, *Brief Des Paulus*, 443–46.

67. Conzelmann, "Briefe," 86–124.

68. Lindemann, *Epheserbrief*, 9–18.

69. Schmithals, "Corpus Paulinum," 107–24.

70. Norden, *Agnostos Theos*, 240–76.

church or syncretize it with a Pauline version of Christianity. Meyer sees Ephesians addressing the glory of redemption and warning against the onslaught of Gnosticism.[71] However, there has been a movement away from the assumption that the authors of the NT were addressing pre-Christian Gnostic myth.[72] Best establishes that there is no evidence in Ephesians that the author was consciously refuting Gnosticism.[73]

A better understanding of the influence of Gnosticism reveals that there may have been a strain of nascent Gnosticism rather than a fully engaged form of it that dominated the conversation of Paul and the churches.[74] In addition, Dupont (and expanded by Ridderbos) does not deny that Paul used the vocabulary of popular Gnostic-Hellenistic philosophy, but maintains that Paul's use of "gnosis" is founded in and explained by the OT.[75] Paul's understanding of divine knowledge does not come from Gnostic systems, Hermetic writings, mystery religions, or a syncretic hybrid with the OT—but squarely from the OT. Arnold establishes a clearer historical understanding of the influence of Gnosticism and the general religious milieu: "The most productive approach is to examine the local religious traditions which were known to be active and influential at the time the letter was written. For Western Asia Minor this would include the phenomena commonly referred to as magic, the Anatolian religions (such as the cults of Artemis and Cybele), astrological practices and astral religions, and the various other local cults . . . A deeper understanding of these traditions provides a firmer basis for interpreting the readers and assessing how Paul may have contextualized his theology to address their needs."[76] Arnold continues: "References to such items as temple, redemption, God's choosing, hope, mercy, promise, wisdom, the Father, sons of men, helmet of salvation, and many more show how deeply steeped the author was in the OT and how the language of the OT influenced his own composition."[77]

---

71. Meyer et al., *Critical and Exegetical*, 302–8.

72. For a discussion of the German historical school's influence on the interpretation of Ephesians: Dahl et al., *Studies*, 457, 463–65. Bultmann's Gnostic view of John 1 is discussed and refuted: Endo, *Creation*, 1–4. For more discussion and refutation: Köster, *Introduction*, 271; Sampley, "And the Two," 63–64.

73. Best, *Critical and Exegetical*, 87–89.

74. Arnold, "Ephesians," 243.

75. Dupont, *Gnosis*, 151–81, 531–34; Ridderbos, *Paul*, 28, 36.

76. Arnold, "Ephesians," 243. Arnold cites within this quote: Arnold, *Ephesians: Power and Magic*, 5–40.

77. Arnold, "Ephesians," 239.

1.3.2 Unity of Jewish and Gentile Christians

Counter to the position of the dominant influence of Gnosticism in Ephesians, Robinson and others understand the epistle from the standpoint of unity.[78] The author of the epistle explains God's purpose for the unity of mankind, which is demonstrated through Christ and the corporate life of the church.[79] O'Brien seems to echo a comparable position, seeing the purpose of the letter as cosmic reconciliation and unity in Christ, resulting in identity formation.[80] Wood agrees with Robinson, saying that the letter captures a vision of the unity of mankind in Christ (Eph 1:9, 10) and the purpose of the world through the church.[81] In view of this inspiration the author also addresses the practical side of Christian living in a hostile society. Schnackenburg considers the letter fulfilling two objectives: internal unity and living a distinctively Christian lifestyle in a pagan environment.[82] E. Scott holds that the letter was to the church at Laodicea and speaks to Jew-Gentile disunity and heresies that were threatening unity.[83] Chadwick proposes that the letter functions to demonstrate to non-Pauline churches the need for unity among churches influenced by Paul.[84] Schmithals sees a similar purpose, maintaining that disenfranchised Jewish Christians had been removed from the synagogue and needed acceptance from Gentile Christians.[85] Muddiman's position is analogous.[86] The Gentile Christians from the Pauline churches were to accept their Jewish brothers from the synagogue and acquaint them with Pauline tradition. Fischer recognizes a situation in which Gentile Christians increasingly despise Jewish Christians.[87] D. Smith considers the letter from the standpoint of reconciliation between arrogant Gentiles and Jewish believers.[88] Similarly, Biguzzi understands the letter as a plea for Gentile Christians not to abandon the

---

78. Robinson, *St. Paul's Epistle*, 10–14.

79. Concerning the emphasis on ἑνότης in Ephesians: Patzia, *Ephesians*, 133–39. Another advocate of unity as the purpose of the epistle is Turner: "Mission and Meaning," 138–66.

80. O'Brien, *Letter*, 56–57. Similarly: Snodgrass, *Ephesians*, 23.

81. Wood, "Ephesians," 17.

82. Schnackenburg, *Ephesians*, 22–35.

83. E. Scott, *Epistles of Paul*, 123–24.

84. Chadwick, "Absicht," 145–53.

85. Schmithals, "Corpus Paulinum," 122.

86. Muddiman, *Ephesians*, 17.

87. Fischer, *Tendenz*, 21–39, 79–94.

88. D. Smith, "Ephesian Heresy," 45–54; D. Smith, "Ephesian Heresy and the Origin," 78–103.

multiethnic church.[89] Martin sees the letter functioning as a prose-poem that directs Gentile readers to appreciate the Jewish heritage of their faith.[90] Along this line of thought, Gentiles had wrongly considered themselves separate from Israel and adopted a lax moral code.

M. Barth recognizes the missive as one that addresses the Gentiles in Ephesus who came to salvation after Paul's ministry there.[91] He sees a Jewish-Gentile conflict that requires resolution, but with Gentiles who felt alienated rather than Jews. Similarly, Thielman understands that the Jewish Christians who predated Paul in the city and the Gentile believers who came afterward required closer connections given the challenges of their day.[92] Bruce considers the epistle to be an explanation of the mystery and Gentiles coming to appreciate their value in the church.[93] Gentile Christians are to understand and walk according to their heavenly calling. Ephesians does speak of the unity of Jew and Gentile with the emphasis on the acceptance of Gentiles rather than Jews (2:11–16; 3:6). Furthermore, there is no evidence that a clear disjunction existed between Pauline and non-Pauline churches which might have produced anti-Semitic sentiments.

1.3.3 *Power Motif*

Arnold understands Ephesians to be stressing a power motif that includes a warning against slipping back into the worship of Artemis.[94] The Christians in Ephesus need not return to their former beliefs because of the complete adequacy and superiority of their faith. In addition, they need not fear what was generally accepted in their cultural milieu: flourishing magical practices, Phrygian mysteries, and astrological beliefs.[95] Divine power is a prevalent theme in the epistle, but questions remain concerning other portions of the letter that do not seem to fit this scenario, namely the emphasis on the unity of Jew and Gentile (Eph 2:12–18), the makeup of God's people (2:14; 3:6; 4:1–6), and Paul's role as arbiter of the mystery (3:1–13). Another potential problem is the nature of the Artemis cult and whether it can be caricatured as demonic powers, which are emphasized repeatedly in

---

89. Biguzzi, "Efesini," 347–64. Cited by Hoehner, *Ephesians*, 100.
90. Martin, *Ephesians*, 5–6.
91. M. Barth, "Conversion," 3–24; M. Barth, *Ephesians, Chapters 1–3*, 10–11.
92. Thielman, *Ephesians*, 28.
93. Bruce, *Epistles*, 245–46. Cf. Schlier, *Brief*, 21–22.
94. Arnold, "Ephesians," 246; Arnold, *Power and Magic*, 123–24, 167–72. Cf. the Colossian situation: Arnold, *Colossian Syncretism*, 228–44.
95. Arnold, *Power and Magic*, 167.

the epistle (1:21; 2:2; 3:10; 4:27; 6:11–13).[96] Related to this view is Moritz who sees Ephesians recontextualizing Colossians to combat the dangers of syncretism, but different from Colossians in that the audience in Ephesus is more Jewish in nature.[97] Arnold admits shortcomings in his proposal,[98] but the merits of his study lie in seeing power as a prominent feature in the letter. This will be examined in the balance of the thesis under passages that speak of these powers.

Kreitzer thinks that the letter was written against those in the church who were attracted to the Demeter and Cybele cult.[99] The licentiousness of the underworld could be in view in the epistle (4:9; 5:12), but given the other emphases in the letter it should not be seen as a central purpose. Themes such as the redemption of the church, the exaltation of Christ, and unity of Jewish and Gentile believers are strong indications that the letter is not only a polemic against paganism.

1.3.4 *Liturgical Origin*

Some speculate that Ephesians is not a letter at all, but rather a theological tract, wisdom discourse, baptismal hymn or liturgical script, or homily written by a disciple of Paul.[100] Dahl understands Ephesians as a means to orient new Christians to their faith and baptism.[101] Kirby sees a renewal of baptismal vows that coincides with the Feast of Pentecost.[102] Luz views the epistle as a "baptismal reminder."[103] Schille holds to the hymnic nature of the letter, which was to be used as a paraenesis for baptism and catechism.[104] The weakness of these positions on baptism is that there is only one clear mention of baptism in the epistle (Eph 4:5) within a section on the importance of unity. Also, liturgical explanations for the letter do not fully explain

---

96. Strelan, *Paul,* 83–86.

97. Moritz, "Ephesians," 315.

98. Arnold, *Power and Magic,* 168.

99. Kreitzer, *Epistle,* 21–48; Kreitzer, "Crude Language?," 51–77; Kreitzer, *Hierapolis,* 73–92.

100. Hoehner, *Ephesians,* 97; O'Brien, *Letter,* 51.

101. Dahl et al., *Studies,* 31–39. Along with baptism, Dahl understands that the letter should be taken in a general faith sense; one of reminder and congratulation; 471 (cf. this chapter, 1.3.9).

102. Kirby, *Ephesians,* 145–61.

103. The German term used by Luz for "baptism reminder" is tauferinnerungsgottesdienst: Luz, "Überlegungen," 376–96.

104. Schille, "Liturgisches," 135–51; Schille, "Autor," 325–34; Schille, *Frühchristliche,* 20–23, 53–60, 102–7.

apostolic and epistolary sections such as 3:2–14, which are too personal (concerning Paul) and too specific for the purposes of catechism.

1.3.5 Canonical Function

Goodspeed and Knox see Ephesians canonically.[105] It was written near the end of the first century as a cover letter to introduce Paul's writings.[106] Mitton has a similar position, understanding the epistle to have a relationship to the Pauline Corpus, but perhaps not as an introduction.[107] The letter addresses a new generation of Christians who should understand the threat of Gnosticism and the value of their Jewish heritage. This theory has been roundly challenged by many and is no longer considered persuasive.[108] One substantive argument against this position is the likelihood that Paul's influence continued immediately after his death through such workers as Timothy, and by the distribution of Paul's letters (2 Tim 4:13). Additionally, the author of Ephesians addresses the pastoral function of some church offices (4:11) but is silent about submission to authority.

1.3.6 Reassertion of Pauline Authority

Similar to the canonical function above, Lincoln considers that the letter was written by a disciple of Paul to fill a vacuum in leadership after the departure of the apostle.[109] The epistle reasserts Paul's authority and seeks to solidify the audience around common Pauline themes. He holds that in light of the departure of Paul and the fading of the Parousia, Christians in Asia Minor need to realize who they are in Christ and live accordingly.[110] Christians who follow the admonition would live a distinctive lifestyle reflected in the numerous calls to moral living in the epistle. The Christ-followers of Western Asia Minor would be set in bold relief against their polytheistic and secular counterparts.

Similarly, Lindemann maintains that the purpose of the letter is to offer consolation and support during the Domitian persecution in AD 96 while enduring the loss of eschatological expectation.[111] In conjunction with

---

105. Goodspeed, *Meaning*, 1–75. Cf. Knox, *Philemon*, 85–92.

106. Patzia, *Making*, 82.

107. Mitton, *Epistle*, 29–31.

108. Such as Bruce, Martin, and Zuntz: Patzia, *Making*, 82. Muddiman gives a succinct argument against Goodspeed's theory: Muddiman, *Ephesians*, 12–14.

109. Lincoln, *Ephesians*, lviii, lxxxv–lxxxvii. Meade's position coincides with Lincoln: Meade, *Pseudonymity*, 148–54.

110. Lincoln, *Ephesians*, lxxiv–lxxxvii.

111. Lindemann, "Bemerkungen," 234–51; Lindemann, *Epheserbrief*, 14–15.

this disappointment there arose a need to establish unity among divergent churches; Ephesians is presented as a means to divert a crisis of authority. Lindemann establishes the political-military aspect of his position on the metaphor in Eph 6. However, this attributes a disproportional influence upon the metaphor. In addition, the imagery there, as well as other portions of the letter, speak of spiritual conflict rather than "blood and flesh" (6:12). Spiritual battles do not require an opposing physical army.[112]

1.3.7 Essene and Anti-Essene Influence

Mussner,[113] Kuhn,[114] and Perkins[115] reveal commonalities between Ephesians and Qumran literature. Associations are found with phrases such as "the working of the power of his might" (Eph 1:19), "children of light" (5:8), "fellow citizens with the holy ones" (2:19), the community as temple (2:21), and ethical dualisms (5:10–11). However, at issue is the setting for the parallelisms with Qumran. Is Ephesians warning against ascetical mysticism as in Col 2:18, or is it seeking to attract displaced Essene Jews in the aftermath of the destruction of Jerusalem (AD 66–70)?[116] Evidence for the intentional use of Essene material is too sparse to mount a convincing case for this to be the the prevailing reason for the composition.

1.3.8 Love and Unity

Hoehner approaches the purpose of Ephesians from the standpoint of corporate ἀγάπη. He sees this emphasis tying in well with the theme of unity.[117] His conclusion is primarily based upon the number of uses of ἀγάπη in the epistle, as well as the account of Paul's message to the Ephesian elders at Miletus (Acts 20:18–35) and Timothy (1 Tim 1:5). However, the lexical evidence for ἀγάπη does not counterbalance the other great themes of the letter, such as understanding and utilizing divine power, and triumph. Certainly love is a key component to the epistle, but as the central purpose it does not adequately account for other important motifs.

---

112. Muddiman discusses Lindemann and other German Protestant scholars such as Käsemann and Conzelmann concerning "early catholicism": Muddiman, *Ephesians*, 14.

113. Mussner, "Contributions," 159–78.

114. Kuhn, "Epistle," 115–31.

115. Perkins, *Ephesians*, 29, 39, 62, 77, 147.

116. Muddiman, *Ephesians*, 16.

117. Hoehner, *Ephesians*, 104–6.

1.3.9 Generalization

The "circular letter" hypothesis, based on the destination problem in Eph 1:1, lends itself to the idea that Ephesians was written with a general purpose in mind. However, not all who embrace a general theme hold to the circularity of the missive. Ellicott thinks that no special occasion prompted the letter; rather, the epistle was written to put forth the origin and progress of the church.[118] Some, like Lincoln, discuss the strengths of this general understanding of the epistle, suggesting that the letter addresses broad Christian principles.[119] Käsemann holds that Ephesians has no central argument and is an appropriation of Pauline traditions undertaken by a follower of Paul.[120] In a novel but related approach, Shkul maintains a sociological-entrepreneurial function by which the purpose of the letter is attained by means of promoting cultural ideology.[121]

1.3.10 Triumph in Christ

The position of a recent author most resembles the one taken up in this present work. Gombis asserts that the central coherence of the letter is the triumph of God in Christ over all competing cosmic powers.[122] After declaring that God has triumphed by seating Christ in the heavenlies (Eph 1:20–23), the epistle continues by demonstrating this fact by the triumphs of God in Christ (2:1–22), the participation of Paul in the triumph despite his suffering and imprisonment (3:2–13), and the strategic role of the church in participating in the triumph (4:1—6:9). Gombis's monograph has merit in that it seeks to explain portions of Ephesians that otherwise appear enigmatic (such as the difficult autobiographic digression, 3:2–13). He demonstrates that the common thread of triumph over the cosmic forces can be maintained throughout the epistle. Similarly, Longman and Reid see an ideological pattern in ancient Near East divine warfare: conflict, victory, kingship, house-building, celebration—elements of which are found in Ephesians.[123] The difficulty of asserting a triumph motif, however, is in subordinating the other major themes such as soteriology, Christology, unity of

---

118. Ellicott, *Commentary*, xv–xvi.

119. Lincoln, *Ephesians*, lxxxi–lxxxiii.

120. Käsemann, "Ephesians," 297. Jeal argues for a rhetorical purpose to the epistle with the author's appeal to sublime truths: *Integrating Theology*, 66–67.

121. Shkul, *Reading Ephesians*, 11–24.

122. Gombis, "Triumph" (2005a), 1–7 For an extended abstract: Gombis, "Triumph" (2005b), 157–60. Cf. Yoder-Neufeld who traces divine warfare throughout Ephesians: *Put on the Armour*, 94–153.

123. Longman and Reid, *God Is a Warrior*, 83–88.

believing Jews and Gentiles, and ethical living. Gombis appears to overcome these obstacles by citing, among other issues, how ethics are treated. By living properly, the early church overcomes the cosmic forces that seek to draw Christians back into their former lives. Another is the relationship between Jews and Gentiles. The demonic powers' interest lies in exploiting an already volatile situation in the church. The powers also utilize ethnic animosities by co-opting the Mosaic law. By showing how these areas relate to triumph, Gombis builds a formidable case.

The limitation of Gombis's study is the handling of the OT. When he considers the OT passages utilized by the author of Ephesians he does not fully account for the OT contextual logic behind the plethora of OT texts in the epistle. Gombis often draws on OT triumph episodes, such as Elijah and the prophets of Baal as well as David and Goliath, but falls short of fully integrating all the OT texts that are specific to Ephesians, especially Isaiah.[124] The deficiency relates to how OT triumph, specifically INE triumph, makes its presence known in the epistle. Gombis mentions exodus passages but does not indicate where the evidence may lead.[125]

In summary, there is considerable diversity among scholars as to the authorship, destination, audience, and date of Ephesians. It is therefore not surprising that a divergence of opinion exists concerning its purpose.[126] However, there remains commonality along broad lines of thought. The consensus is that the letter is a post-Pauline reinterpretation of Paul to a subsequent generation of Christians, much along the lines of section 1.3.6, preceding. However, it will be considered in this current work that the present triumphal aspect of the INE guides the composition of the epistle.

1.4 THE OT AS FOUNDATIONAL TO PAULINE THOUGHT

The OT is integral to Paul's thought world. He was without doubt a "Hebrew of Hebrews" (Phil 3:5); an "Israelite and descendent of Abraham" (Rom 11:1; 2 Cor 11:22); born in Tarsus but brought up and educated under Gamaliel in Jerusalem (Acts 22:3); a "strict Pharisee" (Acts 23:6, 26:5); and immersed in the OT and its traditions.[127] To Paul the OT Scriptures were

---

124. Gombis, "Triumph" (2005a), 69–70.
125. Such as Exod 15: Gombis, "Ephesians 3:2–13," 315.
126. Roberts, "Enigma," 93–106; Snodgrass, *Ephesians*, 22.
127. Ellis, *Recent Interpreters*, 11–33; Ridderbos, *Paul*, 32–43. Both Ellis and Ridderbos trace the transition in the last century from the Greek-Hellenistic focus of Pauline scholarship to the Jewish premises of Paul's ministry and message. Ridderbos rightly maintains a Hellenistic influence in Paul but warns that this is not to be overdone as the Tübingen school maintains: *Paul*, 36. For the Jewish influence on Paul's youth: Unnik, *Tarsus or Jerusalem*, 3–4, 52.

a priori authoritative, and the lens through which he judged his life and ministry.[128] This, however, does not mean that Paul adopted wholesale the rabbinical tradition of his day. Ellis makes the case with others that although Paul was within the mechanics of the rabbinic tradition, it was the apostolic church and Christ himself that primarily influenced his understanding and application of the OT.[129] The influence of Hellenism on Paul should be seen similarly. His frequent use of athletic metaphors was most likely the influence of contemporary athletic games. Paul incorporated these pictures into his writings to describe the Christian life and his apostolic ministry. But the Hellenistic images in Ephesians and elsewhere find their theological alignment in the OT, often directly with Isaiah. An example of this will be seen in the panoply metaphor in chapter 11 of this present work (Eph 6:10–17). In those verses, the author of the letter uses rich Hellenistic imagery that is anchored by and given substance through an Isaianic world view. Paul's theology was soundly founded upon the OT, but he oftentimes communicated through the illustrations and verbiage of contemporary Greco-Roman thinking. It is within these contexts, both Jewish contemporary thought and Hellenism,[130] that Paul undertook the use of Isaiah, Psalms, Genesis, Deuteronomy, and other new exodus passages for his purposes.[131]

Among OT writings, Isaiah plays a pivotal role in the Pauline Corpus.[132] Hays speaks of the primacy of Isaiah for Paul, "I believe that Paul had read and pondered the scroll of Isaiah as a whole, over the years of his apostolic ministry, and developed a sustained reading of it as God's revelation of 'the mystery that has kept secret for long ages but is now disclosed, and through the prophetic writings is made known to all the Gentiles, according to the

---

128. C. Evans and Sanders, *Paul and the Scriptures*, 13–17. Ellis's appendices of OT occurrences in Paul reveal a definitive list of quotations, allusions, and parallels: *Paul's Use*, 150–87. Silva also lists Paul's employment of the OT: "Old Testament in Paul," 631.

129. Ellis, *Paul's Use*, 1–5. Kennedy sees Paul using the OT for proof, analogy, illustration, or general phraseology: *St. Paul and the Mystery*, 154–60.

130. Pfitzner, *Paul and the Agon*, 1–5, 76–195.

131. Flaming, "New Testament Use," 94.

132. Care must be taken when attempting to reconstuct a Pauline understanding of Isaiah. There is little doubt that Paul (or Pauline writers) utilized Isaiah, but despite a better understanding of the LXX-A as the primary source for Paul, questions remain as to the unity of Isaiah in the ancient world. This, in turn, affects the theological ideas that are embraced by later interpreters—built largely from a unified Isaiah, such as the concept of the "suffering servant." For works that help to shape the debate and give reasons for the unity of Isaiah, along with a recent update: Williamson, *Book Called Isaiah*, 94–115, 240; Williamson, "Recent Issues," 21–39. But the unity position is not without critics: Melugin, "Book of Isaiah," 44–45.

command of the eternal God, to bring about the obedience of faith.'"[133] He adds, "Isaiah offers the clearest expression in the Old Testament of a universalistic, eschatological vision in which the restoration of Israel in Zion is accompanied by an ingathering of Gentiles to worship the Lord; that is why this book is both statistically and substantively the most important scriptural source for Paul."[134]

With other NT authors Paul sees a seamless transition from God's redemptive work in the OT with that of the NT. Dodd maintains that OT and NT authors embrace the same world view, with the NT in continuity with the OT.[135] Romans 16:25b-26 (incorporated by Hays, preceding) describes Paul's attitude toward the Isaiah and other prophetic portions of the Hebrew Scriptures: "The revelation of the mystery that was kept secret for long ages but is now disclosed, and through the prophetic writings is made known to all the Gentiles, according to the command of the eternal God, to bring about the obedience of faith."[136]

In Isaiah, Paul saw God working apocalyptically in turning the fortunes of Israel, including Gentile nations, so that Gentiles would come to understand and recognize Israel's God. In addition, to Paul Isaiah's apocalyptic timeline cohered with the incarnation, crucifixion, resurrection, and ascension of Jesus.[137]

From the OT, Paul defines not only his message but his self-understanding. He frequently refers to his calling and how the OT legitimizes his ministry.[138] Both Gaventa and Lyons see Paul proclaiming the gospel and using himself, autobiographically, as a model of the gospel—all deeply rooted in the OT.[139] S. Kim contends that the Damascus road christophany heavily colors and influences Paul's vocabulary and thought.[140] In addition, Kim

---

133. Hays, *Conversion*, 27. Cf., Hays, *Echoes*, 154–92, esp. 162.

134. Ibid., *Echoes*, 162.

135. Dodd, *According*, 133.

136. Unless otherwise noted the New Revised Standard Version is utilized in this thesis: Thomas Nelson Publishers, *Holy Bible*.

137. Several scholars observe Paul's apocalyptic worldview from various perspectives: Beker, *Paul's Apocalyptic*, 29–54; Käsemann, "Justification," 60–78. Käsemann sees Rom 9–11 as central to the theological argument of Romans: God at work apocalyptically in the nation. A. Schweitzer, *Mysticism*, 52–100. Cf. Watson, *Paul, Judaism*, 235.

138. Rom 1:1–2; 10:2–4; 11:1–6; 1 Cor 9:1–17; 15:8–10; 2 Cor 3:4—4:6; 5:16; Gal 1:13–17; Eph 3:1–13; Phil 3:4–11; Col 1:23–29. The Lukan call narratives closely resemble Paul's versions: Acts 9:3–20; 22:6–21; 26:12–18.

139. Gaventa, "Galatians 1 and 2," 309–26; Lyons, "Pauline Autobiography," 171, 226.

140. Seyoon Kim, *Origin*, 51–66.

considers Paul's call narratives echoing those of Moses, Isaiah, Jeremiah, and Ezekiel.[141] Paul sees himself in the tradition of the great prophets: "Isaianic texts and motifs have profoundly shaped Paul's conception of his calling as an apostle."[142] Paul reflects this in Gal 1:15–16: "But when God, who had set me apart before I was born and called me through his grace, was pleased to reveal his Son to me, so that I might proclaim him among the Gentiles, I did not confer with any human being." Critical to Paul's argument in Galatians 1 is that he was a genuine apostle called to a Gentile-focused mission. Validation is added through Paul's choice of words. They reflect prophet-calling passages, such as Isa 49:1: "Listen to me, O coastlands, pay attention, you peoples from far away! The LORD called me before I was born, while I was in my mother's womb he named me." The Galatians passage is also seen in Jer 1:5: "Before I formed you in the womb I knew you, and before you were born I consecrated you; I appointed you a prophet to the nations." Both OT passages speak of divine calling that includes Gentile salvation, which is essential to Paul's argument in Galatians.[143] Kim makes the same discovery, linking not only Paul's general call to ministry to Isaiah but to the Gentile mission as well.[144] Zimmerli observed two types of prophetic commissions in the OT: a visionary type (Isaiah and Ezekiel), and a nonvisionary (Moses and Jeremiah).[145] The former consists of a vision of the heavenly throne; the latter involves a close encounter with Yahweh that includes hesitation and resistance on the part of the soon-to-be prophet. Zimmerli affirms that both aspects are found in the narratives of Paul's call: the former is emphasized in the Lukan narratives, and the latter in Gal 1:13–17.[146]

This is not to say that Paul saw his call and ministry only in terms of the OT prophets.[147] He takes great pains to explain discontinuity with Moses and the old covenant. Also, he never technically refers to himself a "prophet," preferring to be seen within the apostolic mission of preaching the gospel.[148] What emerges from the autobiographical passages is an apostolic ministry that corresponds typologically to the great OT prophets and

---

141. Moses: Exod 3:1–22; 4:1–17; 6:2–12; 7:1–7; Isaiah: Isa 6; 49:1–6; Jeremiah: Jer 1:5–7; Ezekiel: Ezek 1:1–3:15. Seyoon Kim, *Origin*, 18, 92–95.

142. Wagner, "Isaiah," 130.

143. Martyn provides numerous parallels between Galatians and Isaiah: *Galatians*, 156–57, 429.

144. Seyoon Kim, *Origin*, 95.

145. Zimmerli et al., *Ezekiel*, 100.

146. Ibid., 20.

147. Bruce points out the similarities and dissimilarities with Jeremiah: *Paul*, 145–46.

148. Roloff, *Apostolat*, 43–44.

Moses, with a fundamental distinction centered on the advent of Christ and mystery elements of the new covenant.

In summary, the OT formed the world view of Paul, preeminently Isaiah, as a critical authoritative source to explain his call to ministry and his eschatological understanding of the advent of Christ. Paul saw himself within the sweep of divine history and upon the cusp of a new age.

1.5 THE AUTHOR'S OT SOURCES IN EPHESIANS

Concerning the author's use of the OT in Ephesians, key questions emerge: what textual source was used by the NT writer in his employment of Isaiah, Psalms, and other portions of the OT?[149] Second, did the writer use the OT or a written or oral tradition that may have accessed the OT? Third, how did he alter the texts to fit his purposes? Fourth, are changes in the OT text used in the NT due to the writer's source, textual transmission, or to the writer? These are not easily explained.[150] Determining the best possibilities of textual traditions in regard to the LXX, the MT, and other manuscripts and traditions that may have been available to the writer, have significant ramifications.[151] This is an issue that affects both quotations and allusive usages in the letter.

Textual transmission brings questions to light of how a text may have changed, by whom, and when. Explanations might be found among three areas: the source document, transmission texts, or the NT author. Some maintain that if the author of Ephesians uses the OT in a way that is not indicated by the LXX, MT, or later Greek translations, then the change should be attributed to the writer of Ephesians. However, each case varies in complexity. In some situations the wording used by the NT author may indicate a copy of the OT or tradition beyond extant versions.[152] NT

---

149. Silva gives a helpful analysis of the various possibilities of origination for the OT usages in Ephesians: "Old Testament in Paul," 630–42.

150. For example, many decades of scholarship have been dedicated to the origin, history, and textual integrity of the LXX, and how these questions relate to textual transmission, the MT, and usage in the NT: The *Göttingen Septuagint* project has taken place for several decades (1931–2008) and is the most detailed critical edition of the LXX: Rahlfs et al., *Göttingen Septuagint*; cf. Jobes and Silva, *Invitation*, 19–28; Tov, *Text-Critical Use*, 1–5.

151. Barr's review of Jobes and Silva's book cited above illustrates the importance of scholarship's view of the LXX. As Barr notes, Jobes and Silva lean too favorably toward the MT in sorting through OT in the NT questions: Barr, "Invitation to the Septuagint," 1–24. In Barr's critique many Isaianic texts come into play: 5:17; 29:3; 52:15; 53:7, 8, 11; 61:1.

152. For example, this is central to the question of the origin of the cited text in Eph 5:14.

copyists at times had competing options. On the one hand they had a NT manuscript (with the OT citation) before them. On the other they had an OT Hebrew or Greek text, or the memory of an OT Hebrew or Greek text, or an unknown tradition. In transcribing the OT usage in the New they may have made changes from what the NT author indicated by writing what they, the transcriber, best understood the OT to read. Silva makes this case using the example of Deut 25:4 in 1 Cor 9:9.[153]

Scholarship maintains that the author of Ephesians largely based his use of the OT on an Alexandrian Septuagintal (LXX-A) version.[154] The use of the LXX-A by the author of the epistle shall be presumed for purposes of this present study. Concerning Hebrew and Targumic sources, Mortiz observes that there is "little evidence to suggest any significant recourse to Hebrew texts although this can by no means be ruled out. Similarly, the author does not appear to have had knowledge of Targumic traditions."[155] In terms of analyzing other extra-biblical origins, there is value in considering sources such as Qumran (Kuhn), Gnostic (Pokorný), Stoicism or "hellenistic Judaism" (Gnilka), but these should not take away from the predominant and deliberate use of the OT.[156]

In summary, in this present work the understood source of OT material in Ephesians will be the LXX, primarily the Alexandrian, but not without the possibility that Hebrew versions of the OT or other extra-biblical sources were utilized by the writer. Understanding the origin and transmission of the OT text in Ephesians is an ongoing challenge but does not unduly stymie this investigation. Each occurrence will be treated independently as warranted.

---

153. Silva "Old Testament in Paul." Silva also elicits 1 Cor 3:19 quoting Job 5:13, p. 633.

154. Moritz, *Profound Mystery*, 214–15. Ellis cites Roepe, Kautzsch, and Swete who maintain that Paul almost always uses the Alexandrian version of the LXX: Ellis, *Paul's Use*, 4–5, 13–14; Kautzsch, *De Veteris Testamenti Locis*; Roepe, *De Veteris Testamenti Locorum* (Ellis does not supply page references for Roepe and Kautzsch; cf. Swete, *Introduction*, 403. Ellis also recognizes Stendahl who sees the Alexandrian text form as most trustworthy when Paul is citing the prophets: Ellis, *Paul's Use*, 12–15; Stendahl, *School of St. Matthew*, 172. However, although Paul's use of LXX links most favorably toward LXX-A, the Alexandrian, text forms vary considerably and his individual letters cannot always be tied to certain LXX texts: Ellis, *Paul's Use*, 13–14; Vollmer, *Alttestamentlichen*, 13–20, 48. An example of the complexity is the citation in 1 Cor 15:54 (Isa 25:8). It shows affinity with Greek versions of Theodotion, Aquila, and Symmachus, but less with the LXX.

155. Moritz, *Profound Mystery*, 213.

156. Gnilka, *Epheserbrief: Auslegung*, 1–52; Kuhn, "Epistle," 115–31; Pokorný, "Epheserbrief," 43–46.

1.6 UTILIZATION OF A TYPOLOGICAL-HISTORICAL HERMENEUTIC

The history of biblical interpretation includes the study of the use of Scripture within Scripture: the OT in the OT, the OT within the NT, and the NT in the NT. Research in this area has grown voluminously over the past twenty-five years.[157] Scholars such as Eichrodt, Rad, and Fishbane focus on the OT;[158] others such as Goppelt, Lampe and Woollcombe, Amsler, France, and Longenecker emphasize the NT;[159] and still others such as Ellis, Hays, and Silva concentrate on the Pauline Corpus and specifically Paul's use of the OT.[160] In OT in NT studies, questions of typology are the focus of concern in new exodus analysis. The study of typology in biblical studies has a long history and finds general association with the interpretation of literature.[161] In terms of the exodus, the exodus event functions as a type in a historical "promise-fulfillment" sense. That is, the exodus is used in other portions of the Bible not as prophecy-prediction-fulfillment, nor as nonhistorical typology or allegory, but as a fact of the past that has bearing on how God should be expected to act in the future. Underlying the use of typology in the Bible is the conviction that there is an affinity between God's created order and the spiritual world. How God acts in creation and history suggests (or proves) how he will work in a forthcoming time.[162] Foulkes was one of the first to observe that a recurring theme in the Bible (such as the exodus) is the basis of how God will act in the future.[163] In the NT, the new exodus expectation was not considered to be the fulfillment of prophecy but rather a typological history ultimately completed in the antitype events of the eschaton. Foulkes sees that oftentimes the NT author understands an organic link between the type in the OT and its NT antitype counterpart. Goppelt's

---

157. Lindars et al., *Written*, 1–24; Snodgrass, "Use," 209–29.

158. Eichrodt, *Theology*, 227–28, 244; Fishbane, *Biblical Interpretation*, 288–89; Rad, *Old Testament*, xx–xxiv, xxxiii–xxxv, 175–78. Cf. Rad, "Typological Interpretation," 17–39, among other useful essays.

159. Amsler, *L'ancien Testament*, 141–47; France, *Jesus and the Old Testament*, 38–80; Lampe and Woollcombe, *Essays on Typology*, 39–69; R. Longenecker, *Biblical Exegesis*, xiii–xli.

160. Hays considers the following as landmark works on Paul's use of the OT, *Echoes*, 196 n. 25: Bonsirven, *Exegese Rabbinique*; Dodd, *According*; Ellis, *Paul's Use*; Goppelt, *Typos*; Koch, *Schrift*; Lindars, *New Testament Apologetic*; Michel, *Paulus Und Seine Bibel*. Other useful works may be added: Aageson, "Written Also," 152–81; Keesmaat, "In the Face," 182–212; Moyise, "Old Testament," 75–97.

161. Fairbairn, *Typology of Scripture*, 13–163; Foulkes, *Acts of God*, 14; Galdon, *Typology*, 19–29; Goppelt, *Typos*, 1–22; Hugenberger, "Introductory Notes," 331–41.

162. D. Baker, "Typology and the Christian," 313–16, 322.

163. Foulkes, *Acts of God*, 9.

influential work understands typology not merely as the NT's metaphorical or illustrative use of an OT concept, but the eschatological fulfillment of God's redemptive plan.[164] The antitype in the NT does not merely find its image in the OT—it is the historical fulfillment of the OT type. Baker helps to differentiate the typological associations: "There are two main kinds of correspondence here: vertical (archetype and antitype, that is, the relationship between the heavenly and earthly realities) and the horizontal (prototype and antitype, that is, the relationship between the earlier and the later historical facts)."[165] The new exodus has to do with both aspects. Later it will be shown that both Isaiah and the author of Ephesians think in terms of both the vertical and horizontal realms; however, the primary emphasis is upon the horizontal one, which explains that the past actions of God are the basis for future deliverance. This method of interpreting God's actions became an ongoing principle utilized by the writers of both the OT and NT.[166] Hermeneutically, this use of OT imagery is considered historical typology.[167]

Examples of historical typology find origination in the way OT speakers link previous and future OT events.[168] Isbell and Ninow observe typology taking place in regard to the exodus. Isbell traces exodus motifs in OT historical figures such as Balaam, Joshua, Gideon, Samuel, David, and Elijah.[169] Ninow sees exodus typology in both the Pentateuch and the prophets.[170] In the Pentateuch, examples include Exod 15, Num 23 and 24, Deut 18:15–19 and 28–30. Of the prophets, he examines Isaiah, Jeremiah, Hosea, Micah, and Zechariah. Isaiah understands Eden as a type of new paradise (Isa 51:3); Hosea uses the wilderness wandering as a type of future wilderness wandering (Hos 2:14–15; 12:9); Isaiah conscripts the exodus for a new exodus (Isa 11:15–16; 43:16–21; 48:20–21; 51:9–11; 52:11–12); the psalmist incorporates the provision in the wilderness for future provision (Ps 78:52–53; 114:8), and the use of prior triumph in warfare to future triumph (Ps 83:9–11); Jeremiah sees the exodus and wilderness imagery as a new exodus (Jer 16:14–15; 23:7–8; 31:2); and Ezekiel undertakes the exodus as the way God relates to his people (Ezek 20:34–36). Abraham is a type of faithful servant (Gen 15:6); Moses an ideal prophet (Deut 18:15, 18); manna

---

164. Goppelt, *Typos*, 35.
165. D. Baker, "Typology and the Christian," 322.
166. Marsh, *Fulness*, 54–55; Tasker, *Old Testament in the New*, 20–21.
167. Other adjectives are elicited, such as "eschatological" (the Christ advent as the culmination of history) and "canonical" (interpreting individual texts in light of the entirety of the Bible).
168. Foulkes, *Acts of God*, 7.
169. C. Isbell, *Function*, 75–162.
170. Ninow, *Indicators*, 120–236.

a picture of provision (Exod 16:9–27); and David a type of king (Isa 11:1; 53:3–4; Jer 23:5; Ezek 34:23–24). Horace Hummel adds other typological figures and events such as creation week, flood, law, holy land, Jerusalem, temple, the wise man, Edom, Jonah, and Babylon.[171] He sees Israel's understanding of reality as having been acquired in large part from a typological understanding of her history. In a survey of the Old and New Testaments still other typological figures may be added to this listing, such as the use of Adam, Sodom, the plagues, and Jacob and Esau. Typological-historical understanding also involves memorials and feasts, a new Melchizedek, Moses, David, Elijah, the temple, and a basis of prayer.[172]

The typological understanding of events in the OT is replicated by writers and individuals in the NT. The events surrounding Christ became the basis for a typological interpretation of many OT images and events. Hundreds of examples could be cited.[173] A sampling includes NT writers seeing correspondence between the events of Israel's history in Egypt and the birth and baptism narratives (Matt 1–3, Mark 1, Luke 1–3); the rebellion in the wilderness and the church (1 Cor 10:6, 11); the flood and Christian suffering (1 Pet 3:21); the idolatry of Israel and the rejection of Christ (Amos 5:26; Acts 7:43); Moses and Christ (Acts 3:22, 7:37; Heb 3:2); and between the exodus period and final judgment (Rev 5–22). These interpretations enabled NT writers and audiences understand and correlate the Old and New Testaments. Through these events they deduced the meaning of the advent of Christ and the composition and purpose of the early church. Goppelt, Foulkes, and others argue further that OT prophets and NT writers envisioned not just a repetition of OT history but a repetition of expanded proportions. God would act similarly as he had in the past, but on a grander scale and in unprecedented ways. The typology functions in a double aspect: correspondence and increase.[174]

This is not to say that typologies in general and the new exodus in particular correspond uniformly throughout the Bible. The imageries and symbols, along with corresponding types and antitypes, vary. Authors and time periods may have their own typological framework. Farrer establishes this important delimitation.[175] The use of Moses as a type serves as an example. In the OT, Second Temple Judaism, and early Christianity, Moses was considered a type to several individuals: Joshua, Josiah, Jeremiah, Baruch and

---

171. Hummel, "Old Testament Basis," 38–40.
172. Foulkes, *Acts of God*, 19–40.
173. Beale and Carson, *Commentary*, 1163–1223.
174. D. Baker, "Typology and the Christian," 317–18.
175. Farrer, *Glass of Vision*, 45.

Hillel, Peter, Gregory Thaumaturgis, Constantine, Basil the Great, and others.[176] In many ways, Moses's life is seen to prefigure many of these individuals, revealing a multiplicity of uses. Each of these binary types and antitypes must be examined on their own merit. Ellis offers an important caution: "In the final analysis it is unwise to attempt to erect any integrated system of typology even within the Pauline writings; some elements were probably viewed as 'wholes' without reference to any larger scheme."[177] Osborne distinguishes between innate typology and inferred. The former is explicit and is stated as such in the NT; the latter is not explicit but is established by the tone of the NT. Both are legitimate uses of typology in the NT. Often gospel writers will delineate an explicit type (Matt 2:15); whereas in the book of Hebrews a typological assumption underlies nearly the entire work (Heb 7:1–3). It will be found that Paul uses new exodus typology in a variety of ways. For example, there is little doubt that 1 Cor 10:1–6 contains explicit exodus imagery. However, given the nature of the OT usages in Ephesians, it is anticipated that the typology there will be inferred.[178]

This is not to discount the study that follows; rather it sets in place how the new exodus is used in Scripture and the way in which it is likely to occur in Ephesians. In 1 Cor 10:1–6 explicit terms such as "cloud," "sea," "Moses," and "rock" all point unquestionably to the period after the departure from Egypt. But this is not the only way that Paul and NT writers speak of the exodus. Ephesians does not have these obvious markers, but neither are they necessary—especially to audiences familiar with the OT. Other, less explicit new exodus usages from Isaiah and the OT are clearly found in the NT and the Ephesian epistle. An argument will be made that the new exodus is to some degree inferred in the letter. This will be further discussed in chapters 2, 3, and 4 of this present work, and in the exposition of the epistle itself.

1.7 CONCLUSION

For purposes of this work, Paul is considered the author of Ephesians; however, many scholars disagree that the letter came from the apostle's hand. It will also be established that Ephesus was the destination of the epistle, or other cities of Western Asia Minor that resembled the situation at Ephesus. The following will also be understood: The audience was both Gentile and Jewish, with a focus on the acceptance of Gentiles into the blessings that had come upon believing Jews. The perspective of Paul is founded unambiguously upon the OT, primarily Isaiah, and the use of the OT in

---

176. Allison, *New Moses*, 1–39, 73–90, 192–94, 248–53.
177. Ellis, *Paul's Use*, 131–32 n. 9.
178. Osborne, "Type, Typology," 1118.

Ephesians forms the primary distinction with Colossians. The OT shaped Paul's worldview and was the lens through which he couched the advent of Christ, the church community, and human history. It is also understood that he most likely utilized the Alexandrian Septuagintal versions, but not without exception, as it is possible that he relied on Hebrew renderings of the OT whether written or from memory. Furthermore, it is accepted that NT authors and Paul employed a typological-historical hermeneutic by which they explained how the messages of the OT prophets were to be applied to their contemporary situation. The typological-historical approach does not demand explicit term-markers in a text in order to demonstrate the new exodus, although the subtleties of ancient language and culture are often underestimated or lost upon the modern reader. Note that since Paul and other OT and NT writers employed this hermeneutic, Ephesians may demonstrate it as well.[179]

With these introductory thoughts in mind, the task ahead is to survey the exodus theme in the Bible and Second Temple literature, including the formative influence of the new exodus on Paul, and review the history of scholarship relating to the study of the new exodus. In the balance of this work the question of the pervasiveness of the new exodus thinking in the epistle itself will be addressed.

---

179. This opens the possibility that a typological-historical interpretation of Isaiah's new exodus was part of the composition. This remains a proposal; it is not yet clear if the evidence mounts a convincing case.

2

The Formative Influence of the Exodus

UNDERSTANDING THE USE OF the new exodus in the book of Ephesians depends a great deal upon the comparative employment of the motif in other portions of the Bible and Jewish literature. It is especially important to grasp new exodus influence in the Pauline Corpus because it closely coincides with Ephesians. The resemblance of the use of the new exodus among these various sources will form part of the basis from which to judge new exodus influence in the epistle.[1]

2.1 THE NEW EXODUS AND ISAIANIC NEW EXODUS CONCEPTS

The book of Exodus and its images play a powerful role in the Bible.[2] The events leading up to and following the exodus deliverance form an epoch-

---

1. Luke attributes to Paul a brief reference to the historical exodus in the book of Acts (Acts 13:16–18; cf. 39) concerning the failure of Israel and the coming of Christ. Similar negative connotations of the exodus period are undertaken in 1 Cor 10:1–10 and Heb 3 and 8. Cf., Childs, *Exodus*, 233–34.

2. For a general introduction to the exodus motif: Hoffman, *Doctrine*, 60–65, 230–31; K. Kitchen, "Exodus," 2:700–708; Loewenstamm, *Evolution*, 53–68; Wright, *People of God*, 215–23; Zakovitch, "*You Shall Tell*," 46–98. For an introduction to the motif in the OT specifically: Longman and Dillard, *Introduction*, 73–74. Specific to the NT: Beale and Carson, *Commentary*, 14, 102, 112–131.In Beale and Carson's volume the new exodus influence in the NT is seen hundreds of times, and in various books. The editors and writers are keenly aware of the importance of the motif in OT in NT studies. For a history of the scholarship pertaining to the new exodus see chapter 3 of this present work. Apart from the Bible, the story of the exodus has played a major role as a programmatic text in the self-consciousness of peoples: Newton, "Analysis," 56–62; Weiler, "Communities," 63–71. For the resilience and ongoing influence of the exodus: Waltzer, *Revolution*, 7–17.

making pattern that is utilized time and again: God's selection and pity for his people, the emergence of a divinely appointed leader, the confrontation of evil and the demonstration of God's superiority, the flight from Egypt, the crossing of the sea, deliverance by the hand of God, the punishment of the Egyptians and neighboring peoples, the inauguration of the law and nation, the way through the desert, and the entrance into the promised land. The exodus period proper is widely defined, but most scholars consider it the history of the Hebrews from their oppression in Egypt (Exod 1) to their appearance at the Transjordan (Josh 1). However, literary influence of the exodus begins in Gen 1.[3] The liberation of Abraham's family is the historical and theological epicenter of God's relationship with Israel and shaped how the nation perceived itself and its future.

The historical exodus and its subplots served to prove God's intention to deliver his people at a later period during the exile.[4] The story was adopted by Isaiah, Jeremiah, and other prophets to form a related motif—a "new exodus" envisaged eschatologically as a new age and outpouring of God's power and presence among his people.[5] Isaiah depicts Cyrus as God's agent who releases the exiles (Isa 45:1–25), but ultimately it is God who actually redeems them from slavery (Isa 52:3–6). This is likened to the first exodus from Egypt (Isa 43:1–4, 14).[6] To the exilic nation, the new exodus was essentially a projection of the exodus narrative upon the events that faced the nation during and after the sojourn in Babylonia-Persia:[7] "Consciously or unconsciously, they came to shape their anticipation of the great eschatological salvation through the Messiah according to the pattern of the Exodus under Moses."[8]

However, the return from exile did not completely accomplish the new exodus conceived by the prophets.[9] Following the return from Persia, Yahweh's spokesmen saw a still future exodus. Postexilic passages describe the plight and spiritual state of the returning refugees and how the period came short of the idyllic age conceived by Isaiah, Jeremiah, and Ezekiel.[10] For

3. Burns, "Exodus," 13; Nixon, *New Testament*, 5.

4. The exodus was the primal act of God that brought certainty of God's future actions toward his people: Brueggemann, *Hope*, 87.

5. Childs, *Isaiah*, 36–37; Snaith, *Notes*, 146–47, 180, 188; P. Hanson, *Apocalyptic*, 218 n. 33.

6. Morris, "Redemption," 784–85.

7. Fishbane, "'Exodus' Motif,'" 121–40; Iersel et al., *Lasting Paradigm*, xv–46; Piper, "Unchanging," 3, 21; R. Smith, "Exodus Typology," 340–42.

8. Sahlin, "Salvation," 81.

9. Brunson, *Psalm 118*, 153–54; Childs, *Introduction*, 483; Wright, *Victory*, 268–70.

10. Dan 9:4–19; Ezra 9:6–15; Neh 9:5–37; Bar 1:15—3:8; Pr Azar; Sir 36:1–17. The

example, Ezra 9:8–9 speaks of the returnees' present bondage and slavery. The postexilic prophets in general painted a dark picture of the condition of the nation upon its return from Persia. Haggai's message was essentially one of reproof for the people's spiritual indifference toward the temple. Zechariah emphasized needed moral transformation. Malachi rebuked the people for inferior sacrifices and violations regarding divorce. Penitential prayers of the period reflect the lamentable state of the nation. Steck and others argue that Jewish literature in the Second Temple period is replete with the hope of the full restoration of the nation.[11] The extra-biblical literature of the period questions the validity of the Second Temple[12] and the belief that Israel remained in protracted spiritual exile.[13] This still future age is regarded by some as the "third exodus"—that which would fully accomplish the promises of Yahweh to his people.[14] Ultimately, this anticipation would form an overarching metanarrative through which the events of the Gospels, the early church, and final days of redemptive history would be brought into sharp relief.[15] The exodus anticipated in the postexilic period morphed into two successive epochs in the NT, the first inaugurated by the advent of Christ and the second by his return. Of the NT community Vos says, "The age to come was perceived to bear in its womb another age to come."[16] While still in the anticipated new exodus era, Jesus speaks of the Day of the Lord in which he will return and consummate history (Matt 24). The exodus depiction of this apocalyptic is shown in sweeping fashion in Revelation with plague, sea, bride, and other exodus motifs.

In summary, the aspects of the exodus motif in the OT (historical, new, and postexilic expectation) and that in the NT (the postexilic fulfilled and futuristic) came to establish a critical foundation in the writing of the NT and its understanding of the events of Jesus, the early church, and the

---

postexilic prophets anticipated the completion of the vision set forth by Isaiah, Jeremiah, and Ezekiel.

11. Steck, *Israel*, 60–322; Steck, "Problem," 445–58. This anticipation was not universally embraced. Some saw the establishment of the postexilic cult, however meager, as the genuine restoration of Israel. For comments: J. Scott, "Restoration," 797. Cf. later in this chapter: 2.2.3.

12. Dan 3:38 (LXX); Sir 36:14; *1 En.* 89:73; 90:28–33; Tob 14:5; *T. Levi* 16:1–5; 17:10–11; *2 Bar.* 68:5–7; *T. Moses* 4:8.

13. Two companion volumes depict the ongoing paradigmatic influence of the exile, and by association the exodus: J. Scott, *Exile*, 329–87, esp. 334–35, 365–66; J. Scott, *Restoration*, 114–16, 449.

14. Brueggemann, *Theology*, 622–49; C. Evans, "New Testament Use," 72–80; Goldsworthy, "Relationship," 81–88; Waltke and Yu, *Old Testament*, 139.

15. Wright, *People of God*, 126–27; Wright, *Victory*, 154–55.

16. Vos, *Pauline Eschatology*, 36.

culmination of history. The exodus had a formative and central influence on Jews of the first century and the writing of the NT.

2.2 SURVEY OF THE EXODUS THEME IN THE BIBLE AND SECOND TEMPLE LITERATURE

Both the Old and the New Testaments and Second Temple Literature provide ample evidence of the new exodus theme. The degree of new exodus influence upon Isaiah and Paul (and Pauline writings) weighs upon this present study.

2.2.1 *The OT*

Canonically, Genesis is placed before Exodus to explain the uniqueness of Israel and her God, as well as the call of Abraham and the nation in the context of human history. Although Genesis is placed prior to Exodus, it is not superior in influence. Childs argues that Genesis is best understood as a prologue to Yahweh's revelation at Sinai.[17] It serves to prepare readers for the central message revealed to Moses on the mountain. Nixon observes the creation narrative in the shadow of the exodus, while Fishbane aligns the exodus and new exodus with creation.[18] Brueggemann sees the narrative of Genesis, as early as Gen 15:7, suggesting the departure from Ur as an anticipation of the exodus.[19] Genesis demonstrates that the God who created and called the patriarchs is Yahweh who liberated the nation from Egypt, revealed himself at Sinai, and constituted a nation under Moses. Scholars argue that Genesis contains themes suggestive not only of the creation of Israel, but equally important the demonstration of Yahweh's creation power in redeeming his people in the historical exodus.[20] Among many other possibilities these themes include creation stories (Gen 1 and 2), Israel's call to be a witness among the nations (Gen 12:1), and the Hagar-Ishmael narratives (Gen 16–25).[21]

Exodus appears to be the theological center of the Pentateuch, where God most clearly revealed himself and demonstrated his intentions toward Israel and the Gentile nations. An early indication of the usefulness of the

---

17. Childs, *Canonical*, 53–56. Cf. Childs, *Exodus*, 232–39. In this second volume Childs examines NT counterparts to the Exodus passages under question, demonstrating the critical use of Exodus in the NT.

18. Ninow, *Indicators*, 5. Fishbane, "Exodus' Motif," cites Isa 51:9–11 and Hab 3, pp. 135–36.

19. Brueggemann, *Theology*, 177.

20. Dyrness, *Themes*, 64, 76; Goldingay, *Israel's Gospel*, 205–8.

21. Brueggemann, *Theology*, 147, 590.

The Formative Influence of the Exodus   31

exodus story in the Jewish Scriptures is found in Exod 12:41–42, "At the end of four hundred thirty years, on that very day, all the companies of the Lord went out from the land of Egypt. That was for the Lord a night of vigil, to bring them out of the land of Egypt. That same night is a vigil to be kept for the Lord by all the Israelites throughout their generations." The exodus event served as a pivotal, multigenerational lesson to the Hebrews. In the same general context, Exod 13:9 indicates a similar prescient theme: "It shall serve for you as a sign on your hand and as a reminder on your forehead, so that the teaching of the Lord may be on your lips; for with a strong hand the Lord brought you out of Egypt." The exodus event and the Passover observance were historic markers that were to be used throughout the history of the nation.[22] Similarly, Rad captures the significance of the Passover, indicating that the departure from Egypt would supply the basis for numerous lessons throughout the Old and New Testaments:

> The historical acts by which Jahweh founded the community of Israel were absolute. They did not share the fate of all other events, which inevitably slip back into the past. They were actual for each subsequent generation; and this not just in the sense of furnishing the imagination with a vivid present picture of past events—no, it was only the community assembled for a festival that by recitation and ritual brought Israel in the full sense of the word into being: in her own person she really and truly entered into the historic situation to which the festival in question was related. When Israel ate the Passover, clad as for a journey, staff in hand, sandals on her feet, and in the haste of departure (Ex. XII. 11), she was manifestly doing more than merely remembering the Exodus: she was entering into the saving event of the Exodus itself and participating in it in a quite "actual" way.[23]

Through the Passover the past acts of God and his future actions were inextricably linked. Stories and observances were oral, literary, and tangible devices garnered to teach new generations of their origins and expected conduct.[24] Exod 13:14 reveals a clear pedagogical purpose for the exodus, "When in the future your child asks you, 'What does this mean?' you shall answer, 'By strength of hand the Lord brought us out of Egypt, from the

---

22. Goldingay, *Israel's Faith*, 174.

23. Rad, *Old Testament*, II, 104. Ninow speaks of this understanding of present-in-past history as "you-were-there motif": *Indicators*, 115–20.

24. Burns writes how stories in Exodus also served to explain such things as the names of locations in the desert and accompanying theological lessons: "Exodus," 17.

house of slavery.'" The liberation from Egypt became a historical touchstone that was never to be forgotten.[25]

The Deuteronomic reforms also utilized Moses and exodus imagery.[26] A retelling of the exodus story is found in Deut 26:5–9, where preparations are made for the surviving wilderness generation to enter the Promised Land:

> [Y]ou shall make this response before the Lord your God: "A wandering Aramean was my ancestor; he went down into Egypt and lived there as an alien, few in number, and there he became a great nation, mighty and populous. When the Egyptians treated us harshly and afflicted us, by imposing hard labor on us, we cried to the Lord, the God of our ancestors; the Lord heard our voice and saw our affliction, our toil, and our oppression. The Lord brought us out of Egypt with a mighty hand and an outstretched arm, with a terrifying display of power, and with signs and wonders; and he brought us into this place and gave us this land, a land flowing with milk and honey."[27]

This is also seen in Num 24:8, a passage linked with Matthew's messianic use of Hos 11:1.[28] In this passage the history of the exodus is used to prepare God's people to conquer the land: "God who brings him out of Egypt, is like the horns of a wild ox for him; he shall devour the nations that are his foes and break their bones. He shall strike with his arrows." In addition, a widely recognized typological passage having to do with the "new Moses" finds its genesis in Deut 18:15–19.[29] Although it is unclear what Second Temple Judaism anticipated in terms of a Moses figure, Samaritan eschatology[30] and the NT writers[31] certainly found in Moses messianic typology.

The use of the exodus continues through the period of Joshua.[32] As God was with Moses, so he would be with his protégé (Josh 3:7, 4:14).

---

25. Lapide, "Jewish Tradition," 47–48.

26. Hayes, "Golden Calf," 45–49; Teeple, "Eschatological Prophet," 84–94.

27. Kaiser links this Deuteronomic exodus credo with the similar one in Josh 24:16–18: *Toward*, 62.

28. Blomberg, "Matthew," 8.

29. C. Isbell considers the possibility of Joshua, Gideon, Samuel, David, and Elijah, each as a second Moses. He concludes that all of these figures have fundamental similarities with Moses but that Elijah most resembles him: *Function*, 97–162; cf. Ninow, *Indicators*, 144–48.

30. Dexinger, "Samaritan Eschatology," 266–92; J. Macdonald, *Samaritans*, 266–76; Ninow, *Indicators*, 145–47.

31. Kaiser, *Messiah*, 57–60.

32. Noort, "Joshua," 155–70.

"Egypt" is mentioned at least seventeen times in the book, usually as a point of reference concerning entrance into the promised land. The crossing of the Jordan is placed in parallel to the crossing of the sea during the exodus (Josh 4:22–23). Josh 24:5–7 is one example of how the author intones the exodus, "Then I sent Moses and Aaron, and I plagued Egypt with what I did in its midst; and afterwards I brought you out. When I brought your ancestors out of Egypt, you came to the sea; and the Egyptians pursued your ancestors with chariots and horsemen to the Red Sea. When they cried out to the Lord, he put darkness between you and the Egyptians, and made the sea come upon them and cover them; and your eyes saw what I did to Egypt. Afterwards you lived in the wilderness a long time." In the book of Joshua there is a clear fusion between the era of Moses and that of Joshua in terms of leadership, deliverance, ritual, and remembrance of the exodus.

In Judges this is observed as well.[33] "Egypt" is often used in reference to the exodus.[34] One telling example is Judg 2:1: "Now the angel of the Lord went up from Gilgal to Bochim, and said, 'I brought you up from Egypt, and brought you into the land that I had promised to your ancestors.' I said, 'I will never break my covenant with you.'"

The exodus theme continues through the premonarchy, monarchy, and the preexilic, exilic, and postexilic periods. In the premonarchy, 1 Sam 10:18 is indicative of this usage, "[A]nd said to them, 'Thus says the Lord, the God of Israel, "I brought up Israel out of Egypt, and I rescued you from the hand of the Egyptians and from the hand of all the kingdoms that were oppressing you."'" The Philistines are cognizant of the renown associated with Yahweh and how he punished the Egyptians and their gods (1 Sam 4:7–8; 6:6). First and 2 Samuel,[35] 1 and 2 Kings,[36] and 1 and 2 Chronicles[37]

---

33. Hauser, "Songs of Victory," 265–84.

34. It is used seven times. By comparing Joshua, Gideon, Samuel, and Elijah to Moses, C. Isbell theorizes that at each juncture in Israel's history Yahweh provides a Moses-like leader to guide his people through the most tumultuous times: *Function*, 168. Along these same lines, Malachi may reprise Moses in his figure of Elijah (Mal 4:5).

35. Fishbane, "Motif," 121–40; Klein, *1 Samuel*, 60–61; McKenzie, "Time and Space," 76–79.

36. Aberbach and Smolar, "Golden Calves," 129–40; Frisch, "1 Kings 1–14," 3–21; Oblath, "Pharaohs and Kings," 23–42.

37. Although many would dispute his dating of Chronicles, Johnstone places the work in a post–Ezra-Nehemiah setting, asserting that the community was still in exile and to whom God would bring restoration: Johnstone, "Chronicles in Itself," 89–140. This "realized eschatology" in Chronicles is supported by others: Goldingay, "Chronicler," 99–126. But this understanding of Chronicles is disputed and reconfigured as "utopianism" by S. Schweitzer, "Reading Utopia," 30–64. Whereas "realized eschatology" looks to present manifestations of divine promises, "utopianism" sees the present situation of the writer in a better, improved light.

are replete with references to the historical exodus. During the construction of the temple, the exodus theme emerges as a chronological and theological point of reference: "I have not lived in a house since the day I brought up the people of Israel from Egypt to this day, but I have been moving about in a tent and a tabernacle" (2 Sam 7:6). Also, 1 Kgs 8:53, positioned in Solomon's reign, speaks of the ongoing application of the past historical situation to the present circumstances of the nation, "For you have separated them from among all the peoples of the earth, to be your heritage, just as you promised through Moses, your servant, when you brought our ancestors out of Egypt, O Lord God." First Chronicles 17:21 imparts a similar message: "Who is like your people Israel, one nation on the earth whom God went to redeem to be his people, making for yourself a name for great and terrible things, in driving out nations before your people whom you redeemed from Egypt?" Some maintain that Song of Songs employs exodus imagery.[38] Others, such as Childs, dispute non-sapiential theories, not only in Song but the balance of the wisdom corpus.[39] The discussion centers on the question of the literary nature of the book. If Song is sapiential in nature, then it functions much as Proverbs and Ecclesiastes. If it serves an allegorical, historical, or prophetic purpose, then the possibilities of new exodus imagery are more likely. In these latter cases the new exodus coalesces with images of God's love for his people and the divine marriage at Passover and Sinai (Ezek 16:1–14; Hos 2:14–20).[40] However, until new evidence comes forth the new exodus in Song is less than conclusive.

During the Babylonian-Persian exilic periods[41] the exodus is conscripted by the OT prophets—envisaged in the return from exile as a new Egyptian-like exodus, with the Isaiah text leading the way.[42] Childs speaks

38. Among other examples, Ochs links Song 5:2–8 with Exod 4:24: Ochs, "Political Transformation," 129.

39. Childs, *Introduction*, 574–75.

40. Rabbi Akiba's allegorical understanding of the Song sees the work eliciting Yahweh's growing intimacy with his people: Bloch and Bloch, *Song of Songs*, 30; Urbach, *Sages*, 417. Holland, among others, mounts a case for the Passover as the event of God's marriage with Israel. Indirectly this may connect with Song: Holland, *Contours*, 111–39, 226.

41. Of course the concept of exile is closely aligned with the exodus theme. Lorek sees several expressions of an exile pattern in the Hebrew Bible beginning with Adam and finishing with the postexilic prophets: when the nation was outside the land (Jer 50–51), when they were within it (Ezra 9, Neh 9, Dan 9), the expectation of the eschatological exile of Israel from Judah (Zech 13–14), and the post-resurrection exile of some Israelites (Dan 12:2): Lorek, "Exile," 2.

42. Table 12.3 in this work has a compilation of Isaiah's new exodus texts gleaned from prominent scholars. The literature on the new exodus in Isaiah is voluminous. For a sampling: B. Anderson, "Exodus Typology," 177–95; B. Anderson, "Exodus and

of Isaiah undertaking "the appropriation of the language of the exodus from Egypt."[43] Apart from the other prophets, Isaiah indicates a more specific employment of the exodus story in which the departure from Egypt is availed in terms of the return from Medo-Persia, messianic expectation, the reinstitution of Israel, and the arrival of the eschaton.[44] The utilization of new exodus images in Isaiah is not entirely distinct from previous usages, but does apply the exodus to the exiles in Babylonia-Persia and future generations. A key passage is Isa 11:11-14:

> On that day the Lord will extend his hand yet a second time to recover the remnant that is left of his people, from Assyria, from Egypt, from Pathros, from Ethiopia, from Elam, from Shinar, from Hamath, and from the coastlands of the sea. He will raise a signal for the nations, and will assemble the outcasts of Israel, and gather the dispersed of Judah from the four corners of the earth. The jealousy of Ephraim shall depart, the hostility of Judah shall be cut off; Ephraim shall not be jealous of Judah, and Judah shall not be hostile towards Ephraim. But they shall swoop down on the backs of the Philistines in the west, together they shall plunder the people of the east. They shall put forth their hand against Edom and Moab, and the Ammonites shall obey them. And the Lord will utterly destroy the tongue of the sea of Egypt; and will wave his hand over the River with his scorching wind; and will split it into seven channels, and make a way to cross on foot; so there shall be a highway from Assyria for the remnant that is left of his people, as there was for Israel when they came up from the land of Egypt.

Isaiah envisions parallels between the historic exodus and what God will bring about in the current historical situation. Another significant passage on the new exodus theme in Isaiah is found in 43:14-21:

Covenant," 339-60; Ceresko, "Rhetorical Strategy," 42-55; Durham, "Isaiah 40-55," 47-56; Sungsoo Kim, "Exodus Motif in Isaiah," iv-121; Stuhlmueller, *Creative Redemption*, 59-98; R. Watts, "Consolation," 31-59; Zenger, "God of Exodus," 22-33.

43. Childs, *Isaiah*, 299.

44. Isa 4:5; 10:26-27; 35:8-10; 43:16-17; 49:8-13; 50:2; 63:11, 12. Moyise and Menken, *Isaiah*,1-6, 76-78, 115-16, 132, 157, 209-10. This is represented by both older and more recent commentators: Alexander, *Commentary*, I: 77, 57-59, 177, 258, 263, 412; II: 95, 147, 149, 156, 161, 210, 218, 223, 249, 272, 281, 332, 420, 423; Oswalt, *Isaiah, Chapters 1-39*, 145, 286-94, 312, 367-380, 466, 570, esp. 624; Oswalt, *Isaiah, Chapters 40-66*, 86, 93, 101, 134-39, 152-55, 195-208, 235, 258-68, 281-99, 315-20, 341, 364, 372, 443, 553, 604, 614, 622, esp. 155, 200, 208, 609. Oswalt articulates the reserve that interpreters should demonstrate in determining the degree of influence of the exodus in particular passages in Isaiah: 199-200 n. 15.

> Thus says the Lord, your Redeemer, the Holy One of Israel: For your sake I will send to Babylon and break down all the bars, and the shouting of the Chaldeans will be turned to lamentation. I am the Lord, your Holy One, the Creator of Israel, your King. Thus says the Lord, who makes a way in the sea, a path in the mighty waters, who brings out chariot and horse, army and warrior; they lie down, they cannot rise, they are extinguished, quenched like a wick: Do not remember the former things, or consider the things of old. I am about to do a new thing; now it springs forth, do you not perceive it? I will make a way in the wilderness and rivers in the desert. The wild animals will honor me, the jackals and the ostriches; for I give water in the wilderness, rivers in the desert, to give drink to my chosen people, the people whom I formed for myself so that they might declare my praise.

Many other passages could be cited[45] and are listed in the summary inventory located in the last chapter of this present work.[46] Other references to the exodus in Isaiah speak of Israel as a light to the nations and the eschatological Sinai for all peoples.[47] Snaith makes a compelling argument that the new exodus is a controlling theme in Second Isaiah to which all other motifs are subservient.[48] Muilenburg notes that the new exodus is the "most profound and most prominent" motif employed by Second Isaiah.[49] B. Anderson traces exodus typology in Second Isaiah by emphasizing "typology as a means to . . . express the Biblical understanding of history."[50] He sees the new exodus motif in Isaiah (and the NT) not so much from the standpoint of traditional arguments concerning the use of the OT in the New, but how biblical authors choose to relate typology and history. He argues that the first exodus becomes the type of the new exodus that Isaiah envisioned while Cyrus made preparations to free the Jews. Balentine concludes his

---

45. Isa 4:2–6; 12:1f; 19:19–25; 24:23; 35:1–10; 40:3–11, 41:17–20; 42:14–17; 43:1–7; 44:1–5, 27; 48:20–21; 49:8–12; 50:2–3; 51:1—52:15; 55:12; 63:1–19.

46. The Isaianic new exodus texts cited in this present work are a compilation of Ninow, Fishbane, Stuhlmueller, and R. Watts: Fishbane, "Motif," 121–40; Ninow, *Indicators*, 157–95; Stuhlmueller, *Creative Redemption*, 59–98; R. Watts, *New Exodus in Mark*, 367–88.

47. Zenger, "God of Exodus," 29–32.

48. Snaith, *Notes*, 146–47, 180, 188.

49. Muilenburg, *Isaiah*, 602.

50. B. Anderson, "Exodus Typology," 177–95. Anderson cites Kraus's summary: Kraus, *Geschichte*, 432–40.

argumentation along this line remarking, "Second Isaiah employs mythological motifs in his elaboration of the typology of the old and the new exodus."[51]

Similar to Isaiah, Jeremiah was another exilic prophet based in the southern kingdom. He clearly exhibits new exodus imagery (Jer 23:7–8; 31:31–34; 33:4–11).[52] The same can be said of Micah's colloquy with God (Mic 7:14–17).[53] In the northern kingdom, Hosea (Hos 2:16–17, 11:1–11)[54] and Amos (Amos 9:7–15)[55] indicate exodus typology in terms of judgment and restoration. Similarly, Jonah may show intertextual evidence of the exodus with images of the watery deep and rescue (Jonah 2:1–10).[56] There are indications that Nahum had the new exodus in mind as well, echoing Isa 52:7 in Nah 1:15.

Ezekiel, considered an exilic prophet, exhibits the new exodus.[57] In one of the most devastating OT passages on the judgment of Israel, Ezekiel holds out hope couched in images of a Moses exodus (Ezek 20; 36:24–26, 33).[58] Increasingly, Daniel is seen in terms of its use in the NT, including the concepts of μυστήριον and "Son of Man;"[59] resurrection, reward and judgment (Dan 12:2); and the Danielic apocalyptic imagery utilized in Revelation.[60] Although there does not appear to be explicit new exodus terminology in Daniel, these images comport well with the new exodus. Of course, μυστήριον will prove prominent in Ephesians.

In addition, the postexilic prophets are emblematic. An explicit reference to liberation from Egypt is found in Hag 2:5, and another exodus experience is clearly adumbrated (Hag 2:5–6). Zechariah picks up the new exodus theme in keeping with Isaiah (Zech 8:1–8, 11–13, 14–15; esp. 6–8,

---

51. Balentine, "Death of Jesus," 94.

52. Bellis, "New Exodus in Jeremiah," 157–68; Wal, "Themes," 559–66; Yates, "New Exodus," 1–22.

53. Fishbane, "Motif," 125–26; Ninow, *Indicators*, 218–28.

54. Hoffman, "North Israelite," 169–82; Loretz, "Exodus, Dekalog," 217–48; McKenzie, "Hosea," 100–108.

55. Brueggemann, "'Exodus' in the Plural," 15–34; Dijkstra, "Prophet's Pupil," 105–28; Lang, "Amos Und Exodus," 27–29.

56. Hunter, "Jonah 2," 142–58.

57. Hattori, "Divine Dilemma," 413–24; Lust, "Ezekiel," 209–24; Patton, "Gave Them Laws," 73–90; Zimmerli et al., *Ezekiel*, 455.

58. Childs, *Canonical*, 165.

59. M. Casey, *Son of Man*, 51–98; Ferch, *Daniel Seven*, 4–39, 95 n. 2.

60. Beale, "Danielic Background," 163–70.

11; 10:10–12).[61] Perhaps Esther employs the exodus.[62] Nehemiah draws on the exodus as a historical point of reference (Neh 9:9–17; esp. 36–37). A new exodus is clearly sought after in the contexts of these passages. Watts points out new exodus allusions in Malachi and the prophet's connections to the new exodus hope in Isaiah (Mal 3:1).[63]

As a whole, the exilic and postexilic prophets anticipated a new era that included a return from Babylonia-Persia but also vastly exceeded this homecoming: "The prophets . . . do not proclaim a restoration after the destructive exile that simply returns to the old Deuteronomic status quo. Their theological and relational picture of the future is different—and better. There will be a new exodus (Isaiah), a new covenant of forgiveness, written on hearts instead of stone (Jeremiah), and a new presence of Yahweh's indwelling Spirit within individuals (Ezekiel and Joel)."[64] Ninow describes the expectations of the postexilic remnant: "The overall picture is still one of exile and unfulfilled promise; it is still a situation that expects reversal."[65] Zechariah speaks of an exodus that far exceeds the experience in Egypt.

Several Psalms show exodus effects, usually for purposes of worship or warning. Those undertaken for praise and worship include: 77,[66] 105, 106, 114, 118,[67] 135, and 136. God is to be praised for his unerring faithfulness to the exodus generation with an eye to a contemporary application. The crisis of the exodus and the crises of present circumstances are closely aligned. Ps 114:3 ties the crossing of the Red Sea with that of the Jordan.[68] The warning psalms utilize the disobedience of exodus generation in order to caution the current audience: 78,[69] 81,[70] and 85. Other psalms, such as 23,[71] 80,[72]

---

61. Ninow comments on Zech 10:6–12: "It appears as if certain elements that are characteristic of the first coming out from Egypt form a paradigm for the new eschatological exodus": Ninow, *Indicators*, 234.

62. Andrew, "Esther, Exodus," 25–28.

63. R. Watts, *New Exodus in Mark*, 67–74.

64. Pate et al., "Prophets," 96.

65. Ninow, *Indicators*, 234–36. Ninow provides a helpful summary chart of the new exodus in the prophets, 240–41.

66. Kselman, "Psalm 77," 51–58; Stevenson, "Communal Imagery," 215–29.

67. Brunson, *Psalm 118*, 153–79.

68. The same alignment is found in Josh 4:18–24: Macintosh, "Psalm 114," 318–19.

69. Witte, "Exodus to David," 21–42.

70. Loretz, "Psalm 81," 127–43.

71. Milne, "Psalm 23," 237–47.

72. Hieke, "Psalm 80," 551–58.

105,[73] 110,[74] 149,[75] and others, have offered ample images of new covenant and exodus themes for NT writers. Of all the psalms, Psalm 68 most clearly depicts new exodus thought.[76] It explicitly sees a superior messianic deliverance that is first typified in the Egyptian exodus.[77] The exodus-influenced psalms reveal how vibrant the story was to the nation. The variety of dates of the exodus psalms speak of the depth and breadth of exodus consciousness that permeated the minds of those who wrote, transmitted, and received Hebrew hymnic literature.[78]

In summary, the historical exodus is rooted in the book of Exodus, but nearly the entire OT reflects the exodus event in various degrees. Exodus imagery in Genesis relates themes that highlight Yahweh as the God of creation who triumphs over darkness, and calls Abraham and his family to their unique role in redemptive history. Numbers and Deuteronomy recount the exodus in order to motivate the Hebrews to enter the land. In Joshua the exodus theme continues with Joshua as the new Moses, called to lead the nation to complete the intention of the exodus to enter the Promised Land. In Judges the exodus is remembered as a lasting memory for a nation that has lost its way. In Samuel, Kings, and Chronicles the exodus is used time and again for many purposes, ranging from the call of the nation to deliverance and building the temple. The Psalms reveal the ubiquitous nature of the exodus theme in ancient Israel, specifically for use in worship. The prophets undertake the exodus in a variety of ways, but Isaiah stands out as the apex, envisioning a fully developed new exodus. This is supported and enhanced by Hosea, Amos, Jeremiah, and Ezekiel, among others.

---

73. Holm-Nielsen, "Psalm 105," 22–30.

74. Psalm 110 is the most frequently referenced psalm in the NT: Matt 22:44; Mark 12:36; Luke 20:42; Acts 2:34; and Heb 1:13, 5: 6, 7:17. Allusions are made as well: Matt 26:64; Mark 14:62; Luke 22:69; Eph 1:20; Col 3:1; and Heb 5:10; 6:20; 7:11, 15; 8:1. For the use of the psalm in the early Christian era: D. Anderson, *Psalm 110*, 277–90; David, "Messianic Psalm?," 162–63; Hay, *Glory at the Right Hand*, 163–64.

75. Ceresko, "Psalm 149," 177–94.

76. Ps 68 is considered at length in chapter 8 of this present work in the discussion of Eph 4:8.

77. Ellis, *Paul's Use*, 131–32.

78. Other possible psalmic connections include the messianic psalms such as Juel's conjectures concerning Psalm 89's use in the NT: *Messianic Exegesis*, 109. But Hays sees Juel moving too far from the typological hermeneutic: Hays, *Conversion*, 110.

2.2.2 The NT

In the NT the use of the new exodus narrative continues. The synoptics and the Gospel of John all clearly evoke the new exodus.[79] As a sampling, Matt 2:15 reveals a new exodus background from Hosea 11:1 (and Exod 23:30).[80] Blomberg attests that in Matt 2:15 "a new exodus motif is present."[81] Additionally, Matt 3:3 (as well as the three other Gospels) express the new exodus in terms of the forerunner: "This is the one of whom the prophet Isaiah spoke when he said, 'The voice of one crying out in the wilderness: "Prepare the way of the Lord, make his paths straight"'" (Isa 40:3).[82] In Matthew, Jesus is presented as a "new Moses"[83] who, in contrast to OT Israel, demonstrated faithfulness to Yahweh.[84] Like Moses, Jesus is saved in his infancy from an evil ruler, travels from Egypt, lives in the wilderness for a period of "forty" days leads "twelve" followers, presents the law from the mount, and displays miracles.[85] Studies in Mark reveal an Isaianic new exodus structure.[86] R. Watts shows Jesus depicted as the Yahweh-Warrior of Isaiah.[87] Janzen identifies Exod 3:6 and the revelation of Yahweh in the portrayal of resurrection in Mark 12:26.[88] Luke-Acts is heavily influenced by the new exodus,[89] and the specific use of Isaiah is likewise found in Luke.[90] Luke's recorded sermons by

---

79. New exodus works on all the Gospels include: C. Evans and Stegner, *Gospels*, 15–27; Tuckett, *Scriptures in the Gospels*, xxiv; Wright, *Victory*, xviii, 130, 160, 177. For the exodus influence in the synoptics: Swartley, *Story Shaping Story*, 5–7. Early on, Stendahl's influential work on Matthew set the stage for a debate on pesher citation methods of NT authors' use of the OT: Stendahl, *School of St. Matthew*, 13–31. However, Gundry sees no need to resort to pesher explanations of matthean citation methods: Gundry, *Use of the Old Testament*, 172. For exodus imagery in Jesus's life, especially considering his combative relations with the powers, Wink's trilogy is informative: *Naming*; *Unmasking*; and *Engaging*.

80. Piper, "Unchanging," 8.

81. Blomberg, "Matthew," 8; France, "Formula-Quotations," 243–44.

82. Horsley and Hanson, *Popular Movements*, 136–46; R. Webb, *Baptizer and Prophet*, 347.

83. Allison, *New Moses*, 86, 109, 247.

84. Aus, *Virginal Conception*, 30–35.

85. Matt 2:13, 15; 4:1–11; 5:1; 8:1–9:38; 10:1. Cf. Blomberg, "Matthew," 8.

86. Bowman, *Gospel of Mark*, 53, 77, 350; Daube, "Earliest Structure," 174–87; R. Watts, *New Exodus in Mark*, 369–88.

87. R. Watts, *New Exodus in Mark*, 140–56. Cf., Myers, *Binding*, 61–62.

88. Janzen, "Resurrection," 43–58. For a Pauline perspective: Carrez, "Pauline Hermeneutics," 30–48.

89. Mánek, "Books of Luke," 8–23; Pao, *Acts*, 4–17; Strauss, *Davidic Messiah*, 261–336; cf. Park, *Finding Herem?*, 181–82.

90. Sanders, "Isaiah in Luke," 144–55.

Peter, Stephen, and Paul (Acts 3:22, 7:17–43, 13:16–23) confirm the realization of the new exodus. In the Beelzebul controversy (Luke 11:17–22), connection is made between the "finger of God" and the power of God during the plagues and the exodus (Exod 8:19).[91] Mánek asserts that "the passion according to St. Luke is the outline of the Old Testament Exodus in its main phases."[92] Sahlin writes of the exodus influence on the synoptic writers: "The typology of the Exodus was fundamental for the Evangelists, and supplied no merely accidental correspondence . . . Exodus and the Messianic deliverance was not only generally accepted among the Jews in the time of Jesus, but was also taken for granted in serious theological thinking; Exodus typology was, in other words, of a dogmatic character."[93] In portions of the Gospel of John there is a manifestation of the new exodus.[94] John 1:14–18 (coupled with Exod 33:7—34:35 and perhaps Ps 85); 6:35 (with Exod 16); 7:37–38 (with Exod 17); and 8:12 (with Exod 13:21) show Christ fulfilling new exodus expectations, especially in view of the culmination of history.[95] Gärtner has a thorough treatment of Passover imagery in John 6.[96]

Hebrews indicates the new exodus motif.[97] Among many other passages, Heb 4:1–2 is influenced by Ps 95 and Exod 17:1–10. The wilderness generation serves as a type of temporary and provisional situation that is contrasted with a complete and final state of affairs. New exodus investigations are proven fruitful in 1 Peter.[98] Revelation shows extensive evidence and structure from the OT and the new exodus.[99] The garments of the Son of Man in Rev 1:13 echo the garments of Aaron and his sons in Exod 28. Revelation 8:7; 11:19; and 16:21 coincide with the hailstones in Exod 9:22–23. The darkness of Rev 8:12 links with Exod 10:21–23, and Rev 9:3 ties

---

91. Fuller, "Kingdom," 168–69.

92. Mánek, "Books of Luke," 13.

93. Sahlin, "Salvation," 83.

94. Enz, "Gospel of John," 208–15; A. Hanson, "John 1:14–18," 97–109; Mowvley, "Light of Exodus," 135–37; R. Smith, "Exodus Typology," 340–42.

95. Corell, *Consummatum*, 1–6, 84.

96. Gärtner, *John 6*, 17.

97. For the new exodus in the Pauline Corpus, a separate section follows in this present chapter: 2.3, The Influence of Isaiah's New Exodus on Pauline Thought. For the new exodus in Hebrews: Gray, "Desert Sojourn," 148–54; Piper, "Unchanging," 19; Sahlin, "Salvation," 82; Shin, "Hebrews," i; Thiessen, "End of the Exodus," 353–69.

98. Deterding, "First Peter," 58–65; Mbuvi, *Identity*, 11, 42; Scharlemann, "Exodus Ethics," 165–70; Viviano, "Peter as Jesus's Mouth," 226–52.

99. J. Casey, "Exodus Theme," 34–46; Gallus, "Revelation 15–16," 21–43; Mathewson, "Sea Was No More," 243–58; Sanborn, "Risen Lamb," 18–25; Shea, "Parallels," 164–79. Other, more general works contribute to the OT use in Revelation: Beale, *Book of Revelation*, 313, 327, esp. 643–45; Moyise, *Revelation*, 102, 117, 122.

with locusts in Exod 10:12–15. Rev 12:14 (God holding his people on eagle's wings) finds influence in Exod 19:4. Other passages such as Rev 15:3–4 show effect from Exod 15:1–18 (the Song of the Sea); Rev 15:5–8, 21:1–4 and 22 (the tabernacle) refer back to Exod 36:30 and 40:34; and Rev 21:12 and Exod 10:12–15 demonstrate commonality with the twelve tribes motif. Childs sees a skip stone relationship between Exodus themes projected upon Isaiah and ultimately Revelation, especially in the latter chapters of the Apocalypse. He writes, "The most complete resonance of this eschatological theme encompassing the entire book of Isaiah is found in Rev. 21:22–27."[100]

The new exodus clearly permeates many portions of the NT. The Gospels depict Jesus as the messianic figure who was integral to the new exodus conceived by the OT prophets. The sermons in Acts identify Jesus with Moses and see the church within the new exodus heritage. The epistles and Apocalypse in varying degrees reflect the influence of new exodus thinking.

2.2.3 Second Temple Literature

Important connections may exist between the new exodus in Second Temple literature and Ephesians.[101] The writings of this period,[102] including the Apocrypha, OT Pseudepigrapha, Josephus, Dead Sea Scrolls, targumic, rabbinic writings, and other related texts reveal in a variety of gradations an emphasis on the exodus event, demonstrating a multiplicity of uses.[103] Grabbe, in his work on Judaism in the Second Temple Period, discusses the numerous uses of exodus imagery.[104] Strack and Billerbeck observe that in the rabbinic literature of this period it was common to see the exodus event as a type of messianic salvation that included the age to come.[105] Wright and Holland see the perpetuity of the exile in several primary sources throughout the period.[106]

---

100. Childs, *Isaiah*, 36–37. Bruce speaks highly of Revelation as well, "Victory of God," 50.

101. One example among others is the possible targumic influence on Eph 4:8 from Ps 68:18. Another similar effect is Deut 30:12–14 in Rom 10:6–8. This first instance will be explored in the expositional portion of this study in chapters 5–11.

102. For background: Guignebert, *Jewish World*; Moore, *Judaism*, 3 vols.

103. The following give many examples of the exodus effect in Second Temple Period literature: Balentine, "Death of Jesus," 27–30; O. Piper, "Unchanging," 5–6; Sahlin, "Salvation," 81–82.

104. Grabbe, *Judaic Religion*, 56, 67, 72, 86–88. Cf. Jeremias, *Theological Dictionary*, IV, 864.

105. Strack and Billerbeck, *Kommentar*, 1:85–88, 2:481. Cf. Blomberg, "Matthew," 7.

106. Wright investigates *1 En.* 89.73–77; *As. Mos.* 4.5—6.9; 1QpHab. 9.3–7; 12.7–9;

Concerning the Apocrypha, about half of Wisdom of Solomon is a commentary on the exodus (Wis 11–19). There is an ongoing contrast between the righteous and wicked, with the exodus plagues serving as a model of judgment (Wis 10:17–19). If the locus of the work is Alexandria, Egypt, then the exodus imagery, including diatribes against polytheism and animal worship, would certainly be analogous to the original situation in Egypt. Grabbe maintains that Wisdom may have been an attempt to discourage Jewish youth from abandoning their ancestral roots. Cities such as Alexandria and events like the greater Diaspora provided an attractive Greek alternative to the dictates of Jewish tradition. Conversely, Cheon considers Wisdom of Solomon functioning sociologically in the wake of anti-Semitism in Alexandria in the first century AD.[107] Third Macc. 6:4, 10 references the historical exodus and generally refers to the new exodus. Second Esd 15:10–12, 15:60, and 16:1 view a new exodus. First Bar focuses on the return from exile by way of utilizing the second exodus imagery of Isa 51:10–11 (cf. Jer 24, 29).[108] The prayer of Sir 36:10 indicates that Yahweh will restore the inheritance of Jacob, offering details that the event will be akin to the exodus from Egypt. The rebuilding of Jerusalem and the temple, and the inclusion of Gentiles in the new age, is described in Tobit.[109]

Added to the Apocrypha are evidences in the Dead Sea Scrolls and Qumran that are in keeping with the Isaianic expectation of a new exodus.[110] Using the language of Isaiah, Qumran documents provide evidence of messiah figures. They reveal that a Davidic Messiah will build a spiritual temple.[111] The exodus story was so pervasive at Qumran that it functioned as a prototype by which the community conducted its affairs.[112] Josephus contains allusions to the new exodus: the division of the Jordan and entrance into the Promised Land, and miracles and other events in the wilderness.[113]

4Q175., 25–30: *Victory*, xviii, 313. Holland undertakes the Dead Sea Scrolls, Josephus, *Psalms of Solomon*, Tobit, Baruch, and rabbinic writings: Holland, *Contours*, 22–26.

107. Cheon, *Exodus Story*, 150–52. Cf. Winston, *Wisdom of Solomon*, 20–25.

108. Grabbe, *Judaic Religion*, 67.

109. Tob 14:4–7.

110. Wise et al., *Dead Sea Scrolls*, 136, 277, 394–95, 422–23. Holland sees the new exodus in *A Genesis Florilegium* (4Q252), *Joshua Apocryphon*, (4Q522), *The Words of Michael* (4Q434, 436), *The New Jerusalem* (4Q554), *Hymns of the Poor* (4Q434, 436), and *War Scroll* (1QM 11:7c–10a); among others: Holland, *Contours*, 22–24. The noted difference is the Qumran two Messiahs (one as king from Judah and one as priest from Levi) with the NT understanding of one.

111. Wise et al., *Dead Sea Scrolls*, referencing *The Children of Salvation* (Yeshua) and *Mystery of Existence* (4Q416, 418), Fragment 1.

112. Milik, *Ten Years of Discovery*, 51–56; Teeple, "Eschatological Prophet," 84–94.

113. Josephus, *Complete Works*, 20.5.1; 20.8.6; 20.8.10; 20.97–99.

He indicates that popular Judaism hoped for a Messiah who would function as a second Moses and liberate Israel from Roman domination. The *Psalms of Solomon* describe second exodus events as the messianic king comes to seize Jerusalem.[114]

The Rabbinic Writings have references to the exodus and eschatological redemption: the entire imagery of the Passover ritual,[115] the exodus as a model of salvation, a return of the signs and miracles of the exodus, going into the wilderness to meet God,[116] and these events taking place on the Passover[117] under the leadership of a new Moses.[118] The Messiah would correspond to Moses by bringing plagues upon those who afflict Israel and by performing the miracles of water from the rock and the provision of manna.[119] Hannah analyzes the use of Isaiah among the multifarious Judaisms of the Second Temple period just prior to the writing of the NT. While focusing on the most utilized passages (Isa 6:1–13; 10:33—11:10; and the servant songs Isa 42:1–7; 49:1–9; 50:4–11; 52:13—53:12), Hannah undertakes these occurrences in the Qumran manuscripts, *Psalms of Solomon*, the *Similitudes of Enoch*, the *Third Sibylline Oracle*, *Ezra*, and the *Qeduša*. He discovers that the usages are usually messianic and eschatological in nature.[120]

Other, Judaic literature further speaks of the popularity and pervasiveness of the exodus story. The book of *Jubilees* is another apocryphal writing that builds its argument around the exodus event.[121] Jubilees retraces the entire story of the exodus, beginning with creation and ending with the people of God finding rest. God will adopt his people, along with his Messiah as his sons, and redeem them from exile.[122] Additionally, Jdt 5:5–13 makes use of the historical exodus. Jdt 2:11–15 refers to the historical exodus but alludes to the new exodus as well:

---

114. *Pss. Sol.*, Ps. 2, 9, 11, 18. Psalm 2 is a prayer that the king who oppresses Jerusalem will lie slain on a beach in Egypt without anyone to bury him. Psalm 9 is a petition for the intervention of the Lord on behalf of his distressed people. Psalm 11 depicts the return of the captives. The eighteenth Psalm is Christological in nature and pictures the downfall of the Hasmoneans and Romans: Jonge, *Outside*, 160–61; Surburg, *Intertestamental*, 144–45.

115. Exod 3:8, *Pesig. Rab Kah.* 116b.

116. Cited by Holland: Strack and Billerbeck, 1:68, 85; 2:284, 293; 4:55 (model of salvation); 1:85, 4:954 (signs and miracles); 4:939 (meeting God in the wilderness): *Contours*, 26 nn. 15, 16, 17, 19.

117. Sahlin, "Salvation," 82.

118. Jeremias, *Eucharistic Words*, 207.

119. *Pesig. Rab Kah.* 49b; 67b–68.

120. Hannah, "Isaiah within Judaism," 7–33.

121. VanderKam, *Jubilees*, 11–12. Cf. O. Piper, "Unchanging," 5.

122. *Jub.* 1:24. The same may be said of *T. Jud.* 24:3 and 4Q174 1:11.

> And now, O Lord God of Israel, who brought your people out of the land of Egypt with a mighty hand and with signs and wonders and with great power and outstretched arm, and made yourself a name that continues to this day, we have sinned, we have been ungodly, we have done wrong, O Lord our God, against all your ordinances. Let your anger turn away from us, for we are left, few in number, among the nations where you have scattered us. Hear, O Lord, our prayer and our supplication, and for your own sake deliver us, and grant us favor in the sight of those who have carried us into exile; so that all the earth may know that you are the Lord our God, for Israel and his descendants are called by your name.

The work of Ezekiel the Dramatist, dated perhaps in the second century BC, includes a drama on the exodus.[123] The author claims to be Jewish while utilizing the LXX and Greek literary form. Similarly, the *Exagoge* of Ezekiel the Tragedian is a Greek composition, but in contrast to the Dramatist, the Tragedian goes to great lengths to rework the exodus story.[124] The Tannaim typologically connect the historical exodus with the new age described in Isaiah.[125] It appears that 5 Ezra employs the exodus as well.[126]

In summary, the exodus and new exodus are dominant themes in the OT, NT, and Second Temple literature. The saga of the exodus became a prismatic lens through which the Jewish people gained understanding concerning deliverance in the past and how God would act ultimately on their behalf in the future. The exodus provided a timeless archetype of warning and hope. The expectation of an eschatological new exodus was in keeping with Isaiah, Jeremiah, Ezekiel, Hosea, Malachi, and other OT prophets. The exodus and new exodus formed a common theme among biblical and extra-biblical writers, thus establishing the new exodus as a unifying background to the NT.[127] Based on these findings, important connections with Ephesians may exist.

2.3 THE INFLUENCE OF ISAIAH'S NEW EXODUS ON PAULINE THOUGHT

The new exodus credo plays a prominent role in the Pauline Corpus and is central to whether, and to what degree, the new exodus is manifested

---

123. Grabbe, *Judaic Religion*, 72.
124. Ibid., 56.
125. Piper, "Unchanging," 5.
126. Bergren, "Exodus-Review," 34–50.
127. Piper, "Unchanging" 3, 21.

in Ephesians. Michel,[128] Dodd,[129] Käsemann,[130] Ridderbos,[131] Koch,[132] and Stanley[133] recognize the Pauline use of the OT, but Sahlin,[134] Ellis,[135] Hays,[136] C. Evans and Sanders,[137] Wright,[138] Keesmaat,[139] and others[140] go further in order to examine the apostle's use of the exodus motif, or in some cases Paul's use of Isaiah.[141] These latter scholars regard the exodus as a fundamental force in the Paul that functions paradigmatically. Related is Hickling's finding that 26 percent of the time Paul uses Isaiah when citing the OT.[142] This is probably a conservative estimate given the apostle's penchant for subtle usages.

---

128. Michel, *Paulus Und Seine Bibel*, 193–201 for a survey of OT usage in Ephesians.

129. Dodd, *According*. For his survey of Ephesians: 33, 35, 38, 94, 121.

130. Käsemann, *Perspectives*, 45.

131. Ridderbos, *Paul*, 153–58.

132. Koch, *Schrift*, 33, 45–48, 129–32.

133. Stanley, *Language of Scripture*, 3–30.

134. Sahlin, "Salvation," 83–94.

135. E. Ellis, *Paul's Use*, 117, 127, 129–35; esp. 4–5 for a history of scholarship pertaining to Paul's use of the OT.

136. Hays, *Echoes*, 1–24, 25–49; Hays, *Conversion*, 87–104.

137. In C. Evans and Sanders' work, chapters that specifically consider the new exodus are Enns, "Psalm 95 in Hebrews 3:1—4.13," 352–63; Keesmaat, "Paul and His Story: Exodus," 300-333; Swancutt, "Hungers Assuaged," 218–51: *Early Christian Interpretation*.

138. Wright, "New Inheritance," 16, 47; Wright, "New Exodus, New Inheritance," 26–35.

139. Keesmaat, *Paul and His Story*, 35, 39, 41–42, 46–47, 59, 61, 63–65, 72–73, 77–80, 82, 87–90, 93–96, 102, 107, 110, 117–18, 122, 125–26, 131, 134, 136, 139–43, 151, 153–54, 162–64, 169, 170, 172–73, 179, 185, 188, 191–92, 199, 207–8, 213, 220, 222–23, 226, 228, 234–37.

140. Oropeza, "Echoes of Isaiah," 87–112.

141. Wagner, *Heralds*, 2–3, 170–80, 344–46, 356–69; Wagner, "Moses and Isaiah," 87–106; Wilk, *Bedeutung*, 1–15.

142. Hickling, "Paul's Reading," 215–23.

Turpie,¹⁴³ Michel,¹⁴⁴ Koch,¹⁴⁵ Wilk,¹⁴⁶ Ellis,¹⁴⁷ and Silva¹⁴⁸ provide data of the Pauline use of the OT. Ellis deals with both quotation and allusions, whereas Silva, while discussing allusions, lists only what he considers citations. The following survey examines whether and in what manner the Pauline Corpus undertakes the INE. This analysis will provide a better perspective on the Pauline use of the OT, and specifically Isaiah in Ephesians. The use of the INE in Ephesians is omitted in this survey because it is discussed at length in chapters 3 and 4 of this present work, as well as in the expositional section of chapters 5 through 12. The following discussion uses the terms "quotation," "allusion," and "echo." In this study, *quotations* are understood as explicit using several common words from the OT, *allusions* share a mutual word or two, and *echoes* have conceptual correspondence rather than verbal.

2.3.1 Romans

Romans utilizes the OT more than any other NT book, and it contains perhaps fifty-three quotations and twenty-four allusions. Isaiah is incorporated in Romans more than any other OT book, followed by Deuteronomy and Psalms. The epistle is influenced by the new exodus motif and contains

---

143. Turpie lists tables throughout his work with related commentary, dealing with what he considers quotations: *Old Testament in the New*. In xv–xxxii he explains his system of tables.

144. Michel addresses four primary issues in Paul's use of the OT: Paul's understanding of OT (issues of canon and citation technique), his handling of the OT compared to his contemporaries (Rabbinic and Hellenistic exegesis), the meaning of specific OT passages (when used in his writings), and the implication of Paul's use of the OT on the history of the early church: *Paulus Und Seine Bibel*, 112–80.

145. Koch, *Schrift*, for a sampling: 18–19, 70–71, 82–83, 140–41; Hübner regards Koch's monograph as "the best and most solidly founded survey" of Paul's quotations from OT: "New Testament Interpretation," 340.

146. Wilk deals primarily with Paul's use of Isaiah in Romans, 1 and 2 Corinthians, Galatians, Philippians, and 1 Thessalonians: *Bedeutung*, 42–159, 266–339, 388–400.

147. Ellis references Turpie's classifications, but does not use them exclusively. Ellis's appendices include: Quotations in the Pauline Epistles, OT Allusions and Parallels in the Pauline Epistles, Texts of OT Citations (with introductory formulas), Combined Quotations in the Pauline Epistles, and Parallel Quotations (with OT and non-Pauline NT parallels): *Paul's Use*, 150–87.

148. Silva utilizes Michel, Ellis, and Koch with 107 citations: Romans (59), 1 Corinthians (18), 2 Corinthians (13), Galatians (11), Ephesians (3), 1 Timothy (1), 2 Timothy (2): Silva, "Old Testament in Paul," 631. Both Ellis and Silva attempt to determine to what extent Paul's quotations agree with the LXX and MT. Silva regards Wilk's charts as outstanding tools to research Paul's use of Isaiah.

typological-historical uses of the exodus and new exodus.[149] Hays, Wright, and Holland all argue for the impact of Isaiah and other OT themes in this epistle, with Wright and Holland focusing on the new exodus. Although Hays does not address the new exodus in Paul at length, he does lay the hermeneutical framework in Paul's use of the OT, particularly Isaiah in Romans.[150] Holland reveals Paul's extensive use of Isaiah in Romans, demonstrating a systemic use of the prophet by Paul.[151] Seifrid explains how the new exodus is used by Paul in Rom 3 to draw parallels between the liberation of Israel from exile (through the recognition of sin and repentance) and the liberation that comes through redemption in Christ.[152] In terms of the OT in Romans he writes, "The Scriptures, according to Paul, are nothing other than God speaking to his people in the present through his words of judgment and salvation to Israel in the past."[153] Forman completed a recent article paralleling Isa 54:1–3 and the Abraham and Sarah birth narrative with Rom 4:19–21.[154] He argues that Paul is evoking a profoundly sociopolitical message wherein God is at work to liberate his people within a hostile empire. Beale contributes to the study of new exodus echoes in Rom 9 by considering the hardening of Pharoah's heart.[155] Along these same lines J. Piper understands that Rom 9 is connected particularly with Moses's interactions with Yahweh in the desert. God's freedom to choose Israel in the OT typifies his choice, in the era of the church, to incorporate believing Gentiles.[156]

Wagner, in chapters 3–5 of his book, *Heralds of the Good News*, discusses Rom 9, 10, 11, and 15, and the prevailing influence of Isaiah in terms of the position of Israel and the expectation of the Parousia. He sees Paul using both Isaiah and Deut 29–32 in concert to depict a two-stage process in Israel's deliverance: blindness then salvation.[157] Other connections and arguments between Exodus and Rom 9–11 could be cited, such as Abasciano's recent work.[158] He particularly observes the critical role of Exod 32–34

---

149. Keesmaat, "Intertextual Transformation," 29–56; Wright, "New Inheritance," 16, 47; Wright, "New Exodus, New Inheritance," 26–35.

150. Hays, "'Who Has Believed Our Message?,'" 25–49.

151. Holland, *Contours*, 31–34. Hays has a helpful chart on the explicit citations of Isaiah in Romans: *Conversion*, 39.

152. Seifrid, "Romans," 607–94.

153. Ibid., 608.

154. Forman, "Politics of Promise," 301–24.

155. Beale, "Pharoah's Heart," 129–54.

156. J. Piper, "Understanding Romans 9:14–15," 203–16.

157. Wagner, *Heralds*, 359.

158. Abasciano, *Romans 9.1–9*, 1–2, 225–28.

as the background to Rom 9:1–5, and specifically Exod 32:32. He concludes that in Rom 9 Paul indicates a continuation of the OT narrative, and that Israel's failure has not negated the God's covenant with his people or his work of deliverance among the Gentiles.

Hays and others point out the importance of Deuteronomy for Paul.[159] In Romans Paul uses Deuteronomy as a basis for an eschatological vision in which Israel is restored along with believing Gentiles.[160] Deuteronomy in Romans is undertaken much like Isaiah is to support the apostle's typological-historical-soteriological argument. Central to this use is Deut 32 concerning God's election and care for Israel (32: 6–14), Israel's rebellion (32:15–18), God's subsequent wrath upon them (32:19–35), and the ultimate deliverance of his people (32:36–43). There is also the idea of Israel stirred to jealousy (32:21) and Gentiles praising God (32:43). Both J. Scott and Pate understand that Paul is incorporating the Deuteronomic curse-blessing rubric throughout many of his letters.[161] This Deuteronomy tradition essentially runs parallel to Isaiah's new exodus.

Romans incorporates the new exodus in order to put forth a newly designed message that is rooted in Isaiah, Deuteronomy, and Psalms concerning Christ, the nation of Israel, and the eschaton. Just as God hardened and then liberated Israel by returning the nation from Egypt and Babylon as envisioned by Moses and the prophets, he does much the same to those who are redeemed through Christ. Moses and Israel typify the antitypes of Christ and the redeemed church. Those of fallen humanity who come to believe are saved from sin by faith, not by the works of the law. This redemption is manifested by overcoming sin and living righteously, all according to the empowerment of God's Spirit (Rom 7:6; 8:2–27).[162] The Spirit played a key role with God's dealing with Israel during the exodus period and the new exodus envisioned by the prophets, and similarly the Spirit is critical in the NT plan of redemption.[163]

In summary, Romans is Paul's most extensive explanation of the gospel. The main thrust of his message is how the gospel, extended successfully to the Gentile world, correlates with the OT and Yahweh's covenant with Israel. To develop his argument Paul relies preeminently on Isaiah, wherein he finds key support for the depravity of man—including the hardening

---

159. Hays, *Echoes*, 162–63.

160. What might be expected is a pejorative use of Deuteronomy against works-based salvation, which seems to be Paul's intent in Gal 3:10 (Deut 27:26) and 13 (Deut 21:23); but not in Romans.

161. Pate et al., *Story of Israel*, 18–23, 213–19; J. Scott, "Restoration," 800–805.

162. Dunn, "Spirit Speech," 82–91.

163. Beale, "Fruit of the Spirit," 1–38; Dillard, "Effusion of the Spirit," 87–94.

of Israel, Yahweh's provision of redemption, and the dawn of the Parousia—seen in the advent of Christ, the birth of the Christian community, and imminent close of history. As such, the arrival of Christ and the Christian age has an organic bond with Isaiah and the new Egyptian exodus. In addition, Paul saw his own ministry within the Isaianic new exodus messianic age (Rom 10:11–15; 15:21–24).[164] In the exposition of Ephesians later in this study, it will be found that Ephesians and Romans share both common and distinct usages of Isaiah.

2.3.2 1 Corinthians

First Corinthians contains conceivably sixteen citations and eighteen allusions from the OT. As with Romans, Isaiah is foremost then followed by usages from Psalms and the Pentateuch. Studies have surveyed the new exodus typological-historical effect in First Corinthinas,[165] notably the Passover theme in 1 Cor 5:5–7, where the Passover is presented as a new exodus.[166]

Prominent as well is the picture of unyielding hostility between human wisdom and the wisdom of God (1 Cor 1:19 with Isa 29:14; and 1 Cor 2:9 with Isa 64:4).[167] The contexts of 1 Cor 1:19 and Isa 29 share topics such as superficial displays of piety, destruction of evil, wonderful yet shocking things, and messianic overtones. The wisdom of God is expanded and applied in 1 Cor 2:9 (Isa 64). In the Isaianic passage there is an appeal for God's intervention (Isa 64:1) along with a promise that God will indeed act in a dramatic fashion (Isa 64:2–4). Paul sees the promise of intervention fulfilled in the cross. The wisdom-mystery of God is the plan by which the promises of Isaiah are manifested through Christ. This is more than just illustration and imagery since the prophecy of Isaiah and its fulfillment were intended to be historical in nature—predestined and planned throughout the ages (1 Cor 2:7). This is an excellent example of Paul's historical use of typology.

Another exodus aspect is Paul's use of an exodus background for his argument against the factionalism and vices found in the Corinthian church, most notably, sexual immorality and idolatry (1 Cor 6:5–11).[168] In

---

164. Although acknowledged as a prominent point of discussion in recent Pauline studies, no attempt is made in this present investigation to consider the merits of covenantal nomism as put forth by Sanders, Dunn, Wright, and others. For a recent discussion: Husbands and Treier, *Current Debates*. An effort is made by Yee to understand covenantal nomism in Ephesians 2: *Jewish Identity*, 1–33, 84.

165. Parry, "Isaiah 49:1–7," 126–32; Wilk, "Isaiah in 1 and 2 Corinthians," 133–58, esp. 157–58.

166. Fitzmyer, *First Corinthians*, 241–42; Howard, "Christ Our Passover," 97–108.

167. Ciampa and Rosner," 1 Corinthians," 698–701.

168. Ibid., 705–13.

this context he utilizes a Deuteronomic expulsion formula (1 Cor 5:13 from Deut 13:5). The Deuteronomy passage itself harkens back to the original exodus as the basis for the call to shun those who practice false prophecy and idolatry.

Additionally, 1 Cor 10 appeals to Israel's failures in the exodus period as a reason to flee idolatry and other sins that have threatened the purity of the Corinthian church (1 Cor 10:7–8, 18).[169] Paul explicitly informs the reader of his use of τύπος (1 Cor 10:6) from the exodus period. The employment of Moses and the sea are included in his embellishment of the typology. Shortly thereafter are Paul's strong associations between the exodus and the new covenant (1 Cor 11:25).[170]

By using the Passover, human wisdom and God's actions through the cross, and the disobedience of Israel, among other things, Paul is harmonizing the narrative of the OT exodus period and the new exodus of Isaiah with the contemporary situation in Corinth. The antitype to the Passover is Christ, the antitype to Israel's conduct is the church, and the antitype of the wonder and deliverance anticipated by Isaiah is the cross. This does not equate Christ with the Passover or the church with Israel, but it does fit a paradigm found in Romans and other parts of the Pauline Corpus: Paul saw the advent of Christ and Christian community as eschatological antitypes corresponding to the Egyptian exodus, and later the return from Persia. Paralleled as well is the conduct expected of God's people against idolatry and other sins, and what was not to be tolerated in the nation-church. To Paul the actions of God through the wisdom-mystery of the cross, along with the resultant Christian community, became the apocalyptic manifestation of Isaiah's vision.

The distinction between the use of the INE in Romans and 1 Corinthians is that in Romans the new exodus is used more in terms of the reconciliation of Israel's rejection and God's faithfulness; whereas in 1 Corinthians the emphasis is on the contrast between human and divine wisdom, and the ethical conduct required of God's people. Both epistles see the INE as a foundational concept in understanding the church. The ethical aspect of the INE in Paul's epistles is an important discovery because much is said in Ephesians concerning moral living. The question in Ephesians has to do with the way ethical living relates to the triumphal aspect of Isaiah's new exodus. However, at this point, 1 Corinthians already previews the use of Isaiah's new exodus and ethical living. This will be further explored in this present work as the exposition of Eph 4:1–5:9 is undertaken.

169. Other 1 Cor 10 parallels are observed in Enns, "Moveable Well," 23–38.
170. Balentine, "Death of Jesus," 37; Nixon, *New Testament*, 23.

2.3.3 2 Corinthians

Second Corinthians has perhaps nine citations and twelve allusions from the OT. Young and Ford discuss the comprehensive influence that the OT had on Paul and subsequently on his writing of 2 Corinthians, listing many parallels.[171] The letter contains vivid new exodus components.

Second Cor 3:1–18 is a typological-historical use of the OT that juxtaposes the old covenant and Moses with the new covenant and the Lord-Spirit.[172] Paul's purpose is to defend his ministry; and while doing so he contrasts the covenants using a bevy of OT echoes from Exod 31:18, 34:34; Ezek 11:19, 36:26; and Jer 31:31. The old covenant, along with Moses and the tabernacle, were inferior and fading compared with the splendor of the "glory of the Lord" (2 Cor 3:18). As a result, Paul's ministry was one that corresponded with the superior character of the new covenant.

Additionally, 2 Cor 4:13 quotes Ps 116:10 (LXX 115:1) indicating, as in Romans and 1 Corinthians, Paul's understanding that his own ministry was in parallel to that of the Messiah's. In this particular linkage, the Messiah, who survives death, lives and speaks in the psalm. In a similar way Christ speaks through the ministry of Paul. Also, Isa 49:8 is found in 2 Cor 6:2. Here Paul employs Isaiah to portray the willingness of Yahweh to give the servant to Israel. The servant will "apportion the desolate heritages" (Isa 49:8) to his restored people. The chapter also carries an international tone that includes the oft-quoted, Israel—"a light to the nations" (Isa 49:6).

Finally, 2 Cor 6:17 uses Isa 52:11–12 and Ezek 20:34. The usage is part of a broader text that includes 2 Cor 6:14—7:1.[173] The notorious difficulties in this passage include the abrupt change of subject matter and tone from its context and OT origins. These problems are addressed by W. Webb who concludes that rather than the section being a misplaced interpolation it coincides with the thrusts of the OT texts. He maintains that the segment was written by a paulinist who argues for contextual continuity with the OT.[174] Common themes from Isaiah include new-covenant and exilic-return motifs, among others. One specific example of commonality is Isa

---

171. Young and Ford, *Meaning and Truth*, 63–68.

172. Belleville, *Reflections of Glory*, 217–25; Belleville, "Tradition or Creation?," 165–86; Dumbrell, "Paul's Use of Exodus 34," 179–94; Hafemann, *Paul, Moses*, 136–37; Stockhausen, *Moses's Veil*, 169–75.

173. W. Webb, *Returning Home*, 112.

174. Noh is generally supportive of Webb's work but is less persuaded by exodus return motifs in some passages such as 2 Cor 5:1–10, 11–21: "Context for 2 Corinthians 6:14—7:1," 669–70. Although conceding that Webb's work is fundamentally sound, Muller maintains that Webb's search for texts was too narrowly focused on the OT: "New Covenant and Second Exodus," 199–200.

52:11, "Depart, depart, go out from there! Touch no unclean thing; go out from the midst of it, purify yourselves, you who carry the vessels of the Lord." With emotion seldom equaled in the Pauline Corpus (6:11–13), Paul is represented as one who opens his heart to the church with whom he is at odds. The basis of his appeal is the message of Isaiah to the captives whom Yahweh would restore. Just as in the Egyptian exodus (Isa 52:4), the returnees from Persia would carry plunder, but in this superior exodus the booty would be comprised of the dislocated vessels of temple worship (Isa 52:11). Upon their exit from Persia, God's people are to "touch no unclean thing," and instead are to secure the return of the sacred vessels. In the same way, God brings about Isaiah's new exodus through the advent of Isaiah's messianic age. The new Isaianic community at Corinth is to be pure; eschewing pettiness against the apostle as well as any flirtations with divisive teachers.

In summary, 2 Corinthians continues the use of the INE while sharing overarching themes with Romans and 1 Corinthians. The focus of the use of the INE in 2 Corinthians is continuity and discontinuity with the Mosaic covenant, Paul's defense of his apostolic ministry by identifying with the Psalmist's vision of the servant's ministry, and an emotional call to ethical INE communal living.

2.3.4 Galatians

Galatians may contain about ten citations and four allusions from the OT, placing it proportionately second only to Romans in terms of explicit OT usage.[175] In defending the integrity of the gospel message, Galatians is the most polemic of Paul's letters. The OT is employed for this purpose, primarily through allusions in chapters 1–2,[176] and by explicit citations in chapters 3–6. Old Testament and new exodus related studies have been undertaken in the epistle.[177]

J. Scott considers Gal 4:5 to be linked to 2 Sam 7:14 (and Isa 43:6 with 2 Cor 6:18) in an adoption formula. The recitation, "I will be to him a father, and he will be to me a son" came to be applied to the Davidic Messiah, the new exodus, and the eschatological people of God. Scott remarks, "the whole argumentation in Galatians 3–4, together with Pauline parallels, leads unambiguously to an OT/Jewish background."[178]

---

175. Silva, "Galatians," 785.
176. Ciampa, *Presence and Function*, 184–94.
177. Keesmaat, "Paul and His Story: Exodus," 300–33; Pate, *Reverse of the Curse*, 139–231.
178. J. Scott, "Works of the Law," 187–221.

Isa 54:1 in Gal 4:27 has INE overtones.[179] Paul links parallels to the Isaianic personage of Sarah in Isa 54:1 with the bondage of Hagar's children, "present Jerusalem," and the law (Gal 4:21–26). Isaiah converts Sarah from the barren mother-patriarch to a symbol of fertile Israel. Sarah is associated with those who are free and "Jerusalem above" (Gal 4:26). Contextually, Paul adopts the vision of Isaiah in seeing Christ in Isa 54 who brings the fertility of the gospel of grace to those who believe. This is in contrast to Hagar, present Jerusalem, and the law. Isa 51:1–2 mentions Sarah as well. In this context Isaiah calls on the righteous exiles to remember their association with Abraham and Sarah and the blessings that were promised. The further image of desolate Jerusalem undertaken by Paul finds its origins in Isa 64:10. By using images of Sarah and Jerusalem from Isa 51, 54, and 64, Paul could have expected his audience to associate Christ in Isa 54 and a new era marked by the gospel of grace and the righteousness that should accompany such belief. What begins on the surface as a simple allegory of a barren woman taken from Genesis, flowers into Isaiah's vision of the new exodus in which Yahweh redeems his righteous people. In the end, Paul's usage of Isaianic Sarah and Jerusalem is more in keeping with a typological-historical hermeneutic than an allegorical one.

Other parallels between Galatians and Isaiah's new exodus can be cited, such as Paul's stinging words in Gal 5:12. These may reflect the concept found in the exodus ethos of Deut 23:1. Another coupling is Gal 3:10 and Deut 27:26. Scott makes the case that in the Second Exodus Period the curses of Deut 27–32 were understood to have fallen upon Israel (rather than specifically upon the law).[180] The curse would remain until messianic redemption and restoration. This supports the idea that Paul assumed that the advent of Christ and the grace-gospel was in keeping with the INE and the dawn of the new age. Additionally, Gal 5:18 and the continuity and discontinuity of law and spirit are found to mirror the exodus narrative.[181] Beale associates Gal 5:22 with Isa 32:14–18,[182] and argues for the correlation between "true Israel" (Gal 6:16) with Isa 54:10.[183] This latter linkage shows a relationship once again between the Galatian letter and the INE narrative. Wagner points out the connection between Isa 49 and Paul's self-identification as an apostle.[184] Longenecker expounds on the original role of

---

179. Jobes, "Jerusalem, Our Mother," 229–320.
180. J. Scott, "Works of the Law," 221.
181. Wilder, *Echoes of the Exodus*, 249.
182. Beale, "Fruit of the Spirit," 1–38.
183. Beale, "Peace and Mercy," 204–23.
184. Wagner, "Isaiah," 129–32.

Abraham and the nation according to Galatians—that instead of fulfilling God's commission to the nations they became like the nations. The triumph however lies in God's faithfulness in Christ.[185]

Pate summarizes his understanding of Galatians by gathering together several INE themes in the epistle:

> In Galatians 3:1–5 one can detect the Judaizing message that the Spirit, the sign of the age to come, now resides within Christians and empowers them to perform genuine works of faith—in effect, the ethics of the new covenant. Furthermore, according to Galatians 3:6–9, even Gentiles can now become children of Abraham if they believe in Jesus Messiah and submit to circumcision. As such, they, together with Jewish Christians, can experience the Deuteronomic blessings by obeying the Torah, because Christ had taken its curses unto himself, according to Galatians 3:10–14. In other words the eschatological restoration of Israel has dawned, and the nations can participate in Israel's salvation, provided they become like Jews. Gentiles no longer need be enslaved to the curses of the covenant (once pronounced on Israel's enemies) because they do not follow the Torah; now they can experience the new exodus with its spiritual freedom born out of a new-found obedience. All of this has happened in light of the fullness of time, the dawning of the messianic age (Galatians 4:1–7).[186]

As with Romans and 1 and 2 Corinthians, Galatians demonstrates the presence of the INE. Although the diversified use of the Isaiah exodus theme in Romans and the Corinthian letters is not as fully developed in Galatians (such as Paul's specific INE eschatological permutations), it is present in Paul's polemic to defend the grace-gospel, and his efforts to elicit in his audience righteous INE Spirit-living.

2.3.5 Philippians

Philippians may utilize about eight OT allusions along with parallels to the INE. Although the epistle has no explicit citations, it would be a mistake to minimize the influence of the OT on it.[187] Compared to the previously noted letters, the correspondences to the OT in Philippians are fewer and more subtle, but nevertheless weighty in their influence on the letter. Perhaps the lack of polemic (compared to Galatians; and lesser, Romans and

---

185. B. Longenecker, *Abraham's God*, 51–54.
186. Pate et al., "Paul: The Reverse of the Curse," 225.
187. Fee, *Philippians*, 17–18.

1 and 2 Corinthians) is reason for the absence of citations and the number and force of the allusions. It appears that Paul's authority was not being directly challenged. This often brought to bear strong responses along with appeals to the OT (but this cannot be accepted without exception; cf. 1:17). There are threats by false teachers and errant doctrines (Phil 3:2) but the warning is more perfunctory in nature (3:1); a reminder of what the Philippians already knew. It seems that some divisions in the church existed, but these are addressed in a tempered tone (4:2). Scholarship would be amiss to conclude with Harnack and Beker that Paul only uses the OT on a contingency basis.[188] Clearly the Jewish Scriptures played a constitutive role for Paul, which includes letters, like Philippians where the tone is perhaps more moderate, citations minimal, and allusions less direct.

A possible INE allusion is in the *Carmen Christi* in Phil 2:7 (from Isa 53:12).[189] Christ, who "emptied himself" may correspond to "poured out himself" in Isaiah. Support for this is where Paul uses Isaiah later, in Phil 2:9–11, with Isa 45 in mind. The passage says that Christ took the form of a servant: μορφὴν δούλου λαβών. Heriban makes a case for Isa 52:13—53:12 and Isa 45 forming the background for the Christ hymn.[190]

Isaiah 45:23 is found in Phil 2:10–11. The imagery in Isaiah is the nations coming to pay homage to Yahweh who is sovereign ("there is no other god besides me" 45:21).[191] If the author has Isaiah in mind, he envisions the uniqueness and exaltation of Yahweh shifted to Christ. Both the LXX and Paul use the word ἐξομολογήσηται, which further corresponds to the Hebrew, שָׁבַע. Because of the multiple links to Isaiah there is good reason to believe that Paul seeks to equate Christ with the personage in Isa 53 and the exaltation of Yahweh in Isa 45. However, some like O'Brien and Gundry do not entirely agree.[192]

Fee and Silva, among others see Paul in Phil 2:14–16 making a thematic connection with Israel in the wilderness in Deut 32:5.[193] This is similar to Paul's appeal to the Corinthians (1 Cor 10:10), which echos Num 13:1–38.

---

188. Hays, *Conversion*, 183.

189. The correspondences to Isaiah do not diminish the possibility that Paul makes an implicit allusion to Adam in Phil 1:6 (who thus functions as a foil for Christ): Hooker, "Adam Redivivus," 220–34.

190. Heriban, *Retto Phronein*, 160–62. Bockmuehl undertakes a helpful analysis: *Philippians*, 135–36.

191. Wilk suggests that Philippians has other ties to Isa 45 in Phil 1:28, 2:11–12: *Bedeutung*, 325.

192. O'Brien lists objections: *Epistle to the Philippians*, 268–71. Gundry presents an alternative position: "Style and Substance," 271–94.

193. Fee, *Philippians*, 18; Silva, "Philippians," 838.

As in other cases with Paul, the association links the church's behavior with the demeanor of Israel. In Philippians the nation's abysmal conduct during the exodus period is used as a warning.

"A fragrant offering, a sacrifice acceptable and pleasing to God" from Phil 4:18 (and 2:17, 25, 30) corresponds with Exod 29:18 and Ezek 20:41. More than just borrowing the verbiage and style of the Levitical ceremonial system, Paul's theological framework includes the transfer and transformation of that system to the Christian church.[194] Paul's understanding of Christian service corresponds with the type of sacrifice and worship expected of Israel in Exod 29:18 and anticipated by the prophets in the INE. In Ezek 20:41 the restored Israel is personified as a soothing, acceptable sacrifice. A similar picture is in view in Eph 5:1–2.

Philippians does not contain the number and strength of citations and allusions in regard to the INE as the previous Paulines surveyed thus far in this chapter. However, in the few that are found, notably the latter previous two, a reasonable case may be made. In Philippians Christ is placed in the eschatological center of redemptive history. Christ is seen as the divine figure in Isaiah who alone deserves homage from the nations. Also, but more subtle, is the linkage of the church with the OT sacrificial system, as described both in the Pentateuch and INE Ezekiel.

2.3.6 Colossians

Like Philippians, Colossians has no citations, and perhaps half the allusions from the OT. Some work has been done on the use of the OT in Colossians,[195] but it appears that little attempt has been made to connect Colossians to the new exodus.[196]

The first possible INE link is Col 1:6 and 10 with Jer 3:16, 23:3. According to Beale, the phrases "bearing fruit and growing" (Col 1:6) and "bear fruit" (Col 1:10) echo Gen 1:28, "Be fruitful and multiply, and fill the earth." He maintains that the Genesis motif is picked up and repeated in the

---

194. The term λειτουργία in Phil 2:17 and related terminology in 2:25 and 30 may reflect the OT idea of servanthood. Cf. Silva, "Old Testament in Paul," 634.

195. Beale, "Colossians," 841–70; Beetham, "Colossians," 247–51; Fee, "Intertextuality," 201–21.

196. Walsh and Keesmaat attempt to read Colossians as the antithesis both to the first century Roman Empire and contemporary North America. Helpful OT in NT information is given, along with parallels to the INE, but the thrust of the book is to apply the social situation in Colossae with a modern one: *Colossians Remixed*, 7–8. W. Campbell and Henderson provide helpful critiques to the aforementioned mentioned article: "Subverting the Empire," 68–69; Henderson, "Colossians Remixed: Subverting the Empire," 108–10.

OT and the NT.[197] The phraseology is found four times in the NT: Acts 6:7, 7:17, 12:24, and 19:20. With the help of Pao,[198] Beale sees both OT and NT authors transforming the verbiage from the physical progeny of Adam to the new creation. Beale summarizes how this applies to Colossians: "Therefore, believers are the created progeny of the last Adam, who are beginning to fulfill in him the mandate given to the first Adam. The Gen 1:28 language applied by Paul to them in Col 1:6, 9–10 indicates that they are part of the inaugurated new creation and are beginning to fulfill in Christ what has been left unfulfilled in the primordial mandate throughout the ages."[199] A further point may be made concerning passages such as Isa 51:2; 54:2–5; Jer 3:16; 23:3; and Ezek 36:10–11, 29–30. In these the "fruitful and multiply" motif is transformed to both a physical progeny and spiritual blessing. The three prophets depict the coming idyllic age with the fruitfulness of Sarah (Isa 51:2), the stretching out of the inhabitants of Israel (God of "all the earth," Isa 54:2–5), the multiplication and increase in the restored land (Jer 3:16), the regathering of God's flock to their pasture to be fruitful and multiply (Jer 23:3), and the increase of men and beasts on the mountains of Israel along with the multiplication of various types of agriculture (Ezek 36:10–11, 29–30). These passages may indicate that Paul, in Col 1:6 and 10, is utilizing a typological-historical hermeneutic and Isaiah's new exodus.

Subtle INE echoes may appear in Col 1:9–10 with Exod 31:3 and Isa 11:2 with the verbiage, "knowledge, wisdom, understanding, and insight."[200] Col 2:3 is related to the aforementioned, "in whom are hidden all the treasures of wisdom and knowledge" from Isa 45:3, "the treasures of darkness and riches hidden in secret places." The parallels point to Paul envisioning the revelation that accompanies the INE arriving at Colossae. This will be examined later in this present work when Eph 1:8, 17 and the entirety of Eph 3, are disscussed.

Colossians 1:13–14 may coincide with Exod 6:6 and Deut 7:8. "He has rescued us from the power of darkness and transferred us into the kingdom of his beloved Son" finds resemblance with new creational redemption and

---

197. In the OT usages utilize the dual terminology "increase and multiply" and several contain "all the earth": Gen 9:1, 6–7; 12:2; 17:2, 6, 8; 22:17–18; 26:3, 4, 24; 28:3–4; 35:11–12; 47:27; Exod 1:7; Lev 26:9; 1 Chron 29:10–11; Ps 8:5–9; 107:38; Isa 51:2; 54:2–5; Jer 3:16; 23:3; Ezek 36:10–11, 29–30. In the NT the focus is on Acts, where Gen 1:28 is referred to four times: Acts 6:7; 7:17; 12:24; and 19:20.

198. Pao, *Acts*, 167–69.

199. Beale, "Colossians," 845.

200. Ibid., 845, 846–48; cf. Williams, *Wisdom of the Wise*, 55–61.

deliverance from slavery, as well as adopted sonship.[201] These are related to Isaiah's new exodus.

Beale, Watts, and Wright present several other possibilities in Colossians, most containing INE images: Col 1:15 with Gen 1:27, the "first and last Adam"; Col 1:24 with Isa 52:13–14 concerning the servant; Col 1:26–27, 2:2, and 4:3, "servant" and "mystery" motifs; Col 2:3, "treasures of wisdom and knowledge"; Col 2:22 with "human commands and teachings," may find connection with Isa 29:13, "human commandment learned by rote"; Col 3:9–10, "image"; Col 3:12 and "chosen ones" with Deut 4:37 ("he chose their descendants") and 10:15 ("chose you"); and Col 4:5, new creational living.[202]

Colossians may appear on the surface to have little connection with the new epoch envisioned by Isaiah. But in the course of digging deeper, many allusions to both the Egyptian exodus and the new exodus are discovered. In addition, the OT usages in Colossians find common ground with the other previously surveyed letters. For example, there are clear parallels of OT usage by Paul when comparing the use in Colossians with Romans and 1 and 2 Corinthians. Among these are Col 1:15 parallel with Rom 8:20, 29; 1 Cor 11:7, 15:45–49; and 2 Cor 4:4 concerning "image" and "firstborn." Like Romans, 1 and 2 Corinthians, Galatians, and Philippians, Paul uses the INE to make a typological-historical case for his message. The difference with the use of the new exodus in Colossians is subtlety, which would be more in keeping with Philippians (along with an emphasis on Christology). Due to mounting evidence, along with similar methods in other Pauline writings, the use of the INE in Colossians seems quite possible. The repeated references to the INE in Colossians seem to call for an explanation beyond what might be only verbal and style references. Many of these discoveries in Colossians will come into play in the analysis of Ephesians since the two letters are fundamentally linked. Their commonalities involve not only the use of the OT but their eschatology.[203] However, it will be discovered that Ephesians is distinguished from Colossians in the widespread and explicit use of the OT in support of its theme.

2.3.7 1 and 2 Thessalonians

First Thessalonians has no explicit citations from the OT, however eight allusions may be evident; in 2 Thessalonians there are no citations, but

---

201. R. Watts, "Exodus," 485–86.

202. Beale, "Colossians," 848–68; R. Watts, "Exodus," 485–86; Wright, "Colossians 1:15–20," 444–68; Wright, *Climax of the Covenant*, 109.

203. For a comparative analysis of the development of eschatology in Colossians and Ephesians: Achtemeier, "Apocalyptic Shift," esp. 237–38.

perhaps seven allusions. As with the other letters with no explicit usages, there is the presence of the OT with possibly the INE motif.[204] This is the case despite the probability that the Thessalonian church was made up primarily of Gentiles (1 Thess 1:9–10; 2:14).[205]

A major topic in the two letters that reflect the OT is the return of the Lord. One aspect of the return is the gathering of God's people. In his article on 1 Thess 4:13–28 Houwelingen indicates this: "We find this theme with all kinds of variations in the books of Moses (Deut 30:4), in various prophets (Isa 11:12; 27:12–13; Ezek 39:27; Zech 2:10 LXX), and in several Psalms (Pss 106:47; 147:2)."[206] Houwelingen goes on to indicate that the gathering theme is prominent in Second Temple writings as well.[207] During the Egyptian and exile periods the regathering was to take place in the land of promise. In the Second Temple Period this assembling would be the reversal of the Diaspora; and in the NT it would be the gathering of God's people in the new heavens and earth as depicted in the latter chapters of Revelation. The regathering of God's people is fundamental to Paul's eschatology. Houwelingen argues that in 1 Thess 4 this motif is more important than the resurrection. The question addressed is if deceased loved ones share in the glory of the Parousia, not whether they live in the afterlife. This may also be the same question that is addressed in 1 Cor 15 and Rev 14.

Other OT topics related to the coming of the Lord with evidence of the INE are possible. The trumpet blast in 1 Thess 4:16 (and Matt 24:31; 1 Cor 15:52; and Rev 8–9; 11:15) echoes the INE from passages such as Exod 19:16–19; Ps 47:5; Isa 27:13; Joel 2:1, 15; Zeph 1:14–16; and Zech 9:14.[208] It seems that Paul understood that just as Yahweh descended upon Sinai accompanied by loud trumpet blasts, and just as the trumpet would be blown at the INE regathering, Christ would return to the earth. Other possible parallels related to Christ's coming (1 Thess 4:16–17) have to do with the shout (Ps 47:5);[209] clouds and smoke that gather in a foreboding

---

204. Weima, "1–2 Thessalonians," 871–89. Witherington observes several echoes from the OT in 1 and 2 Thessalonians: *Socio-Rhetorical Commentary*, 193, 195, 198, 218. But J. Thompson criticizes him for parallelomania: "1 and 2 Thessalonians," 126.

205. Notwithstanding that there were Jews among the converts in Thessalonica (Acts 17:1–4): Nicholl, *Situating*, 112 n. 92.

206. Houwelingen, "Word of the Lord," 316.

207. Such as in the apocryphal books: *Tob* 13:15; *Bar* 5:5–9; *2 Macc.* 2:7–8; and in the pseudepigrapha: *1 En* 57; *Psalms of Solomon* 11:2–3; 17:26: Cited in Houwelingen, "Word of the Lord," 316. It was regarded a privilege to experience the end of the world: Klijn, "First Thessalonians 4:13–18," 67–73.

208. Beale, *1–2 Thessalonians*, 140.

209. C. Evans, "Ascending and Descending," 238–53.

manner upon Sinai (Exod 19:6–20) or as an apparent means of transportation (Dan 7:13; Rev 11:12); as well as fire seen on Sinai and upon Christ's return (2 Thess 1:7–8). Another is the dwelling motif in which God's people anticipate always being with him, as seen in 1 Thess 4:17. Being with God and dwelling with him are specific exodus and new exodus concepts: Exod 29:45–46; Jer 7:3, 7:7; Ezek 37:27; and Zech 2:10. In the new exodus, the people of God are regathered to dwell in Jerusalem with Yahweh. In the NT, as well as with extra-biblical writers, dwelling with God is an ongoing motif, especially with Paul: John 14:3; Rom 6:8; 8:17; 2 Cor 5:8; Phil 1:23; Rev 21:3; and 1 En 39:6–8; 45:4; 62:14; 71:16. Another related theme is Christ returning "with all his saints" (1 Thess 3:13). The dependence here seems to be upon Zech 14:5: "Then the LORD my God will come, and all the holy ones with him." Although there is some debate as to the identity of the "holy ones"[210] the allusion clearly refers to the return of the Lord to Jerusalem in order to rescue her from the gathered nations. This same wording is used in Matt 25:31, also with reference to the return of Christ. It seems that the holy ones are both angels and saints, but contextually the emphasis is on saints since this provides evidence that deceased loved ones will not miss the Parousia. Added to these associations should be, "Day of the Lord" (1 Thess 5:2; 2 Thess 2:2), which has mass affiliations with the OT and the INE (Isa 2:1–4:6; Jer 46:10; Ezek 30:2–3; Joel 1:15; 2:1, 11, 31–32; Amos 5:18–20; Obad 15; Zeph 1:14–18; Zech 14; Mal 4:5).[211] "Day of the Lord" is used by Paul in Thessalonians to indicate the return of Christ in terms of judgment (cf. 1 Cor 5:5; 2 Cor 1:14). Still another is the connection of "birth pangs" (1 Thess 5:3) with the Parousia, used elsewhere by Paul (Rom 8:22) and seen often in the OT, particularly Isaiah and Jeremiah in INE contexts.[212] In 1 Thess 5:3 the pain of childbirth refers to judgment; in Roman 8 the pain is associated with Christian perseverance. One correspondence concerning the return could be the idea of retribution upon the enemies of God and his people (2 Thess 1:7–8 and 2:1–12 with Isa 66:15; Jer 6:13–15, 8:10b–12; Dan 10–12).[213] In regard to Paul's indictment upon the temple cult and the Day

---

210. Weima summarizes the arguments: Weima, "1–2 Thessalonians," 875.

211. Another similar phrase, "on that day" (2 Thess 1:10) is recurrent in Isaiah, Jeremiah, Ezekiel, Hosea, Amos, Obadiah, Micah, Zephaniah, Haggai, and especially Zechariah: Hiers, "Day of the Lord," 2:82–83; King, "Day of the Lord in Zephaniah," 16–17; Nicholl, *Situating*, 118.

212. Ps 48:6; Isa 13:4–8; 21:3; 26:17–18; 37:3; 42:14; 66:7–8; Jer 4:31; 6:24; 22:23; 30:4–7; 48:41; 50:43; Hos 13:13; Mic 4:9. Gempf, however, seems to downplay his own OT evidence by stating that Paul's eschatology is dependent on gospel traditions: "Birth Pangs," 123–26, 134–35.

213. Aus, as well as Richard and Harrington, and Brown maintain that the Isa 66 usage in 2 Thess 1 is conscious. Aus also brings into view Rev 12:2, 5–6: Aus, "Relevance

of the Lord, Nicholl concludes that "the parallels between Jeremiah 6 and 8 and 1 Thess. 5:3 and 2 Thess. 2:1–12 (cf. 2:3–10) are indeed remarkable."[214]

Another INE theme not directly related to the return of the Lord is Paul's call to "holiness" (1 Thess 3:13, 4:4, 7). It is clear that Paul reflects OT and Jewish moral tradition in his calls for ethical behavior.[215] The idea of holiness is rooted in Sinai (Exod 19:5–25; Deut 26:18–19; Lev 11:44) where the new nation was called to live apart from the other peoples. Holiness is a distinguishing characteristic of restored Israel in the INE: "They shall be called, 'The Holy People, The Redeemed of the LORD'; and you shall be called, 'Sought Out, A City Not Forsaken'" (Isa 62:12). This reoccurring theme in Paul and Pauline writings (Rom 12:1; 1 Cor 3:17; 7:14, 34; 2 Cor 6:6; 7:1; Eph 1:4; 2:21; 4:24; 5:26–27; Col 1:22; 3:12; 1 Tim 2:8, 15; 2 Tim 1:9) gives strong indication that the people of God were called, similar to Israel, to live distinct lives in keeping with God's standards. In 1 Thess 4:8 this conduct is in keeping with the indwelling Holy Spirit. The Spirit and holiness are linked together in conjunction with new exodus thought: "I will put my spirit within you, and make you follow my statutes and be careful to observe my ordinances" (Ezek 36:27); "I will put my spirit within you, and you shall live, and I will place you on your own soil; then you shall know that I, the LORD, have spoken and will act, says the LORD" (Ezek 37:14; cf. Ezek 37:6, 14 and Isa 59:21); and "they rebelled and grieved his holy spirit"(Isa 63:10).[216]

The phrase, "taught by God" (1 Thess 4:9) echoes Isa 54:13 and Jer 31:33–34. It indicates that the new age will be marked by such an intimacy with God that no teachers will be required. God will indwell by his Spirit, write on the hearts of his people, and conduct the teaching (Isa 2:3; Mic 4:1–3; John 6:45; 1 John 2:27). Also, the armor imagery in 1 Thess 5:8 utilizes Isa 59:17. It is Yahweh's armor that is to be taken up by the Christians in Thessalonica (and Eph 6:10–20; cf. other Pauline military imagery, Rom 13:12; 2 Cor 6:7; 10:3–5; Phil 2:25; 2 Tim 2:3–4).

First and 2 Thessalonians furnish evidence of Paul's understanding of the INE, especially in terms of the Christian Parousia. He sees continuity between the gathering and regathering of God's people from the exodus

---

of Isaiah 66:7," 266–67; Aus, "Comfort in Judgment," 113–14; Richard and Harrington, *First and Second Thessalonians*, 315–16. S. Brown argues that 2 Thess 1 and 2 follow the same chiasmus of Isa 66: "Isaiah 66:17 and 2 Thessalonians 2:7," 272–75.

214. Nicholl, *Situating*, 207 n. 36.

215. Carras, "1 Thess 4:3–8," 306–15; Collins, "1 Thess 4:1–12; 5, 12–22," 398–414; Hodgson, "1 Thess 4:1–12," 199–215; Rosner, "1 Thessalonians 4:1–12," 351–60.

216. Beale, "Fruit of the Spirit," 1–38; Dillard, "Effusion of the Spirit," 87–94; Fee, *Holy Spirit*, 154; Fee, *First and Second Letters*, 145–55, 176–77; Wanamaker, *Thessalonians*, 146, 158.

periods in Egypt and Bablylonia-Persia to the final gathering of Christians. There also is correspondence with the conduct expected of Israel in the new age and that of the Christians in Thessalonica. The use of the new exodus in the Thessalonian letters has continuity and added emphases as compared to the other Pauline letters already considered. Commonalities include utilizing the INE as a call to ethical conduct; the added emphasis is the return of Christ.

2.3.8 The Pastorals

Overall, the Pastoral Epistles indicate a less explicit use of the OT compared with Romans, 1 and 2 Corinthians, and Galatians; and are more in league with Philippians, Colossians, and 1 and 2 Thessalonians. However, just as in these latter epistles, the Pastorals show evidence of OT influence, and may contain new exodus tendencies.[217] The use of the INE in 1 and 2 Timothy may hold special significance in this present work if the epistles were written to Timothy while he was stationed at Ephesus (even if Ephesians is taken as circular letter).[218]

First Timothy has one OT citation and seven allusions. Hanson points out several OT uses, and in particular two that may be INE in nature. The first is Paul equating his call and ministry with Moses. Although Hanson regards the Pastorals as written by a later Paulinist, he offers the possibility that the author models Christ's revelation to Paul upon the biblical account of God's revelation to Moses (1 Tim 1:14–16 echoing Exod 34:6 [LXX]).[219] Hanson also argues for the use of Job 9:32–33 and Isa 45:21–22 in 1 Tim 2:3–5. The common factor is the eventual conversion of Gentiles to Judaism.[220] This linkage of Paul with Moses and the conversion of the Gentiles is in concert with the INE.

Another possible INE usage is 1 Tim 2:5. Horbury as well as Towner point out the association of this passage with Num 24:7, 17 (LXX) and Isa 19:20.[221] Commonalities include a vision, Egypt and exodus imagery, Israel's role among the nations, and the concept of ἄνθρωπος as savior and judge. The author uses the INE concepts to reinforce the argument for a universal offer of salvation through Christ. This grand appeal to receive salvation is

---

217. A. Hanson, "Old Testament Pastoral Epistles," 203–19; Nielsen, "Scripture in the Pastoral Epistles," 4–23; Wolfe, "Scripture in the Pastoral Epistles," 48–54.
218. 1 Tim 1:3; 2 Tim 1:18; 4:12. Knight, *Pastoral Epistles*, 72.
219. A. Hanson, "Old Testament in the Pastoral Epistles," 211.
220. Ibid., 212.
221. Horbury, *Jewish Messianism*, 44–45; Towner, "1–2 Timothy and Titus," 892–93.

rooted in the original call of Israel at the exodus as well as the reconstituted call envisioned by Isaiah during the exilic period.

Another is 1 Tim 2:8, "in every place," which appears to be a conscious echo of Mal 1:11, "For from the rising of the sun to its setting my name is great among the nations, and in every place incense is offered to my name, and a pure offering; for my name is great among the nations, says the LORD of hosts."[222] The phrase also appears in 1 Cor 1:2; 2 Cor 2:14, and 1 Thess 1:8. These usages are suggestive of the universality of the gospel. This is in keeping with the general contexts of Malachi and 1 Tim 2.[223]

Others possibilities include the list of aggravated sins in 1 Tim 1:8–10 and the violations of the Decalogue in Exod 21. Knight proposes several parallels that suggest intentionality on the part of Paul.[224] "Household of God" (1 Tim 3:14–15) seems to find association with the assembling of God's people under Moses (Deut 4:10; 9:10; 18:16; 31:30).[225] "Deceitful spirits" (1 Tim 4:1) and "spirit of confusion" (Isa 19:14) ties Paul's warning of end times apostasy with a spirit of error poured upon the Egyptians. Closely following is the author's polemic against heretical food asceticism (1 Tim 4:3–4), admonishing that partaking of forbidden food is acceptable if received with thanksgiving. This gratitude argument is used in 1 Cor 10:26, 30, which follows Paul's lengthy discussion of Israel's food disobedience in the wilderness (1 Cor 10:1–22). One final association is the doxology in 1 Tim 6:16 with Moses's request to see the glory of God (Exod 33:17–33). Guthrie understands the Exodus passage as the foundation for 1 Tim 1:16.[226]

Second Timothy has two quotations and two allusions from the OT, with the possibility of INE usage taking place between 2 Tim 2:19, "But God's firm foundation stands," and Isa 28:16, "therefore thus says the Lord GOD, see, I am laying in Zion a foundation stone, a tested stone, a precious cornerstone, a sure foundation." Both passages utilize θεμέλιος, which indicates firm confidence in God. This corresponds with the household imagery that will follow (2 Tim 2:20), as well as Eph 2:18–22 and other places in the NT. In the face of the gangrenous threat from Hymenaeus and Philetus (2 Tim 2:17) the author reassures Timothy of the church's potency and God's ultimate control. In Isa 28 the writer finds contrast between relying on foreign powers (Isa 28:14–15) and depending on the foundation stone placed in Zion (Isa 28:16–17). The latter reference concerns the messianic age with

---

222. Towner, "The Pastoral Epistles," 333, 335.
223. Towner, "1–2 Timothy and Titus," 893.
224. Knight, *Pastoral Epistles*, 83–88.
225. Collins, *1 & 2 Timothy and Titus*, 103.
226. Guthrie, *Pastoral Epistles*, 129. Cf. Bernard, *Pastoral Epistles*, 101.

similar imagery in Ps 118, and identified as such in Rom 9:33 and Eph 2:20.[227] This probable use of Isa 28 on the part of the author in 2 Tim 2 adds to the idea that the INE finds manifestation in the church. The same assurances offered to Israel are issued to Christian congregations.

Other possible INE uses include 2 Tim 1:10 with Neh 9:12, 19 (LXX, the exodus pillar lighting the way);[228] 2 Tim 2:19 and Isa 26:13 ("name"); 2 Tim 2:19 and Isa 52:11 ("turn away");[229] 2 Tim 3:8, which directly employs the rebellion mounted against Moses during the exodus period (Exod 7:11, 22; 8:7, 18, 19; 9:11);[230] and repeated allusions and applications of Ps 21(LXX) in 2 Tim 4:16–18.

Titus appears to have no quotations but suggests two allusions from the OT. Titus 2:11–14 has several strong echoes of the INE. The context speaks of salvation (Titus 2:11) and Christ who procures redemption. The author conveys the significance of Christ's death in terms of salvation in general, and purification and redemption from lawlessness in particular. "[G]ave himself for us" (Titus 2:14) hearkens back to Mark 10:45 with derivations used in many contexts (Gal 1:4; 2:20; Eph 5:2; 1 Tim 2:6). Combined with "redeem," the Titus passage imports key OT concepts having to do with God establishing his covenant with Moses and Israel: the choosing of a people, the manumission of slaves, substitutionary atonement and Passover, redemption, purity from lawless deeds—all finding their primary origination in the Egyptian exodus.[231] In the OT tradition "redeem" is used for God delivering and freeing his people (Exod 6:6; Deut 7:8; 2 Sam 7:23). Towner says, "It was another way of speaking of God's saving act, and it would have primarily called to mind the OT story of deliverance from Egypt."[232] Additional correspondences in Titus 2:14 include the use of Ps 129:8 (LXX), "It is he who will redeem Israel from all its iniquities"; Ezek 36:25, 28, 29, 33, and 37:23, which have to do with purification and cleansing in the new covenant; and Exod 19:5 and Deut 7:6 in regard to God's people as his "possession."[233]

Another INE use of the OT in Titus is the description of the cleansing of salvation in connection with the renewal of the Holy Spirit in 3:4–6. The pouring out of the Spirit (3:6) comes from Joel 2:28, "I will pour out my

---

227. Other non-Pauline usages of Ps 118: Matt 21:42, Mark 12:10, Luke 20:17, Acts 4:11, and 1 Pet 2:6–8.

228. Quinn and Wacker, *First and Second Letters to Timothy*, 588.

229. Guthrie, *Pastoral Epistles*, 167.

230. Ibid., 171; Quinn and Wacker, *First and Second Letters to Timothy*, 727–33.

231. Collins, *1 & 2 Timothy and Titus*, 354–55; Towner, *1–2 Timothy and Titus*, 249.

232. Towner, "1–2 Timothy and Titus," 913.

233. Guthrie, *Pastoral Epistles*, 213.

spirit on all flesh" (cf. Acts 2:17), and corresponds to promises of the Spirit's activity found in Ezekiel (36:25–27, as mentioned previously).

The Pastorals suggest evidence of INE allusions. In 1 Timothy the INE reinforces the calling to ministry, the universality of the offer of the gospel, and ethics. Second Timothy may share θεμέλιος with Isa 28:16 and uses it within a context of warning against dangerous doctrines that threaten the church. In Titus there are strong allusions to INE paschal redemption. The letter uses promises given to Israel in exile to delineate INE truths concerning the situation on Crete. The challenges faced by the church were to be met with realizing the climactic acts of God in Christ. What was envisioned by Ezekiel and Joel finds fulfillment in the provision of the Spirit for the ministry of the church on Crete. Later it will be discovered that several of these concepts are found in Ephesians, but they are used for different purposes.

2.3.9 Philemon

Philemon is not considered at length in this present work because it appears to have no quotations or allusions from the OT. Some regard Paul employing the OT in terms of Deut 23:15–16 and the treatment of slaves; however, this is not a certainty.[234] Others see an illustration of substitutionary atonement in Paul's offer to pay any expenses (Phlm 18–19),[235] but this is a faint echo of the INE.

It is important to remember, however, that Christianity made possible an entire slave reversal, from the historical situation of the oppressed brick makers in Egypt to those who became spiritually free in Christ (Rom 6:16–20; Gal 4:7). Whether this was on Paul's mind in the writing of the short letter is an open question. Philemon has more to do with a literal slave situation and how Christian love should prevail.[236]

But interestingly, ἀναπαύω (Phlm 7, 20) occurs seventeen times in Isaiah, seven in Job, six in Ezekiel, and in all the other books of the OT (fewer than five times in each). Of the seventeen times in Isaiah, eight occurrences refer to animals resting under the direction of Yahweh, often in restorative conditions (7:19, 13:20, 13:21 [2], 27:10, 34:14 [2], 34:17), five times point to the rest afforded God's people (14:1, 7, 30; 32:16, 18), two speak of Yahweh's dwelling (11:2, 57:15), one to the ceasing of the oppressor (14:4), and one to the inability of the wicked to rest (57:20). Could the

---

234. Beale and Carson, "Philemon," 918; cf. Fitzmyer, *Letter to Philemon*, 17–24.

235. Getty, "Theology of Philemon," 503–8; M. Harris, "Philemon," 336–37.

236. Bruce, *Epistles*, 197–98. In other places Paul commands Christian slaves and masters to live in harmony (the household codes of Colossians and Ephesians), and contentedly (1 Cor 7:20–24).

refreshment demonstrated (Phlm 7) and then expected of Philemon (Phlm 20) have lingered in Paul's mind, since it is mentioned repeatedly in Isaiah in INE contexts, most frequently in a situation in which Israel would enslave the enslavers (Isa 14:2)? Perhaps ἀναπαύω is set in contrast to the conditions of slavery in which Yahweh turns the tables on Israel's oppressors.

2.4 CONSIDERATION OF THOSE WHO QUESTION THE PERVASIVENESS OF THE INE IN THE NT

In the judgment of some, the pervasiveness of the INE and other "way metaphors" in the NT is not a foregone conclusion. Barstad sees no prevailing new exodus motif in Isaiah.[237] He deems the language of Isa 40–55 as strongly poetic in nature, and which cannot be firmly placed in the new exodus camp. Lund maintains that the images in Isaiah are open to a variety of possible readings, not solely the new exodus.[238] Litwak calls into question what is commonly referred to as an echo (whether conscious or unconscious), and how this weighs on the intent of the author, among other concerns.[239]

Hatina argues that the motif as a hermeneutical key or underlying organizing principle has not been proven with certainty.[240] By way of a study of the Gospel of Mark and a critique of R. Watts, Hatina affirms that the INE is undoubtedly a motif in the NT, but stops short in acknowledging the concept as a hermeneutical principle or construct by which the book of Mark is assembled.[241] The following remarks capture Hatina's balanced consideration of Watts's monograph:

> Watts's attempt to integrate Markan structure and themes, particularly the function of Scripture quotations within a structural paradigm, is a valiant effort in responding to notions which reject theological or literary coherence of the Gospel as a whole. And in many ways he tries to fill the same void which in part inspires my own study. I also grant that "the way" or "new exodus" may well be a legitimate reading paradigm even if it differs from my own. The difficulty, however, which immediately presents itself in Watts's reading, is that the metanarrative, so to speak,

---

237. Barstad, *Way in the Wilderness*, 1–3, 109.
238. Lund, *Way Metaphors*, 16–21, esp. 21.
239. Litwak, *Scripture in Luke-Acts*, 47–65.
240. Hatina, *In Search*, 374–80.
241. R. Watts, *New Exodus in Mark*.

of the new exodus overshadows whatever narrative is latent in the Gospel itself.[242]

Hatina's cautions are well-taken and should engender pause on the part of those who would attempt to assemble a hermeneutical hypothesis that fails to reflect a prudent understanding of the intent of NT authors. As Hatina notes, if the underlying message is new exodus in nature, then how does this correspond with any other more explicit message intended from the author?

Scholars such as Hatina, Barstad, Lund, and Litwak are taken into consideration in this present work. However, it is not the intention of this investigation to necessarily prove an underlying hermeneutical INE construct in Ephesians akin to Watts's findings in Mark. The objective here is to ascertain the degree of influence of the OT, and specifically the present triumphal aspect of the INE in the epistle. The influence of the INE upon the author of Ephesians does not necessarily equate into a rigid mesh that underlies the epistle. Given this understanding, it is worth mentioning that the consensus of scholarship understands that there is indeed a new exodus afoot in Isaiah; the question that remains open is the degree of its influence in both Isaiah and the NT.

2.5 CONCLUSION

The INE has influence upon the Old and New Testaments, Second Temple Judaism, and most of the Pauline Corpus. The use of the INE varies, but common themes emerge. Isaianic motifs that most affected Paul are summarized by Wilk. He lists four areas: the message about Christ, Paul's apostolic self-understanding, the position of Israel vis-à-vis the gospel, and the expectation of the Parousia.[243]

Ellis sees Paul's typological-historical use of the OT as drawing from three periods: creation, the patriarchs, and the exodus.[244] He maintains that the exodus typology is built upon the structural framework of the two covenants: the Abrahamic and the new, especially in terms explained in 2 Cor 3 where the law under Moses at Sinai is contrasted with the Spirit that gives life and does not fade. The typology is rooted in the exodus and finds its fuller terminal point (antitype) in Christ and the Spirit. Within the broad structure of the old-new covenant, exodus typology is found in several correspondences: the Passover (1 Cor 5:7, 11:25) under Moses is now completely fulfilled in the paschal death of Christ (Rom 3:24–25) and

---

242. Hatina, *In Search*, 22–23.
243. Wilk, "Zitation," 16–206.
244. Ellis, *Paul's Use*, 129–135.

commemorated in the communal acts of the church. Both the bread and the cup have new exodus significance since they speak not only of Christ's body and blood, but of the Passover meal on the night before the exodus (Matt 26:26–29). The old covenant was inscribed on tablets of stone during the exodus, but in the new exodus the new covenant is placed upon the hearts of men (2 Cor 3:3). Moses and the children of Israel were baptized in the cloud and the sea, those in Christ are baptized through his death and resurrection (1 Cor 10:3, Rom 6:3–4, Gal 3:26). In Judaism, physical baptism allowed proselytes to identify with Israel and the exodus through the sea; in the NT, Christian baptism identifies participants with the new exodus.[245] The food and drink of the historical exodus is now spiritual food and drink in Christ (1 Cor 10:3–4). The wilderness wanderers were accompanied by the tabernacle and Shekinah glory. In the new covenant the presence of God typified in the OT in the cloud, tabernacle, and temple is now within Christians (1 Cor 3:16–17, Hebrews).

The employment of the INE in the Pauline Corpus is a central facet in the messages to the early churches. Paul's immersion in Isaiah and the other prophets informed him that the historical exodus anticipated how God would act in a similar, yet fuller fashion in the new covenant. Paul's thinking concerning the new exodus is set comfortably within the wide stream of OT prophets and contemporary Judaism. He expands upon these generally accepted positions in light of the advent of Christ and the anticipated age. Joseph Klausner's comment about Paul and Judaism may be applied to Paul and the OT, as well as the Pauline incorporation of the INE: "Intensive research over many years has brought the writer of the present book to a deep conviction that there is nothing in the teaching of Paul—not even the most mystical elements in it—that did not come from authentic Judaism."[246] However, balance is required; Ridderbos makes the important point that, in light of his Judaic contemporaries, Paul's OT messianic conceptions and his eschatology maintain a unique character.[247]

The use of the exodus is found throughout the OT, and was a prominent feature in Second Temple Judaism and the NT. Epistles such as Romans, Galatians, and 1 and 2 Corinthians demonstrate a plethora of examples of new exodus usages; but expressions in other Pauline epistles are substantial as well, though less explicit. The new exodus usages demonstrate a broad singularity of thought in the writing of these letters. It is plausible that during

---

245. Sahlin, "Salvation," 90.

246. Klausner, *From Jesus to Paul*, 466. Cited by Ellis with no page reference: *Paul's Use*, 39.

247. Ridderbos, *Paul*, 51–52.

the purported time period directly affecting the writing of Ephesians (from Acts 19–20 to 2 Timothy), Paul had an established understanding of the INE and how it applied to the Christian era. This understanding is reflected, more or less, in the cluster of Pauline material. More weight is added when it is observed that apart from Colossians, Ephesians has strongest theological resemblance to Romans. Because Romans contains a superfluity of OT usage, as well as explicit arguments for the INE, a similar likelihood is expected of Ephesians. This does not exclude other developed nuances to Paul's doctrines, but a reader would generally expect a consistency of OT usage on the part of Paul, and specifically in a fundamental area such as the INE.

It is difficult to overestimate the pervasive force of the new exodus in Paul's thinking. Since the new exodus is prominent in the Pauline Corpus there is a probability that it will be found in Ephesians. This suggests that a case can begin to be made for the influence of the OT in Ephesians along with the possibility of any weight provided by the INE. If the OT and INE are not present in Ephesians, then the letter would stand conspicuously alone with Philemon as an exception among Paul's works. These findings will come to bear in determining the extent and meaning of the new exodus in Ephesians. It is yet to be determined if there is OT and INE influence in the epistle, and whether the influence is to any degree formative.

3

A Review of the Approaches to the Use of the OT in Ephesians and the Works That Have Recognized the Influence of the INE in the Epistle

The study of the OT in Ephesians has not received a great deal of attention. Reasons include claims of Gnostic influences, alleged pseudonymity, lack of verbal parallels with the OT, and shared concepts with the undisputed Paulines.[1] As a result, while other portions of the NT and the Pauline letters have been examined in terms of the new exodus, Ephesians has been overlooked. This is a remarkable state of affairs given that Ephesians is so closely aligned with other Pauline works that have received a vast amount of attention in OT in NT studies, such as Romans, 1 and 2 Corinthians, and Galatians. In addition to these four letters it has been determined in this present work that significant amounts of OT allusions populate the balance of the Pauline Corpus, with the probable exception of Philemon.

There are several general works that have to do with the OT in Ephesians and there are others that deal with the new exodus that are found in a few isolated texts in the epistle. A discussion of these general and new exodus works follows.

---

1. Lincoln explains this neglect: Lincoln, "Use," 17.

3.1 APPROACHES TO THE STUDY OF THE OT IN THE EPISTLE

While some scholars observe a degree of OT influence in Ephesians, others such as Lindemann and Beker see very little, if any.[2] Maurer maintains that the eulogy in Eph 1:3–14 discloses the heavy influence of Gnosticism and concludes that Paul's use of the OT was selective in order to fit the purposes of his Gnostic beliefs.[3] Kuhn[4] and Mussner[5] observe a considerable influence from Qumran rather than the OT.[6] Kuhn recognizes parallels between the paraenetical sections of Ephesians and the Dead Sea Scrolls, and Mussner extends the same discussion to reoccurring themes in the epistle. Perkins finds resemblance to Essene thought throughout the letter.[7]

On the other hand, Schmid in *Der Epheserbrief des Apostels Paulus* considers Paul's use of the OT in Ephesians from the standpoint of authorship.[8] If the epistle is fully Pauline, it must share in the homologoumena, utilizing the OT as in the rest of the Pauline Corpus. In his commentary on Ephesians, M. Barth studies Paul's use of the OT, much as Schmid, for purposes of determining authorship. Barth concludes that, based on the use of the OT in Ephesians, Pauline authorship cannot be ruled out.[9] Sampley presents observations on the use of the OT in Ephesians, primarily in regard to Jewish influence in the book.[10] These works certainly see the import of the OT in Ephesians, and they lay the groundwork for further studies that open the possibility of an Isaianic exodus in the epistle.

Lincoln establishes clear corollaries and patterns from the OT in Ephesians.[11] However, he maintains that the OT plays a supportive role rather than a formative one.[12] He draws this conclusion based on the material in Ephesians that includes a number of authoritative traditions alongside the use of the OT. Lincoln concludes that there are Jewish Christian traditions, liturgical formulations, explicit OT citations, and imbedded OT motifs in

---

2. Beker, *Heirs of Paul*, 93; Lindemann, *Aufhebung*, 88.
3. Maurer, "Der Hymnus," 151–72.
4. Kuhn, "Epistle," 115–31.
5. Mussner, "Contributions," 159–78.
6. Kuhn, "Epistle," 115–31; Mussner, "Contributions," 59–78. M. Barth argues for Paul using Qumran language and style: *Ephesians, Chapters 1–3*, 21.
7. Perkins, *Ephesians*, 29, 39, 62, 77, 147.
8. Schmid, *Epheserbrief*, 131.
9. M. Barth, *Ephesians, Chapters 1–3*, 28–30.
10. Sampley, "And the Two," 101–09.
11. Lincoln, "Use," 16–57.
12. Ibid., 49; Lincoln, *Ephesians*, lxi–lxii; Lincoln and Wedderburn, *Later Pauline Letters*, 89–90.

the missive. He maintains that the extra-biblical traditions do not bear the same authority as the OT, but are utilized as additional sources as the writer seeks to support his arguments. At first glance Lincoln's observations would seem to limit the possibility of the INE in Ephesians; however, he paves the way to delve deeper into the OT usages and possible new exodus patterns. In speaking of the purpose of Ephesians, he draws a tangential point when he writes, "The uses of the OT are spread fairly evenly throughout the letter and serve the major aspects of that purpose. This use of Scripture along with that of other traditions known to the churches has a certain cohesive and unifying function for the churches the writer addresses, and the very fact that the OT is used at all establishes a certain continuity with God's dealings with Israel in the past."[13] Lincoln shows that the author of Ephesians used his epistle to explain certain OT concepts and to elaborate upon them in light of the advent of Christ. These issues center on how the heritage of Israel is seen in the Jewish-Gentile makeup of NT congregations and how the church adopts aspects of God's purposes for the nation. Additionally, Lincoln notes that explanations of the mystery, ethics, household matters, and cosmic warfare have OT foundations that come into play. If the OT is important in Ephesians, as Lincoln maintains, it is possible that the new exodus should be found in Ephesians as well. The new exodus certainly is integral to both OT Israel and the reinterpretation of national promises in the NT.

Lincoln reveals other possibilities of the INE in Ephesians. He chides Maurer for including "broad" OT notions in Ephesians such as, "election, blessing, the relation of the servant of God to the title of 'Beloved,'" as well as other bridge concepts. But Lincoln himself goes on to speak of OT images in Ephesians, such as the idea of the cornerstone and sacrificial imageries, as well as "the general theological influence of OT ideas, such as election, salvation (and) the people of God."[14] Although Lincoln does not explicitly write of the INE in Ephesians, he does observe OT biblical-theological themes in the letter.

3.2 WORKS RECOGNIZING THE INE IN EPHESIANS

Recent studies in Ephesians have been influenced by an upsurge in intertextual analysis. Works since Dodd have now been applied to the Pauline Corpus, including Ephesians.[15] As a result, more emphasis has been placed on the wider, biblical-theological use of the OT in the epistle.

13. Lincoln, "Use," 50.
14. Ibid., 16–17.
15. Smalley's article on eschatology in Ephesians arrived soon after Dodd's,

Qualls and J. Watts survey the influence of Isaiah in Ephesians. They note five sections of the epistle where Isaiah plays a prominent role (Eph 1:4–14, 1:15–23, 2:1–22, 5:3–14, 6:13–17).[16] In each of these sections the theological import is considered. As with Lincoln, they arrive at conclusions that clearly open the way for new exodus evidences in Ephesians: "New Testament exegesis often relies on the Old Testament as a source of authority, and it defines Old Testament prophecy as being fulfilled in the present. But, Isaiah in Ephesians is more than just the typology of prophecy/fulfilment; it is a restatement of the prophetic message in light of new revelation. Thus, when the prophetic message of the Old Testament is incorporated into the realities of the New Testament, it undergoes a metamorphosis."[17]

Moritz's *A Profound Mystery: The Use of the Old Testament in Ephesians*[18] is a thorough exegetical analysis, including the exploration of the use of OT texts in Ephesians. He builds on Lincoln and others by further demonstrating the use of the OT in the letter. Mortiz reveals that Ephesians is engorged with the OT. The "new exodus" does not appear as a sustained line of reasoning in this monograph, but the essential issues and arguments of new exodus evidences make their appearance.[19] Moritz's work significantly adds to the scholarship of the new exodus in Ephesians by opening new avenues of understanding Ephesians through the lens of Jewish Scriptures and second century literature and tradition. As seen in the previous chapter of this present work, the OT and the Jewish second century literature were themselves fully engaged within the new exodus.

O'Brien's commentary on Ephesians is another study of the new exodus in Ephesians. He undertakes a serious attempt to unearth the INE evidences in the epistle.[20] O'Brien's commentary is a helpful tool in understanding use of the OT in the missive, especially because it utilizes the standard scholarly works of the field as they relate to the new exodus.[21] O'Brien, however, does not envisage the INE as a compelling force in the composition of the letter.

According to the Scriptures, but fails to incorporate the OT allusions and echoes that lie in the epistle (Smalley deals only with Ps 68:18 in Eph 4:8). As a result Smalley's work speaks of eschatology in Ephesians but without a thorough OT analysis: "Eschatology of Ephesians," 152–57.

16. Qualls and J. Watts, "Isaiah in Ephesians," 250–56.

17. Ibid., 256.

18. Moritz, *Profound Mystery*. In addition is his summary work on Ephesians: "Ephesians," 315–19.

19. Moritz, *Profound Mystery*, 213.

20. O'Brien, *Letter*, 35, 42, 102, 115–16, 288, 292–95, 304, 346–48, 442–43, and 461.

21. For O'Brien's index of authors: *Letter*, 501–07.

A Review of the Approaches to the Use of the OT in Ephesians 75

Thielman explores OT usage in Ephesians, in particular the incorporation of Isaiah.[22] His intention is not specifically the INE, but as with other similar studies he establishes the use of the OT for purposes that coincide with the hopes of Israel during the exilic period.[23]

A few works are breaking new ground in the study of the INE in Ephesians. Suh's "The Use of Ezekiel 37 in Ephesians 2" directly addresses the issue of a new exodus in Ephesians that mirrors Ezekiel.[24] Yee presents another recent work, *Jews, Gentiles, and Ethnic Reconciliation: Paul's Jewish Identity and Ephesians*, which focuses on the makeup of "Gentiles in the flesh" in Eph 2 and how Gentiles were incorporated into the covenant of Israel.[25] W. Harris in *The Descent of Christ: Ephesians 4:7–11 and Traditional Hebrew Imagery* presents the clear OT background to this much-disputed passage.[26] *Put on the Armour of God: The Divine Warrior from Isaiah to Ephesians* by Yoder-Neufeld analyzes the connection between Isaiah and the panoply metaphor in Eph 6.[27] In *The Story of Israel: A Biblical Theology* one chapter is devoted to "Paul: The Reverse of the Curse"[28] in which Ephesians and Colossians are considered from the standpoint of the reversal of the Deuteronomic curses.[29] Roon sees Ephesians in general as eschatological: "This moderation in the use of eschatological pronouncements by no means signifies that the eschatological structure in Eph. is essentially different than the HP. If it is correct to say that the end of time begins with the death and resurrection of Christ . . . then in Eph. the era in which the apostle and the faithful are living is elevated in the same way as it is in the HP."[30] Roon reminds that Ephesians falls within the broad OT eschatological stream that Paul assumes in 1 Cor 10:11: "These things happened to them to serve as an example, and they were written down to instruct us, on whom the ends of the ages have come." Ridderbos concurs by observing that a fundamental structure of Paul is eschatological or redemptive-historical.[31]

These aforementioned works will be more fully investigated as specific passages in Ephesians are considered.

22. Thielman, "Ephesians," 813–33.
23. Ibid., 814, 817–19 (esp. 819 concerning 3:1–13), 820, 823–26, 830–33.
24. Suh, "Use of Ezekiel," 715–33.
25. Yee, *Jewish Identity*, 1–33, 213–18.
26. W. Harris, *Descent of Christ*, xv–xvii.
27. Yoder-Neufeld, *Put on*, 11–14.
28. Pate et al., "Paul: The Reverse of the Curse," 206–31.
29. Ibid., 222–24.
30. "HP" signifies the undisputed Paulines: Roon, *Authenticity*, 258.
31. Ridderbos, *Paul*, 44.

3.3 A PRELIMINARY SUMMARY OF INE PASSAGES IN THE LETTER

Ephesians clearly utilizes the OT and may sustain correlations with the exodus motif and INE.[32] By way of preliminary summary, ten linkages are suggested:

1. Yahweh's choice of Israel and the inaugural Passover, and Christ's choosing of the church and paschal sacrifice (Exod 12:1–27 and the ubiquitous redemption and salvation motifs in Isaiah such as in 43:14, 44:22 with Eph 1:7, 13, 14; 4:30 [cf. 5:2]; 6:17).
2. Yahweh and his Messiah's royal enthronement, and Christ's enthronement with the church (Pss 110 and 8, with Eph 1:20–2:6).
3. The resurrection of the believing remnant and the remaining judgment on the unbelieving dead in the death-new life metaphor (Isa 26:14, 19 with Eph 2:5f).
4. Nations thronging to honor Yahweh and his servant in Zion, and the integration of the church community based on the new creation motif (Isa 57:19; 52:7 with Eph 2:13, 17).
5. The inferiority of the pre-exilic and postexilic temples, and the church's access through the Spirit to the eschatological temple where Christ is lodged as cornerstone (Isa 28:16; Ezek 37:27 with Eph 2:18–21).
6. The Danielic mystery of the new age and the disclosure of Christian truth by Paul, the apostles, and prophets (Daniel, where μυστήριον is found seventeen times, with Eph 1:9; 3:1–10; 5:32; 6:19).
7. The occasion of Yahweh's triumphant ascension upon Zion where he receives gifts, and Christ's descent and exalted gift giving (Ps 68 with Eph 4:7–10).
8. Ethical living in conjunction with the new age of Israel, and the behavior expected of God's new humanity (Isa 63:10; 60:1; 26:19; Ezek 11:19–20; Zech 8:16; with Eph 4:22—6:9).
9. The restored marriage of Yahweh and Israel, and that realized by Christ and the church (as prototypes of Christian marriage; Ezek 16:4, 9; Gen 2:24; Lev 19:18; Isa 54:5; and Hosea with Eph 5:22–33).

---

32. Ellis considers four usages in Ephesians from twelve sources in the OT. Lincoln sees thirteen uses in Ephesians from thirty-five in Isaiah. Moritz has seven uses in Ephesians from Isaiah, Psalms, and Zechariah. Qualls and J. Watts note five sections of Ephesians where Isaiah plays a prominent role (Eph 1:4–14, 1:15–23, 2:1–22, 5:3–14, 6:13–17): Ellis, *Paul's Use*, 152, 154; Lincoln, "Use," 16–57; Moritz, *Profound Mystery*, 11–96, 178–212; Qualls and J. Watts, "Isaiah in Ephesians," 250–56.

10. Yahweh and his servant's warfare and triumph, and the church's conflict and victory pertaining to cosmic powers (Isa 11:4–5; 49:2; 52:7–15; 59:17 and Eph 6:10–17).

These are suggestions that open up possibilities of correspondence, and serve as an introduction to the arguments that follow in the balance of this work. Other potential linkages with less weight will be forthcoming in the course of the study. The ultimate goal of this current work is to establish the degree to which these images are rooted in the concept of the new exodus; and whether these OT new exodus usages in Ephesians suggest that the triumphal aspect of the INE controlled the composition of the letter.

3.4 CONCLUSION

The use of the OT in Ephesians has been surveyed in the past. In these works many of the OT usages were examined in detail. More recently, some works have looked at aspects of Isaiah and other prophets' new exodus in the epistle, such as Ezekiel in Eph 2, Qualls and Watts's work, as well as the scholarship of Yoder-Neufeld, O'Brien, and Thielman, among others. Credible evidence has come forth from these studies that strongly suggest evidence of exodus influence in Ephesians. However, none of these studies inspect the letter exclusively in terms of Isaiah's exodus, nor do these works examine what aspects of the INE were accentuated in the epistle. There remains a need for a full study of the influence of the new exodus in Ephesians; which is the aim of this current work. Several possible ties between Isaiah's new exodus and Ephesians exist. An assessment of these prospective connections include not only questions as to whether the INE is utilized, but what degree of influence they may have had on the author of Ephesians. Before this assessment can be done, however, an understanding of Paul's idea of triumph will be discussed, and how the idea of triumph might come to bear upon Ephesians.

4

An Introduction to the Triumphal Aspect of the INE in Ephesians

It has been shown that Paul's immersion in the OT, particularly Isaiah, shaped his understanding of the coming of Jesus and the formation of the Christian community. In his mind the INE and accompanying blessings had, in large part, arrived in Western Asia Minor. However, a similar line of broad reasoning could be applied to several portions of the NT, and in particular, Romans and Colossians. In what way did the INE influence the composition of Ephesians that, in turn, sets it apart from the use of the INE in other segments of the NT? If Ephesians is a rewriting of Colossians and was composed days or weeks afterward as some suggest, what controlling factors caused the author to write Ephesians as he did? Also, what INE tendencies in Ephesians distinguish the epistle from the OT eschatological themes found in Galatians or 1 and 2 Corinthians? This current work asserts that there is a possibility, perhaps likelihood, that the central, distinctive thrust of Ephesians is the present triumphal aspect of the INE. In the composition of this letter the writer may have parsed the INE in order that the recipients might focus on its present features, and may have done so in such a way as to distinguish the epistle from the balance of the Pauline Corpus as well as the rest of the NT.

If it is to be discovered that the triumphal aspect of the INE played a distinguishing role in the composition of Ephesians, then two critical issues require attention. First, there should be evidential confirmation that there are INE passages from the OT utilized within the letter in a fashion that suggest triumph. The INE triumphal aspect may be inherent to the OT passage or conscripted by the author of Ephesians to intimate triumph. Cumulative

An Introduction to the Triumphal Aspect of the INE in Ephesians

proof, whether by quotation, allusion, or echo, should be forthcoming. It should be expected that there is evidence of the INE in Ephesians since the phenomenon is evidenced throughout the other letters of the Pauline Corpus. The substantiation of the INE in Ephesians was introduced in chapter 3 of this present work, and it will be expanded upon as particular passages are examined. Secondly, these INE usages, along with the corresponding contexts in Ephesians, should indicate that triumph is a present reality. The audience of this missive should have understood that the INE had arrived in some substantive way.

A section on Pauline triumphalism follows. An understanding of Paul's view of triumph assists in comprehending the nuances of the application of the INE in Ephesians. How did Paul envision the victory of God and Christ? How does it correspond to the vision of Isaiah and the other prophets concerning the new age? Answering these questions will enable a more precise view of this concept in the Pauline Corpus and any distinction found in Ephesians. If the premise of this present work is correct, then Ephesians should emphasize to some degree a prevailing aspect of INE triumphalism.

4.1 PAULINE TRIUMPHALISM: "ALREADY"

Pauline eschatology is integral to contextualizing the concept of the INE triumph in Ephesians.[1] Not all agree, but increasingly scholarship sees the influence of OT eschatology on Paul.[2] Eschatology, and the recognition of a present and future age, was a part of the first century Jewish mindset.[3] Paul

---

1. The standard introductory works on Paul have sections on his eschatology: Bornkamm, *Paul*, 196–227; Bruce, *Paul, Apostle*, 53–61, 104, 300–13; Ridderbos, *Paul*, 44–90, 161–65, 487–562; Whiteley, *Theology of St. Paul*, 233–73. Other more critical studies do as well: Davies, *Paul and Rabbinic Judaism*, 102–8, 147–76, 268–75; Käsemann, *Questions*, 131–36; Munck, *Salvation of Mankind*, 38–40; Schoeps, *Theology of the Apostle*, 88, 112; A. Schweitzer, *Mysticism*, 52–74, 75–100; Vos, *Pauline Eschatology*, passim, esp. 1–61.

2. Beker produced notable recent works on Pauline eschatology with monikers, "contingency" (the changing contemporary situation) and "coherence" (Paul's gospel and central theology): *Triumph of God*, 351–67; *Paul's Apocalyptic*, 29–54; *Heirs of Paul*, 109–12; "Recasting Pauline Theology," 15–24. Additionally, Wright builds on Beker and others, while commenting on Beker's attempts: *Climax of the Covenant*, 258–59.

3. Cf. 4 Ezra 7:50, "The Most High made not one age but two." Dunn cites Zech 14:9: *Theology of Paul*, 465 n. 17. Jewish expectation of the Parousia in first century Palestine was a complex matter, different parts of which were redefined by Paul. For a discussion of this complexity and the skirmishes between the Christian church and rabbinical school: Dunn, *Partings of the Ways*, 22–25. Dunn reflects that one reason Christianity failed to overtake rabbinical influence in Palestine is precisely because of Pauline eschatology. The Messiah provided a present spiritualized triumph and his return was delayed in order to win Gentiles. This did not sit well with Jewish nationalism.

was not far from his first century Jewish contemporaries in regard to end time events. This does not mean he duplicated their thinking, for undoubtedly he introduced novel aspects that centered upon the advent of Christ. The roots of Paul's understanding of eschatology are found in the OT. They hearken back to the soteriological purposes of God in the founding of the nation of Israel and the call of Abraham. It was God's intent that the nation witness to the nations (Gal 3:8, 16, 29). The purpose of the call of Abraham eventuated in the advent of Christ in "the fullness of time" (Gal 4:4 and Eph 1:10) and as an "acceptable time" (2 Cor 6:2). This is explicit in Rom 16:25–26 in Paul's treatment of the μυστήριον motif: " Now to God who is able to strengthen you according to my gospel and the proclamation of Jesus Christ, according to the revelation of the mystery that was kept secret for long ages but is now disclosed, and through the prophetic writings is made known to all the Gentiles, according to the command of the eternal God, to bring about the obedience of faith." The term "mystery" appears in much the same manner in other Pauline letters, and repeatedly in Ephesians.[4] The word refers to certain aspects of the inscrutable nature of the new age, but not the fact that it was unanticipated or an invention of Paul. This novel era is in keeping with the message of the prophets and Jesus: "The time is fulfilled, and the kingdom of God has come near; repent, and believe in the good news" (Mark 1:15).[5] The early preaching of the apostles in Acts reveals their understanding that in the coming of Jesus the consummation of redemptive history was upon them: "In the last days it will be, God declares, that I will pour out my Spirit upon all flesh, and your sons and your daughters shall prophesy, and your young men shall see visions, and your old men shall dream dreams" (Acts 2:17).

Ridderbos contends that, "Nothing less is intended than that the decisive, long-expected coming of God has dawned, the hour of hours, the day of salvation in the fulfilling, eschatological sense of the word."[6] Paul was echoing Jesus and the other apostles in declaring that the new created order predicted in the OT had arrived.

In keeping with Paul's understanding of eschatological, redemptive-history is the triumphal aspect of God's consummation of time.[7] God prevailing over his foes stems once again from Paul's view of divine triumph found in the OT. Prior to the exodus, Abraham's rescue of Lot included the

---

4. Other passages on the mystery include: Eph 1:9; 3:3, 4, 5, 9; 5:32; 6:19; Col 1:26, 2:2–3; 1 Cor 2:7; 2 Tim 1:9, 10; Titus 1:2–3.

5. Cf. "mysteries" in Matt 13:11, 16, and 17.

6. Ridderbos, *Paul*, 45.

7. Reid, "Christus Victor;" Reid, "Triumph," 946–54.

triumphant imagery of Yahweh as Abraham's shield.[8] Upon crossing the sea, the Hebrews acclaim Yahweh as a warrior leading his people in victory against Pharaoh's armies (Exod 14:14; 15:3).[9] The Song of the Sea forms a classic ancient understanding of a celebration that follows the triumph of a king.[10] In other passages Yahweh is seen riding on a chariot in the clouds.[11] Many of the historical high points of Israel involve ascribing military victory to Yahweh, such as those of Deborah and Barak (Judg 5).[12] This is the battle cry of David, who sees Yahweh giving the enemy into his hands (1 Sam 17:47). The triumphant warrior imagery is especially apparent in Isaiah, portraying Yahweh's conquest throughout Isa 60–66, which has ongoing influence in the Pauline Corpus: "For the LORD will come in fire, and his chariots like the whirlwind, to pay back his anger in fury, and his rebuke in flames of fire. For by fire will the LORD execute judgment, and by his sword, on all flesh; and those slain by the LORD shall be many" (Isa 66:15–16).

Other OT passages look to a future cosmological victory on the part of Yahweh and his people.[13] The "Day of Yahweh" is a theme developed by the prophets upon the certainty of God's judgment and triumph on some future day.[14] It is understood that Yahweh will rout his enemies and restore

---

8. Gen 14:19–20, 15:1. Longman and Reid see divine warfare in the Bible in five phases: (1) God fights Israel's enemies; (2) God fights Israel; (3) the future divine deliverer; (4) Jesus fights the principalities and powers; and, (5) the final battle: *God Is a Warrior*, 17. For a review of works on Yahweh as a warrior, from Calvin to Rad and forward: Longman and Reid, 19–26. R. Watts notes the primary literature and discusses Yahweh-Warrior in Isaiah: *New Exodus in Mark*, 140–44, 140 n. 11. Aune considers ancient versions of the combat myth in Rev 11:19—12:17; a widespread understanding that two deities struggle for dominance over the world: *Revelation 6–16*, 668–74. Cf. Fontenrose, *Delphic Myth*, 1–11.

9. Lind, *Yahweh Is a Warrior*, 46–60, 171. Lind's study understands that if Israel truly believed that Yahweh was her warrior, she would have fought less. The responsibility would have fallen to divine miracle apart from human warriors. But Lind's pacifist understanding is not in keeping with the evidence of the biblical text. God's presence as a warrior is the basis for courage in battle but not a substitute for human effort: Rowlett, *Rhetoric of Violence*, 65–67.

10. Gombis discusses the victorious warrior elements in the Song of the Sea: "Triumph" (2005a), 14–18. Cf. Cassuto, *Book of Exodus*, 173; J. Watts, "The Song of the Sea," 371–80. Childs places the Song within its context recognizing "the conquest and possession of the land which culminate in the establishment of the divine sanctuary": Childs, *Exodus*, 244. This has parallels to triumphalism and Eph 2:20–22.

11. Ps 68:4; 104:3–4; Isa 19:1; and esp. Dan 7:13–14. Cf. Pss 29; 110.

12. Millar, "Victory," 830–32. As the nation increasingly disobeys, an appeal is made for Yahweh to act on the people's behalf, not on the basis of merit but because of God's mercy (Ps 74; Isa 63:18; Ezek 39:27).

13. Pss 46, 74, 76.

14. Isa 13:6–13; 19:21; 22:12; 61:2; Jer 25:33; 46:10; 50:31; Lam 1:12; Ezek 13:5;

his people: "Rejoice greatly, O daughter Zion! Shout aloud, O daughter Jerusalem! Lo, your king comes to you; triumphant and victorious is he, humble and riding on a donkey, on a colt, the foal of a donkey. He will cut off the chariot from Ephraim and the war-horse from Jerusalem; and the battle bow shall be cut off, and he shall command peace to the nations; his dominion shall be from sea to sea, and from the River to the ends of the earth"[15] (Zech 9:9–10). In addition, and in conjunction with triumph, it is not surprising that an "already, not yet" understanding of God's program is present in Isaiah. Childs observes this in Isaiah 25–26.[16] This understanding of Isaiah's perception of triumph will have repercussions later in the expositional portion of this present work.

In Christ the day of triumph had appeared; Jesus came as the victorious messiah-king, though without political ambition.[17] Jesus's ministry is clearly seen as a fulfillment of the victory envisioned in Isaiah: "He will not break a bruised reed or quench a smoldering wick until he brings justice to victory. And in his name the Gentiles will hope" (Matt 12:20–21 quoting Isa 42:3). Jesus understood his ministry using triumphant imagery. On one occasion he explains how he overpowers evil: "But if it is by the finger of God that I cast out the demons, then the kingdom of God has come to you. When a strong man, fully armed, guards his castle, his property is safe. But when one stronger than he attacks him and overpowers him, he takes away his armor in which he trusted and divides his plunder. Whoever is not with me is against me, and whoever does not gather with me scatters" (Luke 11:20–23). Although Satan acquired a Pyrrhic advantage at the cross, Christ triumphed there through his death and resurrection, vanquishing cosmic powers. This is Paul's understanding: "erasing the record that stood against us with its legal demands. He set this aside, nailing it to the cross. He disarmed the rulers and authorities and made a public example of them, triumphing over them in it" (Col 2:14–15).[18] Paul sees the cross of Christ leading to cosmic victory. Both Col 2:15 and 2 Cor 2:14 emphatically speak of θριαμβεύω as well as the associated manifestation of triumph, ἐδειγμάτισεν ἐν παρρησίᾳ and φανερόω:[19] "But thanks be to God, who in Christ always leads us in triumphal procession, and through us spreads in every place the

---

30:2–3; 39:8; Joel 1:15; 2:1, 11, 31; 3:14; Amos 5:18, 20; Zeph 1:7; 2:2; 3:8, 14–16; Zech 2:11; 9:16; 14:3, 7, 9, 20–21; Mal 4:1–3, 5.

15. Cf. Isa 45:21. Bruce, "Victory of God," 40–50. Bruce supplies a myriad of OT passages, exodus and new exodus in nature; and a spattering from the NT.

16. Childs, *Isaiah*, 189–90.

17. Matt 2:2; 21:5; 27:11, 42; Mark 15:9; Luke 23:2; John 1:49; 8:37; 19:21.

18. Cf. Col 1:13; Heb 2:14–15.

19. These are the only two verses in the NT where the verb θριαμβεύω occurs.

fragrance that comes from knowing him" (2 Cor 2:14).[20] Paul utilizes OT warfare images in his letters to the churches. He adapted the OT pictures, but with Christ and the church in mind: "In telling the story of Christ, Paul utilized the story of God, Israel, and the nations. The progressive pattern of warfare, victory, kingship, temple building, and celebration was transposed. For Paul, God was in Christ reconciling the world; the actions that the Old Testament and Judaism had ascribed to God, Paul could now ascribe to Christ."[21] Christ's ascension and enthronement, in turn, demonstrate the victory over sin and death.[22] Christ reigns at the right hand of God as Lord over all as a cosmic demonstration of triumph.[23] To him belongs universal obeisance (Phil 2:9–11). In addition, his people reign with him and are the temple of his kingdom.[24]

Although there are detractors, scholarship increasingly understands Paul's preaching as being fundamentally from the standpoint of OT eschatological fulfilment.[25] It forms a foundational element that underlys doctrines such as theology proper, Christology, pneumatology, ecclesiology, soteriology, anthropology, and ethics.[26] According to Beker, the essential thesis to understanding Paul is that the Christ-event is proleptic for the cosmic triumph of God.[27] Christ is the anticipated fulfilment of divine triumph. In this sense Pauline theology is not ultimately Christocentric or Christomonic,

---

20. Duff is certain that in 2 Cor 2:14 Paul sees himself as a prisoner rather than a victor, and argues that Paul uses θριαμβεύω ironically, assuming the position of his detractors and then turning their argument back upon them (2 Cor 5:14). His argument is persuasive but not convincing: "'Led in Triumph' in 2 Corinthians 2:14," 79–92. For a philological attempt at understanding the verb in the two texts (2 Cor 2:14 and Col 2:15): Egan, "Lexical Evidence," 34–62. Whether Paul intends to be seen as a driven captive or accompanying a victorious general (or Dionysus), or whether he utilizes irony with θριαμβεύω, the message is essentially the same: he is a part of Christ's victorious procession: Reid, "Triumph," 948; Ridderbos, *Paul*, 267 n. 34.

21. Longman and Reid, *God Is a Warrior*, 136.

22. Rom 1:4; 4:25; 8:31–34; Eph 1:20; Phil 2:9–11; 2 Tim 1:10.

23. Ps 110:1 and its multiple uses in the NT, as in Eph 1:20. Cf.: Ps 8:6; 1 Cor 15:24–26; Col 3:1; 1 Tim 3:16.

24. 1 Cor 3:16–17; 2 Cor 6:16; Eph 2:19–22.

25. Ridderbos, *Paul*, 44–51, 487–88; J. Scott, "Restoration," 796–805.

26. Kreitzer, "Eschatology," 253–69. Kreitzer observes eschatology surfacing in all of Paul's letters with the exception of perhaps Galatians and Philemon. Cf. Kreitzer, *Jesus and God*, 93–163, esp. 113–29.

27. Beker, "Triumph of God," 351–67. For Beker's summary concerning Pauline triumphalism: 351–63. Beker utilizes Dahl to support his argument concerning the neglect of understanding the NT from an eschatological viewpoint: Dahl, "Neglected Factor," 153–63.

but rather triumph arriving and procured in Christ.[28] Central Pauline doctrines such as the revelation of the righteousness of God and justification by faith, participation in Christ, the life and empowerment of the believing community, the gift and ministry of the Holy Spirit, and the church as a body are subordinate to the overarching theme of Christ as bringing about the anticipated victory of God.[29] A case in point is Col 1:19–20: "For in him all the fullness of God was pleased to dwell, and through him God was pleased to reconcile to himself all things, whether on earth or in heaven, by making peace through the blood of his cross."

Beker objects to Cullmann and others who take the passage to refer to the centrality of Christ. Cullmann's position, Beker contends, leads to ecclesiastical triumphalism rather than the consummation of history. Beker reminds that the focus is on a chronological, futurist culmination of history (that has already begun), aiming at both history and all creation.[30] Paul's view of triumph is apocalyptic in nature; inaugurated, obtained, and ultimately finalized in Christ's person and work. Pauline faith involved not just the certainty of Christ dying for the sins of his people but also the assurance of Christ who triumphantly ushers in final history.

Paul was convinced that with the coming of Christ the long-awaited epoch anticipated by the prophets had arrived and the eschatological program of God found its fulfilment. Christ shares this triumph with his followers by virtue of their association with him, and with them a new order (2 Cor 5:17–19). Rom 8:37 reveals this same conquest language on a corporate level: "in all these things we are more than conquerors through him who loved us."[31] This, of course, did not include physical military victory or literal kingdom building. As his ministry progressed, Jesus clarified the nature of his triumph (John 18:36). Reid therefore argues, "The triumph of God in Christ is not the triumph of brute force, as if to assert a cosmic principle of

---

28. Beker distinguishes his position from that of Cullmann who allows his Christocentric theology to replace eschatology, thus deapocalypticizing Paul; and from Bultmann whose hermeneutic supplants eschatology with anthropology: Bultmann, *Theology*, 1:190; Cullmann, *Christ and Time*, 139. Donfried agrees with Beker in the former's analysis of 1 Thess 2:13–16: Donfried, *Early Christianity*, 196–97. For criticism of Beker's position: Davies, *Paul and Rabbinic Judaism*, 361 n. 16; Martyn, "Apocalyptic Antinomies," 410–24.

29. In his classic work on soteriology, Aulén sees in the atonement Christ overcoming hostile powers that hold humanity in their grip: *Victor*, 146. Among the other aspects of the atonement, he claims that this particular position was held by the early church for the first one thousand years of its history.

30. Beker, *Triumph of God*, 356.

31. Ibid., 363. Beker considers Rom 8:17–39, "Paul's most impressive confession of the triumph of God." Cf. 1 John 2:13–14: "you have conquered the evil one."

'might is right.' It is a triumph of grace in which divine love goes forth in sacrifice."[32] This is in keeping with Paul's understanding, emphasizing the spiritual nature of the triumph of God's program in Christ.[33]

The "already" nature of Pauline triumphalism is clearly established in the Pauline Corpus, and is firmly rooted in the OT, including the present victory envisioned by Isaiah. This may include his usage of the exodus motif as seen in the INE, which will be discussed later. The author of Ephesians may have understood that in the coming of Christ the prophets' INE vision of Yahweh's triumph was in place.

4.2 PAULINE TRIUMPHALISM: "NOT YET"

Alongside the present conquest is the future one.[34] Both are considered triumph, but take place at different times in the divine economy. Future triumph is seen in Christ's return: "And then the lawless one will be revealed, whom the Lord Jesus will destroy with the breath of his mouth, annihilating him by the manifestation of his coming" (2 Thess 2:8). He will return with his people to reoccupy his rightful territory.[35] Adam's death is defeated and reversed by the resurrection of God's people,[36] and in the final eschatological conflagration Christ defeats his foes and reigns as King of kings and Lord of lords (Rev 19:16).

The "Day of the Lord" while present, is yet future.[37] The last day has dawned, but it is not complete. The people of God were to live in these two

---

32. Reid, "Triumph," 952. Cf. C. Moule, "Reflections," 219–27.

33. This is not to say that NT triumph must be exclusively spiritual, but in the Pauline epistles it largely is, save Romans 9–11, where national Israel may be in view. At the end of the church age, it appears that the spiritual nature of the conquest transforms into one resembling that which is found in OT victory motifs, where graphic eschatological war imagery is found on the earth (Rev 20:7). The interpreter of Revelation is then pressed to determine what the apocalyptic author has in mind and whether and to what degree national Israel, in conjunction with the glorified church, is in view.

34. Ridderbos, *Paul*, 45.

35. 1 Thess 4:17. Ridderbos claims that upon Christ's return to earth he does not take his people back with him to heaven, but rather gathers them with him in the clouds to accompany him back to earth in victory. The victory in this passage is expressly earthbound: Ibid., 535.

36. Rom 5:14; 1 Cor 15:22–28, 45, 54–59; 1 Thess 4:16–17; 2 Tim 1:10.

37. The prophets (Amos, Ezekiel, Isaiah, Zechariah, Zephaniah, Malachi, Joel) include in the Day of the Lord both judgment and deliverance. Paul adopted the Day of the Lord motif, shifting the focus to the Day of Christ: 1 Cor 1:8; 3:3; 5:5; 2 Cor 1:14; Phil 1:6, 10; 2:16; 1Thess 5:4–5; 2 Thess 2:2; 2 Tim 1:12, 18; 4:8. Several other terms are used by Paul in association with Christ's second coming: παρουσία (1 Cor 15:23), ἀποκάλυψις (1 Cor 1:7), ἐπιφάνεια (2 Tim 4:1), ἔρχομαι (1 Cor 4:5), φανερῶ (Col 3:4), τέλος (1 Cor 15:24). Qumran literature reveals the anticipated Day of the Lord, but

realities. In commenting on victory over death, Paul was able to couch the triumph presently: "But thanks be to God, who gives us the victory through our Lord Jesus Christ" (1 Cor 15:57).[38] On the other hand the present is seen as evil and transitory: "there is a new creation: everything old has passed away" (2 Cor 5:17) and "the present form of this world is passing away" (1 Cor 7:31). Paul uses different imageries to demonstrate this including, Adam-Christ (1 Cor 15:20–21), first fruits (1 Cor 15:20, 23), and firstborn (Col 1:15–20).[39]

Although there is an absolute sense to the present triumph in Christ, there nevertheless remains a provisional and incomplete aspect to it. God's people live between the victory of the cross and the triumph of Christ's return. There is a present conquest and an ongoing struggle. Reid summarizes: "In the meantime the people of the Messiah live between the two episodes and are engaged in eschatological warfare, enjoying the benefits and advantage of Christ's defeat of the enemy at the cross (Rom 8:37) and yet beset by a hostile foe (Eph 6:10–17) as they await their Lord to descend from heaven (1 Thess 4:16–17)."[40] Pauline triumphalism is seen as a current reality that God's people share, and a future certainty that brings present hope. Both are presented by Paul without any tension or difficulty on his part. In regard to Christ's first and second comings, the author's use of ἐπιφάνεια in 2 Timothy reveals how he could move in and out of the present and future worlds with ease. The first citation demonstrates Christ's first coming; the second two describe the Parousia. All depict aspects of triumph:

> But it has now been revealed through the appearing (ἐπιφάνεια) of our Savior Christ Jesus, who abolished death and brought life and immortality to light through the gospel. (2 Tim 1:10)

> In the presence of God and of Christ Jesus, who is to judge the living and the dead, and in view of his appearing (ἐπιφάνεια) and his kingdom, I solemnly urge you. (2 Tim 4:1)

---

perhaps inaugurated by an angel: 11Q13. It is also seen in *1 Enoch, 4 Ezra, 2 Bar.*, 1QM, and 1QS.

38. Revelation treats this tension by admitting the temporary victories of evil (6:2; 11:7; 13:7) and by the final triumph secured by the Lamb (3:21; 5:5; 12:11; 21:7). Cf. Heb 9:28.

39. Dunn, *Theology of Paul*, 461–98.

40. Reid, "Triumph," 948. Reid adds that many of the Pauline passages that point out Christ's triumph may be hymnic in nature (Eph 1:20–22; 2:14–16; Phil 2:6–11; Col 2:14–16), indicating that like Israel the early church celebrated the triumph of God in worship and "hailed a (future) eschatological event *as a present reality*" (emphasis mine), 950.

> From now on there is reserved for me the crown of righteousness, which the Lord, the righteous judge, will give me on that day, and not only to me but also to all who have longed for his appearing (ἐπιφάνεια). (2 Tim 4:8)

Along a similar vein, 2 Tim 4:17–18 may be added to this trio of citations. In 4:17, Paul declares that he was "delivered" (ῥύομαι; aorist, passive, indicative) out of the lion's mouth as a past event; perhaps as a consequence of an initial acquittal, or his hearing or execution having been delayed in some way. Then, without pause, in 4:18 he anticipates that the Lord will "deliver" (ῥύομαι; future, middle, indicative) him from every evil deed; a future deliverance that coincides with entrance to the heavenly kingdom. It appears that in the mind of the author there is no hard line between temporal and afterlife deliverance. The concept of delivery appears holistically, and includes both temporal and atemporal realms—with ultimate rescue bearing down upon every momentary obstacle: "The Lord will rescue me from every evil attack and save me for his heavenly kingdom" (2 Tim 4:18). It would be a misrepresentation of the text to conclude that Paul was not delivered at his final trial, conviction, and execution since he would consider himself safely ushered ("save;" σῴζω; future active, indicative) to his heavenly abode. A problem erupts if a modern dichotomization of life and afterlife is forced upon text. Death was less of an issue and the afterlife was as real as life; therefore, divine deliverance was timeless with heavenly entrance, capping all other desires for rescue. From the standpoint of the apostle, delivery did in fact take place; as easily as if a modern said that Tuesday followed Monday. Vos speaks of the two ages as an objective shift from one age and world to the next. This is a cosmic transition event that he views as key to understanding Paul's presentation of the gospel.[41] Pauline triumphalism is experienced both in the current age and the one to come. The victory of God is present but not complete.

4.3 SPATIALITY, LINEARITY, AND TRIUMPHALISM IN EPHESIANS

As with Paul in general, Ephesians is best understood with two ages in view, a present and a futuristic one.[42] In the present aspect the focus is on the spiritual benefits of divine blessings (Eph 1:3–7, 9–10, 13, 21a; 2:1–6, 10; 3:5, 10, 18–20; 4:10, 30a; 6:10–11). The future age concentrates on the glory

---

41. For example, Vos's understanding of "new creation" sees salvation as becoming a part of the new era, not just conversion, 2 Cor 5:17: *Pauline Eschatology*, 46–47.

42. Hoehner, *Ephesians*, 281–82.

and exaltation of Christ and the Church's relation to him (1: 10, 14, 21b; 2:7; 4:10, 30b; 5:5, 27; 6:8). One verse clearly has both ages in mind (1:21): "far above all rule and authority and power and dominion, and above every name that is named, not only in this age but also in the age to come." Those passages that appear ambiguous may refer to the present or future, or perhaps both (1:10; 4:10). The two ages are not always seen as exclusive. They can be viewed as the same age, overlapping, or the second breaking in upon the first, such as in 1 Cor 10:11, where Christians of the present age are described as those "on whom the ends of the ages have come."[43] Christians are suspended between two ages, with the latter intruding upon the present. For purposes of this present work, it is essential to consider which passages in Ephesians speak of a present triumph, which are futuristic, and how the use of Isaiah comes into the picture. In Ephesians, Christians are victors in both ages, even in the face of struggles with the powers of darkness. The "already, not yet" eschatology exists within this tension.

Arnold analyzes the time tension in Ephesians from the standpoint of two related schemas, the ποτε-νῦν (Eph 2:1–22; esp. 5:8) and ἐν τοῖς ἐπουρανίοις (Eph 1:13, 20; 2:6; 3:10; 6:12).[44] He discusses Conzelmann and Merklein's view that the spatial idea in Ephesians (ἐν τοῖς ἐπουρανίοις) nearly overtakes the time concept (ποτε-νῦν).[45] The linear time aspect seems to dissolve into a below and above worldview. Merklein writes, "The contrast is no longer present versus future, but under versus above. The Eschaton is no longer in the future but above."[46] Tachau notices that the ποτε-νῦν formula is not developed historically in Ephesians as it is in other Paulines, thus giving way to a spatial emphasis.[47] With Lindemann, Tachau sees time collapsing into a new spatial reality.[48] These are useful insights, helping the interpreter of Ephesians to better understand an otherwise enigmatic problem in the epistle. But Arnold brings the argument back to the evidence in the letter where both the Jewish two-age concept (Eph 1:21; 2:7; 4:30) and the spatial concept are seen (Eph 1:13, 20; 2:6; 3:10; 6:12). Arnold proposes that the writer of Ephesians employs the spatial schema "extensively to emphasize

---

43. Dunn contends that Paul's ages could be one or more, depending on how they are divided. But essentially there are two with an eschatological tension between them, the present and the one to come: *Theology of Paul*, 462–63, esp. 463 n. 7. Dunn notes his indebtedness to Cullmann, 463 n. 11.

44. Arnold, *Powers of Darkness*, 150–51.

45. Conzelmann, "Briefe," 88; Merklein, "Paulinische Theologie," 44.

46. Merklein, "Paulinische Theologie," 44.

47. Tachau, *"Einst" Und "Jetzt,"* 143.

48. Lindemann, *Aufhebung*, 191–92.

An Introduction to the Triumphal Aspect of the INE in Ephesians 89

the absolute transfer of dominions experienced" by the Christian.[49] The focus is upon the unqualified break made with the past and an entirely new position. The spatial cosmological grid emphasizes the massive spiritual changes that have occurred without entirely casting aside temporal markers. This cosmological concept envisions a new heavenly reality alongside day-to-day life in Western Asia Minor. The spatial rubric not only affords a change in the audience's spiritual position; it asserts a new dominance over the cosmic forces below. A change has occurred, the difference now positions Christians in an exalted co-arrangement with Christ (Eph 1:20–23). They are not only in a new spatial reality but one in which they presently reign with Christ over the threatening forces. How the recipients of the letter can exist simultaneously in these two realities will be further developed in this present work, and is central to the argument of this study.[50]

The matter to be addressed in this present work is not whether triumph is seen in Ephesians, for certainly it is found as both present and future. The principal issue has to do with how INE triumph weighs upon the epistle, and whether the present aspect or the future one prevails. Many scholars rightly point out that Ephesians emphasizes a realized eschatology over a futurist one.[51] But not all agree. Dahl wrestles with the ποτε (pre-Christian) and νῦν (post-Christian) elements of the epistle without adopting a firm position (Eph 2:2; 5:8).[52] In speaking of Paul in general, Dunn believes that Beker oversteps his bounds in saying that Paul emphasizes "the already" over the "not yet."[53] But even if Dunn is correct in his assessment of the Pauline Corpus, it is possible that Ephesians stands as an exception.

Bruce considers Paul's eschatology as neither cyclical nor purely linear. It is, "The consummation of God's purpose whether it coincides with the end of the world (or of history) or not, whether the consummation is totally final or marks a stage in the unfolding pattern of his purpose."[54] Bruce understands Paul's eschatology as thematic rather than merely temporal.

---

49. Arnold, *Power and Magic*, 151.

50. As Tachau asserts, the ποτε-νῦν expression is probably not found in the OT, Judaism, or Qumran (2 Sam 15:34; Wis 14:15; 2 Macc 13:10 notwithstanding). He does observe it in *Joseph and Aseneth*: Tachau, *"Einst" Und "Jetzt,"* 68–70. The motif may be novel to Paul, used to designate a definitive break with life before Christ. However, this is not to say that the concept of ποτε-νῦν is foreign to Isaiah, for certainly the expected ethical change in the eschatological age will be seen as prominent. This is captured in the ethical section of the epistle (Eph 4:1—6:9).

51. O'Brien, *Letter*, 23–24, 29–32; Ridderbos, *Paul*, 29–32, 44–90, 159–81; Thielman, "Ephesians," 813–33.

52. Dahl et al., *Studies*, 471.

53. Dunn, *Theology of Paul*, 462–63, esp. 465 n. 17.

54. Bruce, "Eschatology," 362.

Ephesians will be seen to reflect this. For Paul the OT Parousia, the divine consummation of history, has thematically arrived but in another sense the era remains within the confines of time.

There are both vertical (spatial) and horizontal (chronological) features to Paul's eschatology. The following diagrams illustrate how Paul's eschatology developed from the OT view of INE triumph from two ages (triumph predicted, triumph ensues) into a three-stage view (triumph predicted, triumph provisional, triumph complete). The second diagram includes the contemporaneous spatial and linear conceptions in Isaiah and Ephesians.[55] Christians are both above and below, now and not yet. Their heavenly position encroaches upon the present age while in the present age they are destined for the summing up of all things. The "new exodus era" is placed on the second diagram in preliminary fashion. The evidence from Ephesians must support the fact that the author had the INE in mind while discussing spatial and linear issues in the epistle. This will be considered in the balance of this present work.

---

55. Several Pauline eschatological diagrams concerning the spatial "above" and "below," and "now" and "not yet" have been put forth: Dunn contrasts the eschatological outlook from the OT to the New: *Theology of Paul*, 464–65. Wright diagrams from Paul's standpoint of covenanted Israel: plight (of Israel), solution (through the cross and resurrection), new plight (Israel still in exile): *Climax of the Covenant*, 261. Vos and Arnold's diagrams take into consideration the earthly and heavenly realms found in Ephesians: Arnold, *Power and Magic*, 154; Vos, *Pauline Eschatology*, 38.

FIGURE 4.1: PAULINE ESCHATOLOGICAL DEVELOPMENT

Old INE Triumph Schema

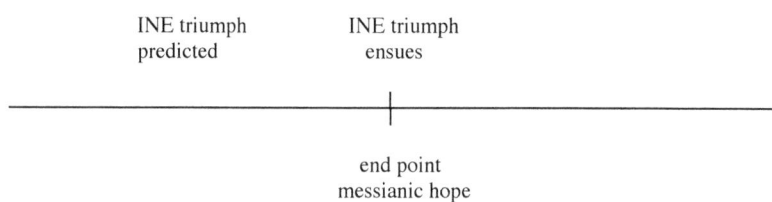

Revised Pauline INE Triumph Schema in Ephesians (1:21)

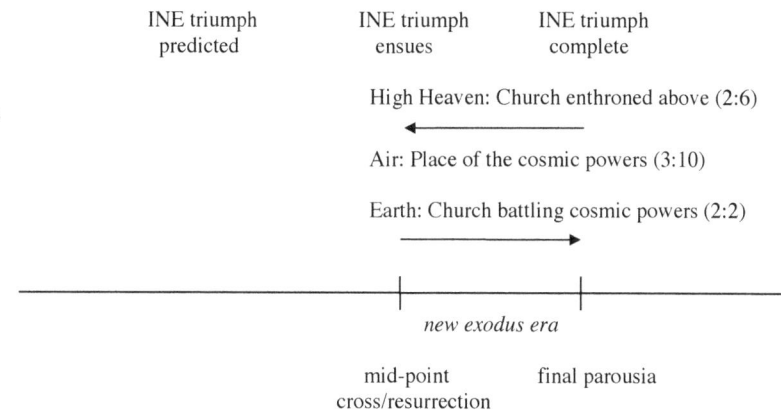

4.4 SPATIALITY AND LINEARITY IN ISAIAH

It is possible that Paul views spatiality and linearity similarly as Isaiah and the other prophets. Yahweh is enthroned above. As the exalted one, he is to be feared and worshipped (Isa 6:1) while others vie for his enviable position (Isa 14:13–14). He is above his creation and is sovereign over all kingdoms (Isa 37:16). Yahweh's exalted position compares people with grasshoppers (Isa 40:22). God's expansiveness above brings into question whether he can dwell in a house made by people (Isa 66:1). Yet, Yahweh does not remain above. From heaven he terrorizes and strikes the earth (Isa 2:19; 11:4; 13:5), and fills it with his glory (Isa 6:3; 11:9). He wars with beings above the earth (Isa 24:21; cf. 13:13). Yahweh's renown reaches from the heavens to the depths of the earth (Isa 44:23; cf. 51:6). As in Ephesians, Isaiah depicts God enthroned in the highest heaven, active on the earth judging sin and intervening on behalf of his people, and at war with cosmic beings between heaven and earth.

In addition to spatial considerations, Isaiah reveals linear conceptions in regard to eschatology, not a one-time event.[56] As noted previously, Isaiah had an "already, not yet" understanding of God's program. Childs observes this in Isaiah 25–26.[57] The new exodus passage, Isa 11:10–16, describes the progressive gathering of people. Travel will take place across great distances through a transformed desert (Isa 35:1–10). There appears to be a time element and progression to Yahweh's actions on behalf of the remnant in new exodus events (Isa 41:17–20; 49:8–12). The desert is renewed with roadways, rivers, and wildlife (Isa 43:16–21). Within this linearity is both difficulty and triumph. Because of storm and rain the pillar of light will shade exodus-like travellers by day and provide fire by night (Isa 4:5–6). This intimates extended travel and the need for protection amidst the rigors of the wilderness journey. Isa 19:19–25 is strongly new exodus: Yahweh's Savior and Champion (Isa 19:20) is dispatched to those who are oppressed in Egypt. Yahweh strikes Egypt, but subsequently heals it. This reveals a period of time in which judgment and repentance take place. In Isa 43:2 new exodus trekkers face the fears of sea crossing and other difficulties. Isa 50:1–3 shows Yahweh arriving to attend to his people. He converses with

---

56. In his discussion of the hermeneutics of the INE in Mark, R. Watts correctly identifies the new exodus in Isaiah as a conceptual cluster made up of a series of events within the founding event. A hierarchical structure is formed in which the initial experience is the dominant theme but can be recalled through any one of several subthemes. Yahweh the Warrior, wilderness journey, arrival in Jerusalem, and other examples are emblematic of the exodus without identifying the historic liberation from Egypt. Audiences are expected to understand the subtleties: R. Watts, *New Exodus in Mark*, 40–45.

57. Childs, *Isaiah*, 189–90.

Israel, claiming to have never divorced or sold her. He declares his strength and power to deliver. Yahweh then dries up the sea, restores the wilderness, and clothes the heavens. Several events transpire in this new exodus episode. The same may be said of Isa 51:1—52:15, a long section with many images of the new exodus. Once again a time element is in view as the remnant is given instructions on how to depart Persia (Isa 52:8–12). Vivid exodus images are found in Isa 63:7–19. The grumbling of the Hebrews in the desert is recounted (Isa 63:10). Just as the budding nation complained of circumstances and enemies in the historic exodus, those of the predicted new exodus may experience the same (cf. Eph 4:30). Yet conversely, in the face of all these challenges, Isaiah declares that in the envisioned exodus warfare will end (Isa 40:1). This leaves open the question of the nature of new exodus triumph and how it was understood by Isaiah and the writer of Ephesians.

Paul may have interpreted these pictures of the new exodus as predictions of a series of events that involve both good and bad outcomes, while on course to ultimate deliverance. Within the Isaianic exodus age there is intense conflict with the enemies of Yahweh, while the era requires great effort on the part of God's people. The apparent discordance between realized and unrealized eschatology in Ephesians can be understood from Isaiah's perspective. In Isaiah, the arrival of the new exodus is marked by a period of judgment leading to restoration. Just as the historical exodus was an era, Isaiah viewed the new exodus as a similar period. As in the historical exodus, the sinning generation is judged and dies, a remnant remains, and entrance into the land is finally realized. This appears to be Isaiah's perception of the purpose and duration of the new exodus. Based on this evidence from Isaiah it is possible to deduce that the Pauline writings understood the new exodus to have a durative aspect. The writer may have considered it to be an era that includes triumph and conflict leading to the final Parousia. If this is the case, then it may provide for Ephesians an explanation for simultaneous existence above and below, now and not yet. Actually, all four of these aspects are found in Eph 1:21 (previously discussed): "far above all rule and authority and power and dominion, and above every name that is named, not only in this age but also in the age to come." Based on these features there is reason to maintain that Isaiah understands the new exodus as involving four components: above and below, now and future. Following closely is the author of Ephesians, whose cosmological and eschatological vision is quadrilateral as well. Isaiah's new exodus should not be viewed as a singular act, but as a progressive era of both struggle and victory, occurring on and above the earth. The epistle's author shares the same view of the final age, but whether there is a direct new exodus linkage is a matter yet to be discussed.

4.5 CONCLUSION

There is the possibility of the INE in Ephesians. The suggested linkages cited in chapter 3 of this present work appear to show the effects of Isaiah's eschatology found in the rest of the Pauline Corpus and in the NT in general. This is not conclusive proof that the INE exists in Ephesians, for the exegetical evidence from the missive must yet be considered. Additionally, Ephesians demonstrates triumphalism using both spatial and linear terms. This view is similar to Isaiah's view of God's actions during the new exodus. This understanding helps to solve the apparent disparities between realized and unrealized eschatology in Ephesians, as well as the durative aspects of Christian life in Western Asia Minor. Looking ahead, the individual INE-triumphant passages will be examined in forthcoming chapters in this present work. This investigation will consider if these passages are indeed INE in nature; whether they exhibit an emphasis on the present aspect of INE triumph; and, if so, to what degree these passage weighed upon the author.

5

Co-enthronement with Christ as Present INE Triumph, Eph 1:1–23

IT HAS BEEN SUGGESTED that Ephesians reflects present triumphal expressions of Isaiah's new exodus. In the first chapter of the epistle, the author appears to encourage his readers in part by demonstrating that their salvation coincides with the present aspect of INE triumph anticipated in the OT.

5.1 PRESENT TRIUMPHAL ASPECTS OF EPH 1:20–23

The compelling vision of the opening section of Ephesians is best understood from the vantage point of Eph 1:20–23. The berakah of praise (3–14)[1] and prayer for understanding (15–19)[2] culminate in the manifestation of

---

[1]. This berakah (also referred to as a cry, outburst, or staccato) is along the lines of typical OT eulogies of praise, such as 2 Chr 2:11–12. The striking feature, which sets it apart from other introductory eulogies in the NT, is the lengthy and comprehensive portrayal of salvation. The closest parallels in the NT are 2 Cor 1:3–4 and 1 Pet 1:3–5. However, these are shorter and do not share the same sublime characteristics. Other, nonintroductory Pauline passages contain a similar focus on soteriology and eschatology, such as Rom 8:28–30. However, the Romans passage is shorter and written for different purposes. Second Cor 1:3–11, Gal 4:1–7, Col 1:3–14, 2 Thess 2:13–15, and Phlm 4–7 contain analogous verbiage, but without the august qualities. M. Kitchen gives insight into the OT concept of blessing, citing Kirby: Kirby, *Ephesians*, 84–89, 126–38; M. Kitchen, *Ephesians*, 42–43. Best includes a comparison with extra-biblical literature: *Critical and Exegetical*, 104–6. Specific to this present work, Hoehner observes that more scholars are understanding the berakah as borne out of a Semitic background, such as Kuhn: Hoehner, *Ephesians*, 157; Kuhn, "Epistle," 116–17. Brunson argues that the prayer of Jesus in John 11 and those of Paul at the opening of his letters share in the hodayoth and berakoth traditions: *Psalm 118*, 365–66.

[2]. Wiles, *Paul's Intercessory Prayers*, 22–44. Unfortunately Wiles limits his

God's power in the exaltation of Christ and co-enthronement of the church (20–23).

5.1.1 The Importance and Present Aspect of Eph 1:20–23

Gombis maintains that Eph 1:20–23 is the thesis statement for the letter.[3] In line with this is Snackenburg's claim that the theological argumentation of the epistle begins at 1:19.[4] Others observe the important connection between what 1:20–23 establishes and the follow-up argumentation.[5] Some see the section as the concluding flourish of the eulogy and prayer, but when aligned with 2:1–6 the implications are far broader.[6] The subject matter in 2:1–6 focuses on how co-resurrection and co-enthronement come to bear on those dead in sin. In Christ's resurrection and enthronement (1:19–20) God made him sovereign over all things (1:21–22). This exaltation is in conjunction with the new community: Christ the Victor, as head over all things, is given "for the church" (1:22–23).[7] This anticipates 2:1–3 where those in sin are made alive, and 2:4–7 where the church, in turn, is raised and enthroned. The writer will draw upon this new elevated position of the church to specify the subsequent blessings and admonitions in the epistle. He has in mind a present triumph based upon the resurrection and exaltation of Christ and the church's current co-enthronement with him. The

---

investigation to the commonly accepted letters of Paul, excluding Ephesians and Colossians. However, he does observe that Paul's prayer-reports (which would apply to Eph 1:15–16) function to anticipate the paraenetic thrust of the letters in which they are found (228–29). In addition, the background of Paul's prayers is Jewish in nature with Hellenistic influence, while marked as Christian. Cf. Harder, *Paulus Und Das Gebet*, 8–9; Miller, *They Cried to the Lord*, 430 n. 38.

3. Gombis, "Triumph" (2005a), 56.

4. Schnackenburg, *Ephesians*, 76.

5. Mouton, *Reading*, 61–65; Roberts, "Pauline Transitions," 96–98; Roberts, *Letter to the Ephesians*, 18–19; Roberts, "Enigma," 100–101.

6. Though not all see 1:20–23 explicitly as the thesis of the epistle, many conclude that the eulogy as a whole (1:3–23) is written to introduce what follows and thus forms the basis for the balance of the letter: M. Barth, *Ephesians, Chapters 1–3*, 55, 97; Caragounis, *Ephesian Mysterion*, 45–52; Castellino, "La Dossologia," 147–67; Dahl et al., *Studies*, 250–65; Maurer, "Der Hymnus," 167–72; O'Brien, "Unusual Introduction," 509–16; O'Brien, *Letter*, 93; Schlier, *Brief*, 72.

7. Ephesians does not argue for a form of "ecclesiastical triumphalism" as if the church is the agent of Christ's cosmic Lordship. Rather, the triumph envisioned concerns the cosmic forces from without, and the fears and lapses of the inner man: Arnold, *Power and Magic*, 85, 142. Arnold focuses on the prevalence of the cosmic power theme in Ephesians. Gombis takes matters a step further by seeing the triumph of God through divine warfare over these powers: "Triumph" (2005a), 67–70.

author speaks of this achievement taking place in both present and future ages (1:21).

"In the heavenly places" (1:20) early on (1:3) focuses readers on a prevailing motif in the epistle. Heaven is the abode of God and Christ, and the place from which the saints are endowed with every spiritual blessing (1:3, 20; 2:6; 4:10; 6:9). Christ ascended above the heavens (3:10), indicating that "heaven" can refer to the space between the earth and God's abode. This lower heaven is also the location of the cosmic powers who seek to disrupt the work of God on earth (1:21; 2:2; 6:12).[8] These locations will be swept up in the ἀνακεφαλαιώσασθαι τὰ πάντα ἐν τῷ Χριστῷ (1:10) in the eschaton. The writer uses these spatial categories to describe the spiritual benefits of the risen Christ.[9] This is strongly suggested in chapter 1 of this work, and is made explicit in Eph 2:6. Lincoln shows that the church has present access to Christ in heaven, and that the heavenly realm is in this sense a current reality. The epistle sees eschatological salvation as twofold: there is an earthly and heavenly reality, both existing as complementary, and without contradistinction. The Spirit plays a key role providing access to the heavenly reality (1:13; 2:18; 4:30) while at the same time supplying wisdom, power, unity, and prayer for the earthly (1:17; 3:5, 16; 4:3–4; 5:18; 6:17–18). The "heaven" motif argues for a present eschatological reality. The future aspect is also in evidence, but in Eph 1 the present heavenly reality is emphasized over the future.

5.1.2 *The Use of Pss 110 and 8*

The author of the epistle utilizes a traditional conflation of Pss 110:1 (in Eph 1:20) and 8:6 (in Eph 1:22), both of which portray messianic triumphalism.[10]

---

8. Dunn, *Theology of Paul*, 108 n. 34. The contrastive use of power by the cosmic entities and God is pictured in Ephesians. The former uses power to dominate, exploit, and gain ascendency; whereas God's power in men is to manifest the love of Christ, place others first, and exhibit virtuous living (Eph 3:16—4:2; 5:1–2): Arnold, *Power and Magic*, 75.

9. Lincoln, "Ephesians and Heavenly," 135–68.

10. It is hard to overestimate the influence of Ps 110 (109 LXX; Ps 8:7 LXX for 8:6) in the NT. It is the most frequently cited psalm in the NT: Matt 22:44; Mark 12:36; Luke 20:42; Acts 2:34; and is often utilized by allusion: Matt 26:64; Mark 14:62; Luke 22:69; Eph 1:20; and Col 3:1. The author of Hebrews quotes Ps 110:4 in affirming the Messiah in the priestly order of Melchizedek in Heb 5:6; 7:17; and makes general reference to the psalm in Heb 1:13; 5:10; 6:20; 7:11, 15; and 8:1. Christ used it self-referentially, and it was immediately taken up by the early church to support his Lordship (Acts 2:34). For Paul's use: Bateman, "Psalm 110:1," 438–53; Harman, "Aspects" 1–23; Moritz, "Psalms in Ephesians," 185. There is also the eschatological role of Melchizedek in 11Q13; a divine being who prosecutes vengeance on the wicked and delivers and restores God's people; as well as the treatment of Melchizedek, a figure presented as the brother of

In Ps 110 Yahweh instructs the Davidic king to take his rightful position as sovereign ruler and priest after the Melchizedekan order.[11] Moritz observes that the power language in these two psalms correspond with the thrust of Ephesians.[12] Metzger considers a tight linkage in the NT between the resurrection and exaltation of Christ, notably in Paul: the apostle concludes that in the exaltation at God's right hand "Christ lives and rules with the authority and power of God himself."[13] J. Kim views Ps 110 as describing the Messiah's eschatological warfare and victory, which are essentially concurrent with the eschatological texts of the Second Temple Period.[14] Huie-Jolly associates the death and resurrection motif in the NT with divine warfare.[15] In the postexilic community Zechariah envisions the close association of king and priest (Ps 110:1, 4) anticipated in the future idyllic leader (Zech 6:13), which was already perceptible in David and his successors (Ps 2:2; 6:8). Additionally, Denny observes a correlation between Isa 9, 11, and 12, and the exaltation of Christ in Eph 1:20–23. He argues that underlying correspondences to Ps 110 are the allusions to Isaiah's vision of the newly ensconced Davidic ruler.[16] This suggests an alignment between the use of Ps 110 with Isaiah's understanding of the new age, and makes an important linkage in the use of the psalm in Ephesians. In Eph 1 the use of the psalm is not set in contrast to Isaiah, nor ancillary, but fits within what is known about the Pauline understanding Isaiah. Ps 110 is understood by the writer of the letter and other NT authors and figures as one that falls within the broad stream of the eschatological age anticipated by the OT prophets. The author of the epistle uses Ps 110 to establish the arrival of the new age anticipated by the prophets, which then anchors the present triumphant aspect of the missive.

Noah in Second Book of Enoch.

11. Consideration should also be given to Ps 110's place in the psaltery. Davis contends that Pss 107–109 speak of the distress of God's people, whereas Ps 110 is God's answer: He has heard their cries for deliverance and shall secure victory from their enemies. This coincides with Ps 110's use in Ephesians: Davis, "Contextual Analysis," 162.

12. Moritz, *Profound Mystery*, 214–15. The power language found in the prayers in Ephesians is in contrast to that in Colossians. Both are about divine knowledge and arguably reflect new exodus thought, but Ephesians focuses more on the power aspect: Marshall, "Ephesians," 382.

13. Metzger, "Christ's Ascension," 122, 128.

14. J. Kim, "Message of Psalm 110," iii, 276–86, 348–53. Cf. Gourgues, *La Droite De Dieu*, 31–44, 63–73; Hay, *Glory at the Right Hand*, 163–64; Hengel, *Early Christology*, 119–250; Loader, "Christ at the Right Hand," 199–217.

15. Huie-Jolly, "Threats Answered," 191–217.

16. Denny, "Significance of Isaiah," 96–104.

Concerning Ps 8, the epistle's originality lies not in understanding the hymn as directly eschatological or messianic,[17] but rather as an implicit reference to pre-fall Adam and the restoration of man's glory.[18] Before the fall, Adam is depicted as a little lower than God, crowned with glory and majesty, with creation at his feet. In Ephesians, the recapture of this glory comes about by the enthronement of the new man, Christ.[19] Moritz understands Ps 8 as an expression of eschatological longing to overcome evil, which is in keeping with what is known of the audience.[20] Kraus points out that "Ps 8:3 sees a way of putting these hostile powers to shame."[21] The author of Ps 8 is answering a larger question as to why God would allow such powers to persist; the answer lies in Yahweh utilizing their antagonism to bring about a demonstration of their shame and inferiority. By utilizing Ps 8:6, the writer of the missive intimates the reinstatement of man's glory through Christ and the church, and domination over the powers. This is evidenced in Eph 1:21; 2:7; 3:10; 4:8; and in some respect 6:17. Keesmaat correlates this loss and recapture of glory with the exodus.[22]

In Eph 1, Ps 110 and 8:6 are utilized in a typological-historical fashion to ground the argumentation as to what the enthronement of Christ means for the church.[23] It is from the standpoint of Christ's completed triumph and the church's association with him that the recipients of the letter are to understand their present situation. The victory is described as Christ's Lordship "over all things for the church," which speaks of the fact of his exaltation and those who are a part of his reign.[24] The church is sharing

17. Childs conducts a hermeneutical and methodological discussion of Ps 8's use in the NT: Matt 21:16; 1 Cor 15:27; Heb 2:6–8; Eph 1:22; but he primarily focuses on Heb 2. The contribution of his article is how the NT writers adapted the psalm's message in a variety of ways: "Psalm 8," 20–31.

18. As seen in Rom 5:12–21 and 8:21; cf. Phil 3:21. In his comments on Paul's use of Ps 8 Moritz cites 1QS 11.20–22 where Ps 8:5 is linked with Gen 2:17: *Profound Mystery*, 17–18. Similarly, Thielman points out the Qumran connection: Thielman, "Ephesians," 816.

19. Lincoln, "Use," 41.

20. Moritz, "Psalms in Ephesians," 87–88.

21. Kraus and Crim, "Enemy Powers," 128.

22. Keesmaat, *Paul and His Story*, 85.

23. Ps 110 is Luke's most important OT passage confirming Jesus's exaltation and enthronement (Acts 2:34–35; 5:31; Luke 20:42–43): Strauss, *Davidic Messiah*, 300. Strauss also places Ps 110 into the flow of the entire Deuteronomistic promise tradition and Yahweh's victory over his enemies, 36–37.

24. "Which is his body" (1:23; 4:12) is imagery used several times by Paul, but it is only here in Ephesians that the image is utilized in a triumphant context. Cf. Rom 12:5 (unity and diversity); 1 Cor 10:16 (misuse of communion); 1 Cor 12:12, 27 (unity and diversity); and Eph 4:12 (giftedness and building up) and 5:23 (comparison to

the completed victory, spoken of as τὸ πλήρωμα τοῦ τὰ πάντα ἐν πᾶσιν πληρουμένου (1:23b).[25] In this victory the church manifests the plenitude of God, his presence, power, and glory.[26] The saliency of the letter's use of Ps 8 is found in the turnabout in the face of the unseen powers; for now the church has, in Christ, not only recaptured glory but dominion over astral authorities. In comparison to the balance of the Pauline Corpus, Ephesians emphasizes the association of the ἐκκλησία with the triumph, as a universal triumphal church concept, versus merely a geographical or local expression. This is a significant point given that in the epistle the triumph of God over the cosmic forces takes on widespread proportions.[27]

Moritz warns against the popular position that the Ephesians adopt wholesale the early Christian use of these psalms.[28] He contends that when the author's use of the psalms is compared to their adoption in other portions of the NT, unique features appear. Lincoln concurs.[29] For one, the employment of Ps 110 (and the parallel use in 1 Cor 15:24–28; cf. Heb 2:8 and 1 Pet 3:22) goes far beyond the rest of the NT in the development of κάθου ἐκ δεξιῶν μου (Ps 109:1 LXX).[30] In Eph 1:20 there is certainly the standard understanding of Ps 110's emphasis on the enthronement of the messiah; but nuanced is the accentuation on enemies, the superiority of God and his chosen one, and the heavenly dimension.[31] Of special note is the comparison of Ps 110's use in 1 Cor 15. There the subjugation of the king's enemies is seen as a future event, whereas Ephesians understands the conquest as having already occurred—a small but important difference that highlights

---

marriage). Dunn offers the possibility that Pauline body imagery helped Gentile churches better understand their equal standing with Jewish Christians before God, without undertaking nation imagery (Rom 9—12:4). The source of the metaphor for Paul probably goes back to sacramental usage (1 Cor 10:16–17 and Luke 22:19): Dunn, *Theology of Paul*, 548–52.

25. Overfield, "Pleroma," 384–96.

26. Lincoln recognizes that the final three clauses in Eph 1:22–23 are among the most challenging in the epistle with the introduction of difficult concepts such as "head," "church," "body," and "fullness": Lincoln, *Ephesians*, 53–54, 66–67. These particular interpretive difficulties do not undermine the argument that the theological underpinnings of the letter are found there.

27. Cf. Dunn, *Paul the Apostle*, 563 n. 155.

28. Moritz, *Mystery*, 19–22.

29. Lincoln, "Use," 41–42.

30. In Matt 22:44; Mark 12:36; Luke 20:42; Acts 2:34; Heb 1:13.

31. One other possible use of Ps 110 in Eph 1 may be considered. Underlying the exaltation of the Messiah may be his function as both high priest and sacrifice, as in Hebrews (Heb 2:17–18; 7:26–27; 9:25). In this scenario, Ephesians presents the exalted Melchizedekan Priest (1:20), flanked on both sides as the Paschal redeemer (1:7, 14 and 2:13; 4:30).

a distinction in Ephesians concerning present triumph.³² By combining the two psalms, the writer weaves OT triumph with a sympathetic understanding of the frailties of the audience by indicating to them that their king is now enthroned and they are exalted with him.

This coincides with the understood needs of the readers of the epistle. Arnold establishes that there was widespread fear in Asia Minor.³³ Luke's narrative of Paul's encounter with the inhabitants of Ephesus bears this out (Acts 19). Life in Ephesus reflects divination, powers in association with planetary bodies and stars, zodiacs, horoscopes, and magic.³⁴ Isaiah also shows elements of astrological and magical powers that are pitted against God.³⁵ Rochberg-Halton demonstrates that the astrological beliefs that form the background to the fears of those in first-century Asia Minor link back in part to the astral challenges faced by the Hebrews in Babylon.³⁶ This means that there was a significant degree of similarity between Isaiah and the audiences of Asia Minor in regard to fear of mystical powers. Isaiah and Ephesians do not treat mysticism and fear in exactly the same manner, but generally speaking mysticism represented the powers mounted against God, which was then crushed by his redeeming actions. As a result the people of God, whether in Babylon or Western Asia Minor, should have found comfort rather than fear in facing these powers. As with Isaiah's audience, conquering the cosmic forces would find resonance with the recipients of the letter to the Ephesians. Those at Colossae also required reassurance over

32. Thielman, "Ephesians," 816.

33. Arnold, *Power and Magic*, 47, 56–58, 64, 121–24, 167–69. Arnold sees the cosmic forces appearing at strategic points in Ephesians (1:20–23; 3:10; 4:8; 6:12) forming a prominent theme. They are the primary objects of the present triumph. Gombis observes the cosmic powers theme in the magical papyri, Greco-Roman intellectual thought, and Second Temple Judaism, concluding that his survey, "demonstrates the ubiquity of the sense of enslavement to cosmic powers in the ancient world": Gombis, "Triumph," (2005a), 36–51; quote taken from 51. Cf. Dunn, *Theology of Paul*, 104–10; Kotansky, "Demonology," 269–73; Lichtenberger, "Spirits and Demons," 14–21.

34. There may be a subtle linkage between Eph 1:21 and Acts 19:13–16 with the reference to the "name" of Christ. The seven sons of Sceva wrongly thought that they could utilize the God of Paul by invoking his name. In Ephesus there was a clear association between the name of a deity and its power. To trifle with, or misuse a deity's name was to tempt death. Acts 19:17 reveals this trepidation: "When this became known to all residents of Ephesus, both Jews and Greeks, everyone was awestruck [φόβος]; and the name of the Lord Jesus was praised." The use of "every name that is named" (1:21) reveals Christ's supremacy amidst the abject fear that gripped the region.

35. Concerning mysticism: Isa 2:6; 3:2–3; 8:19; 19:3; 29:4; 44:25; 47:12–13; cf. Dan 2:2, 4–5. Concerning fear: Isa 35:4, 10; 40:1; 41:10, 12, 13, 17; 43:1, 5; 49:14, 20; 51:3, 7, 12–13, 14, 21–22; 57:1, 11. For further discussion see section 7.1 of this present work.

36. Rochberg-Halton, "Elements," 51–62.

the powers (Col 1:13, 16), but in Ephesians the writer takes quite a different approach. In distinction to Colossians he roots his reassurance in explicit and repeated uses of the OT. He also emphasizes the realized aspect of divine victory.

5.1.3 The Question of the Eschatological "Now" in Eph 1:10 and 14

It was seen that Eph 1:20–23 stresses the present aspect of triumph and sets the tone for the epistle. Two other verses in the first chapter require further consideration in regard to the timing of the section: ἀνακεφαλαιώσασθαι (1:10) and ἀπολούω (1:14). There is a difference of opinion as to which age is referred to in 1:10. Is this a future event, or a current one? O'Brien makes it clear that the author is not saying that the implementation of the divine plan is not underway.[37] However, he adds that the writer would not deny a future summing up. If this is the case, the gathering up of all things in verse 10 includes a present or initial implementation, as well as a future fulfillment.

The end has come, but not completely. The letter intimates that both the mystery and fullness combine in an era in which the end of all things arrives, but still involves a final conflagration. The future Parousia will mark the summation of things, but in 1:10 the emphasis includes a present reality. The "gathering up" in the verse is a short preview of what shall be enunciated at the end of Eph 1 as a present reality (1:20–23). Triumph is clearly in view in 1:10 but scholarship is unsure as to whether present or future enthronement is in mind. It could mean both since, as it was observed in chapter 4 of this present work, there is evidence in the Pauline Corpus that Paul moves effortlessly between the ages.[38] For purposes of this present work the latter passage, 1:20–23, is more explicit in terms of describing present triumph and as such it is unnecessary to insist, as does Lindemann, that 1:10 offers strong evidence for present triumph.[39] Taken as a whole, Eph 1 gives explicit evidence that the final age had already arrived in the first coming of Christ.[40]

The pregnant term, ἀπολούω (1:14) should be taken as forthcoming, but it need not throw the entire section into the future. It is used here to

---

37. O'Brien, *Letter*, 114.

38. While pointing out the emphasis on realized eschatology in Ephesians, Wright adds balance by remarking, "Paul . . . was well aware of the future dimension, and had not collapsed the tension of inaugurated eschatology into a spirituality in which the End had already arrived, full and entire, in the present" *Resurrection*, 236.

39. Lindemann, *Aufhebung*, 209–10; Lindemann, *Epheserbrief*, 30–31.

40. Moritz takes "gather up all things" (ἀνακεφαλαιώσασθαι τὰ πάντα, 1:10) as the pivotal point of the berakah, which topically coincides with 1:20–23. He sees 1:20–23 functioning as the central thesis of the epistle: Moritz, "Summing up," 96. Cf. Heil, *Empowerment*, 65–66; O'Brien, "Summing up of All Things," 206–19.

close the eulogy, completing an inclusio that begins with divine choosing in the past (1:4) and ends with God's possession of his chosen in the future (1:14). This should produce a present hope on the part of the audience (1:18).[41] The broad portrait of redemption would be expected to include a future heavenly aspect; however, 1:14, 18 furnish a supporting role rather than a central one.

One other observation concerning timing may be made in 1:20–23 concerning the berakah and its culmination. Ephesians is unique among the Pauline letters in that rather than thanksgiving following a greeting, an extended expression of praise is launched after the welcome.[42] In verse 15 the thanksgiving follows. This replacement of praise for introductory thanksgivings has been associated with the questions of authorship and source materials. However, it appears the writer is concerned with emphasizing the immediacy of triumph. His normal course of correspondence in offering thanksgivings is interrupted by his driving concern to establish the present victory of Christians.

In summary, the letter announces victory in two ages in 1:20–23, but it is the present facet that dominates the section. The triumph is directed at the readers' persistent fears of the cosmic forces that significantly align with the fears of Isaiah's audience. Concerning this segment of the epistle, Lincoln rightly concludes: "Here in Ephesians it is from the perspective of realized eschatology, as the ὑπέταξεν is to be taken in a straightforward sense indicating that the subjection is seen as having already occurred."[43] This is not to say that other places in the NT (particularly by Paul) do not announce triumph, but the other occurrences (such as in Rom 8; Phil 2:10–11; 3:21; and Col 2:15) are in contexts significantly different from Ephesians. It is the contention of this present work that the overall thrust of Ephesians is the present application of the eschatological age, whereas Romans, Philippians, and Colossians include present triumph, but not as the primary concern.

---

41. Vos speaks instructively of Pauline hope: "So far from resembling a quiescent, nonproductive capital, merely carried out pro forma on the ledger of consciousness, it contains energy and actual no less than potential force": Vos, *Pauline Eschatology*, 40. Pauline hope is not idle or passive; it brings to bear the force of existential triumph into present consciousness.

42. In 2 Cor 1:3–4 the eulogy replaces thanksgiving but obviously the contextual and volume dissimilarities with Ephesians are significant. First Pet 1:3–12 is the only other book in the NT that has a eulogy following a greeting. Neither 1 nor 2 Pet has introductory thanksgivings: Hoehner, *Ephesians*, 162.

43. The tense of ὑπέταξεν is aorist, translated "he put": Lincoln, "Use," 42. Cf. "Paul's aorists again and again call his readers to that initial stage and to its character as determinative for their ongoing discipleship": Dunn, *Theology of Paul*, 324.

Apart from Eph 1:20–23 demonstrating immediate realized triumph that sets the eschatological tone for the letter, there are several evidences of the section manifesting the Isaianic new exodus.

5.2 CHOOSING AS A FUNCTION OF PRESENT INE TRIUMPH IN EPH 1:4, 5, 9, 11

The terms ἐκλέγω (Eph 1:4) and προορίζω (Eph 1:5, 11) are to be understood from the standpoint of the OT and their covenantal significance.[44] In speaking of the Pauline use of the terms, Das remarks, "This is the Jewish Scriptures language for Israel."[45] Dunn comments similarly, "'beloved by God,' 'called to be saints,' 'God's elect,' that is, using epithets which had marked out the distinctiveness of Israel's self-understanding."[46]

5.2.1 Choosing as Exodus Triumph in Isa 14:1; 41:8–9; 43:10; 44:1–2; 49:7

Divine selection is closely associated with the exodus experiences and favor imparted to the Hebrews through Moses,[47] which is seen most prominently in covenantalism found in Deuteronomy.[48] Divine choice certainly includes the call of Abraham (Gen 12), but the central referent in Deuteronomy is the wilderness generations and their activities during the Passover, the crossing of the Red Sea, the encampment at Sinai, the wilderness wanderings, and during the preparations to enter the land of promise.[49] Choosing also har-

---

44. Biblical theology has demonstrated that it would be a mistake to attempt to define election in pure Augustinian or Reformation terms. In commenting on a work by Rowley, Stendahl notes the difficulty of reading systematic theology into the biblical model. An understanding of the OT background is essential: Stendahl, "Called," 65. This is also not the place to engage in an expanded discussion on corporate and individual election. Although it is clear in Ephesians that the author primarily has in mind the church corporate, individual applications are not negated. Barrett's remarks on the corporate versus individual question should engender pause: "The Pauline conception is delicately balanced and impossible to express in simple and rigid terms": Barrett, *From First Adam*, 118–19. Cf. M. Barth, *Ephesians, Chapters 1–3*, 108.

45. Das, *Paul*, 111.

46. Dunn, *Theology of Paul*, 44–45.

47. Newman, "Election and Predestination," 244 n. 7. He considers Deut 7:6–11 as the *locus classicus* of OT election tradition. Several works comment on how the election of Israel is taken up and reflected in the theology of the NT: C. Barth and Bromiley, *God with Us*, 38–55; Bruce, *New Testament Development*, 51–67; Childs, *Biblical Theology*, 426; Rowley, *Biblical Doctrine*, 144.

48. The term בָּחַר ("to choose," "to select") reflects OT covenantal thinking and language: Deut 4:37–38; 7:6–7; 10:15; 14:2: Muddiman, *Ephesians*, 67.

49. "Ancestors" were chosen, but more specifically, "their descendants" and those

kens back to Genesis and creation, but is applied to the nation and codified by Moses at Sinai.[50] The blessing that stems from election is often presented in terms of how God had acted in the exodus from Egypt, which became the basis of how he would act in the future. Passages in Isaiah share both choosing and new exodus motifs.

> But the Lord will have compassion on Jacob and will again choose Israel, and will set them in their own land; and aliens will join them and attach themselves to the house of Jacob. (Isa 14:1)

> But you, Israel, my servant, Jacob, whom I have chosen, the offspring of Abraham, my friend; you whom I took from the ends of the earth, and called from its farthest corners, saying to you, "You are my servant, I have chosen you and not cast you off." (Isa 41:8–9)

> You are my witnesses, says the Lord, and my servant whom I have chosen, so that you may know and believe me and understand that I am he. Before me no god was formed, nor shall there be any after me. (Isa 43:10; consider the INE context in Isa 43:5–6, 14–21)

> But now hear, O Jacob my servant, Israel whom I have chosen! Thus says the Lord who made you, who formed you in the womb and will help you: Do not fear, O Jacob my servant, Jeshurun whom I have chosen. (Isa 44:1–2; once again, consider the INE context referenced immediately above and in Isa 44:3–5)

> Thus says the Lord, the Redeemer of Israel and his Holy One, to one deeply despised, abhorred by the nations, the slave of rulers, "Kings shall see and stand up, princes, and they shall prostrate themselves, because of the Lord, who is faithful, the Holy One of Israel, who has chosen you." (Isa 49:7; consider the INE inferences in Isa 49:5–6 and 8–12; especially if "Sinim" [Isa 49:12] is considered the south or Egypt)

According to Ninow, the most explicit new exodus passages in Isaiah are Isa 4:2–6; 11:10–16; 35:1–10; 40:3–5; 41:17–20; 43:1–3, 16–21; 49:8–12;

"brought . . . out of Egypt" were the objects of Yahweh's choice (Deut 4:37).

50. Lindeskog and Danell link creation and election together, tracing this connection back to both Genesis and Deutero-Isaiah: Danell, "God's People," 23–36; Lindeskog, "Theology of Creation," 2–7.

and 51:1—52:15.[51] Two observations may be made. First, each of the preceding five passages previously quoted that pertain to God's choice of Israel (Isa 14:1; 41:8–9; 43:10; 44:1–2; 49:7) correspond either directly or contextually with the primary new exodus passages identified by Ninow. The five cited passages that concern divine choice and those of the new exodus enumerated by Ninow fall within areas of Isaiah that speak of God's faithfulness to the nation based on their corporate election. Yahweh's choice through Abraham leads directly to preservation and liberation in a reenactment of the exodus. Both choosing and liberating took place in Egypt and would occur similarly in the exilic period. The second observation is that the clustering of the choosing passages and the new exodus sections in Isaiah indicate that choosing and the new exodus are closely aligned in the prophet. By comparing Ninow's new exodus passages in Isaiah with those concerning divine choosing there is reason to see correspondence between the choice of God's people and the promise of a new exodus. Because Israel was chosen, she was assured of a new exodus. Her sins would certainly be judged but a cleansed remnant would remain. The preservation of the remnant indicates God's covenantal faithfulness toward the nation. God upholds his promised covenantal blessing to his chosen in new exodus, historically from Persia and ultimately in a still future deliverance.

A correspondence between election and blessing is found in Psalms,[52] Jeremiah,[53] Ezekiel,[54] Nehemiah,[55] Haggai,[56] and Zechariah.[57] Isaiah, Jeremiah, and Ezekiel tie the concept of divine choosing with the anticipated eschatological restoration of the nation after the return from exile. Nehemiah (quoting Ezra), Haggai, and Zechariah speak of the original choosing as the basis for God's continued faithfulness once the returnees are back in

---

51. Ninow, *Indicators*, 157–96. New exodus passages beyond Ninow's citations could be added. As noted in ch. 2, the Isaianic new exodus texts observed in this work are a compilation of Ninow, Fishbane, Stuhlmueller, and Watts.

52. For example, Strauss and others see προορίζω stemming from Ps 2:7: Strauss, *Davidic Messiah*, 63 n. 1.

53. Jer 33:25–26. Ninow identifies the new exodus in Jer 23:5–8 and Jer 30–31. As with Isaiah the proximity links election and new exodus: Ninow, *Indicators*, 196–206.

54. Ezek 20:5–6. The context is explicitly new exodus (Ezek 20:34–36) and is closely linked with divine choosing in Ezek 20:5–6.

55. Neh 9:7, 32. In this postexilic situation another new exodus is clearly sought after in an election context (Neh 9:9–17; 36–37).

56. Hag 2:23. Once again, the circumstances are postexilic and a new exodus experience is anticipated (2:5–6); and based upon Yahweh's choosing of the nation (2:25).

57. Zech 1:17; 2:12; 3:2 (choosing) with Zech 10:10–12 (new exodus). For the Psalms, several may be cited that indicate choosing and exodus within the same context. As a sample: Ps 106:5 (choosing) and Ps 106:6–12, 47 (new exodus).

the land. The prophets appeal to the sovereign selection of the nation as the basis for reassurance and hope. This expectation was seen as future restoration that included the return from Persia along with a distant future state in which the original call of Abraham is fulfilled.[58]

The choosing of the people of God in the OT was fraught with expectation and contained specific connections between the historical exodus, and reentering the land, and the new exodus.

5.2.2 Choosing as Exodus Triumph in Eph 1:4, 5, 9, 11

The concept of divine choice in association with the INE, and that which is carried into the NT, including the Pauline Corpus, comes to bear in Eph 1:4, 5, 9, and 11: "just as he chose us in Christ before the foundation of the world" (Eph 1:4), "He destined us for adoption as his children through Jesus Christ, according to the good pleasure of his will" (Eph 1:5), "the mystery of his will, according to his good pleasure" (Eph 1:9), "having been destined according to the purpose of him who accomplishes all things according to his counsel and will" (Eph 1:11). These passages in the berakah have several terms that combine to reflect God's intention toward his people: ἐκλέγω (4), προορίζω (5, 11), υἱοθεσία (5), εὐδοκία (5, 9), ἀγαπάω (6), θέλημα (5, 9, 11), πρόθεσις (11), and βουλή (11). This cluster describes God's sovereign act of specifying the recipients of his favor.[59]

Rom 9–11 sheds light on the correlative aspects of eschatological blessings with the choice of Israel and the church.[60] Israel's sovereign elec-

---

58. Second Temple period writings reflect the choosing of Israel. Bar 3:27 says of other nations in the Promised Land, "God did not choose them, or give them the way to knowledge." Second Macc 5:19 has, "But the Lord did not choose the nation for the sake of the holy place, but the place for the sake of the nation." Second Esd 3:13–17 speaks of choosing and the historical exodus in the context of postexilic restoration: "And when they were committing iniquity in your sight, you chose for yourself one of them, whose name was Abraham; you loved him, and to him alone you revealed the end of the times, secretly by night. You made an everlasting covenant with him, and promised him that you would never forsake his descendants; and you gave him Isaac, and to Isaac you gave Jacob and Esau. You set apart Jacob for yourself, but Esau you rejected; and Jacob became a great multitude. And when you led his descendants out of Egypt, you brought them to Mount Sinai."

59. In the LXX the counterpart to בָּחַר is ἐκλέγω and is found in three Pauline cognates: the verb ἐκλέγομαι in Eph 1:4, the noun ἐκλογή in Rom 11:7 [referring to Christians and a remnant of Israel], 28 [referring to Israel]), and the adjective ἐκλεκτός in Col 3:12. Related also are προγινώσκω (Rom 8:29), προορίζω (Rom 8:29), and πρόθεσις/ προτίθημι (Rom 8:28; 1:13).

60. Other Pauline passages support Israel's privileged position and special relationship with God, brought across, and in great measure, applied to the NT community (Rom 9:4, 26; 2 Cor. 6:18). The author's use of election in Ephesians stands with Rom

tion is in view, which inevitably leads to ultimate future blessings upon the nation. Schrenk outlines several uses of ἐκλογή by Paul in Romans: divine selection in the history of the patriarchs (Rom 9:11), the election of all Israel in the fathers (Rom 11:28), God's selecting of a part of Israel out of the whole of Israel (Rom 11:5), and a chosen remnant obtained what hardened Israel sought after (the verb is passive in Rom 11:7).[61] This last usage speaks of the blessings that accompany election. In Romans the election of Israel and the incorporation of Gentiles into the people of God place the church within the stream of what Israel expected in the anticipated new age. Israel's election led to the hope of eventual restoration and renewal during the exilic periods; NT authors and Paul draw the same unavoidable conclusion that the church, elected as a people of God, shares the anticipated future blessings of Israel. It appears that a replacement of the nation by the church is not in view; rather, the new Christian community has equal share of the nation's blessings. In speaking of Ephesians, Dahl remarks, "The author did not embrace the idea that Israel had been rejected and replaced by the Christian church as the people of God. The vision of unification in Christ is a modified version of a point of view which is likely to go back to the earliest years of Christian history: through the death and resurrection of Jesus, the Christ, God confirmed his promise and redeemed his people Israel, with the consequence that Gentiles who believed in Christ were added as associates (e.g., Rom 15:7–12; Acts 3:25–26; 15:13–18)."[62]

Beyond election, other terms in Eph 1 are utilized in a similar manner; both υἱοθεσία and ἀγαπάω. The source of the Pauline understanding of adoption is not entirely clear. Scholars disagree as to the precise origination and meaning, as well as the weight given to either Hellenistic sources or the OT.[63] But apart from this debate, O'Brien, Gamer, and others make strong

---

8:28–30 and 2 Thess 2:13–15 where Christians are inspired by divine election to understand the comprehensiveness of salvation amidst the challenges of the Christian experience. A similar usage is not found in Colossians or other Pauline letters.

61. Concerning ἐκλογή and Paul's discussion of election in Romans, Schrenk concludes, "The whole of the divine work, salvation, and new creation, from its pretemporal origin ([Rom] 8:28–30) to the final glorification, is summed up in the one term. Because the community consists of the ἐκλεκτοὶ θεοῦ, there is no more accusation or condemnation, since, grounded thus, it cannot be separated from the love of God": "Ἐκλογή," 4:189–90.

62. Dahl et al., *Studies*, 446.

63. For the OT side of the debate: Daube, *Exodus Pattern*, 42; Rossell, "Graeco-Roman or Semitic," 233–34; J. Scott, *Adoption as Sons*, 61–117; J. Scott, "Adoption, Sonship," 15–18; Theron, "'Adoption' in the Pauline Corpus," 6–14. For the Hellenistic argument: Burke, *Pauline Metaphor*, 21–31.

cases for the concept utilizing both Hellenistic and the OT as backgrounds.[64] While υἱοθεσία does not occur in the LXX, the concept of adoption in OT exodus contexts is arranged in line with other terms that are unambiguously INE. The other expression, ἀγαπάω, may align with Isa 5:1 and the love Yahweh has for Israel or his servant. It appears to echo passages such as Deut 33:12; Isa 5:1, 7; and Jer 11:15; 12:7. In the early church it had messianic overtones.[65] Election leads to those who are ἁγίους καὶ ἀμώμους (1:4), which has exodus connotations. In Ephesians the terms depict the intended outcome of divine choosing and are observed in the exodus narratives. In Exod 19:5–6 both the choice of God ("out of all peoples") and the intended outcome ("holy nation") coalesce.[66] The writer indicates another tie between divine initiative and holy living in Eph 2:10, "For we are what he has made us, created in Christ Jesus for good works, which God prepared beforehand to be our way of life."

When the election and new exodus language of Eph 1 is aligned with the choosing of Israel, along with the anticipated eschatological new exodus associations, and is further correlated with the present triumphal aspect of Eph 1:20–23, it appears that God's choice of his people in the letter was a signal that the eschatological new exodus age had arrived. It brings to bear the "blessings" of Eph 1:3 to the recipients of the letter and to the entire Christian community who are elected to faith (Eph 1:4; 1 Thess 1:4). Just as Israel was elected according to the purpose of God through Abraham, the church's election and purpose is made possible through Christ. This intended result, articulated in these terms, is exodus in nature and contributes to the INE background of Ephesians.

Choosing in the OT is repeatedly correlated with the anticipated restoration and blessing of the new exodus. Election was used to encourage and motivate the wilderness wanderers and exilic generations. Isaiah promises a new exodus based on Yahweh's choosing of the nation. In Ephesians, choosing is used similarly. The concept is a recurrent and conspicuous feature in the berakah. The author understood that the choosing of the saints at

---

64. Gamer, "Adoption in Christ," 102. Davids, "Adoption," 25–26.

65. Cf. 1 Thess 3:13. O' Brien, *Letter*, 105. In Eph 1:6 the term likely refers to God's adoring love for the Son and his work: M. Barth, *Ephesians, Chapters 1–3*, 82. Christ is the central figure of redemption and was met with God's love, approval and blessing, which in turn is now projected upon the chosen who are the beloved. Cf. Matt 3:17, Mark 1:1; 9:7; 12:6; Luke 3:22; 20:13; and Col 1:13. For divine love and election couched within the context of the historical exodus cf. Deut 4:37.

66. Stendahl sees the NT concept of election defined in large part by the OT, indicative of a collective group that retains individual responsibilities having to do with righteousness: "Called," 69. O'Brien explores the OT background of "holy and blameless": *Letter*, 100–101. Cf. Col 1:22; 1 Thess 3:13; Heb 7:26; Wis 2:22; 10:15.

Ephesus and other cities of Western Asia Minor was to be emphasized as a present reality. These are current blessings in which to rejoice: "so that we, who were the first to set our hope on Christ, might live for the praise of his glory" (Eph 1:12). The emphasis is on the current life of the church. The purpose of choosing is to rouse the recipients to understand and apply this aspect of their heavenly riches. It appears that the recipients of the letter are participants in the new exodus. The focus is on the realized aspect of the eschatological new exodus rather than a future one. Just as the desert wanderers in Deuteronomy and the exilic returnees described in the prophets required encouragement and motivation, the writer reminds his audience that they are the chosen people of God. As with Israel, the choosing is based on God's love and devotion toward his people—but now for the Ephesians, ἐν Χριστῷ.

In summary, at several points in the berakah (1:4, 5, 9, and 11) the letter elicits language in keeping with Yahweh's call of Israel that leads to the triumph of the nation. This sense of victory is associated with both the historical exodus and Isaiah's return from exile. Wright describes Eph 1:3–14 as "the story of the sovereign God and of Jesus as an exodus narrative . . . and the story of God's victory in the Messiah over all the powers of the world."[67] The audience is to be encouraged that they are chosen and are a part of a new triumph in Christ. In Eph 1 this triumph is also seen in the idea of redemption.

5.3 PASCHAL REDEMPTION AS A PRESENT INE POSSESSION IN EPH 1:7–10

After establishing election as the first blessing of the berakah, the writer continues by showing how election becomes a reality in the lives of the recipients through redemption. The terms ἐν Χριστῷ, ἐν ᾧ, ἐν τῷ κυρίῳ are used in total thirty-eight times in Ephesians. By incorporating ἐν Χριστῷ and the related terms the author says that Christ is the central means by which ἀπολύτρωσις (Eph 1:7, 14) is achieved.[68] It is obtained "through His blood, the forgiveness of our trespasses" (Eph 1:7, 14; Col 1:14; Rom 3:23). The basic NT meaning of ἀπολύτρωσις is to set free on the basis of the payment of a ransom.[69] The redemption motif has deep roots in exodus and new exodus thought, and is applied to the original exodus generation (Exod 6:6), the surviving wilderness generation (Deut 7:8), and the new exodus during the

---

67. Wright, *Resurrection*, 237.
68. Allan, "'In Christ' Formula," 54–62; Hoehner, *Ephesians*, 103.
69. Büchsel, "Λύω, Κτλ.," 4:351–56; Foerster and Fohrer, "Σῴζω, Κτλ.," 3:199–200.

exilic period (Isa 43:14; 52:3).[70] The reoccurring use of the concept in Isaiah forms a dominant theme.[71] The motif is adopted by the Gospel writers and applied to the death of Christ. Furthermore, the book of Acts, Hebrews, the General Epistles, and Revelation attest to Christ's death correlating to the Passover ritual. The Pauline Corpus has a similar understanding of Jesus's death. O'Brien acknowledges the exodus roots of the idea of redemption: "The Pauline concept of redemption has its antecedents in the Old Testament, where it describes the release of slaves (Exod 21:8; cf. Lev 25:48) and more particularly God's mighty deliverance of his people from the bondage of Egypt (Deut. 7:8; 9:26; 13:5; 1 Chr 17:21; and more)."[72] Thielman has a similar understanding, maintaining a linkage between redemption and the exodus event: "God came powerfully to the rescue of his people just as he had done in former times when he rescued them from the Egyptians, the Babylonians, and other nations. Paul saw this climactic rescue effort, accomplished through the death of his Beloved Son Jesus Christ, as a measure of God's lavish grace."[73] More important for this present study, J. Casey understands redemption not just in terms of the efficacy and power of blood sacrifice, but the consummation of history.[74] This was also observed in the preceding analyses of the new exodus in Isaiah and the prophets where the historical exodus is inextricably tied to future ones. Redemption is indeed soteriological, but it is also freighted with eschatological expectations. Daube sees redemption as "recovery" both in the original exodus narratives and in Isaiah. Yahweh acts according to ancient law by recovering his

---

70. Dunn discusses the possible Hellenistic roots of Paul's use of ἀπολύτρωσις, but regards the stronger influence to be that of Israel and the exodus: Dunn, *Theology of Paul*, 227–28.

71. This does not mean ἀπολύτρωσις is used extensively in the OT, for its only occurrence in the LXX is Dan 4:34 regarding the release of Nebuchadnezzar from his madness. However, synoptic equivalents are undertaken: Deut 7:8; 9:26; 15:15; Pss 25:22; 31:5; Isa 43:1, 14; 44:22–24; 51:11; and 52:3. Cf. Isa 1:27; 29:22; 35:9; 41:14; 44:6; 47:4; 48:17; 48:20; 49:7, 26; 50:2; 51:10; 52:9; 54:5, 8; 59:20; 60:16; 62:12; 63:4; 63:9, 16. Cf. Jer 15:21; 31:11; 50:34; Lam 3:58; Hos 7:13; 13:14; Mic 4:10; 6:4; Zech 10:8; Ps 19:14; 26:11; 34:44; 44:26; 55:18; 69:18; 72:14; 74:2; 77:15; 78:35; 78:42; 103:4; 107:2; 119:134, 154; 130:7; 10:8; Neh 1:10; 1 Chr 17:21. The general overtones of the contexts (as per Dodd and others) in both Paul and the OT that furnish the new exodus-redemption connection, not solely the data for ἀπολύτρωσις.

72. O'Brien, *Letter*, 105–06.

73. Thielman, *Ephesians*, 59–60, quote from 60.

74. J. Casey, "Exodus Theme," 35. In addition, Gombis sees the consummation of history depicted in Revelation and its related associations with life in Asia Minor. He comments on the Frieze of the Great Altar of Pergamon as a background to life in Asia Minor (and thus Ephesus, Rev 2:1–7; and Laodicea, Rev 3:14–22); specifically, that the region was familiar with combat myth: Gombis, "Triumph" (2005a), 29–37.

next of kin who are suffering under cruel conditions. God witnesses the condition of his chosen and adopted people and redeems them. Just as God interdicts Pharaoh and redeems the Jews, the church enters into God's family as the terminal outworking of the recovery of Yahweh's family. As in the original exodus and later with the exiles, the law of recovering kin under cruel conditions comes into play.[75] Redemption is not only forensic payment but triumphant emancipation and recovery. Balentine summarizes: "It is the presumption of the New Testament as a whole, and preeminently the Gospels, that Jesus's death is the redemptive act inaugurating the new eschatological Exodus of salvation."[76]

As with divine choosing in Eph 1, redemption has strong connotations that suggest present triumph within Isaiah's new exodus imagery. The writer calls upon the recipients of the letter to understand their redemption, much as Israel did in the exodus and new exodus. In Ephesians the emphasis is on the present realization of redemption: "we have redemption" (1:7) that "he lavished on us" (1:8). Büchsel comments that "ἀπολύτρωσις is not just the object of hope. It is also a present possession, an existing reality."[77] Exodus redemption has come upon the missive's audience through the paschal sacrifice of Christ. In Ephesians the redeemed experiences both atonement for sin and rescue from plight.

5.4 INE TRIUMPH SEEN IN MYSTERY, WISDOM, AND INSIGHT IN EPH 1:8, 17

In Eph 1, divine election and redemption are presented as concepts to be understood "with all wisdom and insight he has made known to us the mystery of his will" (Eph 1:8). The terms σοφίᾳ καὶ φρονήσει (1:8) function as a hendiadys specifying that which God grants the church in order to comprehend the mystery.[78] Later a similar phrase is used, indicating the goal of the

---

75. Daube, *Exodus Pattern*, 13, 22, 27–28, 42.

76. Balentine, "Death of Jesus," 30.

77. Büchsel, "Λύω, Κτλ.," 4:353.

78. Because of form, structure, and setting issues, Lincoln sees "wisdom and insight" applying to the preceding phrase—what God lavishes in grace: Lincoln, *Ephesians*, 29. Cf. Alford, *Greek Testament*, 3:74; Best, *Critical and Exegetical*, 132–33; Eadie, *Greek Text*, 45. On the other hand there are those who consider wisdom and insight referring to the phrase that follows: God providing the wherewithal to grasp his redemptive plan. Among these is Hoehner who sees wisdom and insight referring to that which God gives the elect in their understanding of mystery revelation: Hoehner, *Ephesians*, 212–13. This seems to fit the context best; namely, that in both Eph 1:9 and 17 the author highlights the fact that God's chosen are to understand the mystery. It correlates with Col 1:9, "For this reason, since the day we heard it, we have not ceased praying for you and asking that you may be filled with the knowledge of God's will in all

petition for the recipients of his letter, but as σοφίας καὶ ἀποκαλύψεως (1:17). The petition is that the wisdom given by God (1:8) might be fully found in the readers (1:17). In the second couplet πνεῦμα (1:17) is introduced as the way in which the prized knowledge might come to abide in the recipients. "Wisdom and insight" and "wisdom and revelation" have connections to Isaiah.[79] Isaiah 11:2 speaks of, "The spirit of the Lord shall rest on him, the spirit of wisdom and understanding, the spirit of counsel and might, the spirit of knowledge and the fear of the Lord."[80] Childs understands the Isaiah context involving the coming shoot from the stump of Jesse.[81] Three couplets form a trilateral endowment upon Jesse's special progeny: "wisdom and understanding," "counsel and might," and "knowledge and the fear of the Lord." Delitzsch considers these as the whole creative fullness of divine gifts.[82] They speak of governing rightly, distinguishing good and evil, sagacious diplomacy, power to maintain righteous governance, and reverence and worship (Isa 6:3). The stump of Jesse rises as an extraordinary messianic figure with a reign featuring remarkable, spirit-imbued faculties. The difference between the spirit of wisdom and insight in Ephesians and that in Isaiah has to do with who receives the knowledge. In Ephesians, the author transfers the Isaianic attributes of the messianic figure to that which the church should ardently possess. As in cases elsewhere, because the saints enjoy affinity with Christ they share his blessings and endowments. The interchange of identity in Isaiah amongst Yahweh/servant/Israel, is similar to the exchange employed between the church and Israel (1 Cor 10:1–11; Gal 6:16), and the church with Yahweh/servant/Israel/Christ (Eph 6:1–17). In this way the writer follows the hermeneutic of Isaiah and other writers and speakers in the OT. This hermeneutic of identity exchange is born out of the solidarity understood between God and his people.

---

spiritual wisdom and understanding." Cf. Eadie, *Greek Text*, 46; Ellicott, *Commentary*, 12; Schnackenburg, *Ephesians*, 56–57.

79. Lincoln acknowledges the linkage between Isa 11:2 and Eph 1:8: *Ephesians*, 29. O'Brien notes Exodus passages as well: *Letter*, 108 n. 87.

80. In the LXX and NA27 σοφία is the common word between Isaiah and Ephesians, whereas the accompanying φρονήσει ("insight" in Ephesians) and συνέσεως ("understanding" in Isa 10:13; 11:2; 40:14) diverge. However, the distinction is not significant and may spell the difference between categorizing the usages as allusions rather than quotations. Regardless, σοφία is found in close association with φρονήσει in other LXX contexts: Prov 1:2; 3:19; 8:1; 10:23; Jer 10:12; Dan 2:21; 4 Macc 4:18.

81. Childs understands that this is the one upon whom God dons "charismata suitable to the Messiah's high office": Childs, *Isaiah*, 102. For more on the Isaiah context: J. Watts, *Isaiah 1–33*, 171.

82. Keil and Delitzsch, *Isaiah*, 282.

Closely connected with wisdom and insight is what they bring about. They assist in revealing "the mystery of his will" (1:9). Because μυστήριον occurs six times in Ephesians, the concept forms a theme in the letter (1:9; 3:3; 4, 9; 5:32; 6:19). It also occurs four times in Colossians, four in Revelation, and six in 1 Corinthians. The word reflects Semitic roots[83] along with INE implications, found seventeen times in Daniel (the only OT book). The "mystery" in Daniel is considered a veiled disclosure of the future events that God will bring about (Dan 2:28–30). The concept embodies a secret that only God can divulge (Dan 2:28, 47), and he will do so through his spokespersons (Dan 4:9). Balz and Schneider consider μυστήριον in Daniel as an eschatological secret that looks forward.[84] Gladd demonstrates a link between the use of μυστήριον in Daniel (and Second Temple Judaism) and its use in 1 Corinthians.[85] The link may be similar to the relationship between Daniel and Ephesians (and perhaps Revelation and Colossians). The tie could center on the disclosure of the eschatological mystery-truth of the Son of Man (Dan 7:13; 8:17), including the anticipated triumph that accompanies it. In Ephesians this is extrapolated as the revelation of what the Father purposed in Christ (1:9), the disclosure of the mystery-truth to the author and other apostles (3:3–5, 9), the relationship of Christ and the church (5:32), and the mystery's bold proclamation (6:19).[86]

There are mysterious elements to be understood.[87] These are in keeping with Daniel's vision of the Parousia. The eschatological revelation included the triumph of God and the Son of Man. In Ephesians the writer speaks of the mystery as having arrived in Christ, and having been disclosed through God's spokespersons, the apostles. The author utilizes the mystery as that which heavenly wisdom makes clear, and which finds its terminus in the revelation of Christ and the triumph that arrives with him. "Wisdom and insight" aids in understanding the mystery. Though donned by

---

83. Bornkamm, "Μυστήριον," 4:824; R. Brown, *"Mystery,"* 1–30, 56–66; Caragounis, *Ephesian Mysterion*, 121–35.Cf. Marcus's understanding of μυστήριον from the standpoint of Mark's gospel: *Mystery of the Kingdom*, 89–100.

84. Balz and Schneider, *Exegetical Dictionary*, 2:447. The word is also used extensively in the Apocrypha, Qumran, Philo, and Josephus, often in apocalyptic contexts and in keeping with the disclosure of divine secrets. In Qumran it is connected with the Teacher of Righteousness and in Philo, Moses: 1QpHab 7:4f; Philo, *De Cherubim*, 49.

85. Gladd, *Mysterion*, 51–107.

86. Additionally, σοφία often occurs in context with μυστήριον both in 1 Corinthians (1 Cor 2:1, 4–7, 13) and Ephesians (1:8–9, 17; 3:3–10). The term is prominent in Daniel (1:4, 17, 20; 2:20, 21, 23, 30; 5:14), and linked with μυστήριον specifically in Dan 2:30, and contextually in seven additional verses in Dan 2:18–19, 27–30, 47; 4:9.

87. Caragounis, *Ephesian Mysterion*; 136–37. Caragounis sees one mystery, God in Christ, with several applications. Cf. Roon, "Ephesian Mysterion," 143–44.

the Messiah in Isaiah, the correspondence in Ephesians is directed to the church, where wisdom and insight is put forth as the goal of the author's intercessory prayer in 1:17. First anticipated by Isaiah in the stump of Jesse, "wisdom and insight" is fleshed-out by the writer of the epistle as a component of Christian understanding and growth. These are the elements of the new age, prefigured by Isaiah, and brought into eschatological relief by the author. If the writer understands that Isaiah's new exodus has arrived, he is concerned that his readers fully grasp and appreciate the present triumphal aspects of it. It is possible that he views this disclosure process in terms of both the church's adoption of the Isaianic endowments upon the stump of Jesse and the revelation to the church of a Danielic-like mystery. In addition, wisdom, insight, and mystery may mark the Pauline counterpart to the mystery religions of Ephesus and Asia Minor. Certainly the author sought to demonstrate how God's mystery (and the wisdom required to understand it) was superior to the pagan counterparts. But too much may be made of this connection. Like other Pauline arguments that combine the OT with Hellenism, the underlying structure is the OT, not a Hellenistic one. The OT and the revelation of Christ are the fundamental thoughts that guide the writer's worldview and theology; Greek thinking supplied ancillary verbiage and imagery.

The use of the couplet in 1:8 may refer to some Jewish readers who are perplexed by the overwhelming number of Gentiles who have come into the church. In this sense, wisdom and revelation are needed on the part of the Jewish audience to explain the OT basis for the inclusion of Gentiles in the eschatological age. Aspects of the Messiah's coming and the inclusion of the Gentiles were troublesome in a number of ways, and so required an extended explanation in the epistle. The clarification of this topic included putting forth the "fullness of time" (1:10) that coincided with God's intentions toward the "nations."[88] In Ephesians the "mystery" and "fullness" aspects of the new eschatological age were anticipated and fully accounted for through Paul and the apostles (Eph 2:20; 3:7–9; 4:11–12).

In summary, by using σοφίᾳ καὶ φρονήσει and πνεῦμα σοφίας καὶ ἀποκαλύψεως from Isaiah (two times in close proximity in Ephesians), the letter suggests that the prophet plays a significant role in the development of Ephesians 1. The use of the shared terms is not extraordinarily strong when taken in isolation, but if seen within the cluster of other Isaiah uses in Ephesians (to be seen later), and when coupled with the other explicit OT demonstrations of eschatological material in the epistle, it is difficult to

---

88. "Nation" or "nations" is a prevailing motif in the prophets and Psalms (Psalms has 64 occurrences; Isaiah, 83; Jeremiah, 88; Ezekiel, 89), especially as the peoples of the earth find themselves part of Yahweh's eschatological program.

conclude that the use is merely shared language. The writer also adopts the wisdom and insight passage (Isa 11:2–5) in the panoply section (Eph 6:14, 17). This indicates that Isa 11 was very important to the writer in the composition of the letter. He uses Isa 11 to both open and close his epistle. By this he indicates the type of messianic-like wisdom that Christians should acquire in order to understand the mystery along with the type of armor (again from Messiah) they are to adopt. These uses of Isaiah cannot be coincidental or merely accorded to common verbiage. Espousing Isa 11 twice in chapter 1 and twice (depending how the accounting takes place) in chapter 6 alone suggests that the author had the eschatology of Isaiah in mind as he composed his letter.

Lincoln's words reinforce the present advantages of wisdom and insight: "With these words the grace with which believers have been highly favored in the Beloved is elaborated on in terms of some of the present benefits of salvation which they have in him."[89] M. Kitchen adds, "What was set out as his plan in 1:3–6, is here carried out for the believers to experience."[90]

5.5 INHERITANCE AND THE SPIRIT AS EXISTING INE PROVISIONS IN EPH 1:10B–14

The letter transitions from divine choosing (Eph 1:3–6) and redemption (1:7–10a) to the inheritance of the readers (1:10b–14). Once again, there are suggestions that INE triumph elements are present.

In Eph 1:11 and 14 the terms κληρόω (1:11, 14), προορίζω (1:11), πρόθεσις (1:11), and βουλή and θέλημα (1:11) hearken back to God's choice of Israel and the church (Eph 1:4), and the accompanying blessings that come vis-à-vis the eschatological age to those who are God's own. "Inheritance" picks up OT imagery[91] beginning with Abraham (Gen 21:10; 31:14) and continuing in the historical exodus (Exod 32:13; 34:9; Josh 11:23) and new exodus (Isa 57:13; 65:9). Eph 1:11 speaks of either that which Christians inherit, or Christians inherited by God.[92] If it is the latter, an echo may be seen as Israel inherited by God, whereas the nations are apportioned to angelic beings (Deut 32:8–9). This latter interpretation is preferred in that it is a better understanding of the passive voice and is in keeping with the ongoing choosing motif.[93] Additionally, the change from first person plural (1:3, 4, 6, 7, 8, 9, 11, 12) to second person (13, twice) is best taken as

89. Lincoln, *Ephesians*, 27.
90. M. Kitchen, *Ephesians*, 48.
91. Dunn, *Theology of Paul*, 329.
92. O'Brien, *Letter*, 115. Cf. Deut 4:20; 9:29; 1 Kgs 8:51; Ps 33:12; 106:40.
93. Contra Lincoln: *Ephesians*, 9, 36–38.

a distinction between the writer (and fellow Jewish Christians) and Gentiles.[94] The inclusion of Gentiles as an Isaianic eschatological concept lines up well with the previous section of this present work (5.2) in regard to divine choosing, and that which follows (2:11–19). The author reveals the intent of God's sovereign plan, including first the Jewish Christians and then expanding to Gentile believers. For now he is satisfied to introduce the topic in conjunction with the praise due to God and Christ.[95] Other terms found in 1:13 indicate OT influence such as "word of truth" (Ps 119:43; cf. Col 1:5); and perhaps as an Isaianic allusion, "gospel of your salvation" (Isa 52:7; 61:1; cf. Rom 1:16). Aside from σωτηρία being understood in terms of general well-being, Dunn explains that "in a Jewish context, thought of the exodus from Egypt or the return from exile in Babylon would be prominent."[96] As Wright says in speaking of this passage in Ephesians, Christian inheritance is "given coherence and theological power by the Exodus story."[97]

A further indicator of Isaiah is the role of the "promised Holy Spirit" (1:13; Gal 3:14), which joins with divine choice and redemption, and is heavily eschatological and Isaianic in nature.[98] Beker writes, "[I]n the prophets the Spirit has a clear eschatological referent."[99] If the Gentiles are the referent in 1:13 ("you," two times), they received the genuine Spirit that was Israel's. The Spirit would play a prominent role in the new era (Isa 42:1; 44:3; 48:16; 61:1; 63:10–11). These various passages in Isaiah fall contextually within new exodus imagery (Isa 41:17–20; 43:1–3, 16–21; 49:8–12; 51:1—52:15). When the Spirit passages are interwoven with the key new exodus passages it becomes clear that the Spirit would play a major role in the new era, facilitating on behalf of Yahweh key elements of the new exodus. As an example, Isa 44:3 combines the new exodus and the participation of Yahweh's Spirit: "For I will pour water on the thirsty land, and streams on the dry ground; I will pour my spirit upon your descendants, and my blessing on your offspring." Ezek 36:26–27 demonstrates that in the new age there will be a new intimate relationship between God's Spirit and his people. Ezek 9:4, 6 anticipates a distinguishing designation placed upon God's people. To be "marked with the seal" of the Spirit (Eph 1:13) speaks

---

94. O'Brien, *Letter*, 116.

95. Other aspects of the berakah prefigure ancillary themes teased out in the balance of the letter.

96. Dunn, *Theology of Paul*, 329.

97. Wright, *Resurrection*, 30. Also, Denton, "Inheritance," 157–62.

98. Exod 31:3; 35:21, 31; Isa 11:2–3; 63:10–11; Jer 31:33; Ezek 11:19–20; 18:31; 36:26–28; 37:1–14. The common term for "spirit" (πνεῦμα) appears 52 times in Ezekiel, 51 in Isaiah, 18 in Jeremiah. Cf. Fee, *Spirit*, 9–10.

99. Beker, *Triumph of God*, 281.

of ownership, protection, and guarantee. In Acts 19:2 the Lukan record reveals that Paul asked some disciples in Ephesus if they had received the Holy Spirit. The question was posed to determine the genuineness and validity of their Christian experience. This may form part of the background of the use of the term in Eph 1:13. A similar idea is found in Rom 8:9–11 (the indwelling Spirit validating Christian identification and sanctification), 2 Cor 1:22 ("by putting his seal on us and giving us his Spirit in our hearts as a first installment"), and Gal 4:5–7 (where the giving of the Spirit is connected with adoption and inheritance). The "promise" (Eph 1:13) probably refers to the promised Holy Spirit in reference to the OT (Gal 3:14), which is poured out at Pentecost (Acts 2:33). The Holy Spirit is associated with promise and the glory to come (Eph 4:30).

"The pledge of our inheritance" describes the Holy Spirit and what he accomplishes as the guarantor of redemption. "Pledge" (ἀρραβών) is used only by Paul and always in reference to the Spirit.[100] The term has commercial connotations indicating "down payment" or "first installment." The word "inheritance" is used once again, but now appropriately applied, it appears, to both Jewish and Gentile Christians ("our," Eph 1:14). What began as an exclusively Jewish experience in the sovereign plan and choice of God now includes Gentile believers. This leads to the second use of "redemption" (1:14). In the first use (1:7) redemption is seen as a completed action, but here it most likely refers to future glory. Both believing Jews and Gentiles have the surety of God's choice of them and the certainty of every spiritual blessing, which includes the future aspect of redemption. The phrase, "as God's own people" (or "possession") is best understood as God's people versus what God's people possess. Similarly, the OT speaks of Israel as God's possession.[101] The idea of the church as God's possession coincides with the people of God as God's inheritance, as stated earlier, and once again emphasizes God's sovereign choosing and care for his people.

Although redemption in 1:14 emphasizes the future aspect of redemption (as in 4:30), and does indicate future triumph, this is not the primary thrust of the berakah, for redemption is also presented as a past action (1:7). In addition, the promise of future redemption is for present purposes. It is the impartation and sealing of the Spirit that endows Christians with a token of eternal glory. Ultimate eschatological redemption is brought to bear in present redemption through the sealing of the Spirit. In speaking of the Spirit, O'Brien summarizes, "In giving him to us God is not simply promising us our final inheritance but actually providing us with a foretaste

---

100. 2 Cor 1:22; 5:5. Cf. Rom 8:23.
101. Exod 19:6; Deut 14:2; 26:18; Mal 3:17. Cf. 1 Pet 2:9.

of it, even if it 'is only a *small fraction* of the future endowment' . . . Because of the ministry of the Spirit to their hearts and lives, they can begin to enjoy this everlasting possession *now* [emphasis in the original]."[102] As a whole, inheritance and the work of the Spirit is in keeping with OT language, and specifically with the triumphal facets of Isaiah's new exodus.[103] The writer assumes that his audience participates in this triumph; he turns to pray for their full awareness of it.

5.6 A PRAYER FOR PRESENT REALIZATION IN EPH 1:15-19

With the truths of the berakah now in place, the author directs his focus to how such truths should be received. His desire is that the general spiritual realities of redemption might become understood in the new community. Bruce notes, "[P]rayer is offered that the ideal set forth in the *eulogia* may be realized in their experience—perfectly in the resurrection age but in measure at present through the ministry of the Spirit."[104] This is to be expected because the divine plan involves wisdom and insight into the mystery of God (Eph 1:9). Paul and the founding apostles and prophets received this revelation (3:3-5), but the goal is that the church understand it (1:8, 15-19) and proclaim these truths to the astral powers (3:10). It will be seen that the prayer is in keeping with motivating readers to realize the triumphal aspects of the eschatological age.

Once again, "wisdom and understanding" (similarly in Eph 1:8 from Isa 11:2) is in view (v. 17). These are to be the possession of the new spiritual community.[105] In Eph 1:8 these were abilities understood as those granted by God to the chosen in order to provide insight into the mystery of God's will. However, in 1:17 they are abilities that are given as a result of the prayer of the writer. What appears as factual in 1:8 is potential and progressive in 1:17. Comparatively in Isaiah, "wisdom and understanding" seem to have the former (1:8) thrust: when the stump of Jesse comes he will already possess these extraordinary endowments. This use of the couplet in Isaiah corresponds with present triumph in that those who embrace Jesse's child

---

102. O'Brien, *Letter*, 121. O'Brien quotes, Lightfoot, *Notes*, 324. Vos adds, "the eschatological state is preeminently a pneumatic state": *Pauline Eschatology*, 170.

103. Cf. the focus on eschatological praise and glory: Isa 42:8-12 (esp. 8, 10, 12) and Jer 13:11; 33:9. Bruce considers "to the praise of his glory" (1:6, 12, 14) a possible echo of Isa 43:20-21: "The wild animals will honor me, the jackals and the ostriches; for I give water in the wilderness, rivers in the desert, to give drink to my chosen people, the people whom I formed for myself so that they might declare my praise": *Epistles*, 267.

104. Bruce, *Epistles*, 269.

105. The use of σοφία is the common thread, along with corresponding synonyms.

adopt his sagacity—as an existential fact, notwithstanding the progressive element in Eph 1:17.

The parallels between Isaiah and Ephesians involve some of the same concepts as seen in the previous couplet, but more may be added. Both involve new, extraordinary capabilities in perceiving previously undisclosed spiritual truths. The stump of Jesse has received this insight and the same should be found in the new community. This insight is understood to stand in contrast to the knowledge found in the mystery religions of the Asia region (Col 1:9–10).[106] Divine insight was granted to Yahweh's servant in Isaiah and should become a reality in the hearts of the new mystery-community in Christ. This insight takes place through the ministry of the Spirit and the teaching gifts that are claimed to have been given to Paul and the resident teachers in the church (Eph 2:20; 3:3; 4:11–13). The passages reflect a common means by which God's people understand how to combat their spiritual enemies. The stump of Jesse will lead God's people with these endowed capabilities. As in Isaiah, the church utilizes this insight to both know and combat "authorities in heavenly places," evident in Eph 3:10.

In summary, "wisdom and revelation" in Eph 1 demonstrate a connection with the present triumph of the exodus. The spiritual and sagacious abilities of the stump of Jesse are vivified in Eph 1 in the manner in which the mystery is revealed and progressively understood by the church. The extraordinary insight of God's servant in Isaiah, within the context of the new exodus, is portrayed in the revelation of the mystery and in the understanding of New Testament saints.

5.7 HEAVENLY PLACES AS THE VANTAGE POINT OF INE TRIUMPH IN EPH 1:3, 10, 20

The phrase, ἐν τοῖς ἐπουρανίοις (1:3, 10, 20) is found only in Ephesians in the Pauline Corpus[107] and has correspondence with Isaiah and the new exodus. The term, ἐπουράνιος is found thirty-three times in ten Pauline epistles and features heavily in Revelation.[108] In Ephesians it is found nine times,[109] more

---

106. Lincoln offers the possibility that the household codes in Colossians indicate a Pauline "wisdom mode" that is effectually superior to the wisdom from below: Lincoln, "Household Code," 112. This means that wisdom and insight extend from knowing the mystery to practical conduct in the Christian community. This anticipates Eph 4:1—6:9.

107. There is an adjectival form in 1 Cor 15:40, 48 that refers to Christ as the "heavenly man": Muddiman, *Ephesians*, 66.

108. "New heavens" is a motif in Revelation in context with new exodus themes: J. Casey, "Exodus Theme," 35–43.

109. Eph 1:3, 10, 20; 2:6; 3:10, 15; 4:10; 6:9, 12. Cargal, "Seated in the Heavenlies," 804–21; Lincoln, "Re-Examination," 468–83.

than any other Pauline book. Of the nine occurrences it refers to a place of spiritual blessing (1:3),[110] the location where all will be summed up in Christ (1:10), the royal abode of Christ's enthronement (1:20; 2:6), the dwelling of the evil rulers and authorities (3:10; 6:12), the place from which every family derives its name (3:15) and above which Christ ascended (4:10), and the location from which God oversees masters and slaves (6:9). In Ephesians the author sees ἐπουράνιος as a descriptor of the lower heavens (3:10; 6:12) and the higher (1:3, 20; 2:6). The lower were populated with hostile powers that could possibly block access to the abode of God.[111] In the LXX of Isaiah the term occurs forty-one times, in position after Psalms (80), Daniel (69), Deuteronomy (46), and Genesis (44). The portrayal of ἐπουράνιος in Isaiah includes the place of God's abode,[112] a place where conflict and judgment occur,[113] including where pagan diviners look for guidance,[114] and a place that is physically above the earth—the atmosphere, space, metaphorically a great distance—and that is often the object of God's creation and re-creation.[115] The correspondence between Isaiah and Ephesians with regard to ἐπουράνιος involves three parallels. First, both understand ἐπουράνιος as the abode of God and the place from which he reigns. In Isaiah, Yahweh is clearly in view; in Ephesians it is the place where both God and Christ are enthroned. Second, in the heavens the power of evil is at work against God. He battles evil in and from heaven. In Isaiah the king of Babylon is pictured as an angelic being falling from heaven, signaling a judgment that comes upon those in heaven and those on earth. Similarly, in Ephesians the devil and his entourage battle in and from the heavenlies, and engage the people of God in spiritual warfare. Third, the heavens are a place where God will triumph over evil. It is from the heavens that the proclamation of victory over God's enemies comes: "Sing, O heavens, for the LORD has done it; shout, O depths of the earth; break forth into singing, O mountains, O forest, and every tree in it! For the LORD has redeemed Jacob, and will be glorified in Israel" (Isa 44:23). The same thought is emphasized in Isa 66:1 and 22 where God will reign over the new heavens and earth. In Isa 40:22 Yahweh is said to sit upon the circle of the earth; just previously in 40:3–5 a voice cries out to make a way in the new exodus wilderness. Similarly, in

110. "Heavenly places" in 1:3 and 2:6 reveals that a spiritual resurrection has already taken place: I. Marshall, "Ephesians," 381.

111. Dunn, *Theology of Paul*, 108.

112. Isa 40:22; 63:15; 64:1; 66:1.

113. Isa 24:21; 34:4–5.

114. Isa 14:12–13; 24:4, 18, 21; 34:4–5; 47:13; 51:6.

115. Isa 1:2; 7:11; 13:5, 10, 13; 37:16; 40:12, 22; 42:5; 44:23–24; 45:8, 12, 18; 47:13; 48:13; 49:13; 50:3; 51:16; 55:9–10; 65:17; 66:22.

34:4–5 the sword of Yahweh will drink its full in the heavens. Nearby in 35:1–10 the reader is told of a highway and streams in the desert. Both Isa 40:3–5 and 35:1–10 are reminiscent of the exodus, and occur in proximity with Yahweh's activity in the heaven. Because ἐπουράνιος occurs frequently in Isaiah, with occurrences spread throughout the book, and specifically at explicit new exodus locations, the imagery has Yahweh executing the new exodus from the heavens. It is from the vantage point of the heavens that Yahweh judges his enemies and rescues his people from bondage. In Ephesians the triumph over God's enemies is found in Eph 1:21–23 where Christ is seated as victor over all things. Similarly, his triumph is found in 2:6; 3:10; 4:10; and 6:12.

Similarities exist between Isaiah and Ephesians in the treatment of ἐπουράνιος. Just as Isaiah envisaged the new exodus activity of God in the heavens, the writer sees God's victory as taking place through Christ. In both books God triumphs over cosmic forces in the heavens in order to bring about a glorious future for his people. That which was predicted by Isaiah concerning the exilic community finds its terminus in the advent of Christ. God brings this about from the heavens.

5.8 CONCLUSION

Ephesians 1:20–23 serves to sculpt the subject matter and tone of the epistle. Because of Christ's resurrection and enthronement he has triumphed over the cosmic powers (1:20–21). His victory is shared with the church, which sits with him (1:23; 2:6). Although there are small reminders of a still future age (1:14, 21) the overall emphasis in Eph 1 is present triumph. The writer anchors 1:20–23 with Pss 110 and 8 (table 12.5). Psalm 110 anticipates the unequivocal triumph of the Messiah and his intercessory role as a Melchizedekan priest. Psalm 8 speaks of the reinstallation of man in God's creation order.

However, it appears that the psalms function in a supportive rather than central role. The grander eschatological vision may be Isaiah's new exodus. This is observed in the allusive use of Isa 11:2 in Eph 1:8 and 17 (tables 12.1, 12.2). Although Isaiah 11:2 is not an explicit expression of the new exodus, it is found in close proximity to INE passages (tables 12.3, 12.4). When linked with the quotation of Isa 11:4–5 in Eph 6:14 and 17, there is evidence to suggest that a thematic inclusion based on Isaiah's use in the opening and close of the epistle exists (tables 12.1, 12.3). A further determination on this possibility depends on the other occurrences of the OT in the letter.

Additional reasons imply that Isaiah's new exodus may be a source of inspiration for Eph 1. The choosing of the people of God that leads to exodus triumph is clearly an OT motif, particularly in Isaiah (Isa 14:1; 41:8–9; 43:10; 44:1–2; 49:7). Paschal redemption (Eph 1:7) was inaugurated at the exodus and is ubiquitous in Isaiah. At the time of Paul the term had not become an entirely Christianized technical concept void of its OT roots. Its use in the NT and particularly the Pauline Corpus suggests that it was still linked to the historical exodus (Eph 1:7; 2:13, 16; esp. 5:2). In the OT, redemption is applied to the exodus generation (Exod 6:6), the survivors in the wilderness (Deut 7:8), and the new exodus during the exilic period (Isa 43:14). The concept of inheritance (Eph 1:14) is a foundational OT thought, beginning with Abraham (Gen 21:10; 31:14), continuing in the exodus (Exod 32:13; 34:9; Josh 11:23), and anticipated in the new exodus (Isa 57:13; 65:9). The Spirit (Eph 1:13) would play a prominent role in the new era, facilitating on behalf of God the new exodus (Isa 42:1; 44:3; 48:16; 61:1; 63:10–11). The prayer for the audience (Eph 1:16–19) asks that they fully comprehend present eschatological triumph (Eph 1:20–23). The prayer itself emphasizes the present aspect of triumph in that it reflects urgency. The heavenly places (1:3; 20) correspond with Isaiah's use of spatial imagery. It is from the heavens that Yahweh deploys his might, wars with his enemies, and achieves the new exodus (Isa 34:4–5).

Based on these findings there is evidence that the author, to some degree, gained his inspiration of present triumph from Isaiah's new exodus, which anticipated such a victory. The OT blessings are in accordance with Yahweh's covenant with the nation and the miracles in Egypt and the wilderness. Isaiah adopts the exodus imagery and translates it into his message to his generation. What was envisaged for Israel is enacted in the church. It may be that from this standpoint that the author reassures the recipients of the letter that INE triumph had arrived. Ridderbos, citing Eph 1, aptly summarizes how the writer's conception of salvation is anchored in Christ and is the realization of the prophets' vision: "A most basic conception of Christ's advent and work lies at the root of this whole appeal and use, that of the divine drama being realized and fulfilled in his advent and work; this fulfillment was not only foretold by the prophets, but signifies the execution of the divine plan of salvation that he purposed to himself with respect to the course of the ages and the end of the times (Eph 1:9, 19; 3:11). This is the fundamental redemptive-historical and all embracing character of Paul's preaching of Christ."[116] Ephesians 1 has significant ties to Isaiah's new exodus, particularly the present triumphal aspect, but how formative the INE

---

116. Ridderbos, *Paul*, 51. Cf. Beker, "Triumph of God," 81–82.

was to the writer remains an open question. What lies immediately ahead is how present Isaianic triumph plays out in reference to the communal effects of sin.

6

Present INE Triumph Observed in Redemption, Reconciliation, and Temple Building, Eph 2:1–22

THE PRESENT REALIZATION OF INE triumph appears to have played a role in the composition of the praise eulogy, the first apostolic prayer, and the announcement of Christ's enthronement. Aspects of this opening message in Eph 1, especially those found in Eph 1:20–23, are highlighted in 2:1–22. The author applies the triumphal effects of salvation to the spiritually dead (2:1–10), announces how spiritual transformation unites former enemies (2:11–18), and considers the erection of a spiritual temple in keeping with a triumphant warrior (2:19–22). The relationship between 1:20–23 and 2:1 has been the subject of much debate[1] due in part to the absence of explicit grammatical and topic indicators.[2] However, the consensus opinion is in favor of seeing 2:1 as a continuation of the blessing, prayer, and exaltation sections of 1:20–23. If M. Barth may speak for the majority, 2:1–6 belongs under the affirmations of 1:20–23.[3] This present

---

1. Commenting on the transition from chapter 1 to the first section of 2, Dahl writes, "The gift aspect is complemented by transfer terminology: those who were dead have been made alive in Christ and given seats of honor in the high heavens," *Studies*, 443. Dahl discusses the various interpretive permutations in light of Conzelmann, Merklein, M. Barth, and Best: *Studies*, 5.

2. Hoehner deals with the grammatical features of the text, recognizing that the use of καί in 1:22 (2 times) is not merely continued with the καί that begins 2:1. Rather, the latter opens a new thought: in 1:20–23 God is acting in relation to Christ, in 2:1f he is acting on behalf of sinners: Hoehner, *Ephesians*, 305. This does not result in a major bifurcation of the section (1:20—2:10), but simply subdivides it into two parts.

3. M. Barth, *Ephesians, Chapters 1–3*, 212. Lincoln and others generally agree:

study suggests that 1:20—2:10 is the center of the epistle, with 1:20–23 depicting the apex of Isaianic new exodus redemption and 2:1–10 recognizing the immediate salvific effects of spiritual deliverance.

Chapter 2 shows ample evidence of OT influence. Moritz views Isaiah as the entire backcloth of Eph 2.[4] The multiple verbal and conceptual parallels in the salvation section, such as Isa 26:19 (in 2:5), coupled with the quotations from Isa 57:19 and 52:7 (in 2:13, 17), as well as the cluster of OT temple imagery in 2:18–22, make a compelling case not only for Isaiah's general influence in Eph 2 but for the possibility of Isaiah's new exodus. Building on Martin's work, *Reconciliation*,[5] Suh makes a convincing argument for the use of Ezekiel in Eph 2.[6] He observes verbal, structural, and thematic parallels from Ezek 37. The echo of "two becoming one" in Ezek 37:22 is said to appear in the unification of Jews and Gentiles in 2:15: "one new humanity in place of the two." The vivid eschatology in Ezek 37 is in keeping with Isaiah's new exodus understanding of the restoration of the nation, with the former focusing on the reunification of the northern and southern tribes. From Ezek 37, Suh tracks the resurrection and gift of the Spirit, walking in the way of the Lord, the unity of the people of God, the Messiah, and a covenant of peace. Both Ezek 37 and Eph 2 conclude with God's everlasting new sanctuary in which he dwells among his people.[7] Noteworthy is Suh's affirmation that the Davidic Messiah (in Ezekiel) was expected to undertake a messianic war, instituting God's rule over Gentile oppressors and establishing unity and peace for his people.[8] Zimmerli observes an emphasis in Ezek 37 that contrasts human inability with divine omnipotence, along with a dead-in-sins motif, grace, and power over the cosmic forces; all are prominent in Eph 2.[9] Evans makes a strong case for Ezek 37 as well, noting that the repeated formula, "You shall know that I am Yahweh" (Ezek 37:13–14, 28; cf. Eph 2:7; 3:10) is exodus in nature.[10] These observations are in keeping with the overall thrust of Ephesians thus far, and the possibility of the influence of Isaiah's new exodus.

Hoehner, *Ephesians*, 305; Lincoln, *Ephesians*, 85–86; O'Brien, *Letter*, 153–54.

4. Moritz, *Profound Mystery*, 29–53.
5. Martin, *Reconciliation*, 190.
6. Suh, "Use of Ezekiel," 715–34.
7. Ibid., 716, 723, 732–33.
8. Ibid., 728. This is observed in the Jewish Scriptures and later Judaism: Hengel, *Zealots*, 229–312; Klausner, *Messianic Idea*, 384–86.
9. Zimmerli et al., *Ezekiel*, 2:260.
10. Cf. Ezek 37:6, 13, 14, 28; and J. Evans, "You Shall Know."

In his recent study, Gombis considers Eph 2 from the standpoint of both the OT and Ancient Near East divine warfare ideology. He sees a complete cycle in the chapter: the triumphs of God over the powers that hold humanity captive to death, the raising of believers to an exalted state, dismissal of the divisive sociological effects of trespasses and sins, a new understanding of the law that has been hijacked by the powers, and temple-building befitting a conqueror.[11]

6.1 PRESENT INE TRIUMPHAL REDEMPTION IN EPH 2:1–10

As the preceding investigation of redemption (Eph 1:7) has shown, the present triumphal facet of paschal-emancipation is suggested in the epistle. Future redemption is also kept in mind (1:14) but not given the emphasis afforded the present aspect. What changes in 2:1–10[12] is how triumphal redemption demonstratively liberates sinners from the prince of the powers of the air (2:2). The term "redemption" is not explicit in this section, but the concept is clearly present with vivid references to the former and present state of the redeemed.[13] In short, "redemption through his blood" (1:7) is now articulated in terms of the sinful state from which the redeemed are freed along with the cosmic results of the emancipation.[14] Redemption is a present triumph that includes a fundamental, internal, ontological transformation.

Moritz considers the language of 2:5–6 to be primarily explained as dependent on Isa 26:19.[15] Added to his comments should be Isa 26:14 where the unbelieving dead are buried. The shared language is νεκρός (Isa 26:14,

---

11. Gombis, "Triumph" (2005a); esp. ch. 2, "The Pattern of Divine Warfare," 8–37. Gombis investigates warfare patterns in the OT, and Ancient Near East documents such as *Enuma Elish*.

12. Ch. 2:1–10 is flanked on each side by περιπατέω, occurring in vv. 2 and 10, forming an *inclusio*. The focus is an enslaved way of life radically changed through co-resurrection and enthronement. Each time περιπατέω is used in Ephesians the reference is to ethical living (2:2, 10; 4:1, 17; 5:2, 8, 15).

13. Wright, *Resurrection*, 239.

14. The believing "children of wrath" (Eph 2:2) have experienced ontological reversal. Once under the judgment of God (τέκνα φύσει ὀργῆς), they find themselves in a new state of affairs: ensconced with Christ over the powers in the heavenly realm. Hoehner shows the multiple layers of "sons of disobedience" (υἱός, 2:2) and "children of wrath" (τέκνα, 2:3): *Ephesians*, 315–24. Speaking of the idea of final judgment in Paul, Kreitzer remarks, "The wrath is primarily future, but it is not without present implications as well," citing Eph 2:3: *Jesus and God*, 99. Darko recognizes thirteen uses by Paul of God's ὀργή, both present and future: *No Longer*, 46. As with divine blessing, God's wrath, as both now and not yet are nearly indistinguishable.

15. Moritz, *Profound Mystery*, 109 n. 40.

19; Eph 2:1, 5). Conceptual correspondence is also found: συζωοποιέω (Eph 2:5) and συνεγείρω (Eph 2:6); related to ζωή (Isa 26:14), ἀνίστημι (Isa 26:19), and ἐγείρω (Isa 26:19). Contextually, Isa 26 expresses a song of trust from the standpoint of the prophet. He rejoices that Yahweh has restored Judah. A reversal of fortunes has come about as those who dwell on high are laid low (Isa 26:5). The feet of the afflicted will trample the dust where the once proud lay (Isa 26:6). The callous and unjust are put to shame (Isa 26:10–11). In a complete turnabout, the devastation meted out (Isa 26:14; "the dead do not live") is reversed among the redeemed remnant: their corpses shall rise. Sinful Judah and the nations will remain in their graves, but the surviving remnant awake from the dust while peace is established (Isa 26:3, 12; cf. 27:5). In Eph 2 there are also two types of dead people: those under the domination of the prince of the air (Eph 2:1–2) who do not rise because they are under the wrath of God (Eph 2:3) and those who are made alive and raised with Christ (Eph 2:5–6). As in Isaiah, Eph 2 depicts a complete reversal where peace is established (Eph 2:14, 15, 17). One other possible link is πάντα γὰρ ἀπέδωκας ἡμῖν (Isa 26:12) and οὐκ ἐξ ἔργων (Eph 2:9): Yahweh graciously renders to the believing remnant what God mercifully demonstrates through Christ. There is an emphasis in Isa 26 on the remnant waiting solely upon Yahweh's actions for rescue (Isa 26:4, 8–9, 12, 13, 18). This dependence is extended to the remnant's decomposed bodies (Isa 26:19), and as in Ephesians they are at the complete mercy of God (Eph 2:8–10). Based on these associations there is reason to agree with Mortiz that Isa 26:19 (and 26:14) are utilized in Eph 2:5f. In addition, it will be seen later in chapter 10 of this study that Isa 26:19 is probably on the author's mind in Eph 5:14.

This argumentation coincides with the startling descriptive, "new creation" (Eph 2:10, 15; cf. 2 Cor 5:17; Gal 6:15), which Hubbard regards as, "Paul's crucial soteriological matrix . . . It is impossible not to hear echoes of Jeremiah and Ezekiel at this point. Their analysis of the human predicament was remarkably similar to Paul's, and it is hardly surprising that the inner renewal foretold by them is often summarized with the phrase 'new creation.' With respect to his anthropology, Paul's theological ancestry can be traced directly to these prophets."[16] While taking into consideration other prophets, Hubbard argues forcibly that Paul's understanding of new creation was birthed out of Isa 40–55 and new exodus thought. He demonstrates how new creation and redemption in Isaiah are virtually interchangeable.[17]

---

16. Hubbard, *New Creation*, 233–39.
17. Ibid., 12–15; 23–24.

Present INE Triumph Observed in Redemption, Reconciliation, Temple

Keesmaat maintains the same, arguing from Rom 8:14–30, while noting that the exodus deliverance is ultimately for the sake of all creation.[18]

Integral to the exodus story and its subsequent NT usages is liberation from slavery. The extraordinary parallels in the NT, specifically the Pauline Corpus, open the question as to the concept's origination. As noted in the previous discussion of redemption, Daube asserts that Yahweh observed the cruelty of the Egyptians toward the Hebrews and acted on their behalf, functioning as their near kinsman and proceeding upon his own law.[19] Yahweh utilizes the cruelty of Egyptian bondage to first demonstrate the superior ethic of Yahweh monotheism, and then formally encodes it at Sinai.[20] Daube shows that slavery was generally practiced in the Ancient Near East but could be taken to unacceptable lengths, as in Egypt. Yahweh's emancipation of the Hebrews was not just a demonstration of power, as is so often emphasized in connection with the exodus, but a moral expression of his law. Subsequent to the liberation of the Hebrews, an appeal is made for Israel to show the same compassion that they received from Yahweh toward foreigners, strangers, and slaves. The basis of their compassion was that they were to remember that they once were ill-treated. Based on this it is not surprising to see linkage between the new exodus and ethical conduct, since this is observed in the aftermath of the historical exodus and the codification of Yahweh's law. This will be explored in detail in this present study in the ethical section of the epistle (Eph 4:17—6:9); however, in Eph 2, just as in the exodus, God works ethically on behalf of his people.

Arnold parallels the rescue and redemption motif in Exodus (Exod 6:6; 14:30) with the Pauline understanding of both forgiveness and deliverance (1 Cor 1:30; Col 1:13; 2:14; Rom 3:24; 1 Tim 2:6).[21] Keesmaat comments on the phrase πνεῦμα δουλείας in Rom 8:15 and sees its application to Eph 2. After considering the roots of this verbiage she remarks concerning Rom 8, "It seems more likely that in vv. 14 and 15 Paul is echoing one of the Old Testament's confessional statements about the nature of God . . . a statement which characterized God primarily as the one who led the people

---

18. Keesmaat, "Intertextual Transformation," 44; Keesmaat, "Creation, Exodus," 97–135.

19. Daube, *Exodus Pattern*, 11–15.

20. In Exod 20:2 Egypt is called, "the house of slavery." Several terms and phrases are utilized in the exodus narrative that turn upon the intolerable conditions of the Hebrews.

21. Arnold, *Powers of Darkness*, 111. Arnold cites the Jewish document, *Testament of Zebulun* 9:8, dated second century BC: "He will liberate every captive of the sons of men from Beliar, and every spirit of error will be trampled down."

out of Egypt in the exodus, who freed them from bondage."[22] Keesmaat understands that in Paul's bondage-to-freedom phraseologies he is most likely reflecting a pervasive motif in the LXX—freedom from bondage in Egypt.

In terms of the second exodus described in Isaiah, the conditions in Babylon parallel those that were in Egypt.[23] The kingdoms of Egypt and Babylon may be compared to Paul's understanding of the kingdom of principalities and powers. The books of Daniel and Revelation portray world rulers empowered and incited by cosmic forces. Isaiah utilizes the exodus template showing the abiding compassion of Yahweh toward his people. He rescues them from cruel bondage, redeems, and restores. The new order spoken of in Isa 65:17 and 66:22 shall become a reality through the work of God's servant.[24] Isa 65:17 says, "For I am about to create new heavens and a new earth; the former things shall not be remembered or come to mind." Isa 66:22 is similar, "For as the new heavens and the new earth, which I will make, shall remain before me, says the Lord; so shall your descendants and your name remain."[25] The eschatological redeemer in Isaiah is in keeping with the function of Christ in Ephesians. Concerning the new order that redemption has brought about in Eph 2, Moritz notes that when one takes into consideration the use of Isaiah in Eph 2:17, "the author shows awareness of what he perceived to be a fulfillment of Isaiah's prophecy."[26]

Emancipation and new order are demonstrated in Eph 2. The helpless condition of the slave, this time under the encumbrances of sin, calls for divine initiative and love. God performs through the intercessory action of Christ what the enslaved cannot do. As in the exodus, God acts in mercy and

---

22. Keesmaat, "Intertextual Transformation," 42–43.

23. Also, Ps 96:5 LXX, "for all the gods of the nations are demons." Arnold (*Powers of Darkness*) comments on cosmic powers in Isaiah (57, 78, 98) and Babylon (49, 57, 61, 98). Arnold's chapter, "Judaism" (55–74, esp. 55–56), discusses the OT perspective on cosmic evil and considers it embedded in Paul. Concerning the ethereal world in the OT from which Paul acquired his view: "writers and readers apparently shared a common awareness," 56. Similarly, Stendahl: Paul's "appearing before Caesar and confronting the heavenly principalities and powers blend into one": *Paul among Jews and Gentiles*, 120.

24. Cf. Paul's old and new in 2 Cor 5:17.

25. There may be an echo of Isa 43:14 among Eph 2's emphases upon redemption, the breaking down of barriers, and the humiliation of God's enemies—where Isaiah has the original and new exoduses in view: "Thus says the Lord, your Redeemer, the Holy One of Israel: For your sake I will send to Babylon and break down all the bars, and the shouting of the Chaldeans will be turned to lamentation. I am the Lord, your Holy One, the Creator of Israel, your King. Thus says the Lord, who makes a way in the sea, a path in the mighty waters."

26. Moritz, *Profound Mystery*, 215.

love (Eph 2:4–7).²⁷ Just as Yahweh initiated a plan to save his people in the Egyptian and Isaiah exoduses, he does so again through the church's common enthronement with Christ (2:5–6).²⁸ The exodus scenarios in Egypt and Persia were for liberation purposes but ultimately served demonstrative aims, indicating to God's people and their adversaries Yahweh's superiority, compassion, and justice. Exodus-like conditions coalesce in Eph 2 and are used by the writer to likewise "show the immeasurable riches of his grace" (2:7) to the cosmic forces. God's initiative to save his people in Egypt corresponds with the exiles' need in Babylon, and again in Eph 2. It appears that the exoduses of Moses and Isaiah are conjoined in the author of Ephesians, depicting people in desperate need and God in mercy acting on their behalf.

If INE triumph is in view in Eph 2:1–10, is it considered present? The emancipation is considered a past event (2:1–3), and the new life and common enthronement a present reality (2:4–10). The Christians in Western Asia Minor are seated in "heavenly places" with Christ (2:6); a place of spiritual riches (1:3) and sovereign power (1:20). Penner remarks: "The striking feature of this chapter is its apparent 'realized' eschatology. The cosmic church, the body of Christ, is already seated in the heavenly places in Christ." The cosmic powers listed in 2:2 are now working in the disobedient, but for believers they are conquered.²⁹ These ethereal forces kept death in force among mankind, but in cosmic reversal Christians have been made alive. Standing in the face of the enslaving powers is the reality of triumph that arrived in Christ. The brief statement in 2:4–6 serves to etch upon the minds of the audience the astonishing triumph over sin and death that is theirs through God and Christ's mercy.

The author continues emphatically, "but now" (2:13; cf. 3:5, 10; 5:8), underscoring the present aspect of reconciliation. The eschatological "now" is found in several places in the Pauline Corpus.³⁰ Many of these have reference to new revelation, but others, like Ephesians, speak of the new, current

---

27. O'Brien, *Letter*, 164–65. There are many passages in the Pentateuch indicating mercy and love as key motifs of the Egyptian exodus era.

28. Gombis, "Triumph" (2005a), 68. Gombis relates that the "brief" announcement of triumph (encompassing only 2:4, 5b, 6) is in keeping with the ancient divine warfare pattern found in the OT and extra-biblical literature: "Much more space typically is devoted to the development of the threatening situation, setting the backdrop against which the great power of God in salvation can be emphasized . . . a brief statement of the conflict and victory serves to emphasize the stunning and dramatic deliverance." Additionally, 2:4–6 is an extension of what has already been elaborated upon in the eulogy.

29. For specifics on Eph 2:2: Arnold, *Power and Magic*, 59–62, 69, 167–72.

30. Rom 5:9; 6:22; 7:6; 8:1; 11:30–31; 13:11; 1 Cor 15:20; 2 Cor 5:16; 6:2; Col 1:22, 26; 3:8; 2 Tim 1:10.

state of affairs for Christians. The other occurrences share with Ephesians an emphasis on realized eschatology; but what sets Ephesians apart is the accentuation on current triumph. As seen earlier in this present work (section 4.3) Ephesians displays a distinct form of realized eschatology that other Paulines do not share: an unparalleled emphasis on the arrival of triumph, and is put forth soundly as OT fulfillment.

The "already" eschatological aspect is true to the extent that the audience must be warned against boasting (2:9). They are to exult in the present triumph but not construe it a result of human effort.[31] The "works" connected with the new life have already been prepared (2:10) and assumed to be entered upon. The use of σῴζω (2:8) is understood to be a parenthetical outburst,[32] indicating that the audience was and continues to be redeemed by grace (cf. σῴζω in 2:5). The term σῴζω has a variegated field of meaning, but fundamentally depicts rescue from danger.[33] In this particular context the act of redemption rescued believing sinners from the wrath of God. When σῴζω is used in conjunction with ἀπολύτρωσις, as in Ephesians, it is reminiscent of paschal redemption during the exodus era and ultimately in the new exodus.[34] The perfect, passive participle of σῴζω is found in both 2:5 and 2:8. The perfect is more in keeping with a realized state of affairs. In reference to the two occurrences in Eph 2, Hoehner remarks, "the perfect tense expresses a completed action with continuing results in the present time."[35] Vos also recognizes the few instances in the Paulines where salvation is spoken of as unequivocally applied to the present, namely Eph 2:5, 8. Vos observes that comparatively the present tense does not have the same convincing force of the perfect.[36] The emphasis in Eph 2 is on the initial and ongoing fact that the addressees are saved.[37] The ubiquity of σῴζω in Isaiah

---

31. Das, *Paul*, 271–72.

32. Hoehner, *Ephesians*, 331.

33. Foerster and Fohrer, "Σῴζω, Κτλ.," 7:965–1024; Mundle et al., "Redemption," 3:205–23.

34. For ἀπολύτρωσις and the INE see ch. 5 of this present work.

35. Hoehner cites numerous grammarians: *Ephesians*, 333. Dunn seems to mistakenly categorize both occurrences as aorist, attempting to affiliate them with Rom 8:24–25 while making a point about assurance: *Theology of Paul*, 438 n. 129.

36. Vos also lists Titus 3:5 and 2 Tim 1:9 which are both aorist. But Greek scholarship no longer views the aorist as clearly indicating past action. Thus, Eph 2:5 and 8 stand as the only uses of σῴζω in Paul that emphasize present salvation. Vos considers other possibilities such as Rom 10:9 and 2 Cor 2:15 but acknowledges that they are ambiguous on this point: *Pauline Eschatology*, 53.

37. Commentators have wrestled with the time element of σῴζω, creating an authorship issue. Some claim that if the audience is now saved there is an undue emphasis on realized eschatology in the epistle, bringing into doubt genuine Pauline authorship.

Present INE Triumph Observed in Redemption, Reconciliation, Temple 133

is impressive, and usually has to do with divine deliverance in the future with eschatological connotations.[38] Of particular interest is Isa 19, 43, 49, and 51 with several occurrences of σῴζω. According to Fishbane these four chapters (among others) are INE in nature.[39] Isa 60:16 combines σῴζω and ἐξαιρέω in personifying God. In 63:9 σῴζω is used with λυτρόω to describe God's gracious actions towards his people. Isa 66:19 appropriately ends the book of Isaiah by stating that "survivors" (σεσωσμένους, perfect passive participle of σῴζω) will be sent as emissaries to the nations to declare God's glory.

The terms ἀπολύτρωσις and σῴζω combine to produce important motifs in both Isaiah and Ephesians that intimate paschal-exodus and eschatological deliverance. The writer's typological-historical understanding of the OT exoduses may see Christ, the triumphant redeemer, as the realized antitype terminus whereupon NT believers are enriched beneficiaries (Eph 1:3).[40]

6.2 THE INCULCATION OF THE GENTILES IN EPH 2:11-18

Contrary to Käsemann and Schlier's Gnostic arguments, v. 2:11f is clearly presented from a Jewish perspective.[41] The section deals with Gentile inclusion, which is integral to the new exodus.[42] Yahweh's intention from his inaugural covenant with Abraham was to include non-Jews in the redemptive plan.[43] This plays into the author's argument in Ephesians. Not only

---

But this is an unnecessary conclusion. The degree of realized eschatology in the epistle does not mount a persuasive argument against Pauline authorship as comparisons with the undisputed Paulines demonstrate: Gombis, "Triumph" (2005a), 70–71; 71 n. 82.

38. Isa 1:27; 10:20; 12:2; 14:32; 19:20; 20:6; 30:15; 31:5; 33:22; 35:4; 37:20, 22, 35; 38:6; 43:3, 11, 12; 45:17, 20, 22; 46:4; 49:25; 51:14; 59:1; 60:16; 63:8–9; 66:19.

39. Fishbane, "Motif," 121–40. For a study of the LXX usage of σῴζω along with Hebrew equivalents: Foerster and Fohrer, "Σῴζω, Κτλ.," 970–80.

40. In this same vein Yoder-Neufeld observes similarities between Ephesians and apocalyptic literature: Yoder-Neufeld, *Ephesians*, 339–41.

41. Moritz, *Profound Mystery*, 29.

42. Yee analyzes Jewish and Gentile issues in Ephesians from the standpoint of the new perspective on Paul. Apart from the new perspective controversy he brings an appreciation for Jews and Judaism into the thorny interpretive issues of Ephesians, esp. Eph 2: Yee, *Jewish Identity*, 3–4.

43. This is an example of Ephesians and Romans parting ways. Whereas the center of gravity for Romans is chapters 9–11 as an apologetic for God's faithfulness toward Israel despite Gentile inclusion; Ephesians considers Gentile inclusion and equality a towering triumph over the cosmic powers: Stendahl, *Paul among Jews and Gentiles*, 28. Romans explains and defends God's actions, whereas Eph 1–2 announces the present triumph of his actions and declares the communal effects.

did Isaiah's triumph mean present redemption and its concomitants, but the inclusion of Gentiles into the commonwealth of Israel. M. Barth considers Paul to be making a grand announcement.[44]

The effects of redemption are profoundly racial and serve as a crucial application for the writer to the local issues in Western Asia Minor. The epistle introduces the extraordinary privilege of Christian Gentiles who now have equal access to God along with their Jewish counterparts. This is not simply a new outgrowth of Judaism, but a new spiritual organism comprised of both Jews and Gentiles. W. Campbell makes the salient and somewhat controversial observation that in the reconciliation texts neither Ephesians nor Paul negates or replaces Israel. The new humanity is not "in opposition to, or displacement of" the covenant nation, rather these texts assume and affirm the ongoing identity of the OT people of God, with Jewish and Gentile Christians forming a new humanity as co-heirs with Israel.[45] This involves the creation of a new humanity that is coincidental with the eschatological age. Yoder sees that the breadth of the recreation is societal, involving Jews and Gentile, over individual concerns.[46] Several terms and concepts in Eph 2 point to the Gentile inclusion envisioned in the eschatological age: "far off, brought near" and "blood of Christ" (13), "peace" (14–15), "dividing wall" (14), and "far off . . . and near" (17). In the end of the chapter the common Gentile and Jewish community is metaphorically presented in temple imagery (Eph 2:20–22). Among the usages of the OT in Eph 2:11–22 is the little recognized evidence of the abolition of the law and its new creation replacement (2:15). Because the Torah is linked to the act of creation, Christ replaces the Torah and brings about a new world.[47] In Ephesians and Colossians the stipulations of the Torah are replaced by faith in Christ alone.[48]

Embedded in this section of Ephesians is the use of Isa 52:7 (Eph 2:17a) and 57:19 (Eph 2:17b, cf. 40:9).[49] Isa 52:7, "How beautiful upon the

---

44. M. Barth, *Ephesians, Chapters 1–3*, 266.

45. Campbell, "Unity and Diversity," 23–24. Cf. Campbell, *Christian Identity*, 169–70; Campbell, *Paul's Gospel*, 110–13.

46. Yoder, *Politics of Jesus*, 222.

47. A modification of this position is Mussner's, who sees Qumran parallels to re-creation, but his view appears to outrun the evidence: Mussner, "Contributions," 174–76.

48. Pate et al., *Story of Israel*, 222.

49. Lincoln reasons that the key to understanding the relationship between Ephesians and Isaiah in this section is determining whether the writer of Ephesians utilizes an ancient Christian hymn. If a hymn is in view the next question involves the degree to which Isaiah is used. But it could be that no traditional Christian material is undertaken and that the writer has a more straightforward use of Isaiah. Lincoln's position is

mountains are the feet of the messenger who announces peace, who brings good news, who announces salvation, who says to Zion, 'Your God reigns,'" and Isa 57:19, "Peace, peace, to the far and the near, says the LORD; and I will heal them" appear to have continuity with the prophet's vision of the new exodus (Isa 49:5–6).[50] The far and near imagery is repeated in several other places in Isaiah.[51] Concerning the use of these OT passages, Moritz interacts with the breadth of scholarship. Ultimately, Moritz establishes sound reasons for the author's conscious inclusions of Isaiah.[52] He chides Gnilka, Stuhlmacher, and others for their failure to adequately include the Isaiah material in their reconstructions. In view of the changes the author of the epistle made between the texts of Isaiah and Ephesians, M. Barth comments on the perspective of the author: "He probably assumed that such changes would offer an authentic interpretation of the prophetic text."[53] Thielman suggests that the author's thought in the use of these Isaiah texts is probably more expansive than the two passages alone indicate: "Paul probably was thinking of the broad literary contexts of which both of these quotations occur in Isaiah."[54] Wright sees the eschatological import of this section of Isaiah: "These passages (Isa 40:9; 52:7), in company with others, are among the climactic statements of the great double theme of the whole section (Isaiah 40–55): YHWH's return to Zion and enthronement, and the return of Israel herself from her exile in Babylon."[55] Actually, the phrase in 57:19, "near

---

that Eph 2:14–16 may have incorporated Christian traditional sources, but 2:17 and 18 do not. He argues that the OT concept is not integral to the traditional hymnic context in 14–16, and the length of 18 does not provide easily reconstructed hymnic lines. Besides, 2:17 picks up nicely from 2:13. In addition, the section parallels Col 1:15–20 and the reconciliation concepts there. However, there is good reason to see that verbal and thematic similarities between 2:14–16 and 2:17–18 speak of a common writer and source, but not an ancient hymn. On the other hand (and in Lincoln's favor) the entire passage (Eph 2:14–16) does not read as a specific exposition of the Isaiah passage. To sum up, it is possible that the author utilized traditional material for 2:14–16, but in 17 turned to focus on the OT. It is likely that the emphasis on the new situation between Jews and Gentiles and the verbiage "far" and "near" point to origination in Isaiah vis-à-vis the author of the epistle, even if a hymnic remnant is utilized in 2:14–16: Lincoln, "Use," 25.

50. The phrase, εὐηγγελίσατο (Eph 2:17a) is from Isa 52:7, and εἰρήνην ὑμῖν τοῖς μακρὰν καὶ εἰρήνην τοῖς ἐγγύς (Eph 2:17b) is from Isa 57:19.

51. Isa 5:26; 18:2, 7; 29:13; 33:13; 46:13; 57:19. Cf. other places in the Bible: for "far": Deut 28:49; 29:22; 1 Kgs 8:41; and Jer 5:15; "near": Ps 148:14; both: Deut 13:7; 1 Kgs 8:46; Esth 9:20. For NT usages: Acts 2:39 and 22:21.

52. Moritz, *Profound Mystery*, 23–28.

53. M. Barth, *Ephesians, Chapters 1–3*, 276.

54. Thielman, "Ephesians," 817–18.

55. Wright, "Gospel and Theology," 222.

and far" has origination beyond Isaiah. In OT passages the Gentile nations are said to be "far" or "near" based on their proximity to Israel (Deut 13:7; 20:15). However, the author of the epistle has demonstrated a penchant for Isaiah; this tips the scale of evidence toward Isa 57:19 as the point of origination. Some consider the two groups as both Jewish, those in the land and those in exile, others see them as those who are righteous and those in sin, but the passage is also understood to apply to other groups such as Gentile proselytes.[56] Childs comments that Isa 57 falls within the grand purview of the magnificent universal promise in Isa 56:1–8, specifically, an explicit invitation that includes both foreigners and eunuchs (56:3–8).[57] Marshall notes, "To 'bring near' seemingly functions as a technical term in Jewish proselytism meaning to accept an outsider as a full member of the Jewish community (which included circumcision)."[58] The proclamation of peace (Isa 52:7) hearkens back to what was first announced in Isa 40. The herald of the good news leads his people in peace back to Zion: "God has forgiven his people and announces his imminent salvation to the exiles languishing in Babylonian captivity."[59] The exodus-like return from Persia, and the still future idyllic exodus, takes on an international scope that involves multiple nations coming to experience Yahweh's peace. The combination of the two Isaianic passages brings into view two prevalent eschatological motifs: the proclamation of peace and the inclusion of the Gentiles. That is, the writer selects the passages from Isaiah to validate that the Isaianic triumph includes the present application of peace and Gentile inclusion in the church. In Eph 2 εἰρήνη coincides the cessation of war with the cosmic powers that has been brought about through Christ's triumph, and specifically through his person (he is the εἰρήνη, 2:14). "Peace" is in keeping with the messianic title in Isa 9:6 and Mic 5:5. In Eph 2:14–17 εἰρήνη is an eschatological peace personified in the Messiah, that as Usami asserts, "exists now."[60]

However, the letter understands the incorporation of outsiders taken to a new level: both Jew and Gentile will be on the same footing before God.[61]

---

56. Lincoln, "Use," 27–28; McMahan, "Wall," 264–65.

57. Childs, *Isaiah*, 472.

58. M. Marshall, "God's New Humanity," 191. On Isa 52:7 pertaining to the Jews and the land: O'Brien, *Letter*, 207. Moritz also comments: "The terminology of Eph 2 can of course be compared to Jewish proselyte discussion. This is to be explained in the light of the influence Isaiah exercised": *Profound Mystery*, 54. Additionally, O'Brien (*Letter*, 191), on Exod 18:5 where he sees traditional proselyte language.

59. Childs, *Isaiah*, 406.

60. Usami, *Somatic Comprehension*, 57–58, 69–70. Cf. p. 57, n. 288. Quote is from p. 57.

61. Concerning the adaptations the author makes in distinction to contemporary

"Access in one Spirit" (Eph 2:18) recalls the eschatological work of the Spirit (Eph 1:14). The appearance and role of the Spirit is a signal of the new age. In the present context the Spirit facilitates the common access of Jews and Gentiles to the Father. Both the Father and the Spirit not only endorse but facilitate common access.

Eph 2:13 offers proselyte terminology. The emphasis is the author's portrayal of the new multiracial Christian community.[62] Just as Ps 110:1 and 8:6 capped the eulogy, prayer, and enthronement section; Isa 57:19 and 52:7 endorse the triumphal redemption and Gentile section. Both the writer of Ephesians and Isaiah see one eschatological community, made up of all nations and races coming to God to worship: "all the nations shall stream to it" (Isa 2:2–4; 66:18–21). Isaiah considers outsiders such as foreigners and eunuchs as accepted—"these I will bring to my holy mountain" (56:3–8, esp. 7). The difference between the Isaianic usage and Ephesians is the Christological fulfillment. His death was certainly propitiary (emphasized in Eph 1, esp. 1:7; and ch. 2, "the blood" and "the cross," 2:13, 16) but the focus in chapter two is on the sociological impact of redemption in the local Christian community. Ephesians declares that the enmity that once existed between Jews and Gentiles is now abolished. The death of Christ brought about the death of enmity and provided eschatological harmony.

Both Isaiah and Ephesians have an emphasis on the new work of God for his people and the Gentiles. God is aware of the extraordinary problems of his people while in Egypt, Babylon, and Western Asia Minor. He enters into history and redeems them with mercy and grace. This exceptional deliverance includes those outside the fold of Israel and forms a new, otherwise unknown entity. Redemption brings Jews and Gentiles together through Christ with equal status before God.

Does this use of Isa 57:19 and 52:7 point to Isaiah's exodus? There is evidence that their usage is in keeping with Isaiah's new exodus. Ninow identifies Isa 51:1—52:15 as explicitly new exodus.[63] Isa 57:19 fits securely into the new exodus stream of thought that envelops Isaiah. In Isa 57 the wicked are condemned, but suddenly (57:13b) the audience is told that those who trust

---

Jewish exegesis, M. Barth makes clear that Paul understood that the blood of Christ, not the circumcision blood of Gentiles, brought the "far" "near." The "far" were dead in their sins and no amount of circumcision or Sabbath keeping would save them. Jewish writers saw them as hopelessly wicked Gentiles (not pious, God-fearing foreigners who might merit inclusion): *Ephesians, Chapters 1–3*, 276–79.

62. Arnold offers, "Another possible hymnic fragment appears in Ephesians 2:14–18, although this identification is disputed by P. Stuhlmacher who regards it as a Christian midrash on Isaiah 57:19": Arnold, "Ephesians," 239.

63. Ninow, *Indicators*, 186–93.

Yahweh shall inherit the land and Mount Zion. The startling turn of events causes mourners to rejoice (57:18). Yahweh announces peace to those far and near (Isa 57:19). This synchronizes with Isaiah's new exodus.

There is reason to see that in the paschal death of Christ the historical exodus experience of Moses and the new exodus vision of Isaiah are fulfilled within the communal context of God's people. If this is the case, then the integration of Jews and Gentiles into a new community is a present manifestation of the Isaiah's new exodus. Christ's triumph (1:20–23) is shared with his redeemed people as they currently co-reign with him (2:6). "But now" (2:13) signals the present aspect of the integrated races that have been brought near through Christ. The actions of God seen as imminent in Isaiah are realized in Western Asia Minor. Peace has arrived (ποιῶν εἰρήνην, Eph 2:15) through the servant-messiah. Paschal redemption "in Christ" has eradicated ancient animosities having to do with circumcision (2:11), the covenants of promise (2:12), and the law (2:15).[64] The emphasis in Eph 2 is on a completed state of affairs. The cosmic powers have been neutralized, especially in terms of their proclivity for stirring racial animosities. The recipients of the letter had been enslaved by the "prince of the power" to their own ill-conceived notions of ethic division. Currently the church members are "no longer strangers and aliens" but "citizens with the saints and also members of the household of God" (Eph 2:19). Like saints that are victoriously co-seated with Christ, the triumph is patterned after the Isaianic vision of eunuchs and foreigners coming to Zion. A part of this victory in Asia Minor is that Christ's triumph over the principalities and powers overcame their ability to wreak havoc between peoples. The INE triumph over the cosmic powers brings reconciliation with God (Eph 2:1–10) and former ethnic enemies (2:11f), both toward Isaiah's audience and those of the missive.

6.3 A SPIRITUAL TEMPLE BEFITTING THE TRIUMPHANT WARRIOR IN EPH 2:19–22

The work of redemption has further ramifications for the newly formed union of Jewish and Gentile believers. The focus is on the Gentile believers

---

64. Participation in circumcision, the covenants, and the law was the outward manifestation of what it meant to be a child of Abraham. These had the capacity to produce ethnic animosity. But all is upended in Christ. "Circumcision" (2:11) is now only a physical distinction between Jew and Gentile (cf. John 7:22): Muddiman, *Ephesians*, 117–18. The "covenants" (2:12) were made with Israel, but in the new era God is not solely aligned with a national entity: Stanley, "'Redeemer,'" 124 n. 23.The "law" (2:15–16) is directly involved in creating ethnic ill will, but now it is abolished and subject to the newly created order: Moritz, *Profound Mystery*, 40–41.

in particular ("you," Eph 2:19) and the access they gain in the spiritual community. Citizenship, household, and temple images are employed to communicate this new reality.[65] As stated earlier, the new situation is considered a present benefit.

The tabernacle and temple were the national locus for worship ritual in ancient Israel going back to the exodus period and perhaps further.[66] When the Solomonic temple was destroyed by the Babylonians, the prospect of its reconstruction and role in the new exodus came to prominence. Although the postexilic temple of Zerubbabel was built after the return from Persia, it came about under the thumb of Jewish oppressors. The temple was considered inferior and fell short of the sanctuary envisaged by the prophets. As a consequence a new and better temple was predicted in which worship would take place in purity, without the interference of outside powers.

The temple has an eschatological function in the OT and a specific role in the prophets, most notably in Ezek 40–48. Beale has established that the OT prophecies concerning the temple are in large part fulfilled by Christ's body as the temple and cornerstone, and his church the structure, along with God dwelling for all eternity among his people.[67] The anticipated eschatological temple is set within a larger theological rubric of God's expanding presence among his people. Temple terminology facilitates this fundamental "dwelling place" theology seen in Eden, the Sinai tabernacle, the Solomonic temple, and eventually the eschaton. The temple becomes the cosmic symbol of what God desires to do for all people. Concerning the NT church and Paul, God is no longer constricted to a physical temple but makes his presence known expansively through his spiritual presence in the church. O'Brien notes that some in the Second Temple Period had already conceptualized the people of God being the holy dwelling of God, much in keeping with the idea in Eph 2:21–22.[68] In addition, the temple would be a gathering place for Gentiles: "According to Old Testament prophecy the temple at Jerusalem was to be the place where all the nations at the end time

---

65. "Citizenship" and "household" were common terms that spoke of status and privilege in the first century. The images are utilized to represent the advantages of participation in God's family. For the benefits of being a part of a household, especially in terms of Paul: Towner, "Household Codes," 418.

66. As will be discussed, Beale sees temple imagery within broad biblical bookends, Gen 2 and Rev 21:1—22:3. Ephesians falls into this wide stream but contains its own idiosyncrasies.

67. Beale incorporates the OT, and literature from intertestamental, Qumran, rabbinic, and apostolic fathers. He has extensive treatments of Isa 66, Ezek 40–48, Dan 2, and Zech: *Dwelling Place of God*, 25, 201, 385. For a summary and critique of Beale's work: McDaniel, "Dwelling Place," 187–88.

68. O'Brien, *Letter*, 220 n. 272.

would come to worship and pray to the living God (Isa 66:18–20; cf. Isa 2:1–5; Mic 4:1–5)."[69] This has correspondence with the eschatological peace that will prevail when Israel and the nations are united as one worshipping community in Jerusalem.[70]

The author uses the eschatological temple (ναός) motif in his understanding of the heavenly manifestation of the church. The foundation of the temple is the immediate disciples and apostles, and Christ (Eph 2:19–22).[71] This houses the new community of both Jews and Gentiles. Garnering symbolism from the OT temple of literal stone, the new temple is a growing organism,[72] configured by Christ himself[73] as the corner piece,[74] built with multiracial Christians as the stonework,[75] and indwelt by God and his Spirit. Rather than being "far off" (2:17) and segregated by a wall (2:14), Gentile Christians are part of the very materials that make up God's edifice. This is a heavenly residence that corresponds with prior announcements of heavenly riches (1:3) and a heavenly abode (1:20; 2:6). In Eph 2 the temple metaphor is utilized to shape the final eschatological goal of a unified, Spirit-indwelt edifice. The mixed community of Christians resides in this heavenly world, triumphant over the powers of this realm, and unified as fellow members of the spiritual family.[76]

---

69. O'Brien, *Letter*, 220 n. 272. Cf. Holland, *Contours*, 21–23.

70. Eph 2:14–15, 17; Isa 2:4; 57:19; Mic 4:3. Cf. McKelvey, *New Temple*, 111–12.

71. In 1 Cor 3:9–17 the foundation is laid by Paul and the other apostles; in Eph 2 the foundation is laid upon these same early church leaders but with Christ as the cornerstone.

72. Gärtner observes that the picture in Eph 2:19–22 is a compound image, both static and organismic. The building illustration is utilized again but combined with body imagery in Eph 4:12, 16: Gärtner, *Temple Symbolism*, 66.

73. The personal pronoun, αὐτοῦ, is understood as emphatic, emphasizing the integral and personal involvement of Christ who configures the building in which the unified multiracial residents find equal access to God.

74. Jeremias, Lincoln, and others make a case for ἀκρογωνιαῖος being a top stone, and thus a picture of Christ superior to the apostolic founders of the church. Best is uncertain: Best, *Critical and Exegetical*, 286; Jeremias, "Κεφαλὴ Γωνίας-Ἀκρογωνιαῖος," 264–80; Lincoln, *Ephesians*, 154–55. But Hoehner and O'Brien following McKelvey are critical of Jeremias's thin substantiation and maintain that the base of a building is in mind: Hoehner, *Ephesians*, 404–5; 404 n. 5; McKelvey, "Cornerstone," O'Brien, *Letter*, 217.

75. Different from today, no mortar was used in ancient stonework. This required much more elaborate and precise fittings. The painstaking process involved meticulous cutting and exact shaping. The spiritual correspondences are clear: Hoehner, *Ephesians*, 409.

76. Hoehner understands the indwelling in 2:21–22 as individual, but the author of the epistle has the corporate church in mind in Eph 1:23 and 2:22. There is no indication of individualization, but rather the bringing together of disparate ethnic parties.

O'Brien makes a case for the use of ἀκρογωνιαῖος and θεμέλιος alluding to Isa 28:16.[77] It is the only place in the LXX where ἀκρογωνιαῖος is used and like the current passage in Ephesians it integrates θεμέλιος (two times in the Isaiah text). The Isaiah passage and its architectural imagery have been difficult to understand. The meaning of cornerstone has several possibilities including the temple, Zion, the Davidic dynasty, the remnant, or faith.[78] But Childs sees more than just the physical temple in view, or David for that matter: "God is in the process of laying a new foundation stone that is unmovable before the overwhelming scourge of coming judgment."[79] In other places Isaiah has a building motif, indicating a restored city (1:26), and God as a sanctuary and stone (8:14–15). Childs continues: "The initially ambiguous foundation stone of 28:16 serves as a metaphor unifying central themes that have been nuanced in different ways throughout the book . . . The symbolism of the stone encompasses the reality of the new community, a faithful remnant, which is a foretaste of the coming righteous reign of God and which is ushered in by the promised messianic rule of Zion."[80] Isaiah 28:16 is in keeping with Eph 2 and how the writer aims to engage his audience. The Isaiah passage serves to buttress the argument that the eschatological rebuilding of Zion is seen in part in the heavenly household. Combined with Isaianic passages seen just prior in Eph 2:17 a stronger case is made for Isaiah's vision being adopted by the writer, this time with Isaianic edifice terms that undergird and enhance his rationale. Lock makes a case for Ps 68 influencing Eph 2:22.[81] Triumphant exodus imagery is clearly in view in this Psalm (68:7–10, 22), emphasizing Yahweh dwelling victoriously in his sanctuary along with his rescued people (68:5–6, 10, 16–18, 24, 29, 35). In addition, it is possible that the use of cornerstone in Eph 2:20 stems from Ps 118:22 or Christian tradition. But the emphasis is not

---

It is natural to see the same in 3:19. The writer of the epistle considers the corporate nature and triumph of the church. This does not negate the individual appropriation of faith: *Ephesians*, 482.

77. Contra Jeremias and Lincoln. Hoehner is unsure: *Ephesians*, 405–6; cf. O'Brien, *Letter*, 217.

78. Childs, *Isaiah*, 209.

79. Ibid., 209.

80. Childs speaks further of Isaiah: "At times the stone is a pledge of security for faith; at other times it is a rock of stumbling for unbelief (8:11ff). Some texts of the corpus lay emphasis on the remnant as the creation of God, others on the remnant as a sign of the eschatological community. The error of earlier interpreters has been in trying to isolate only one feature from within this larger whole without adequate attention to the dynamic interplay of texts that together comprise the truth of the prophetic proclamation": Ibid., 209–10, quote from 210.

81. Lock finds echoes of Ps 68 throughout Ephesians: *Ephesians*, 11.

on rejection and glory; rather, the stress is upon the cornerstone's stability and basis for measurement (i.e., justice and righteousness; Isa 28:17). This understanding seems to point in the direction of Isaiah. Given these uses of Isaiah and psalms there are reasons to suggest that the Lord's return to the eschatological temple (Eph 2:21) and the indwelling of the Spirit (Eph 2:22) is in keeping with the new exodus seen by Isaiah and the prophets. Certainly Suh's recent investigation advocates more involvement between the eschatological vision of Ezek 37 and Eph 2 than previously acknowledged.[82]

Temple eschatology in Ephesians seems to also coincide with Qumran studies. Gärtner says the language of Eph 1:20–22 "suggests that the relationship between this text and the ideology of Qumran was particularly intimate."[83] McKelvey also observes parallels in Qumran to temple symbolism.[84] In both Qumran and Ephesians, an earthly and heavenly community is formed in which God resides. However, the use of temple imagery in Ephesians is distinguishished from Qumran in that the temple signals the present arrival of the eschaton, the inclusion of Gentiles, and spiritual (not physical) triumph. God is said to have a κατοικητήριον there, which according to the LXX connotes the dwelling place of God upon his holy mountain, in the temple, in Jerusalem, and in heaven.[85]

Gombis considers the place of the temple in connection with the triumphant warrior motif.[86] He undertakes a discussion of Eph 2, maintaining that the pattern of divine warfare is clearly seen in the chapter along with vindication for Christ who is installed as cosmic Lord (cf. 1:20–23). Gombis's outline of the motif in Eph 2 is as follows: Lordship (1:20–23), conflict-victory (2:1–16), victory shout (2:7), celebration (2:18), and house-building (2:20–22).[87] Gombis concludes: "Just as triumphant deities in the ANE had temples built in their honor, so here in Eph 2, the triumphs of the exalted cosmic Lord Christ are memorialized with the building of his temple, the people of God made up of both Jewish and Gentile believers."[88] Tangentially, Kreitzer suggests that Eph 2 deliberately presents Christ as the New Solomon who, as a peaceful ruler, builds his temple.[89] This theory

---

82. Suh, "Use of Ezekiel," 729–30. Cf. Ezek 37:6, 13, 14, 28.

83. Gärtner, *Temple Symbolism*, 64. First Pet 2:4 along with Ephesians, 1 Corinthians, and the Qumran texts reveal an early, widespread tradition of understanding the temple symbolically in a myriad of ways.

84. McKelvey, "Cornerstone," 352–59; McKelvey, *New Temple*, 37, 49, 97.

85. Gärtner citing Schlier: Gärtner, *Temple Symbolism*, 65; Schlier, *Brief*, 145.

86. Gombis, "Triumph" (2005a), 84–86.

87. Ibid., 52.

88. Ibid., 86.

89. Kreitzer, *Hierapolis*, 131.

has merit in that it incorporates the common themes of royalty, peace, and temple-building, but it lacks any specific correspondence to Solomon, or for that matter a Solomonic Christ.

6.4 CONCLUSION

The echo from Isa 26:14, 19 in Eph 2:5; quotations from Isa 57:19 and 52:7 in Eph 2:13, 17; and allusion from Isa 28:16 in Eph 2:20 suggest evidence for the presence of the current triumph of Isaiah's new exodus (tables 12.1, 12.2). Admittedly, both the echo of the death and life metaphor (Isa 26:14, 19 in Eph 2:5) and cornerstone allusion (Isa 28:16 in Eph 2:20) have remote association with INE contexts (tables 12.3, 12.4); however, they fall among passages from Isaiah (19:19–25; 24:23; 35:1–10) that are recognized as new exodus in nature (table 12.3). In these chapters (Isa 19–35) an exodus-like judgment is measured upon the Egyptians (Isa 19–20). Ethiopia (Isa 20), Babylon (Isa 21), Edom and Arabia (Isa 21), and the fall of Tyre (Isa 23) all follow. The judgment upon Jerusalem and her rescue are found within this cluster (Isa 22). In Isa 24 the Lord measures out judgment upon the earth where he will reign with his elders (Isa 24:7–23). This leads to Judah's song of praise for God's favor (Isa 25:1–12) and a song of trust (Isa 26:1–21). It is within this latter passage (Isa 26:1–21) that the echo in Eph 2:5 is positioned, the death to life metaphor. The point to be made is that the contexts of the INE indicators in Isa 19:19–25 and 24:23 build naturally to the employment from Isa 26:14, 19 in Eph 2:5. It proves difficult to bifurcate the underlying exodus judgment in Isa 19:19–25 and 24:23 from the death to life picture utilized by the writer of the epistle in Isa 26:14, 19. In addition, the INE passage in Isa 35:1–10 lies ahead of the usage and would appear to reinforce the new exodus motif.

The other parallel, an allusion (Isa 28:16 in Eph 2:20) is similar to Isa 22 in that a turnabout is witnessed from judgment to rescue. Isa 28 reveals the captivity of Ephraim (Isa 28:1–15), but reciprocation is announced precisely at the usage, Isa 28:16, with the laying of the cornerstone. Once again, there is continuity in the Isaiah text from the INE recognized passages (Isa 19:19–25; 24:23) to the usage in Ephesians (Isa 28:16). If there is strength in this line of reasoning it lies in the cohesive argumentation that is found in Isa 19–28. The usages in Eph 2 fall within these chapters, and their Isaiah contexts are influenced by the INE.

The quotations from Isa 57:19 and 52:7 in Eph 2:13, 17 form stronger evidence since Isa 52:7 is precisely from an INE section (tables 12.3, 12.4). This provides a degree of substantiation in that the author of the epistle saw the Jewish and Gentile new humanity as being a part of Isaiah's new exodus era. Additionally, the echo or conceptual parallels imported from Isaiah and the prophets are noteworthy as well: spiritual reversal (Eph 2:1, 3–4), triumph over enemies (Eph 2:2), slavish conditions reversed (Eph 2:3), enthronement as a display to the enemy (Eph 2:5–7), divinely initiated salvation and righteousness (Eph 2:8–10), proselytization of the nations (Eph 2:11–17), paschal redemption (Eph 2:13, 16), replacement of the Torah by Christ as the means of new creation (Eph 2:15), and the new eschatological temple made up of diverse racial entities accessed through the Spirit (Eph 2:18–22).

It may be maintained that both Eph 1 and 2 utilize the OT to speak of various aspects of present triumph. In addition, to some degree, Isaiah is used in a fashion that suggests the adoption of the prophet's new exodus motif. Concerning Eph 1, the author undertook Isaiah and Pss 110 and 8 to focus on the recipients grasping their current co-enthronement with sovereign Christ. Isaiah 11:2 is used allusively in Eph 1:8 and 17, and is in close proximity to INE passages and may link with the use of Isa 11:4–5 later in the close of the epistle (Isa 11:4–5 in Eph 6:14 and 17). In Eph 2, as seen previously, the echo (Isa 26:14, 19 in Eph 2:5) and allusion (Isa 28:16 in Eph 2:20) have remote association with the INE but nevertheless fall under the influence of INE contexts. The quotations from Isa 57:19 and 52:7 in Eph 2:13, 17 are substantive indicators of new exodus thought that undergird the second chapter of Ephesians, especially in that they provide Isaiah's vision of Jewish and Gentile equality in the church. Suh maintains the influence of Ezek 37 in Eph 2, but given the repeated and clear (and at times explicit) presence of Isaiah, both in the chapter and the epistle thus far, it appears that although Ezekiel provides considerable weight it does not exceed the influence of Isaiah. The same may be said of the use of Pss 110 and 8.

The query ahead concerns the means by which the author of the epistle can make such astonishing claims about the integrated nature of the people of God, and how this new state of affairs coincides with the present triumphal aspect of Isaiah's eschatological exodus.

7

The Author's Explanation of Apostolic Ministry in Accordance with Present INE Triumph, Eph 3:1–21

THE REMARKABLE DISCLOSURES CONCERNING the relationship between Christian Jews and Gentiles in the eschatological temple (Eph 2:18–22) prompt further explanation. As was the case during the evangelism efforts in Acts, those steeped in OT thought and tradition would brace at the God's intentions toward the Gentiles.[1] Those sensitive to Jewish custom would wonder how the author's statements in Eph 2 could be in keeping with the Hebrew Scriptures. What qualified the writer to speak so boldly of a present eschatological triumph that was to be enjoyed equally by Israel and the Gentile nations? In addition, if there is indeed present triumph in view, questions remain concerning Paul's state of affairs. The epistle suggests that the audience was aware of his sufferings as a prisoner (3:1, 13; 4:1; 6:19–21), which resulted in a degree of discomfort for audience (6:22).[2] How are these circumstances experienced by the apostle compatible with Isaiah's vision?

Eph 3 has puzzled commentators.[3] The position that commentators typically hold is that the author of the epistle mounts a defense of Paul's

---

1. Acts 10, 11, and 15.

2. The self-designation, ὁ δέσμιος, with the article may indicate special status as a prisoner. Paul was not any detainee, but a key participant in the revelation of the mystery to the Gentiles: Cassidy, *Paul in Chains*, 96.

3. Some like M. Kitchen who hold to pseudonymity wonder why so much space is devoted to Paul's status: *Ephesians*, 29–30. Muddiman considers Eph 3 second only to 6:21–22 as mounting the strongest case for genuine Paul: *Ephesians*, 147. Others view

ministry and credentials.[4] In Eph 3 key areas come under review: Paul's qualifications and circumstances in revealing the mystery (3:1–13), the second apostolic prayer for inner power and love (3:14–19), and the second doxology (3:20–21).[5] The author's intent in Eph 3:1 is to present a prayer that the participants in the eschatological temple might experience the power of God to love across ethnic lines,[6] but for the moment he is diverted to speak of his credentials and experience as a steward of the mystery to the Gentiles.[7] Aspects of Isaiah's new exodus should accord with the explanation and prayer.

Eph 3 demonstrates no OT quotations or allusions, only echoes from Isaiah and other portions of the OT.[8] Moritz does not dedicate a section to Eph 3 in *Profound Mystery*. He addresses the chapter across a broad spectrum to support the use of the OT in other portions of the epistle.[9] Apart from these instances, he mentions 3:8–12 as Christ replacing the Torah in providing access to God.[10] He also notices that the new man (3:16) is

---

the section as an effort to undergird Paul's authority whether he wrote or an imitator: Houlden, *Paul's Letters*, 294–95; M. MacDonald and Harrington, *Colossians and Ephesians*, 260. Some consider the section an effort to strengthen the author's bond with his audience: Lincoln, *Ephesians*, 171; O'Brien, *Letter*, 225–26. Still others who accept Paul's authorship regard it a pointless digression. For an article arguing against this position: Gombis, "Ephesians 3:12–13," 313–23.

4. Arnold, *Power and Magic*, 86; Best, *Critical and Exegetical*, 292–93.

5. Bruce and Wood suggest that the first prayer (διὰ τοῦτο, 1:15–19) never really ended and is taken up once again in 3:14–19. They also see the initial berakah continuing in 3:14–22. Although this is possible thematically, structurally it remains questionable: Bruce, *Epistles*, 309; Wood, "Ephesians," 44. Most of Eph 3 is parenthetic in nature, "syntactically a digression within an intercessory prayer" that begins in 3:1 and concludes in 14–19. Τούτου χάριν (3:1) . . . Τούτου χάριν (3:14): O'Brien, *Letter*, 224. However, Fay sees no digression but rather an intentional argument that emphasizes the unity of Jews and Gentiles: "Empowered Prisoner," 532–61. Best argues that the author did not cleverly plan the digression: *Critical and Exegetical*, 294. M. Barth discusses Chrysostom and Beza who understand 3:1 as an asyndeton, not a broken sentence: "For this reason I, Paul, am a prisoner . . .," but then argues for a digression based on the article before prisoner: M. Barth, *Ephesians, Chapters 1–3*, 327.

6. Hendriksen, *Ephesians*, 149–50; Hodge, *Commentary*, 100; Lincoln, *Ephesians*, 167.

7. Muddiman, *Ephesians*, 147.

8. Isa 11:10 and 66:18–19 may be echoed in Eph 3:5–6; Isa 45:23 in Eph 3:14; Isa 63:11–12 in Eph 3:16. But it appears that the echoes simply share general language and concepts, and are not conscious. The author does not use the OT directly in making his argument.

9. Moritz, *Profound Mystery*, 3, 4, 20, 24, 42, 49, 68, 70, 76, 84, 88, 134, 145, 150, 174, 190, 200, 204.

10. Ibid., 76.

strengthened through the Spirit in the inner man, which indicates, as noted previously, the eschatological ministry of the Spirit.[11] This completes Moritz's OT investigation of the chapter. Lincoln does not deal with the OT aspects, and mentions Eph 3 while passing on to other points.[12] Lock observes echoes of Ps 68 throughout Ephesians but finds nothing of considerable substance, with the exception of course of Ps 68:18 in Eph 4:8.[13] Qualls and J. Watts closely follow Lincoln, linking Eph 3:1–12 with Isa 49:6, but this is a thematic echo indicating restored Israel as a light to the nations.[14] Based on these observations there is no need to explore specific OT usages in this section. One exception is Ps 103 in Eph 3:14–19, which is commented upon in due course in this present work. Although there appears to be a paucity of OT evidence in Eph 3, it would be shortsighted to dismiss the influence of the Hebrew Scriptures in the chapter.

7.1 APOSTOLIC QUALIFICATIONS AND CIRCUMSTANCES IN REVEALING THE MYSTERY AND THE MESSAGE'S COMPATIBILITY WITH PRESENT VICTORY IN EPH 3:1–13

Thielman approaches his analysis of Eph 3:1–13 from the standpoint of continuity and discontinuity with the OT.[15] The author of Ephesians seems to argue for continuity with the OT in Eph 2 only to emphasize discontinuity in Eph 3. Because Ephesians is eschatological in nature, indicating the present triumphal fulfilment of Isaiah's vision, how is this considered a novel mystery since the era was anticipated by the prophets? On one hand Isaiah is used to predict the union of Jew and Gentile (Eph 2:13, 17), and on the other the pre-Christian era was a time of ignorance ("not made known," 3:5).[16] Many focus on the adverbial conjunction ὡς in 3:5, and whether it functions as a comparison of kind rather than degree. Thielman, Lincoln, Best, Schnackenburg, Bockmuehl, and others argue for the former, which appears to be the preferable understanding.[17] The writer does not have

---

11. Ibid., 88. The ministry of the Spirit in the eschaton is not solely that of empowering (3:16); it is also one of sealing (1:13), access (2:18), and revelation (3:5): Dunn, *Theology of Paul*, 431–32.

12. Lincoln, "Use," 46.

13. Lock sees Ps 68 in the following places: Ps 68:9 in Eph 1:18; Ps 68:10 in Eph 2:10; Ps 68:16 in Eph 2:22; 3:17; Ps 68:28, 35 in Eph 3:16 and 6:10; and Ps 68:4, 32 in Eph 5:19: *Ephesians*, 11. Cf. W. Harris, *Descent of Christ*, 29 n. 112.

14. Qualls and J. Watts, "Isaiah in Ephesians," 257.

15. Thielman, "Ephesians," 818–19.

16. S. Kim, *Origin*, 351.

17. Best, *Ephesians*, 305; Bockmuehl, *Epistle*, 201; Hoehner, *Ephesians*, 439; Lincoln,

in view the degree of revelation in the NT as simply more than what was revealed in the OT; rather, it is markedly different. How is this balanced with the fact that the OT openly and emphatically predicts the inclusion of Gentiles in the final age (Isa 2:2–4; 19:19–25; 25:6–10; 56:6–8)? The best explanation seems to lie in what is specified in the following verse: "Gentiles have become fellow heirs, members of the same body, and sharers in the promise in Christ Jesus through the gospel" (Eph 3:6). The key is in the manner of Gentile inclusion.[18] They would not only gain entrance but would find equal footing with their Jewish counterparts, precisely the writer's argument in 2:11–22. Thielman concludes that although Eph 3 explains new, previously unknown information concerning the Gentiles, these explanations are in keeping with the eschatological thrust of Eph 2. The inclusion of the Gentiles was no secret, but the equality they would share with Israel in the eschatological temple was novel and thus required further explanation. Thielman summarizes:

> Paul's implicit claim in 2:11–22 that the unity of the Jews and Gentiles in Christ fulfilled Isaiah's expectations for the eschatological inclusion of the nations in the worship of God is not inconsistent with his claim in 3:5, that this mystery was withheld from previous generations only to be revealed to NT apostles and prophets in the present. The mystery of 3:3–4, 9 is not the entire argument of 2:11–22, but rather one element within that argument. Now that the eschatological age has begun, Jews and Gentiles do not merely worship together; they are united with each other, occupying the same level of privilege before God.[19]

This agrees with the majority opinion on what is referred to in Eph 3:3 concerning what the author of the epistle had previously written.[20] Most see "as I wrote above" as what immediately precedes, and thus ties Eph 3 more firmly with the tenets of Eph 1 and 2 and the uses of Isaiah and Psalms there.

Ephesians, 177; O'Brien, *Ephesians*, 232; Schnackenburg, *Ephesians*, 133–34. Thielman provides a detailed analysis arguing from the standpoint of the use of ἀποκαλύπτω and μυστήριον in Dan 2: "Ephesians," 819.

18. Bruce, *Epistles*, 314; O'Brien, *Letter*, 232.

19. Thielman, "Ephesians," 819.

20. As in Heb 13:22 and 1 Pet 5:12. M. Barth notes, "It is advisable to see in 3:3 an allusion to 1:9–10 or any other brief passage within Eph 1–2 which speaks about the grace and power of God, his eternal decision, revelation, the adoption of the Gentiles, the one body formed, the involvement of the principalities and powers, or free access to the Father": *Ephesians, Chapters 1–3*, 329.

Best points out that the writer had covered the mystery in brief (Eph 1:9) but had not distinguished Paul's personal role in it.[21]

Does Eph 3:1–13 reflect a triumphal aspect? It seems clear from 3:10 that it does: "so that through the church the wisdom of God in its rich variety might now be made known to the rulers and authorities in the heavenly places." The tone is one of victory in which God's superior wisdom in the μυστήριον is displayed before the cosmic powers (cf. Eph 1:21; 2:7). This produces boldness, as well as confident access and faith (Eph 3:12). Is the present aspect of the triumph in view? As argued previously, Eph 3 is inextricably linked with Eph 1 and 2. Inasmuch as Eph 3 is in keeping with Eph 1 and 2, it has present triumph in view. Additionally, 3:5 explicitly states that the mystery has "now been revealed" to the apostles and prophets.[22] Eph 3:10 says that the revelation "might now be made known" to the cosmic powers. The audience presently has "access to God in boldness and confidence" (3:12), comporting with 2:18, which is in the shadow of the Isaianic quotes there.[23] The description of the Gentiles as fellow partakers and Paul as a steward is spoken of a present state of affairs (3:6–9). The writer presents the situation as currently taking place. The fact that the church exists and proclaims the mystery indicates that the author has in mind the current demonstration of triumphant mystery, not just its content.[24] The church's existence validates that the mystery had been revealed and was incorporated in the Christian community.[25] The summary of all things had, in large part, become a reality. Ephesians 3 is a further explanation of the unity of believing Jews and Gentiles introduced in 2:11–12, and the timing in view is the same as Eph 2. What Isaiah prophesied concerning the Gentiles in the eschatological age, and what the writer saw fulfilled in the current church community, is explained in terms of Paul's ministry in 3:1–13. The setting and timing have not changed.

Gombis contends that Eph 3 is neither a digression nor simply an explanation of how Paul came to preach his message or to indicate aspects of the mystery.[26] Rather, Eph 3 concerns demonstrating victory over the

---

21. Best cites Percy: Percy, *Probleme*, 350; Best, *Critical and Exegetical*, 302.

22. Dunn says that 3:3–6 is "presumably understood as the means by which God will sum up all things in Christ" (1:9–10). Dunn codes this "'revelation' terminology": Dunn, *Theology of Paul*, 180 n. 94.

23. "Boldness and access to God that cannot be hindered by the hostile powers and authorities": O'Brien, *Letter*, 249. Also, "access can be seen as one no longer impeded by the menace of hostile principalities and authorities": Lincoln, *Ephesians*, 191.

24. Dunn, *Theology of Paul*, 526.

25. Gombis, "Triumph" (2005a), 96.

26. Fay and Heil argue that Eph 3 is no digression but a section strategically placed

powers. The author explains the situation to show that despite the apostle's circumstances he remained victorious.[27] The focus, therefore, is 3:1 ("prisoner," cf. 4:1) and 3:13 ("you may not lose heart over my sufferings for you; they are your glory;" cf. 6:20–22).[28] They form bookends, suggesting that the section is about Paul's condition as a prisoner and the audience's concern for his well-being. The strong inferential conjunction (διό, 3:13) begins the apodosis of the long conditional sentence that commenced in 3:2. Because the audience knows of Paul's ministry, they are in a position not to lose heart.[29] The audience's ability not to lose heart is tied directly to their knowledge of certain details of Paul's ministry. These details involve Paul as a recipient of divine disclosures about the Gentiles (3:2–9) that were given in order that God's wisdom might be made known (γνωρίζω, 3:10) to the cosmic powers. The explanation of Paul's ministry to the Gentiles and the subsequent suffering he experiences serves to illustrate the central point of Eph 1:20–23: victory over the cosmic powers, both for the church and Paul. This is also in part the point of 3:10 that God has "made known to the rulers and authorities."[30] The making known is an indication of the present status of God's plan, that he has acted decisively in Christ and procured cosmic victory.

A further point may be made that suggests that Eph 3 aligns with Isaiah's new exodus. This present triumph correlates with the INE that takes place in the midst of the remnant's fear and suffering. As explained earlier, there is a great deal of emphasis in Isaiah on fear (section 5.1.2). It may be added that many of these occurrences take place in exodus sections.[31] The term φοβέω alone occurs thirty-one times in Isaiah. In the face of this sense

---

in the epistle: Fay, *Empowered Prisoner*, 532–61; 667–83; Heil, *Empowerment*, 134–35.

27. Gombis builds on OT and ANE war ideologies. The pattern that emerges is conflict, victory, kingship, house-building, and celebration, all seen in Ephesians: Gombis, "Ephesians 3:2–13," 314–15.

28. Dunn adds that Paul's sufferings were a part of his "already, not yet" worldview. The sufferings were the shared sufferings of Christ and "an integral feature of the eschatological tension": Dunn, *Theology of Paul*, 482–84; quote from 484.

29. The third class condition of εἴ γε may be rendered, "indeed," 3:2: Hoehner, *Ephesians*, 467.

30. Some have seen γνωρίζω (3:10) in league with 1 Pet 1:12 and Mark 13:32 and the need to inform angels concerning the knowledge of the new age. But these parallel passages would intrude on the treatment of the cosmic powers in the Pauline Corpus and Ephesians in particular. The cosmic powers do not include elect angels but are evil and placed in subjection to the enthroned Christ (1:20–22).

31. Cf. section 5.1.2 of this present work. For fear in new exodus passages or near contexts in Isaiah: Isa 35:4, 10; 40:1; 41:10, 12, 13, 17; 43:1, 5; 49:14, 20; 51:3, 7, 12–13, 14, 21–22. For fear connected with the historical exodus: Exod 1:14; 5:21; 14:10–13.

of foreboding is the promise of new exodus and Yahweh's inevitable victory. Connections may also be made with the historical exodus and the fears felt there. This appears not to be lost on the author of the epistle who perceives the apprehensions of the audience, whether they are borne out of news of Paul's circumstances or the cosmic powers in general.

In summary, although Paul is presented as a prisoner, the author explains that the apostle's ministry is in keeping with Isaiah's vision of Gentile inclusion. Paul's ministry also serves the purpose of facilitating the proclamation of present Isaianic victory over the powers and any fear they may hold upon the audience.

7.2 AUTOBIOGRAPHY FUNCTIONING AS ESCHATOLOGICAL RHETORIC

Gombis and others are correct in maintaining that Eph 3 is neither a digression nor biographical filler about Paul's ministry.[32] Others have demonstrated that Paul's biographies serve as rhetorical tools, none of which are intended to merely convey personal information. They are didactic in nature, and are integral to the arguments put forth in his letters. Often they are utilized to defend against critics (2 Cor 3–4), but there is no evidence of this type of usage in Ephesians. In Eph 3 the biographical information coincides with the thrust of the letter seen thus far in Eph 1–2. The author does not seek to merely establish Paul's credentials[33] any more than for the other apostles and prophets who are mentioned (3:5). The writer's goal is to confirm the revelation of the mystery (3:2–7a), highlight the power involved (3:7b), and focus on the accomplishments of Christ over the rulers and authorities (3:8–10). This working of God's power (κατὰ τὴν ἐνέργειαν τῆς δυνάμεως αὐτοῦ) forms an ongoing theme in Ephesians[34] that is central to the letter's argument concerning Isaiah's concept of eschatological victory. The emphasis on triumph comports with identifying Paul as a prisoner rather than an apostle in this section (cf. 1:1; 3:1; 4:1).[35] Although he is considered "the very least of all the apostles" (3:8), his calling and situation has turned out to reveal the OT prophetic vision of the inclusion of the Gentiles that coheres with Christ and the God of Israel's final and complete victory, which is a demonstration of God's "power" (3:7) and "boundless riches"

---

32. Barclay, " Theology as Testimony," 133–56, esp. 135; Gaventa, "Galatians 1 and 2, 309–26; Taylor, "Apostolic Legitimacy," 65–77.

33. Contra Muddiman: *Ephesians*, 147–49.

34. Eph 1:19, 21; 2:2; 3:4, 7, 10, 16, 20; 4:16; 5:5; 6:11–13, 16.

35. In addition to physical deprivations, prisoners in the first century carried an appalling stigma: Rapske, "Prison, Prisoner," 829–30.

(3:8; cf. 1:3, 7, 18; 2:4, 7). If the audience is worried about the imprisoned apostle, the author puts them at ease by applying the message of present triumph to Paul's current situation. Rather than Paul (and the Christians in Western Asia Minor) suffering under the dominance of the enemy, the powers are "devastatingly foiled."[36] The turn of events has upended the actions of the cosmic powers and subjugated them at the feet of sovereign Christ and his church.

The paradox of Paul's imprisonment and contemporaneous triumph is neither a problem nor contradiction to the writer in view of his understanding of eschatological victory.[37] On the contrary, Paul's humble and weakened state is an opportunity to display God's strength and triumph.[38] This follows the Pauline understanding of the paradoxical pattern of Christ, who in suffering and death defeated the menacing powers who had brought death and division to mankind (Eph 2:13–17; 4:8–10).[39] This is precisely the argument of Col 1:24: "I am now rejoicing in my sufferings for your sake, and in my flesh I am completing what is lacking in Christ's afflictions for the sake of his body, that is, the church." The same logic is found in Eph 3:11–12. Although Paul is said to be in chains (Eph 6:20), the announcement is made that the apostle has "access to God in boldness and confidence" (Eph 3:11–12; cf. Eph 2:18). Paul and the audience are neither tethered nor encumbered by hostile powers that hold others in bonds of death (2:1–2). This leads to the inevitable conclusion that Paul's sufferings are understood as a glorious benefit to the audience (3:13). It is through the apostle's sufferings that his ministry bears fruit in the conversion of the Gentiles. His inner weaknesses and external persecutions are in keeping with God's eschatological program. The apostles' tribulations have actually enhanced his ministry: God's grace (2:7) and power (3:7) have been displayed because of the inclusion of the Gentiles and Paul's ministry to them. Keesmaat sees Paul understanding his sufferings eschatologically, the apostle interpreting his misfortunes with a view to the final age.[40]

Gombis maintains that a similar rhetorical strategy is at work in the OT in which God uses weak human agents.[41] He cites David and his battle with Goliath (1 Sam 17), along with Gideon fighting the Midianites (Judg

---

36. Arnold, *Power and Magic*, 64.

37. As seen in ch. 4 of this present work. Also, Penna, "Apostle's Suffering, 232–58. Paul's theology of personal suffering is probably most eloquent in 2 Cor, esp. 4:16—5:15; and 12:7–10.

38. Phil 3:7–8; 1 Cor 19:1–27; 2 Cor 12:9–10.

39. Gombis, "Ephesians 3:2–12," 322. Cf. Gombis, "Power," 117–28.

40. Keesmaat, "Creation, Exodus," 120–21.

41. Gombis, "Triumph" (2005a), 92.

6–7). However, there may be better OT examples of Paul's humility and service in Eph 3, especially ones that bespeak the new exodus. One possibility is Moses, who is utilized as an example in other portions of the Pauline Corpus.[42] The Moses paradigm is most clearly seen in 2 Cor 2:14—4:7 where Paul seeks to defend his role as an apostle by utilizing Moses as a model of his ministry. It is also reflected in Rom 9:3–4 where Paul portrays himself in the mold of Moses, willing to be "cursed and cut off from Christ" (cf. Exod 32:31–33).[43] But Paul uses the Moses paradigm in 2 Corinthians in defense of his ministry, which is not in view in Ephesians; and the usage in Romans depicts sacrifice for the sake of Israel. Another possibility is the servant motif in Isaiah. This has been seen in Paul's self-awareness[44] and in his aligning himself within the broad stream and tradition of the OT prophets.[45] However, Ephesians shows no palpable evidence for this particular use of the OT prophets.

A Danielic approach provides possibilities for the understanding of Paul's view of himself and his service in Eph 3. This is strengthened with the technical use of μυστήριον in Ephesians (particularly in the immediate context: 3:3, 4, 9; cf. 1:9; 5:32; 6:19), which finds roots in eschatological portions of Daniel. What is specifically known of Paul from Ephesians is found in 1:1 ("apostle"), 3:1 ("prisoner," 4:1), 3:8 ("very least of all the saints"), and 6:20 ("an ambassador in chains"). The particular designation in 3:1 ("I, Paul") finds strong parallels in Daniel—nine times, all introducing a section of revelation (Dan 7:15; 28; 8:1, 15, 27; 9:2; 10:2, 7; 12:5).[46] They are also associated with Daniel's prayers and prayer reports, and the reception of mysteries in association with wisdom (Dan 2:20, 21, 23; 5:11, 14) and the Spirit (Dan 4:8–9; 4:18; 5:11; 6:3). Furthermore, both Paul and Daniel were in the hands of the enemy (Paul in chains while Daniel was in exile). During these times they received God's messages. Additionally, the purpose of the mysteries had to do with demonstrating to Gentile peoples the uniqueness and sovereignty of Yahweh and his eschatological plan (Dan 2:28). The uses of ἁγίοις and πνεύματι in Eph 3:5 have possible connections with Daniel. Commentators have puzzled over the use of ἁγίοις in Eph 3:5 because it is

---

42. 1 Cor 10.

43. Stockhausen notes, "In answer to a reproach about his lack of external epistolary recommendation, Paul has proclaimed himself to be the 'new Moses's of God's covenant in Christ'": Stockhausen, *Moses's Veil*, 175. Cf. Belleville, *Reflections of Glory*, 172–79; Hafemann, *Paul, Moses*, 1–16; W. Webb, *Returning Home*, 101.

44. P. Fredriksen, "Judaism," 235–60.

45. Phil 2:16; 1 Cor 9:16 (Jer 20:9 and Amos 3:8); 2 Cor 10:8; 13:10 (Jer 1:10).

46. Much of this discussion of Daniel in Eph 3 is indebted to Asumang, "Vehicles," 1–26.

not found elsewhere in this way. The explanation may be that Dan 4:8–9, 18; 5:11 refer to Daniel (by his pagan counterparts) as possessing the spirit of the holy gods. The commonalities lie in that the recipients of the mystery in Ephesians are "holy" and "in the Spirit." Although his Jewish contemporaries thought differently, Jesus saw Daniel as a prophet (Matt 24:15; Mark 13:14), and it is likely that Paul and his followers observed this as well. Worthy of consideration is Daniel's five uses of ἅγιος (Dan 7:18, 21, 22, 25, 27) and its nine appearances in Ephesians (1:1, 15, 18; 2:19; 3:8, 18; 4:12; 5:3; 6:18). The Danielic occurrences are associated with possessing the kingdom, waging war and victory, and wearing out while struggling in war. In Ephesians the uses include the addressees, the recipients of communal love, recipients of divine inheritance, Paul as the least of them, believing Gentiles who co-populate God's household with believing Jews, shared comprehension of God's power, those who are equipped, those among whom improper things are not mentioned, and the objects of prayer. If there is a common thread it may be that saints are a distinguished group whose interests are God's, who struggle against evil, and who are promised God's kingdom.[47] The self-understanding in Eph 3 appears to find correspondence with the Danielic paradigm. In Ephesians it may be that Paul is seen as understanding his calling and ministry most particularly in conjunction with Daniel.

Although Eph 3:1–13 offers no OT quotations, the passage does suggest allusions and echoes of OT subject matter that has been established in Eph 1 and 2. Eph 3 is tied to Isaiah's eschatology and timing that finds expression in the first two chapters.[48] The autobiographical digression concerning Paul's stewardship of the μυστήριον and his personal circumstances serve to maintain exodus triumph. The author may be suggesting a Danielic eschatological association with his ministry. In the balance of Eph 3 the author is said to pray that the readers fully realize their situation.

7.3 SECOND PRAYER: REQUEST FOR POWER AND LOVE IN ORDER TO FULLY EXPERIENCE INNER TRIUMPH IN EPH 3:14–19

Whereas the first prayer focuses on the audience comprehending the hope of their calling, their inheritance, and the greatness of God's power toward

---

47. Cf. Bockmuehl, *Revelation and Mystery*, 43–48, 201. Other possibilities include Eph 3:8 and Dan 4:17; Eph 3:14 and Dan 6:10; 1 Cor 15:32; 2 Tim 4:17 and Dan 6:16.

48. Jeal argues that from the opening of the chapter τούτου χάριν is not a disruption of the prayer that commences in 1:14, but rather is rooted firmly in what has preceded and brings rhetorical force to what the author requests of the audience: *Integrating Theology*, 111.

them (Eph 1:15–19), the second centers on strengthening the inner man for purposes of God dwelling in love in the new community (3:14–21).[49] The distinctive focus of the second prayer is that readers might have the power to fully grasp God's triumph in Christ in the inner man manifested in interpersonal love.[50] It forms a fitting transition from the highly theological section of the epistle to the paraenesis (chs. 4–6) that summarizes important theological truths while considering their application in the Christian community.

The opening phrase of the prayer, τούτου χάριν (3:14), picks up where the digression began, τούτου χάριν (3:1). After alluding to his solemn prayer posture[51] there is the recognition that God is the sovereign head of creation (a theme already developed in 2:15; 2:22; 3:9). The one to whom it is said that Paul prays is both an intimate "Father" and triumphant creator-God who unflaggingly reigns over the cosmic powers and who is able to answer the supplication at hand.[52] Already it has been shown that God (as Father) is the one to whom both Christian Jews and Gentiles have access (2:18), and that he is the creator of all things (3:9).[53] In 3:14 he is the sovereign creator who names all families, which includes those of both Jewish and Gentile

---

49. O'Brien, *Letter*, 254. However, in many respects the second prayer is a reiteration or further application of the themes of the first prayer.

50. Contra Arnold who sees the point of the prayer as power: Arnold, *Power and Magic*, 87.

51. Conceivably this is an echo of Isa 45:23 since in other similar "bowing the knee" passages by Paul (Rom 14:11; Phil 2:10) the use of the Isaianic passage is explicit. As Wagner explains, Isa 45:23 is INE in nature, declaring that Yahweh alone is God and that in the future restoration the nations will give praise to him: "Isaiah," 127. Conversely, Asumang makes a case for bowing the knee in prayer with Daniel: Asumang, "Vehicles," 16–17.

52. Debate has taken place over the meaning of πατήρ. The term may refer to God as the Father of creation (3:15) who sovereignly names and rules his handiwork, including the hostile powers. But (contra Gombis who includes the hostile powers: "Triumph" [2005a], 101), in comparison with the use of πατήρ in 2:18, it seems the term evokes a pleasant and inviting tone to participants in the eschatological temple. It is from the bounty of the Father's riches (3:16) that he is able to abundantly answer the prayer for the addressees.

53. Moritz points out that the creation language in Ephesians (2:15; 3:9, 15) has parallels in Isaiah and ultimately Gen 1. The Hebrew term בָּרָא in the expression "create the fruit of the lips" (Isa 57:19) is in direct proximity to the creation of one new man and the preaching of peace in Eph 2:17: *Profound Mystery*, 34, 42–43. Moritz admits that one cannot know to what extent the author would have been aware of the precise Hebrew usage in the Isaianic text; however, there seems to be a linkage between the announcement of peace and creation. If so, the new creation in Eph 3:9 and 15 would be in keeping with Isaiah's eschatological vision seen in Isa 57:19 and Eph 2:16–17.

descent.⁵⁴ This is the God who is accessed in prayer. He is able to grant the audience the required strength for inner transformation and communal love. The prayer is a series of requests that are preceded with an introduction (3:14–15) and culminate in an ultimate request (3:19).⁵⁵

The first petition asks for a granting of power according to the "riches of his glory" (3:16; cf. Phil 4:19). This harkens back to 1:3 where the recipients had received all the spiritual blessings of the heavenly realm. It is from this heavenly trove that it is said that Paul asks God to grant power to comprehend.⁵⁶ The sphere of the strengthening is the inner man (ἔσω ἄνθρωπος),⁵⁷ in contrast to the outer man that is affiliated with the flesh and is perishing (Rom 7:22; 2 Cor 4:16). The inner man is where deep spiritual transformation takes place (Rom 12:2). This is also a locus of the cosmic threat and where the armor of God is applied.⁵⁸ Vos comments that the strengthening of the ἔσω ἄνθρωπον has an eschatological sense. When compared to 2 Cor 4:16–18 the inner man is being renewed in contrast to the decaying flesh. This renewal and decay suggest ultimate transformation.⁵⁹ The old flesh is making room for the new body that will enfold the already-new inner man.

The empowering is facilitated through the eschatological ministry of the Spirit (3:16). With the resultant power comes the wherewithal for Christ to dwell (κατοικέω)⁶⁰ in hearts through faith that includes a grounding in love. Eph 3:18 describes the ultimate object of the prayer in picturesque, spatial terms. The breadth, length, height, and depth are governed by one article (τὸ) and should be viewed as one.⁶¹ The terms do not have a specific referent and have been the object of considerable speculation. Some see the

---

54. Stott, *God's New Society*, 133.

55. O'Brien, *Letter*, 256–64.

56. The power language has parallels with Qumran genitive constructions: Kuhn, "Epistle," 117.

57. Jewett, *Paul's Anthropological Terms*, 460.

58. Eph 6 describes the parts of the panoply that serve as types of the inner locations and spiritual resources of the Christian. The primary battlefield with the cosmic forces is the mind; however, the forces that seek to intrude upon the mind inhabit the heavenly places: Cf. Fee, *Holy Spirit*, 695–96.

59. Vos, *Pauline Eschatology*, 203–4.

60. Fee, *Holy Spirit*, 696; Michel, "Κατοικέω," V:153.

61. For an in-depth discussion: Hoehner, *Ephesians*, 486–88. Strauss aligns ὕψος in Eph 3:18 with the abode of God (as in Eph 4:8), but this is off the mark considering that the term is grouped with the other three. It may be that the writer primarily has in mind immensity rather than location: Strauss, *Davidic Messiah*, 103. Roon offers: "It becomes probable that the quadruple formulation of Eph. 3:18 is in reality indicative of the four immeasurable dimensions which, according to ancient geocentric cosmological theories, defined the frontiers of the cosmos": *Authenticity*, 263.

expressions referring to the vertical and horizontal quadrangle conception of below and above, now and not yet (1:21), the spiritual building (2:21), God's wisdom (3:10), divine power (3:16), and Christ's love (3:17).[62] The power option is commendable in light of 1:19 where God's might is immeasurable. In Rom 8:39 the power of God is referred to in terms of "height" and "depth," within a heavenly powers context. In a spatial aspect Christ is exalted by power far above all things (1:21; 4:8).[63] Dahl traces the possible influences upon Eph 3:18 from Jewish wisdom literature to Stoic and Gnostic philosophy, and magical papyri. He sees a combination of factors at work, mainly that of biblical and Platonic phraseology. According to Dahl, the author of Ephesians links the immeasurable dimensions of the universe with wisdom and knowledge concerning God. He observes that the theme of revealed knowledge is more prominent in Ephesians than any other Pauline letter. He concludes that Eph 3:18 serves as a preamble to 3:19, referring to the unreachable knowledge of the plenitude of God. The author of the epistle sets this sought-after knowledge in contrast to the winds of doctrine in 4:14.[64] On the other hand, an argument can be made that the terms refer more directly to what is taking place in the epistle itself; namely, pointing back to the architecture of the eschatological temple in 2:21. If this is the case, then the comprehension referred to in Eph 3:18 is to be made in concert with the multiracial saints there.[65] By extension, what may be in view are the dimensions of the eschatological temple depicted in Ezekiel and Revelation. This expansive and corporate knowledge is the preferred interpretation in this current study, however, this interpretation is not held dogmatically. If this is the case, then the knowledge aspect of the second prayer is in keeping with that of the first, only with an emphasis upon an internal knowledge of divine love and power that leads to practical expressions of the Christian life (Eph 4–6).

At the close of the prayer, paradoxically, the audience cannot fully know (3:19b) what they are being told to comprehend (3:18–19a). The prayer culminates in an appeal to know the love of Christ, which actually surpasses knowledge.[66] To know Christ in this way is comparable to God's

---

62. Hoehner, *Ephesians*, 486–88.

63. Arnold sees reference to magical papyri but Gombis does not accept his evidence as convincing: Arnold, *Power and Magic*, 90–95; Gombis, "Triumph" (2005a), 103 n. 43.

64. Dahl et al., *Studies*, 366–68.

65. "Internal fellowship between the faithful is a condition for full participation in the pleroma": Roon, *Authenticity*, 257.

66. Paul, with all his rhetorical skill cannot escape his own paradox: Foulkes, *Epistle of Paul*, 105.

fullness dwelling among his people (19).⁶⁷ This is also in keeping with God's fullness filling his body (ἵνα πληρωθῆτε εἰς πᾶν τὸ πλήρωμα τοῦ θεοῦ, 3:19). The term πληρόω is used as a noun in Eph 1:10, 23; 4:13. In this present passage the noun is used with the aorist passive verb resulting in "filled with fullness." It speaks of the plenitude of God including his presence, life, and power.⁶⁸ Christians find themselves looking to a "full" era (1:10), while in a "full" state of being seated with Christ in the heavenlies (1:23), and yet in this prayer fullness is a potential to be acquired through spiritual knowledge (3:19), and fullness remains an aspect of spiritual maturity that comes at the hands of church leaders (4:13).⁶⁹ Once again, the dual eschatology, "not yet" and "already" is evident. To be both full and not full, or full and potentially fuller, both now and in the life to come finds no contradiction in the Pauline Corpus. All are clearly present in Ephesians, with the emphasis upon the present aspect.⁷⁰

The question of this current study is whether the present aspect is emphasized in the second prayer. The answer is best understood from the standpoint of the first prayer (1:15–19). There the petition is found between the berakah (1:3–14) and the first doxology (1:20–23). It was shown that both the berakah and doxology demonstrate present triumph. It was also shown that Eph 3 is in many ways an extension of the praise and prayer of Eph 1. The prayers in both chapters are not so much concerned with the matter of timing (whether "now" or "not yet"), but on the vital matter of present comprehension. The first prayer is meant to grasp the power that brought Christ back from the dead and seated him with the church at the right hand of God. The emphasis there is upon the result of the power in cosmic hierarchy. The second prayer for power is similar but comes after an explanation of the ministry to the Gentiles and how it coincides with a proclamation to the cosmic forces. The difference found in the second prayer is that it emphasizes the inner locus of comprehension of God's power and love. This is in preparation for the admonitions in Eph 4–6 where the audience will be called upon to live triumphantly in a world beset by spiritual difficulties. Both prayers emphasize the realization of present eschatological victory.

---

67. The ἵνα introduces the final purpose of the prayer: Hoehner, *Ephesians*, 490.

68. O'Brien, *Letter*, 265.

69. Bruce, *Epistles*, 329.

70. Ridderbos and Bruce demonstrate this duality in their studies of the epistle. Ridderbos discusses the present aspect of πλήρωμα in Ephesians: *Paul*, 44–45. On the other hand, Bruce links mystery and fullness eschatologically in the futuristic sense: *Paul, Apostle*, 439.

As stated earlier concerning previous portions of Eph 3, it appears that no OT quotations are in view; this includes Eph 3:14–19.[71] However Ps 103:11–14 suggests several parallels.[72] In this hymn Yahweh makes his forgiveness known to Moses and Israel in accordance with the height of heaven and the expanse between east and west. This is afforded by God as a compassionate Father who knows the frailties of his children. There are striking similarities between this psalm and 2 Cor 1:3–4. Both speak of God as a comforting father who addresses the afflictions of his people. The commonalities between Ps 103 and Eph 3 include an emphasis on redemption from sin (Eph 1–2; Ps 103:3–4; 8–12); a multi-dimensional expression of the immensity of God (Eph 3:19; Ps 103:11–12);[73] comfort articulated in familial terms from a divine father toward his afflicted children (Eph 3:1, 13, 14; Ps 103:13); acknowledgement of God in multi-generational and infinite terms (Eph 3:21; Ps 103:17); and demonstrated before a heavenly audience (Eph 3:10; Ps 103:20–21). Both are doxological (Eph 3:20–21; Ps 103:1–2, 20–22) that situate God sovereignly enthroned in the heavens (Eph 1:20–22; 3:15; Ps 103:19) and gracious in his actions toward his transitory people (Eph 3:1, 13; 6:20; Ps 103:14–17). Finally, exodus thought and language are explicit in the psalm (Ps 103:7–8).[74] If there is a link to the new exodus in Eph 3 it may come by way of the author's use of Ps 103. This is a possibility, but it depends on the likelihood of the author consciously utilizing Ps 103 as well as adopting the new exodus permutations of the psalm. This is held out as a possibility but not a certainty.

In summary, the triumph considered in Eph 1 and 2, and applied to Paul's circumstances in 3:1–13, has potential application to the readers. The writer already stated that the triumph arrived (Eph 1 and 2), but he wants his audience to fully realize it. In terms of power, the first prayer is meant to realize the supremacy of God that has been experienced through co-resurrection and co-reigning in the heavenlies; the second is meant to fully comprehend the power internally though the Spirit.[75] God has caused the victory to take place, but the locus for understanding such triumph is in the hearts of the believing community. Present triumph is still in view, but it

---

71. Bruce offers Job 11:8–9: "It is higher than heaven—what can you do? Deeper than Sheol—what can you know? Its measure is longer than the earth, and broader than the sea": *Epistles*, 328. Dahl lists Job 38:1; 40:1; and Isa 40:12: "Cosmic Dimensions," 368.

72. H. Moule, *Studies in Ephesians*, 99.

73. In reference to Ps 103:12, "The psalmist uses the spatial sense in order to give expression to the legal concept" of forgiveness: Gregory, "Legal Background," 551.

74. Gaiser, "Sins Are Forgiven, " 81; Rice, "Exposition of Psalm 103," 57–58.

75. O'Brien, *Letter*, 256.

must be grasped. The new exodus may have influenced the composition of Eph 3 with Ps 103 functioning as a possible avenue.

7.4 SECOND DOXOLOGY EXTOLLING VICTORY IN EPH 3:20–21

Best observes that although a doxology is usually inserted near the end of an address, it may come at any time, especially at important junctures.[76] The adversative δέ moves the focus of the address from the human audience to God.[77] As with the first doxology (1:3–14), the author demonstrates exuberance; however, in contrast to the first he is brief and centers on ascribing glory to God for the unimaginable inner power he is able to provide. Lincoln suggests that the doxology picks up where the first prayer digressed into the announcement of Christ's exaltation (1:20–23), by further describing the power of God.[78] The doxology follows the prayer but is also integrated with it, expanding on the theme of power.[79] In his prayer the writer had asked for inner strengthening; the doxology ascribes praise to God who is able to provide it. This power is already at work in the lives of the audience. The words for power link the passage with previous ones (1:19, 20, 21; 2:2; 3:7, 10, 16, 20) and will continue (6:10, 12) to be a major theme in the epistle.

In the seven ascending stages, the author describes God's ability to answer the prayer.[80] He tests the limits of language by a dramatic buildup of thought. The pointed focus of the petition, as in the immediately previous prayer, is ἐν ἡμῖν (3:20). The object of the intercession—inner power by means of the Spirit—is now the object of praise: God is able to provide unimaginable inner strength (Eph 3:16, 20–21). The power theme affords the audience the opportunity to overcome their fears about Paul's circumstances and the cosmic threats. The heavenly forces that brought havoc and death are no match for the "Father" (Eph 3:14) who is able to accomplish far more than can be asked or imagined.[81] "Glory in the church" (3:21; cf. 1:12, 14, 17; 3:13, 16) reminds the audience that the corporate church shares in ascribing praise to God for power in believers and the victory over hostile powers (Eph 1:23). This is also reflected in 3:18 where the desired compre-

---

76. Best, *Critical and Exegetical*, 349.

77. Contra Best, *Critical and Exegetical*, 349. God is the nearest referent (3:19) and is distinguished from Christ (3:21): Hoehner, *Ephesians*, 492.

78. Lincoln, *Ephesians*, 215.

79. O'Brien, *Letter*, 267.

80. Lincoln, *Ephesians*, 216; Stott, *New Society*, 139.

81. "A fitting and moving conclusion to the prayers and the entire first half of the epistle, which brings the power of God into bold relief": Arnold, *Power and Magic*, 100.

hension is practiced in the Christian community with "all the saints."[82] A surprising feature is that the church is placed parallel to Christ. Some transcribers sought to correct this by switching the terms,[83] but the church plays a co-role with Christ, though of course without a hint of equality. It is the church that makes known the victory over the rulers and authorities (3:10) and which is co-resurrected and enthroned with Christ who is sovereign over all things (1:23; 2:6). Christ and the church are indissolubly linked so it is therefore understandable that the church would participate "in Christ" (Eph 3:21) in ascribing glory to God.[84]

In consideration of the timing that is in view, the doxology ascribes praise to God for what he is presently able to do in the hearts of his people: κατὰ τὴν δύναμιν τὴν ἐνεργουμένην ἐν ἡμῖν (Eph 3:20) indicates a power that is presently at work in the lives of the audience. This harkens back to the present tense of ἐνεργέω in Eph 1:11 where early on in the epistle God is said to already be at work.[85] Hoehner comments: "Thus, it is appropriate and right that God should be praised not only for past activity, but also for his powerful work in the hearts of believers (vv. 16–17) at this present time."[86] The author walks a line between what God has definitely done in terms of present victory (1:20–23), and how that triumph is experienced in the life of the Christian. It is a victory that has taken place in which the believer is a part, but one that may be prayed for in terms of full realization.

In summary, the function of the second prayer is the full comprehension of divine triumph. The role of the second doxology is that God should be praised for what he is presently doing to fulfill the aforementioned prayer.[87] The second prayer and doxology declare both triumph and God's ability to

---

82. "The Apostle has spoken of experiences possible only in the *sanctum* of the individual 'heart,' but he reminds the reader here that these are never to terminate in themselves. The individual, as he is never other than a 'member' of Christ, is never other than a 'member' of his brethren" (emphasis in original): H. Moule, *Studies in Epheisans*, 99.

83. Best, *Ephesians*, 350.

84. Wood, "Ephesians," 53.

85. Best, *Ephesians*, 350.

86. Hoehner, *Ephesians*, 493. Hoehner cites Mauerhofer, "Brief an Die Epheser," 19. O'Brien sees ἐνεργουμένην (Eph 3:20) in the passive voice (as in Col 1:29), thus God is the source of the action. But even with the middle voice the point is still made. God's power is at work in the Christian: O'Brien, *Ephesians*, 267.

87. The final phrase τῶν αἰώνων, ἀμήν contains similar terms as 1:21; 2:7; and 3:5 and 9. Some have attempted to ascribe an underlying meaning to the phrase suggesting a reference to demonic forces, or a conflation of ages into one. However, it is best to take the terms in 3:21 as simply time spans or eternity, without any hidden meaning. The praise that God is to receive through the church and Christ should take place now and forever. Cf. M. Barth, *Ephesians, Chapters 1–3*, 376.

reveal the victory internally. The only thing lacking is the Christian's full realization of what has already occurred. In Ephesians the triumph of God is a present reality in the heavens but is not fully grasped by the readers. The prayers function to bring the readers' minds in line with the heavenly reality. The challenges and difficulties of present life in Western Asia Minor do not negate this biblical conception since the eschatological era includes both progress and shortfalls while engaging the enemy powers.[88]

In some respects the first half of the epistle ends as it began: an ascription of praise to God. The change however is from general praise to God for his rich blessings to praise for God's power that is appropriated in the Christian's life and the church corporate. This is an appropriate transition to the practical exhortations that follow in the second half of the epistle.[89]

7.5 CONCLUSION

Although Eph 3 clearly contributes to the present triumphal aspect of the epistle and has general correspondence to Isaiah's eschatological vision, it does not appear to offer substantive quotations, allusions, or echoes. The possible exceptions may concern the influence of Daniel and Ps 103.

In Eph 3 the author supplies an explanation of Gentile inclusion that was made clear through the use of Isaiah in Eph 2. This comports with the eschatological ministry of the Spirit in revealing a mystery of the church age. The mystery refers to Gentiles as fellow-heirs, a fact foreseen by Isaiah but not fully explicated. For this reason and others Eph 3 is inextricably linked with Eph 1 and 2 along with the present, triumphal, and Isaianic aspects evidenced there. This revelation and Paul's participation in it is reminiscent of Daniel's eschatology in that the technical use of μυστήριον in Ephesians may find roots in the revelatory and eschatological portions of Daniel. Several other factors appear to find commonality such as struggle against evil, and Daniel and Paul's self-identification. In terms of Ps 103 there are many parallels between the song and Eph 3. The psalm is found to express vivid new exodus imagery that may be in play in its usage in Eph 3; however, the conscious use of the hymn cannot be maintained with certainty.

The audience should harbor no concern that existing triumph is inconsistent with the circumstances of Paul. Also, they should not think that the announcement of novel mystery runs contrary to the previous citations of Isaiah and Psalms. The triumph is intact but is not entirely realized by the audience. This appears to be the reason behind the second prayer. The resounding truths of Eph 1–3 are to be fully comprehended and utilized by

---

88. Ch. 4 of this present work.
89. Cf. Lincoln, *Ephesians*, 220–21.

the hearers. Immediately after the prayer, praise is directed to God while acknowledging that he is already working in them, demonstrating a degree of present triumphal realities. God, Christ, and the church have triumphed, and this unfading accomplishment is currently working in the audience; but what is lacking is their complete consciousness of victory.

The author turns his attention to how the triumph anticipated in the OT (now a present reality), and finds practical outworking in the daily life of the audience. Further influence from Isaiah is investigated as well.

8

The Present INE Triumph of the Ascended and Gift-Giving Christ, Eph 4:1–16

IN THE SECOND MAJOR section of the epistle, the writer turns to specific matters of the Christian life (Eph 4:1—6:9). Although it is distinct from the first it is thoroughly built upon what has preceded, but does so in terms of practical Christian living.[1] Readers are called to live in accordance with the benefits that have been described: to "walk worthy" of all that divine triumph has provided (4:1). Five areas of conduct are addressed: unity (4:1–16), holiness (4:17–32), love (5:1–6), light (5:7–14), and wisdom (5:15—6:9).[2] Once again present triumphal aspects of Isaiah's new exodus will be considered.

It would be shortsighted to see 4:1–16 merely as a rhetorical bridge from the doctrinal to the practical section of the epistle,[3] or to see these verses as being primarily about unity in the church.[4] Unity is vitally important as are the development and growth that stem from it (4:13–16), but the segment contributes to a larger theme that is grounded by the quote in 4:8. Just as the initial unity of believing Jews and Gentiles (2:13–22) came about as a result of the enthronement of Christ and the church over the inimical powers (1:20—2:6), ongoing communal unity results from the triumph of Christ (4:8), particularly in regard to his distribution of gifts (4:7). The co-habitation of multi-ethnic saints in the household of the eschatological

---

1. Best, *Critical and Exegetical*, 359–60. However, Jeal argues that there is no direct support for Eph 4–6 in 1–3, but this is a minority opinion: *Integrating Theology*, 179.
2. Hoehner, *Ephesians*, 581.
3. M. Barth, *Ephesians, Chapters 1–3*, 499; Bruce, *Epistles*, 354.
4. Gombis, "Triumph" (2005a), 106–7.

temple (2:19–22) should become a daily reality in the churches of Western Asia Minor. This represents the "fullness" of God motif that is repeated in the epistle and is explicitly stated in the current section immediately following the OT citation (4:10).[5] Also, the demonstration of triumph in Paul's life and ministry (3:1–13) is to become a corporate experience for the Christian community. The power of God will continue as a theme, but what was once "within us" (3:20) now must be manifested "among us" in terms of unity.[6] The cosmic powers that seek to divide among race (Eph 2:15–16) must not gain the upper hand. Contemporaneously, the church's role is cosmic in nature; the church is the primary means by which the triumph of Christ is displayed and communicated to the cosmic powers (1:23; 3:10; 4:10). Therefore, the epistle's argument leading up to 4:1 prepares readers to see that the church is the locus in which present triumph is displayed. This is specifically seen in the church's unity.[7]

8.1 THE PRESENT TRIUMPH OF THE ASCENDED CHRIST IN EPH 4:1–10 AND PS 68

In the unity section, Paul is presented as ὁ δέσμιος (4:1) and therefore exhibits the self-giving humility that the audience will be called upon to demonstrate (4:2–3; cf. 5:25). The immeasurable blessings just recorded (3:14–21), which come by virtue of redemption and reconciliation, should engender modesty rather than boasting (2:9). In addition, as in Eph 3, Paul's status as ὁ δέσμιος proves no encumbrance to the sort of life expected of those who experience present victory.[8] Unity is built upon the oneness of God, the Spirit, and the solidarity of the Christian faith (4:4–6).[9] Baptism should be taken not as the theme of the epistle but as a public demonstration of cohesion

---

5. Eph 1:10, 23; 3:19; 4:13. Overfield, "Pleroma," 384–96.

6. Eph 1:19; 3:7; 3:30; 6:10.

7. Muddiman does not see an explicit argument in this section, but rather a general and elusive one: *Ephesians*, 188.

8. "This cryptic reference, then, is the means whereby the author holds before his readers the paradox of glorious calling and a shameful present existence. The writer presents Paul's own life as an *instance* of the triumph of God and his readers must replicate this pattern in their communal life" (emphasis in the original): Gombis, "Triumph" (2005a), 110.

9. Dunn sees Eph 4:4–6 echoing the Shema (Deut 6:4–5): *Theology of Paul*, 32. For a treatment of the Shema in the NT: Tan, "Shema," 181–206. M. Kitchen writes of the fundamental nature of Christian harmony: "Unity pervades the whole structure of faith, and is rooted in the oneness of God himself": *Ephesians*, 74. Dahl offers that the difference between the pneumatology of Ephesians and that of Qumran is the emphasis on the unifying power of the Spirit over the twofoldness of the spirits: *Studies*, 131–32.

with the corporate community.¹⁰ Although one body, God has distributed a diversity of gifts to his people (4:7–8). These endowments provide the means for corporate "fullness" marked by spiritual maturity and the proper functioning of the body of Christ (4:12–13), and are often associated with grace (3:7–8; 4:7).¹¹ In order to establish the letter's teaching on unity and gift-giving, the author appeals to the OT (Ps 68:18 in Eph 4:8). The utilization of the Hebrew Scriptures is introduced with διὸ λέγει, the only such formulation prior to an explicit OT usage in the epistle.¹²

Eph 4:7–11 is among the most difficult to understand in the letter.¹³ The complexity of the challenge is compounded by the problematic use of Ps 68:18.¹⁴ Most of the arguments begin by wrestling with the reversal of language, taking the "receiving gifts" in Ps 68:18 and producing "giving gifts" in Eph 4:8,¹⁵ which will be discussed shortly. Albright, Dahood, Charlesworth, Kidner, and others recognize the difficulty of understanding the structure and historical setting of Ps 68.¹⁶ However, Terrien finds a spectacular literary structure with poetic sequence and adherence to rigorous meter.¹⁷ He considers the psalm to be a diverse song of triumph, written either by David in regard to one of his victories, or by a postexilic writer extolling the triumph of the Jews in returning to the land. There is a particular focus on Deborah and Barak's victory over Sisera. Terrien goes to lengths to justify a correlation between the soldiers hailed by Deborah and the courage that

---

10. Although not the theme of the epistle, baptism in Ephesians should not be taken lightly. A case can be made that NT baptism reflects the exodus event: Holland, *Contours*, 141–54.

11. Dunn, *Theology of Paul*, 322.

12. The lack of use of an introductory formula in Ephesians does not indicate that the OT is not used. Hays shows that the lack of a citation formula may in fact indicate a greater use of the OT: *Conversion*, 2 n. 4; 16 n. 37; *Echoes*, 21. Without the use of an identifiable noun to specify the OT per se (4:8 and 9), the writer most likely assumed that the audience had an awareness of what he meant: Israel's sacred texts. The introductory formula in Eph 5:14 and its implications upon this present passage will be discussed there. For now it is understood that διὸ λέγει usually signals a use of the OT.

13. O'Brien, *Letter*, 293.

14. Ps 68:18 is found in MT 68:19; LXX 67:19. Cf. G. Smith, "Use of Psalm 68:18," 181–89.

15. Such as Moritz: *Profound Mystery*, 56–57.

16. "Widely admitted as textually and exegetically the most difficult and obscure of all the psalms": Dahood, *Psalms II: 51–100*, 133. "No psalm remains so obtuse to the exegete and theologian as Psalm 68": Charlesworth, "Psalm 68," 351. "Considered with justice as the most difficult of all the Psalms": Albright, "Hebrew Lyric Poems," 7. Cf. Albright, *Notes*, 1–12; Emerton, "Mountain of God," 24–37; Kidner, *Psalms 1–72*, 238–45; Weiser, *Psalms*, 481.

17. Terrien, *Strophic Structure*, 489.

the psalmist seeks to evoke in his audience (Judg 5:19; cf. 4:6). Zebulun and Naphtali (as northern tribes) proved conspicuously strong in the Deborah campaign. Benjamin and Judah, as southern tribes, held out for more than a century against the Assyrian juggernaut. If this emphasis is correct, and if the author understood it, a point is made between the confidence the writer seeks to engender and the battlefield courage that will be more fully developed in Eph 6:10–17. Ps 68's use in Ephesians could intimate not only present divine triumph, but the associated courage of God's warriors: "the power of Adonai is thus magnified together with the bravura of the ancient clans."[18] The psalm has to do with the victory of God over his enemies and the reign from his temple. God is to be praised for scattering his enemies and supporting his people.[19]

Ps 68 contains many images of the historical exodus. Verse one is a reference to Num 10:35: "Whenever the ark set out, Moses would say, 'Arise, O Lord, let your enemies be scattered, and your foes flee before you.'" The fourth verse speaks of God's presence in the desert, which is reminiscent of the historical exodus (Deut 33:26) and the new exodus (Isa 40:3; 57:14; and 62:10). Immediately following (Ps 68:5), the psalmist elicits the same thoughts as Deut 10:18 and 26:15. In 68:6, "he leads out the prisoners to prosperity" in keeping with the exodus. There is the mention of the desert in 68:4 and 7 where the Lord "rides through the deserts" and "marched through the wilderness."[20] Ps 68:8 focuses on Sinai and the quaking of the earth.[21] Sinai is mentioned again in reference to Yahweh being present in Jerusalem as he was at the mountain of God (Ps 68:17). There is the probability that verse 9 looks to Deut 11:11 and the plentiful rain of the Promised Land. In verses 11 and 25 reference is given to Exod 15:20 where Miriam

---

18. Several factors warrant this point: the OT intertexual quote in Ps 68:18 from Judg 5:12; the use of "Zalmon" Ps 68:14 from Judg 9:48; and the mention of Zebulun and Naphtali in Ps 68:27 from Deborah and Barak's song in Judg 5:18. Terrien, *Psalms*, 494–96; quote from 496.

19. Contra G. Smith who sees the psalm as the movement of God's presence instead of a successful military campaign. He understands that the gifts are associated with the Levites who are given to the nation (Num 8:14): "Use of Psalm 68:18," 181–89. This idea is refuted by Gombis who accepts a military emphasis while viewing the Levites in an ancillary role: "Triumph" (2005a), 115–16.

20. For a recent and rich addition to the literature on the use of OT wilderness narratives: Pomykala, *Wilderness*; Lee, "Concept of Wilderness," 1–16.

21. Tangentially, Kreitzer discusses earthquakes in Asia Minor and their effects on the populations in the region and allusions in Paul's writings. For Ephesians, his strongest suggestion is rebuilding the temple (2:20–22). Kreitzer theorizes that because of the destructive earthquake of AD 60, pagan temples in the region were in need of rebuilding at the time of Paul's correspondence. He cites numismatic evidence among other data from the time period: "Lycus Valley," 93–106.

and the women rejoice at the crossing of the sea. "Kings and armies that flee" (Ps 68:12, 14) could speak of Israel's exploits with Joshua, and possibly Deborah, during the period of the Judges (Josh 10:16; Judg 5:19, 30; cf. Ps 68:18 and Judg 5:12).

The letter uses the ascent and descent images in the psalm and employs them in speaking of Christ and the gifts given to the church. The psalm's use in Eph 4 is seen from a variety of angles.[22] Two possible new exodus parallels emerge. In the first, the leaders of the nation conquer the enemies of God. The leaders may have been Moses or Moses-like leaders, such as Joshua or David. In the postexilic period perhaps Cyrus and the release of the exiles are in view. The image in Ps 68:18 is the Lord ascending the temple mount with the captives and the spoils of war. Generally speaking, this could be what the author has in mind regarding Christ ascending in triumph and gifting the church.

The second main possibility turns on seeing Eph 4:8 as the historical ascension of Moses at Sinai, based on the epistle's paraphrase of the *Targum Psalms* reading of Ps 68:18: "You have ascended to heaven, that is, Moses the prophet; you have taken captivity captive, you have learned the words of the Torah; you have given it as gifts to men."[23] This scenario "you" of 68:18 refers to Moses, not God. Moses ascends Sinai or heaven, receives the Law, and returns with it. Similar to this position is that of Lincoln who maintains that the influence of Pentecost is used in Ps 68:18 stating, "As we have seen, the Psalm citation was connected with Moses and the giving of the law, and Pentecost, besides celebrating harvest, was more and more coming to be regarded as the feast which commemorated the law-giving at Sinai."[24] In this understanding, the quotation is not from the *Targum* on the Psalms, but rather finds its origin in an earlier rabbinic tradition. Lincoln sees the author of Ephesians adopting the tradition and applying it in a midrash pesher fashion to Christ. He adds that there was good reason to see these renderings of the OT text in the second century BC, the Qumran community, and the synagogue liturgy at the time of Christ. Therefore, Christ is functioning

---

22. For surveys of the positions: Moritz, *Profound Mystery*, 73; O'Brien, *Letter*, 289–93; Thielman, "Ephesians," 820–24.

23. *Tg. Ps.* 68. W. Harris has the most recent and thorough work supporting this position: W. Harris, *Descent of Christ*, 141–42. From the standpoint of Ephesians, M. Barth has an extensive discussion of the extra-biblical evidences: *Ephesians, Chapters 4–6*, 472–76. Other sources warrant consideration: Lindars, *New Testament Apologetic*, 52–54; Ross, "Psalms," 843.

24. Lincoln, "Use," 18–24. Moritz also sees the influence of a rabbinical tradition: *Profound Mystery*, 74–76. Similarly, Harris evokes an early anti-Moses tradition, but sees the descent of Christ as that of the Spirit at Pentecost: *Descent of Christ*, 198–214.

as the new Moses[25] and delivering Sinai-like gifts from God in order to bless his people.[26] Both Lincoln and Caird view the gifts, in turn, as bestowed by the Spirit on the Day of Pentecost, as indicated in Acts 2.[27]

Tied to both of these possibilities is the most significant issue regarding the change in the OT text. The author alters the third verb in Ps 68:18 from ἔλαβες ("you received") to ἔδωκεν ("he gave"). Not only has the person changed, but the subject acts in an opposite manner. Explanations include an early Christian polemic against Moses ascending Sinai and receiving the law of God, and those who see the modification of the text in keeping with the thrust of Ps 68. The polemic against Moses and the Torah takes into view the history of exegetical development and a theological explanation for the change. The problem is that there is a great deal of uncertainty as to whether the particular difficulties faced by the early church with Judaism are the focus of Eph 4:8. The other possibility centers the argument on the texts in Psalms and Ephesians rather than on a historical and exegetical tradition.

Ultimately, it is difficult to discern exactly why the writer opted for a change in the text; whether he did it himself or if the change was adopted by an early church convention.[28] In addition, it is unclear which of the options for Ps 68:18 best describes the evidence: Yahweh or Moses. There is a chance that the writer sees both in view, Jesus functioning as, or supplanting Moses by delivering a superior law; and Jesus functioning in Yahweh's place as the triumphant warrior. But it appears that the warrior option is more in keeping with the prevailing theme of triumph in Ps 68, as well as the numerous parallels with the OT text in Ps 68 as already noted.[29] Although there is evidence in other Pauline letters of strong warnings against the excesses of the law (such as in Romans and Galatians), there is little data in Ephesians that can be understood as an anti-Mosaic polemic. Ephesians

---

25. Whether Jesus or Paul functioned as a new Moses is beyond the scope of this study. However, inasmuch as the text of Ephesians will allow, certain parallels between Moses and Jesus, and Moses and Paul, are drawn. For further study: Balentine, "Death of Jesus,"29; Croatto, "Jesus, Prophet," 451–65; Glasson, *Moses*, 16; Knox, *Acts of the Apostles*, 85–86; R. Smith, "Exodus Typology," 334–38.

26. Daube considers another parallel with the exodus: captives and gifts related to the gifting of released slaves, and the plundering of the Egyptians by the departing Hebrews. But one wonders how this comports with ascending: *Exodus Pattern*, 70–71. O'Brien sees the OT roots in the concept of God receiving gifts to pass them on to someone else: *Letter*, 292–93.

27. Caird, "Descent of Christ," 541; Lincoln, "Use," 23.

28. Thielman discusses the problems and options in detail: "Ephesians," 819–24.

29. Lincoln, who opts for the alteration of a Moses rabbinic reading in Eph 4:8–10, admits to Ps 68's use in the epistle as Christ over the powers: "It certainly fits his earlier depiction of Christ's exaltation over the powers in 1:21, 22": "Use," 19.

2:15 ("He has abolished the law") is mentioned on the way to establishing Jewish and Gentile unity, and the law is employed in a positive fashion for ethical purposes in 5:31 and 6:2–3. On the other hand, there is confirmation in the psalm that supports the change in the text in Ephesians—whether Yahweh is receiving or giving gifts, and whether gifts are given to his people. It is found that gifts were received by both Yahweh (Ps 68:18, 29) and his people (Ps 68:12). Following this line of thinking, Christ's giving gifts in Eph 4 implies that he first had to receive war bounty. If the writer saw Yahweh as a triumphant king returning from war with gifts, and receiving gifts, it is not too far afield to see the king giving gifts, especially when the psalm explicitly states that the populous will enjoy the spoils of war (68:12).[30] This reasoning renders less difficult the picture of Yahweh receiving gifts in Ps 68:18 and Christ distributing gifts in Eph 4:8. Thielman concludes, "Here too good of a case can be made that although Paul's changes to the Greek text of Scripture are dramatic, they are consistent with the overall theological direction of the psalm from which his citation comes."[31] The author of the epistle's emendation of the text is in keeping with the overall thrust of the psalm. He uses Ps 68 to suit his argument without violating its central message. Penner would agree with Thielman's assessment that the use of the psalm coincides with the general thrust of the hymn: "Ephesians appears to allude to the general theology of Ps. 68."[32]

Another matter warrants discussion. The first section of the psalm opens with a call that God's enemies be scattered (68:1–3), then moves to God's care and protection of orphans and the poor (68:5–6), and God's past dealings with his people from the exodus to the establishment of the temple (68:7–18). The second section begins with an outburst of blessing to God for his daily care and salvation (68:19–20) and assurances that God will bring back his people (68:21–23). The balance of the second section describes the

---

30. "The prevailing custom that the victor divides the spoil is recognized also in Scripture": Hendriksen, *Ephesians*, 191. Hendriksen goes on to mention Abraham (Gen 14), David (1 Sam 30:26–31), Israel's enemies (Judg 5:30), and Isa 53:12, "he shall divide the spoil with the strong."

31. Thielman, "Ephesians," 823. Also, Thielman, *Ephesians*, 268. Hoehner illustrates the use of the psalm with the idea of a news reporter (Paul) summarizing an event (Ps 68): *Ephesians*, 528. As Thielman ("Ephesians," 823) notes, this is in keeping with Paul's pattern in Rom 1:17 and Gal 3:11 in his use of Hab 2:4. Similarly he utilizes Deut 30:12–14 in Rom 10:6–8.

32. Penner, "Enthronement," 16. For his entire thesis: Penner, "Enthronement Motif," Moritz maintains contra Penner that the central verse of Ps 68 should be 19, or better 35, rather than 18. But Moritz seems to focus on the central passage of the psalm without considering fully the entire thrust of the song as a triumphant warrior hymn and how it aligns with Ephesians: *Profound Mystery*, 69.

procession of worshippers to Mount Zion (68:24–27) and a prayer for the day when all kingdoms will submit to God's rule (68:28–31). The psalm moves from calling on God to act, to praising God for the past, and finally to a prayer for his faithfulness in the present. It is at the end of the first section that the writer of the epistle selects his material (68:18), which is the climax of the recounting of God's past faithfulness.[33] The verses in Ps 68 and Eph 4 show the reoccurring "captivity captive" from Judg 5:12 where Deborah and Barak sing of God's faithfulness in overcoming Sisera.[34] Psalm 68:18 freezes the moment of the conquering king ascending Mount Zion with his captives and receiving gifts. This section focuses on the culmination of the exodus, which is the establishment of the temple in Zion. The parallels with Ephesians converge upon the triumph of God, the subjugation of his enemies, temple dwelling, and the exchange of gifts. There is dwelling verbiage that pertains to God (68:5, 15–16, 18, 29, 35) and his people (68:6, 10, 13), and the scattering of the enemy (68:1, 2, 12, 14, 30). God's dwelling in Sinai is transferred to Zion (68:17–18). It is understandable that the author of the letter would select such a passage to begin the practical section of the epistle. It gathers together previous themes in the letter, but now will focus on an application to Christian living.

The implication is that the divine warrior of the psalm is adopted by the writer and applied to Christ. Miller points out that the protagonists of Ps 68 were the aerial powers of the cosmos, not just physical figures that ruled nations,[35] while Kraus says much the same.[36] This belief has correspondence with Canaanite myths of Baal defeating the gods of Yam and Bashan (Ps 68:15, 22).[37] This is in keeping with Arnold's understanding of hostile pow-

---

33. Terrien finds eleven strophes in the Hebrew of Ps 68: five ascending strophes (2–16) and five descending (20–36). The core strophe on the Zion sanctuary is the capstone (17–19): *Strophic Structure*, 489. The literary structure of ascent and descent reflects the theological content of the hymn.

34. The following readings add to the "captivity captive" analysis: NRSV: "lead away your captives." MT: Ps 68:18, שָׁבִיתָ שֶּׁבִי; Judg 5:12, וּשֲׁבֵה שֶׁבְיְךָ. LXX, Ps 67:19: ᾐχμαλώτευσας αἰχμαλωσίαν. Eph 4:8: ᾐχμαλώτευσεν αἰχμαλωσίαν. The OT intertexual citation from Judges could also comport with "snowing in Zalmon" (Ps 68:14): referring to a battle won due to the use of tree branches from a mountain near Shechem in the Judges period (Judg 9:48); God's preference for Zion over nearby mountains (Ps 68:15–16); or to fallen corpses and their weaponry scattered like snowflakes. For a discussion of the final possibility: VanGemeren, "Psalms," 447.

35. "The polytheistic impulse of surrounding cultures tended to produce the conception of the divine assembly marked by specificity, complexity, independence, and democratic rule": Miller, *Divine Warrior*, 102–11; quote from 74.

36. "Hostile powers that rage through nature and history": Kraus and Crim, "Enemy Powers," 125–36; quote from 128.

37. Charlesworth, "Psalm 68," 371.

ers in Ephesians. As noted earlier in this present work, there was widespread fear in Asia Minor concerning ethereal entities.[38] Lunde and Dunne's perceptive article validates the author of Ephesians' use of Ps 68:18 in conjunction with the entire context of the psalm, adding that the psalmist recounts the exodus as a basis for God's further actions on behalf of his people.[39] This coheres with previous discussions in this present work concerning the typological-historical use of the exodus in anticipating God's deliverances in the exodus actions of Christ (ch. 2). The added element in the current passage is that the author of the epistle enjoins a psalm that is comprised not only of present triumph but of the exodus as well. Although an explicit case for the author of the epistle consciously utilizing the new exodus aspect of Ps 68 cannot be made, it is reasonable to conclude that the author had the entire context of hymn in mind, including the typological correspondence within the psalm (historical exodus and future deliverance) and the linkage to the first-century situation (OT deliverances typifying Christ triumph and gifting).

In summary, in much the same way that Pss 110 and 8 solidly ground the opening berakah in the present triumphal thought of the OT prophets (Eph 1:20–23), Ps 68 does the same for the second portion of the epistle that focuses on applying the truths of the opening eulogy. The difference between the uses of a triumphant psalm in Eph 4:8 and that in Eph 1:20–22 is that Yahweh the victor distributes gifts for the practical outworking of his conquest. This is understandable given the change in subject matter at 4:1. When these three psalms are considered with the previous citations and allusions from Isaiah (Eph 1:8, 17; 2:5, 13, 17, 20) and other OT uses distributed fairly equidistantly in the epistle, a pattern emerges. The author addresses the apprehensions of the audience, and does so by incorporating key OT sources that appear to depict Yahweh as the indomitable exodus warrior. The people of God are invited by the author to comprehend and demonstrate Yahweh's victory in the daily affairs of the church community.

What is the timing of the victory in Eph 4:8–10? The triumph depicted is considered a past event with current implications for the audience.[40] Gunkel identifies Ps 68 as an eschatological hymn: "While the typical hymns

---

38. Arnold, *Power and Magic*, 167–72.

39. Lunde and Dunne, "Creative and Contextual," 107.

40. Several scholars see the aspect of triumph in the use of Ps 68 in Eph 4:7–10. Gombis takes things a step further by developing the ideology of divine warfare in the use of the psalm. This present work accepts Gombis's basic approach but would appeal more to correlations with the present arrival of Isaiah's vision rather than extra-biblical ideologies, such as *Enuma Elish*: Gombis, "Triumph" (2005a), 124. It is likely that the writer had Isaiah more closely in mind than Mesopotamian myths.

rejoice over divine deeds which have happened, the eschatological hymns praise the great deeds of God which belong to the future. In this context the historical tenor of the typical hymn takes on the significance of the anticipatory *prophetic perfect"* (emphasis in the original).[41] The military leader returning from battle with captives gives every indication of present triumph with a corresponding view to the future. The vision includes God destroying his enemies, caring for his people, and being enthroned in Jerusalem; similarly the vision includes what took place in the exodus period and perhaps during the time of the Judges.[42] The writer of the missive utilizes the psalm in a typical-historical fashion as he did Pss 8 and 110 in Eph 1, and Isaiah in Eph 2 (at Eph 2:5, 13, 17, 20). He employs Ps 68 to speak of the fulfilled victory of Christ and the distribution of gifts.[43] The conjunction διὸ (Eph 4:8) informs the reader that grace was already given according to the measure of Christ's gift (Eph 4:7), and demonstrates that the actions portrayed in Ps 68:18 have come to pass.[44]

In terms of the new exodus, the triumphant warrior-king in Eph 4:8 finds its immediate source in Ps 68, a hymn with explicit exodus imagery, but coincides with the same developed metaphor of the new exodus of Isaiah. This is in step with the role of Yahweh as warrior in Isaiah who acts on behalf of his own interests and those of his people. However, in Isaiah new exodus triumph is developed with a new eschatological horizon in sight. Isaiah views the deliverance from Babylon, but moves beyond Ps 68

---

41. In contrast to eschatological "Zion songs" or "enthronement songs": Gunkel and Begrich, *Religious Lyric*, 251 n. 2; quote is from 263.

42. Some see Ps 68:17–18 describing a military campaign in which God drives from before him all his enemies throughout the region from Mount Sinai to the temple mount. Terrien remarks that during Yahweh's military campaign his "power hurls the kings of the earth into a chaotic rout": *Strophic Structure*, 485–96; quote from 493.

43. The balance of the section, Eph 4:9–10, that immediately follows the quotation explain the past events in the ministry of Christ that culminate with his enthronement in the heavenlies (4:10). The descent in 4:9 has been interpreted as a descent into Hades (*descensus ad inferos*, Rom 10:6–7; 1 Pet 3:18–19; 4:6; Jude 12–13); or the descent of the pre-existent Christ in his incarnation; or, and finally, the descent of the exalted Christ in the Spirit at Pentecost. In this current study the descent is taken simply as the death of Christ that corresponds with his humiliation (and Paul's, 3:1, 4:1, 6:20), which places in bold relief his triumph. From the standpoint of Ephesians, Christ's death is momentary (1:20; 2:13; 5:2) only to contrast with his eschatological glory. A parallel is Phil 2:6–11, but there Christ's humiliation is emphasized for other purposes. Hodge sees Isa 44:23 behind the descent-ascent imagery: "Sing, O heavens, for the Lord has done it; shout, O depths of the earth; break forth into singing, O mountains, O forest, and every tree in it! For the Lord has redeemed Jacob, and will be glorified in Israel": *Commentary*, 133.

44. Moritz offers that διὸ "tends to be used in Ephesians to advance an argument from the level of abstract theology to parenetic significance or vice versa" (Eph 2:11; 4:25; 5:14): "Psalms in Ephesians," 192.

to perceive something far greater.[45] It will be an exodus of such magnitude that it will not be accomplished by a human king.[46] Psalm 68 is useful for displaying the triumphant warrior; but Isaiah exceeds this triumph and develops an entirely new nation—a new world. The epistle is not merely saying that Christ triumphs and gives gifts; it appears that he is using Ps 68 in conjunction with what the psalm utilizes in terms of the new exodus, and for that matter Isaiah, declaring that Christ ushers in an entirely new order. It will be, as B. Anderson says, "a radically new event."[47] Psalm 68 functions to highlight a particular part of the departure from Egypt but not the spectacular new exodus of Isaiah. This is especially noticeable in the first section of the psalm (68:1–19).[48] Both Isaiah and Ps 68 use the new exodus but their usages serve different eschatological purposes.

Finally, it would be shortsighted to see Eph 4:7–9 solely from the standpoint of gift-giving, as much as it would be to arrive at the same conclusion concerning Ps 68. The generous bounty is only made possible by virtue of triumph over the supramundane powers.[49] The picture is one in which the enemy is brought into complete subjection.[50] In taking the captives, Christ defeats the hostile powers that provoke disharmony in the church, whether in issues of ethnicity (2:15), anger (4:26–27), or familial affairs (5:22—6:9).[51] The path of ἀναβὰς εἰς ὕψος (4:8) is to undertake a course through the war-strewn atmosphere and emerge in absolute triumph. The writer speaks of Christ's victory in 4:10 as being "far above all the heavens."[52] His victory is presented as an excessive, exorbitant, over-the-top affair. It includes all the heavenly powers seen elsewhere in the epistle (1:21; 2:2; 3:10; 6:12), but now suffering further defeat. The triumph calls to mind nearly identical language

---

45. This is the observation of Hill, who argues for unity in Isaiah based on an understanding of the multiple exoduses that are in view. Isaiah 10–39 builds upon the historical exodus from Egypt to predict the release from Babylon (the second exodus) and Isa 40 and following builds upon the same historical exodus to envision the eschatological era (the third exodus): "Reading Isaiah," 100–107.

46. D. Carr, "Light in the Darkness," 306; Hasel, *Remnant*, 348; Ninow, *Indicators*, 161.

47. B. Anderson, "Exodus Typology," 191.

48. G. Smith, "Use of Psalm 68:18," 181–89. Cf. O'Brien, *Letter*, 292.

49. Arnold, *Power and Magic*, 56–57.

50. Ibid., 68.

51. M. Barth, *Ephesians, Chapters 4–6*, 477.

52. Lincoln: "The unique status ascribed to Yahweh in the OT and here in v 6 to the exalted Christ ('above all') as the high God whom the heavens cannot contain is now ascribed to the exalted Christ": *Ephesians*, 248. Cf. Jer 23:24, "Do I not fill heaven and earth? says the Lord;" and Bruce, "Now, part of the exaltation conferred by the Father on the Son is the sharing by the Son in the Father's ubiquity": *Epistles*, 345.

in Eph 1:21 (ὑπεράνω πάσης ἀρχῆς), which is a part of the central passage of the epistle that establishes present triumph. In many respects 4:8–10 is a re-explanation of 1:20–23, the only adjustment being that present triumph applies to gifting the church for carrying out victory in the daily affairs of the ἐκκλησία. Corresponding also is πλήρωμα, presented as a fact in 1:23; and in 4:10 where it is offered once again (ἵνα πληρώσῃ τὰ πάντα), but with the verb πληρόω serving as an aorist subjunctive, indicating the potential of greater fullness as church members attain to the mature man (Eph 4:13). What 1:20–23 did for grounding the first half of the epistle, 4:8–10 does for the second, with a subtle but noticeable caveat: the treatment of the victory in terms of gifts functioning in the church for purposes of unity and maturity.[53] Yahweh's enthronement in Ps 110 and supersession over his enemies in Ps 8 is rejoined in Ps 68 with Yahweh being the supreme head of the cosmos; he who provides his people with warfare plunder. Inextricably linked with these psalms is the striking vision of Isaiah offering revelatory insight, life from the dead, and the new multiracial composition of the spiritual temple (Eph 1:8, 17; 2:5, 13, 17, 20). In terms of this study, one of the outstanding features of this section of the letter is the utilized psalm's affiliation with the new exodus. When the new exodus function of Ps 68 is understood in Eph 4:8, there is reason to believe that the shared cosmic triumph (πληρώσῃ τὰ πάντα, 4:10) of Christ and his church is new exodus in nature, and that Christ's gifts are the ancillary benefits of the redeemed.

8.2 PROTAGONISTS OF TRIUMPH DISPLAYED IN CORPORATE FULLNESS IN EPH 4:11–16

Having established the triumph of Christ over the powers as the basis for unity and the distribution of gifts to the church, the author now lists several benefits of the victory that promote the maturity and stability of the Christian community (Eph 4:11–16). These benefits are necessary in the battle against the menacing powers that seek to sow discord (Eph 2:2, 15) and doctrinal instability (4:14).[54] The apostles and prophets, with whom the

---

53. Best suggests that ἵνα πληρώσῃ τὰ πάντα (4:10) is an aside that provides a fitting conclusion to 4:9. But a case can be made that the author is intentional here, indicating that present triumphal Christ filling the universe is manifested in the working of the gifts he provides. This would be a manifestation of the gift-giving feature in Ps 68: Best, *Critical and Exegetical*, 388.

54. Childhood, wind, and wave imageries (4:14), coupled with severe descriptors of those engaged in deceiving, provide insight into the strategies of the cosmic powers and their *modus operandi* in stifling the church's progress toward fullness. Their deceit is in stark contrast to "living and loving truth" (4:15): H. Moule, *Studies in Ephesians*, 112. Hodge provides a colorful discussion of the contrasting images: *Commentary*, 142–44.

eschatological temple is established (2:20) and who reveal the mystery (3:5), now take their place among others to equip church members (4:11).[55] As would be expected in a segment on unity, this section has an emphasis on love (4:15 and 16; cf. 4:2). Both God's love and human love are mentioned previously in the epistle (1:4, 15; 2:4; 3:17, 19) and later (5:2, 25, 28, 33; 6:23, 24).[56] Once again body imagery is used, but now as a living and growing organism.[57]

The author is not addressing giftedness for the entire church as he does in Rom 12 and 1 Cor 12.[58] In Eph 4 the gifts in view are people who serve for the purposes of equipping. The role of leaders in combating cosmic forces prevents the miscalculation that triumph is individualistic or based solely on one's direct connection with Christ. The outworking of practical victory in the Christian life is made possible within the corporate household of the eschatological temple (2:20–22) and through Christ's endowed intermediaries. This demonstrates once again that victory is one that is played out in a communal setting. The address is to the corporate "new man" (Eph 2:15) who participates with "all the saints" (3:18) "until all . . . come to the unity of the faith" (4:13). The phrase εἰς ἄνδρα τέλειον (4:13) portrays the objects of maturity with singularity, most likely with the church as a whole in mind rather than individuals. Through the work of the assigned leaders, the established πλήρωμα of the church (1:23) becomes a progressive reality (4:13; also 4:10 and 3:19).[59] Arnold makes the important observation that

---

Also, Bruce, *Epistles*, 351–52; Foulkes, *Epistle of Paul*, 122–23; M. Kitchen, *Ephesians*, 80–81.

55. The structure of 4:11, τοὺς δὲ . . . τοὺς δὲ . . . τοὺς δὲ, delineates four types of persons without attempting to contrast them; however, they all work with one goal in mind: Hoehner, *Ephesians*, 538; Robertson, *Grammar*, 424, 1152. Generally speaking, apostles usually bore special authority and established new work, prophets received revelation, evangelists focused on winning converts, and pastor-teachers cared for local assemblies. Yet M. Barth sees all four with a specific "ministry of the Word"; they describe men with something to say: *Ephesians, Chapters 4–6*, 483. This oversimplifies the distinctions.

56. The multiple references are a primary reason Hoehner sees love as the central message of Ephesians: *Ephesians*, 105.

57. Dunn, *Theology of Paul*, 548–52.

58. "The gifts are not gifts made to people but gifts of people": Best, *Critical and Exegetical*, 388. This is contra Wood who sees the listed leaders as those who receive gifts: "Ephesians," 58.

59. "The building of the body is inextricably linked with his intention of filling the universe with his rule, since his church is his instrument in carrying out his purposes for the cosmos": O'Brien, *Letter*, 297.

even the work of these intermediaries comes about through the ἐνέργεια (4:16) of God.[60]

Eph 4:11–16 does not contain an overt usage of the OT,[61] but the passage does echo earlier themes in the epistle, such as the body metaphor (4:12, 16), the fullness of Christ (4:13), and Christ's headship (4:16).

8.3 CONCLUSION

Eph 4:1–16 begins the parenetic section of the epistle. The exhortations find their basis and temporal setting in the first half of the letter. The section proper is grounded by the use of Ps 68:18, a hymn that predicts new exodus triumph, enthronement, and Yahweh's gift-giving. Psalm 68 fulfills a vital purpose in Ephesians by emphasizing present triumph through Yahweh's and Christ's largesse. The images of the psalm are in correspondence with Isaiah's new exodus primarily because the psalm itself adopts explicit exodus imagery to convey its message. Ps 68, however, does not contain the entirely new cosmos seen in Isaiah. As with Pss 110 and 8, Ps 68 appears to fill an important but supplemental role in the epistle. Once the entire letter is considered, a firmer statement can be made concerning the relative impact of the three psalms in comparison with the cumulative force of Isaiah.[62]

The picture in Eph 4 is one of completed triumph and the sovereign enthronement of Christ. In his royal capacity he endows the church with leaders that facilitate maturity and stability. This contributes progressively to an already-declared fullness. The writer carefully nuances the balance between the already and the not yet, choosing μέχρι with the subjunctive in order to introduce the temporal clause, καταντήσωμεν οἱ πάντες (4:13). The prospective and final force envisions both the potential nature of Christian sanctification and its finality in eternity.[63]

---

60. Arnold, *Power and Magic*, 160.

61. This does not prevent speculative forays. Some, such as G. Smith, see Ps 68 linked closely with Numbers and the giving of Levites as gifts to Israel. These Levites may correspond to the personnel listed in Eph 4:11–12: G. Smith, "Use of Psalm 68:18," 181–89. Other possibilities are Isa 44:26 in Eph 4:15 (with ἀληθεύων and ἀληθεύοντες, respectively), and Isa 57:20 in Eph 4:14 (sea and storms as a metaphor for life apart from God); but these appear to utilize common language without an attempt on the part of the writer to consciously adopt particular points from the OT.

62. It is the contention of this present work that Isaiah is used consciously in Eph 1:8, 17; 2:5, 13, 17, 20; 4:22, 30; 5:14; and 6:14–17.

63. Blass et al., *Grammar of the New Testament*, 383.2; Wallace, *Exegetical Syntax*, 479–80.

9

Manifestations of Present INE Triumph in Ethical Renewal, Eph 4:17—5:20

IN THE SECOND MAJOR portion of the epistle, the author establishes the present triumph of Christ over the powers as the basis for unity and the distribution of gifts to the church (4:1–16). Central to the argument in this section is the author's strategic mining of Ps 68. The particular verse utilized accords with the hymn's present new exodus triumph, which in turn coincides with the central investigation of this present work. Following the citation in the epistle, several ethical admonitions are put forth (4:17—5:20).[1] The ethical section has come under criticism from commentators who have wrestled with determining its place in the epistle.[2] Several possibilities as to its purpose and makeup have been put forth. Muddiman and Best see it as moralizing and not up to the standards of the genuine Paulines.[3] Jeal distinguishes no logical connection

---

1. For discussions on Paul's understanding of ethics: N. Baker, "Ethics in Ephesians," 39–55; Mott, "Ethics," 269–75. Older and general, but useful: Murray, *Biblical Ethics*, 214–21.

2. As suggested previously, the "doctrinal" and "ethical" delineations oversimplify the subject matter of the epistle. The "doctrinal" section does include aspects of behavior, and the "ethical" portion has references to theology. In the letter, the sections have not "been placed in two separate, watertight compartments": O'Brien, *Letter*, 272. H. Moule states, "the main stress of thought is now on the effects rather than on the cause": *Studies in Ephesians*, 103. M. Barth also resists the aforementioned nomenclature, preferring to see chapters 1–3 as doxological rather than doctrinal: *Ephesians, Chapters 4–6*, 426. Wood understands the first chapters as doxological as well, adding, "Theology is not left behind but interwoven with the moral exhortations": "Ephesians," 54. Cf. M. Kitchen, *Ephesians*, 71.

3. Best, *Critical and Exegetical*, 95–96; Muddiman, *Ephesians*, 32.

between this section of the epistle and the former, saying the second does not build from the first and each is able to stand on its own.[4] Lincoln suggests that the ethical portion is loosely connected with the first half of the epistle in that it is tied together with the rhetorical use of an epistolary sermon or synagogue homily.[5] Fee finds difficulty in seeing how chapters 4–6 fit together.[6] Some consider the ethical section to be a disconnected pastiche of ethical admonitions.[7] However, there are reasons to see a relationship between the doctrinal portion of the epistle and the parenetic section, and to identify clear argumentation and cohesion throughout the balance of the letter.

9.1 INE COHESION AMID THE DOCTRINAL AND PARENETIC SECTIONS IN EPH 1–3 AND 4–6

If present INE triumph inspires the composition of Ephesians, then it should be apparent in both divisions of the letter (chs. 1–3 and 4–6). A profound disconnection between the major sections would bring into question whether the author maintains a consistent argument. If cohesion is not established, then the case for the INE is undermined. The intent of this section of this present work is to demonstrate how the second half of the epistle consistently flows from the foundational elements of Eph 1–3, leading to a climactic closing in 6:10–20.[8]

Three points support cohesion between the doctrinal and ethical sections. First, Beker speaks of the "apocalyptic substratum" of Paul's gospel,[9] which is the apostle's view of the Christ-event and how it translates into the triumph of God over the cosmic powers. Beker says that this understanding of Paul's eschatology is the very element that brings coherence to the apostle's entire message, which includes his repeated summons to

---

4. Jeal seeks to understand Ephesians as an adept rhetorical homily: a specialized form of sermonic oratory meant to move an audience: *Integrating Theology*, 74. On the rhetoric in Ephesians: Witherington, *Socio-Rhetorical Commentary*, 221–3.

5. Lincoln does not see 4:1–16 having a clearly defined form: *Ephesians*, xxxix; xl-xli; lxxxi; 224.

6. Fee, *Holy Spirit*, 709.

7. Gombis, "Triumph" (2005a), 32–33.

8. Best outlines 4:1—6:20 in the following way: discussion of the church as the proper basis for ethical admonition (4:1–16); contrast of the present life of Gentiles with their former life (4:17–24); certain sins that can destroy communal life (4:25—5:2); similar listing of sins as in 4:25—5:2 but now within the context of God's judgment (5:3—14); and specific behaviors expected in particular households rather than the larger church community (5:15—6:9): *Critical and Exegetical*, 354.

9. Beker, "Triumph of God," 62–63.

ethical conduct. According to Beker's understanding, the calls to principled behavior need not be forced or awkwardly added to the austere benefits of salvation. Rather, a new way of living would be expected to flow from the apostle's apocalyptic message and the anticipated new age. Paul's emphasis on renewed living in the eschaton is after the order of the prophets (which are further argued in the following sections of this present work) and is in keeping with the entire vision of the final days. To speak of Paul unduly adding ethical sermonizing to Ephesians is akin to wondering why the prophets spoke repeatedly of ethical conduct in conjunction with the coming age. Contrary to those who see Eph 4:17—5:20 as isolated miscellany, Beker observes a coherent message that is connected together by Paul's apocalyptic vision. Lincoln agrees with Beker (along with Ridderbos and Sanders) on the importance of realized eschatology in Ephesians.[10] He also sees the bold and explicit references to present triumph in Ephesians, more than in any other place in the Pauline Corpus. Lincoln notes the change made at Col 3:1–3, where what is implicit concerning the church's triumph in Colossians is made strikingly clear in Ephesians (Eph 2:5–6).[11] Despite this agreement, Lincoln does not take the eschatological framework to its logical conclusion in understanding the place of the ethical admonitions. Beker does so by explaining that the inclusion of the parenetic section is in keeping up with the apocalyptic perspective. Understanding the close connection between present eschatological triumph and ethical behavior is vital in seeing how the major divisions of Ephesians complement one another and support the eschatological vision of the INE.[12]

Second, early on, the second section of the letter gives precise signals that flow logically and practically from the first subdivision. The ethical admonitions actually begin in Eph 4:1–3 where the writer calls on the

---

10. Lincoln, *Ephesians*, lxxxix–xc.

11. This is made more critical if Ephesians is dependent on Colossians. Also, in contrast to Ephesians is Rev 3:21 that envisions co-enthronement as definitively future: "To the one who conquers I will give a place with me on my throne, just as I myself conquered and sat down with my Father on his throne." In contrast to Revelation and other early Christian literature, Ephesians stands out in its emphasis on realized eschatology.

12. O'Brien notes that πραΰτης (Eph 4:2) is the designation for the poor and oppressed of the OT. It is found, among other places, in Zech 9:9. This may point back to Paul the prisoner in 3:1 and 4:1, and anticipate Eph 4:25 where Zech 8:16 is used: O'Brien, *Letter*, 276. M. Barth discusses the OT roots of the Hebrew term, עָנָו, with Israel viewing herself in this way after the exile including several passages from Isaiah, Psalms, and Zechariah, citing both OT texts and Qumran: *Ephesians, Chapters 4–6*, 458 n. 174. Two of the passages cited, Isa 41:17 and 49:13, are found directly in new exodus contexts, adding support to the assumption on the part of the prophets that Isaiah's new exodus included ethical renewal. The others depict God comforting and restoring his people from an eschatological perspective: Isa 29:19; 54:11; 61:1.

audience to live in a manner worthy of their calling. Dahl maintains that the ethical section is from 4:1 to the end of the epistle.[13] Hoehner notes that the conjunction οὖν draws an inference or result from what precedes (Eph 4:1).[14] Whether οὖν refers back to what immediately precedes or ventures further back is not crucial because the latter portions of Eph 1–3 build an argument that refers to previous material.[15] Additionally, παρακαλῶ ... περιπατῆσαι (4:1) carries imperatival force. In 4:2 the construction does not involve imperatives but rather two prepositional phrases (μετὰ πάσης ταπεινοφροσύνης καὶ πραΰτητος, μετὰ μακροθυμίας) followed by two participial clauses (ἀνεχόμενοι ἀλλήλων ἐν ἀγάπῃ ... σπουδάζοντες τηρεῖν τὴν ἑνότητα τοῦ πνεύματος ἐν τῷ συνδέσμῳ τῆς εἰρήνης). However, these prepositional phrases do function as imperatives because they relate back to περιπατέω in 4:1.[16] The construction depicts the listed expectations naturally flowing from τῆς κλήσεως ἧς ἐκλήθητε mentioned in Eph 4:1. This calling was referenced as far back as 1:18 and further integrates the second half of the epistle with the first.[17] The preposition μετὰ (4:2) speaks of the close association or attendant circumstances that are part of a worthy walk. If 4:1–3 does begin the ethical portion, or at least anticipate it, a stronger argument can be made for ethics fitting into the overall argument of the epistle.[18] In this respect 4:1–3 functions as a bridge from the doctrinal section to the practical, pointing the audience to what was already anticipated.

In the third place, the unity of the ethical section itself lends support to the cohesion and linkage between the first half of the epistle and the second. If the second half of the epistle has clear unity and intentionality, then there

13. Dahl compares Qumran and the ethical section, revealing similarities and dissimilarities: *Studies*, 132–35.

14. Hoehner, *Ephesians*, 502–5.

15. Ibid., 502.

16. Schnackenburg agrees with Hoehner in seeing the prepositional phrases referring back to περιπατέω, but also observes a conceptual connection with the participial clauses that follow: *Ephesians*, 162.

17. O'Brien discusses further similarities, notably love, but the theological indicatives in chapters 1–3 (1:4; 2:4; 3:17, 19) are interwoven with the practical imperatives of 4–6 (4:2, 15, 16; 5:2, 25, 28, 33; 6:24): *Letter*, 272.

18. Lincoln understands 4:1–16 to begin with an exhortation, but then diverges into a theological basis for unity, only to return to the exhortative in 4:17. He (as well as O'Brien and Bruce) cite Bjerkelund, who considers παρακαλέω (4:1) transitioning to a new section of the epistle but not necessarily to the parenetic segment: Bjerkelund, *Parakalô*, 34–74; Lincoln, *Ephesians*, 226. Cf. Breeze, "Hortatory Discourse," 313–47; Mullins, "Petition," 46–54. Best explains that the author needed to further explain aspects of the church before speaking about how they are to live together: "4:2–16 thus sets all that follows within the corporate frame of reference": *Critical and Exegetical*, 354.

is greater likelihood that there is a logical link to the previous section. A recent work by Darko approaches 4:17—6:9 from a rhetorical perspective.[19] He addresses the apparent inconsistency; namely, that the author argues for withdrawal from the world (4:17—5:20) and yet exhorts his audience to adopt Greco-Roman moral traditions (5:21—6:9). Darko concludes that the ethical section does not urge the recipients to withdraw; rather, the author's point is to foster group identification and standards that are in keeping with the audience's new status in Christ.[20] Furthermore, Darko asserts that the commonalities with Greco-Roman codes are largely shared by secular moralists; the difference, however, is the ideological framework in which the codes are couched, including worldview, self-understanding, moral values, and perception of outsiders.[21] From a rhetorical perspective Darko demonstrates consistency and unity in this section of the epistle.

In summary, some have argued that the relationship between the major sections of Ephesians reflect incoherence rather than rationality. They cite the apparent pastiche-makeup of the epistle.[22] But Darko and others reveal that this is not the case, particularly in the ethical section. This suggests that the entirety of Ephesians was composed with a central purpose in mind.

9.2 THE "NOT YET" OF ETHICAL RENEWAL, AND THE QUESTION OF COMPATIBILITY WITH INE TRIUMPH

The ethical expectations anticipated early on in the epistle (2:10) and made explicit in Eph 4-6 are not from the author's isolated imagination. They come about from what appears to be his occupation with Isaiah's vision. Ethical living is in keeping with the prophet's expectations of the new age, something that is overlooked in Isaianic studies as well as in Isaiah's use in the NT.[23] The eschatological triumph of God includes neutralizing the

---

19. Darko, *No Longer*, 29–31.

20. "Thus, they are set apart by virtue of this new identity in Christ but not instructed to withdraw socially from the rest of society": Darko, *No Longer*, 129.

21. This is largely Lincoln's position concerning the commonalities between Paul's lists and those found in secular literature: Lincoln, *Ephesians*, 297.

22. Goodspeed and his procession trumpet the argument that Ephesians was a cover letter of sorts for the Pauline Corpus, composed of an appropriation of Pauline homologoumena: *Meaning*, 1–75; Mitton, *Epistle*, 29–31.

23. In discussing Isa 56–58 Childs makes the case not only for Yahweh's victory but triumph on behalf of the righteous (those who live ethically). It is not a universal salvation for all since the victory is quite selective, bringing judgment upon the iniquitous and securing the welfare of the righteous: "There is no peace, says my God, for the wicked" (Isa 57:21): *Isaiah*, 472–73. In light of the verse just cited, cf. Isa 57:19, which is situated two verses prior and quoted in Eph 2:17. If the writer of the epistle was drawing consciously upon the Isaiah context, then the Christian Isaianic peace of

deadly effects of sin in the lives of his people.[24] In order to emphasize practical moral behavior in the second half of the epistle, the writer undertakes eschatological quotations, images, and echoes from Isaiah and other triumphant portions of the OT, while inculcating forceful ethical admonitions from Isaiah, Zechariah, Psalms, and the Pentateuch. All of these various places of the OT are resourced for moral purposes. While doing so the writer does not violate his primary trust of present victory, but rather reinforces it. It will be seen that the letter's approach falls within the broad stream of practice by the prophets and particularly Isaiah. As viewed in chapter 4 of this present work, the concept of triumph in the new exodus era is not necessarily absolute in nature. Both Isaiah and Ephesians agree that there is often a progressive sense to an era spoken of in potential terms. The first and second prayers of the epistle (Eph 1, 3) speak of potential knowledge and power that may be acquired by the audience (1:17–19; 3:16–19). In the same way it will be found that present triumph as conceived in the OT is not incompatible with a call to ethical development. This emphasis on ethical progress comports with the analysis of the INE in chapter 2 of this present work as well as the nature of the new exodus era observed in chapter 4 of this present work. The argumentation, following, concerning the OT use in Eph 4:22—5:14 suggests that ethical living is expected of those who participate in the new exodus. Such behavior includes times of both progress and regression. This will be seen when the OT usages in the ethical and panoply sections are discussed.

By way of introduction to Eph 4:17f proper, Christians are cautioned to no longer live like the Gentiles (4:17) and to put away former lifestyles (4:22). The warnings are situated in contrast to the expectations of the worthy walk introduced at the onset of the parenetic section (4:1), and speak of behavior that is influenced by the cosmic powers (2:2), and which exacerbate ethnic animosities (2:14–15). The actions are associated with errant doctrines (4:14) and ignorance (4:18) that stand in contrast to the truth that is in Jesus (4:20–21).[25] The phrase εἴ γε (4:21, as in 3:2) assumes the audience has heard and been taught that which follows in 4:22–23, that they put

---

racial reconciliation (Eph 2:17) is set in contrast to those whose wickedness is akin to a frothing sea that churns up refuse, bereft of peace (Isa 57:19–21).

24. Noticeably with Paul, the problem of humankind is the singular "sin" (predominantly in Romans), and the problem with ethical living is "sins" (Eph 2:1), but not without exception (Eph 4:26).

25. Properly understood, this is the eschatological Jesus who is the Christ, and the revelation that fell to the apostles, prophets, and other church leaders to divulge and explain (Eph 2:20; 4:11). The truth about him reveals an entirely new order of living, including Christians ensconced with him in the heavenlies rather than amongst the death and futile darkness of the former life (Eph 1:22—2:1; 4:17–19).

aside the former ways and adopt new creation life.²⁶ In this context the truth of Jesus is an ethical one that puts off the former life and embraces the new one.²⁷ This harkens back to Eph 1:13, indicating that the application of truth began with the audience's initial embrace of the gospel, but now should find fruition in ethical conduct. The former life should be rejected because it is a dark and bleak existence.²⁸ The epistle now enunciates what is expected of the church's heavenly citizenry, juxtaposed against earlier depictions of living death (Eph 2:1).²⁹ These grim elements are the very behaviors that break down the new creation community.³⁰ The language of Eph 4:17–19 is reminiscent of Ecclesiastes and perhaps Pharaoh's hardening.³¹ Although this passage depicts the unconverted, the description reminds the audience that the present triumph does not mean complete practical victory. The addressees still struggle with the possibility of returning to their former way of living.³²

In summary, present triumph is not incompatible with ethical potential. As seen in the analysis of the new exodus in Isaiah in chapter 2 of this

26. Hoehner, *Ephesians*, 594–95. Also, Ὑμεῖς is in the emphatic position: "(But) you did not!" H. Moule, *Studies in Ephesians*, 117.

27. Bruce finds difficulty in seeing a clear distinction in emphasis between "Jesus" and "Christ": *Epistles*, 357. The writer may have sought to emphasize the entire teaching about the Messiah, seen in both his humanity and deity: Stott, *New Society*, 179. Cf. those that see a tradition of teaching associated with the historical Jesus: Best, *Critical and Exegetical*, 429–30; Lincoln, *Ephesians*, 281–82; Wiles, *Paul's Intercessory Prayers*, 81–82; esp. 82 n.1. Perhaps Dunn has the last word when he compares Eph 4:21 to Phil 2:10 and its image of universal obeisance to the exalted Jesus: "Hardly expressive of a particular interest in the life of Jesus": *Theology of Paul*, 196.

28. The present active infinite of περιπατέω (Eph 4:17) denotes habitual action. Avoiding the debauchery of the former life was to be their custom: Fanning, *Verbal Aspect*, 332–33, 382–83.

29. M. MacDonald, "Citizens," 271.

30. Houlden, *Paul's Letters*, 320.

31. Gombis, "Triumph," 2005a, 141 n. 18; O'Brien, *Letter*, 320. The hardness and callousness of heart (Eph 4:18–19) reminds the interpreter of the state of Pharaoh's heart during the exodus period, but as of yet there is no evidence to establish this in the consciousness of the author of the missive. Cf. R. Watts who remarks on the hardening motif in Isa 6 and 29 that is undertaken in Mark: *New Exodus in Mark*, 218.

32. Gombis views the conflict as not between two natures that reside within each Christian (a theological construct), but between the church and the rulers of the cosmic forces. This is based on observing a conflict between powers and the church (2:1–2; 3:10; 6:12), and the activity of the powers on the old humanity (4:17–19). His rationale is that there is no direct instruction in Ephesians on church members relating with those outside the Christian community (cf. Eph 4:17), and from the writer's viewpoint Paul's ministry faced powers rather than people (3:2–13): "Triumph," 2005a, 140–42. This coincides with the nature of the struggle enjoined in the panoply metaphor and is an added distinction between Ephesians and Colossians (Col 4:5).

present work, the nature of the new exodus era in chapter 4 of this present work, and the argument that follows, ethical living is expected of those who participate in the present triumphal new exodus.

9.3 INE TRIUMPH IN NEW CREATION IN EPH 4:22-24

The transformation anticipated in Eph 1–3 and facilitated through Christ's gifts to the church (4:1–16) is now set in contrast to the former manner of life (4:17–21).[33] This new perspective is a way of life rather than repeated, putting off and putting on events.[34] The new being is created (κτισθέντα) in righteousness and holiness (24); whereas the corrupt old self is in demolition. Its corruption is in accordance with deceitfulness, much like the doctrines spoken of in Eph 4:14 and in contrast to the repeated emphases on truth (Eph 1:13; 4:15, 21, 25; 6:14).[35] Renewal takes place as a creative activity of God in the locus of the mind (τῷ πνεύματι τοῦ νοὸς, 4:23).[36] The

---

33. The truth that is taught in Jesus (4:21) is made clear with three infinitives (ἀποθέσθαι, 22; ἀνανεοῦσθαι, 23; ἐνδύσασθαι, 24) which are dependent upon, or function epexegetically in relation to ἐδιδάχθητε (21), that is, they further explain the content of the teaching. The infinitives in this passage have been understood as imperatives, indicatives, the content of the instruction, the purpose of the instruction, or the result of the instruction. The differences among the listed options are slight: Hoehner, *Ephesians*, 599–602; Lincoln, *Ephesians*, 283–84; O'Brien, *Letter*, 326–27; esp. 327 n. 230. Robertson, Parsons, Bruce, and others see infinitives of indirect discourse functioning as indicatives: Bruce, *Epistles*, 358; Parsons, "New Creation," 3–4; Robertson, *Grammar*, 1089. Best does not agree and prefers the imperative sense: *Critical and Exegetical*, 430–31. Although the infinitives should be considered as functioning as indicatives they do have implied imperatival force.

34. It involves putting away the old life (aorist middle, τὸν παλαιὸν ἄνθρωπον, 22), being internally renewed (present passive, ἀνανεοῦσθαι, 23), and being clothed with the new self (aorist middle, τὸν καινὸν ἄνθρωπον, 24). The former life is in the process of corruption and the new being is made after the likeness of God (κατὰ θεὸν, 24). Clothing imagery is used repeatedly by the author and will be discussed later concerning INE affiliations. For an in-depth analysis in Paul and Romans in particular: M. Thompson, *Clothed*, 151. To be clothed with Christ is to take on Christ's behavior in the new age and to eschew the provisions of the flesh. Cf. Moo, *Romans*, 818–19.

35. In terms of contrast Larkin explains Eph 4:22–24 as an antithetical parallelism: Larkin, *Handbook*, 85. Also, the articles accompanying τὰς ἐπιθυμίας τῆς ἀπάτης ("*the* lusts of deceit," 4:22) and τῆς ἀληθείας ("*the* truth," 4:24) highlight the contrast as to their character and value: Hendriksen, *Ephesians*, 215 n. 126.

36. Based on the reoccurrence of πνεῦμα in the epistle (1:17; 3:16; 4:3; 5:18; 6:18), and none referring to the human spirit, many take the term as the divine Spirit: "Be renewed by the Spirit in your mind": Houlden, *Paul's Letters*, 316–17. Cf. Titus 3:5; and 2 Cor 3:18. However, Muddiman and others see the term referring to the human spirit: Best, *Critical and Exegetical*, 436; Fee, *Holy Spirit*, 710–12; Foulkes, *Epistle of Paul*, 130; Hoehner, *Ephesians*, 608; Lincoln, *Ephesians*, 287; Mitton, *Epistle*, 165; Muddiman, *Ephesians*, 220; O'Brien, *Letter*, 330. Since in other places in Ephesians the divine

phrase in Eph 4:24, κατὰ θεὸν κτισθέντα, and other creation language in Ephesians (κτίζω in 2:10; κτίζω in 2:15; κτίζω in 3:9; and ἀνανεόω in 4:23) are reminiscent of Gen 1:26.[37] An entirely new creation is probably in view, with "become new" preferred over the weaker "be renewed."[38] The parallel usage in Col 3:10 emphasizes man's original creation in Adam after *imago Dei*,[39] but in Ephesians the focus is on the creation of man after the pattern of God himself, which affects the controlling interior principle of life.[40] This comports nicely with the thrust of Eph 4:24 and 5:1–2. The intended result is δικαιοσύνῃ καὶ ὁσιότητι (4:24), terms that together refer to virtuous living.[41]

Using new creation imagery, the author describes a radical break with the former life (4:17–19). In cosmic spatial terms the old life is still under the rulers of the cosmic forces, whereas in Christ the new creation has been undertaken.[42] Creation and new creation were already seen in the use of Ps 8 in Eph 1:22. Ps 8 suggested the restoration of man's place in God's creation. Eph 2:10–15 was also viewed in this manner. There the new creation takes place in the sphere of Christ and is manifested in good works. Also, Christ abolishes the historic divisions between Jews and Gentiles to create a new spiritual entity. These are newly created people (Eph 2:15) with accompanying good works (Eph 2:10), housed in a new eschatological temple (Eph 2:19–22).[43] The μυστήριον as part of the new creation was clearly seen in

---

πνεῦμα is accompanied by τῷ ἁγίῳ (1:13; 4:30), and τοῦ νοὸς ὑμῶν is the place of the activity, it is probably best to see the reference as the human spirit.

37. Schnackenburg's effort to distinguish ἀνανεοῦσθαι (cognate from νέος, Eph 4:23) and καινὸν (Eph 4:24) is refuted by Hoehner and O'Brien: Hoehner, *Ephesians*, 607; O'Brien, *Letter*, 329 n. 243; Schnackenburg, *Ephesians*, 200. The terms most likely function synonymously.

38. M. Barth, *Ephesians, Chapters 4–6*, 508. Abbott envisions absolute novelty, not mere rejuvenation: *Critical and Exegetical*, 137–38.

39. "The phrase 'according to God' means 'in the image of God'": Bruce, *Epistles*, 359.

40. Hodge takes τῷ πνεύματι as the animating and governing principle of the mind, as in 1 Cor 2:12: τὸ πνεῦμα τοῦ κόσμου. This inner working was previewed in Eph 1:18 "eyes of your heart;" and 3:16 "inner man": Hodge, *Commentary*, 156–58. Cf. 2 Cor 4:16: "our inner nature is being renewed day by day." Larkin concludes that the coherence of Eph 4:17–19 "is maintained by vocabulary from the semantic domain of attitudes and thoughts" (verbiage in all three verses) and by the use of second person plural pronouns: *Handbook*, 85.

41. Wild, "Imitators of God," 127–43. Best remarks, "a word pair describing personal piety in accordance with God's will": *Critical and Exegetical*, 437. Rom 12:2 is a close parallel as well, indicating renewal (ἀνακαίνωσις) in the mind (τοῦ νοὸς) that contrasts with conformity to the world (αἰών).

42. Gombis, "Triumph," 2005a, 132–42.

43. Thielman, "Ephesians," 825.

Eph 3:9. The locus of the new creation is inner renewal (no doubt corporately with individual applications; Eph 3:16–17) that demonstrates itself in the utilization of gifts in the body and spiritual maturity (Eph 4:12–16). The new "good works" (Eph 2:10) that are briefly touched upon, and the new corporate entity (Eph 2:15) are demonstrated in Eph 3:1–13 where Paul's situation is an opportunity for good works toward the Gentiles, as well as an occasion to explain how the creation of the new ethnic entity came about. However, the opportunity to more fully explain the good works arrives with the moral exhortations of Eph 4:17—5:20.

Hubbard points out how essential it is to understand the Jewish apocalyptic matrix behind Paul's theology of new creation (καινὴ κτίσις, 2 Cor 5:17).[44] Creation and new creation is a prevalent motif in the OT.[45] These indicate that the eschatological age involves a hearkening back to God's activity in the Garden and reworking of his creation after its original pattern. It is seen prominently in several new exodus passages.[46] They establish a clear linkage between the new exodus and new creation. In Isaiah the new exodus is contemporaneous with new creation, both arriving in the eschatological age. Isa 43:16–19 is an example of both motifs in close proximity: "Thus says the LORD, who makes a way in the sea, a path in the mighty waters, who brings out chariot and horse, army and warrior; they lie down, they cannot rise, they are extinguished, quenched like a wick: Do not remember the former things, or consider the things of old. I am about to do a new thing; now it springs forth, do you not perceive it? I will make a way in the wilderness and rivers in the desert." Isa 19:16–25 is a description of the renewal that will take place among the people of Egypt and Assyria. Both nations become devoted worshippers of Yahweh and share Israel's blessings (Isa 19:25). In Isa 66:18–23 the recreation involves both the cosmos and community. New creation takes place in both domains. Paul views the Isaianic eschatological age in a similar fashion, reflecting soteriological, sociological, and cosmological ramifications. With Christ "all things become new" (2 Cor 5:17; Gal 6:15), in the sense of a present reality in the inner heart of the converted (2 Cor 4:16), but also in the community of believers (Eph 2:15), and eventually in the Parousia (Rom 8:17, 9–23). In Ephesians the focus on newness bears on the creation of a new spiritual entity from diverse ethnicities

---

44. Hubbard, *New Creation*, 1–10. Hubbard's analysis does not include Ephesians and Colossians since he considers them disputed, but he offers helpful analysis in spite of this (7 n. 26).

45. B. Anderson, *Creation to New Creation*, 233–45.

46. Such as Isa 42:9–10; 43:19; 48:6; 62:2; 65:17–18; 66:17–23; Jer 31:15–22, 31; and Ezek 11:19; 18:31; 36:26.

(2:15), and the outworking of the new creation in ethics (4:23–24).[47] As Hubbard remarks, this is "strongly reminiscent of the ethic and eschatology of Jeremiah and Ezekiel."[48] Brueggemann surveys new creation theology in the OT including Isaiah and the prophets. He notes that the language concerning God's promises during the time of the exile changed to that of "intimate connection to and solidarity with Israel that is to be expressed as presence."[49] God himself led the Israelites through the desert during the first exodus (Exod 3:11–12), but there is a renewed and pointed emphasis on this motif in the prophets. Not only would the nation find renewal and homecoming but a national change of heart toward intimacy with God. The author of Ephesians reflects this eschatological emphasis, understanding the new creation as inner transformation, and also as a renewal that takes on communal effects. In another volume Brueggemann understands Isa 1–39 as being primarily focused on the old empty life, and Isa 40–55 and 56–66 as being concerned with the new life. He discusses the transformative power of righteousness in Isaiah, first seen in Yahweh and replicated in the corporate life of his people.

Brueggemann surveys all of Isaiah, but considers Isa 61:3 to be the most informative text, which includes clothing images and righteousness.[50] The donning and removal of garments (Eph 4:22, 24) are seen in conjunction with Gnostic texts and mystery religions, as well as rabbinic literature.[51] However more importantly, OT texts demonstrate a donning clothing motif. The imagery illustrates the adoption of moral and religious qualities, such as strength (Isa 51:9; 52:1), righteousness (Ps 132:9; Job 29:14; Isa 61:10), majesty (Ps 93:1), honor (Ps 104:1; Job 40:10), joy (Ps 30:11), praise (Isa 61:3), and salvation (2 Chron 6:41; Ps 132:16; Isa 61:10); or dishonorable traits (Ps 35:26; 109:18, 29; 132:16).[52] The Isaiah passages picture Yahweh dressing with strength (Isa 51:9) and Zion clothing herself with beautiful garments of strength (Isa 52:1). Isaiah 60:17–18; 61:3, 10–11; 62:1–2; and 63:1 reveal a cluster of passages having to do with salvation and righteousness while utilizing clothing imagery. In Isa 63:10 clothing is conceived as both salvation and righteousness.[53] The speaker rejoices in Yahweh who has clothed

47. Hubbard, *New Creation*, 97. Cf. Col 3:9 and Rom 6:6.

48. Ibid., 236.

49. Brueggemann, *Theology*, 171. Cf. Jer 11:4; 24:7; 30:22; 31:33; 32:38; Ezek 11:20; 14:11; 36:28; 37:23, 27; Isa 7:14; 8:8; 41:17, 20; Hos 2:23.

50. Brueggemann, "Righteousness as Power," 27–48; esp. 40, 46, 48.

51. Lincoln, *Ephesians*, 284–85; O'Brien, *Letter*, 327.

52. Best, *Critical and Exegetical*, 431; O'Brien, *Letter*, 327.

53. This is the case with the MT, but not completely with the LXX. The MT has both salvation (יֶ֫שַׁע) and righteousness (צְדָקָה), however, the LXX has only salvation

him (passive) with the accoutrements of both bride and groom. These are in contexts that are clearly suggestive of the new exodus age. Childs speaks of the use of Isa 61 in Luke 4: "A case can be made that Jesus himself ushers in the acceptable year of the Lord, and thus the citation of Isa 61 encompasses the entire mission of the servant, including his life, death, and offspring."[54] This same conception of Isa 61 is not far from what is put forth in Ephesians. In reference to the application to the advent of Christ, Childs adds: "'Today' is the fulfilled time. The new age of salvation has arrived."[55] If there is a conscious connection here on the part of the author of the epistle, then the awakening and putting on of new clothing are in keeping with Isaiah's use of awakening and the investiture of Yahweh and his people. This aligns well with how Yahweh's armor in Isaiah is to be adopted by the audience in Eph 6. The writer makes direct use of Isa 11:4, 5; 49:2; 52:7; and 59:17, explicitly using the Isaianic donning metaphor. In summary, Isaiah's eschatological vision of Yahweh's people clothed with salvation and righteousness may be on the writer's mind in Eph 4:23–24.[56]

Has the "new creation" of Isaiah, Jeremiah, and Ezekiel arrived according to Ephesians? Eph 2:10 and 15 indicates that the new creation has appeared. The language depicts completed action. On the other hand, 4:22–24 shows a mixed picture. Of the three infinitives the first (4:22) and the third (4:24) are aorist, denoting the action is complete or is an undifferentiated whole.[57] The taking off and putting on can be seen as having taken place; the audience had already been taught these truths about their new spiritual condition. Concerning this passage M. Barth writes, "[T]he aorist tense . . .

(σωτήριον) with righteousness following in 61:11 (δικαιοσύνη; cf., Isa 60:17; 61:3, 8; 62:1–2; 63:1). Therefore, the preceding argument depends on several possibilities: Paul understanding the Hebrew text, changing 61:10, alluding to 61:11 (or 61:3; 62:1–2; or 63:1) as well, or utilizing another version of the LXX.

54. Isa 61:1–2a is found in Luke 4:18–19 with Jesus identifying himself as the servant figure: Childs, *Isaiah*, 508.

55. Ibid., 507.

56. Cf., Isa 61:10 and the bride and bridegroom imagery in Eph 5:27. In both eschatological settings God has adorned a glorious bride (further discussed at Eph 5:22–33). Sampley says that a study of ενδύω in the LXX reveals an association with priestly vestment and suggests priestly purity, citing Isa 61:10; among other passages, 2 Chron 6:41, and Ps 132:9, 16: Sampley, "Scripture and Tradition," 103 n. 10. The common motifs are God's priests and people clothed with salvation, righteousness, and joy. The writer of the epistle could have had these in mind. Another parallel with the same motifs is Zech 3:1–4 where Joshua the high priest, once clothed with filthy garments, is given a change of apparel while the heavenly messenger rejoins, "I have taken your guilt away from you, and I will clothe you with festal apparel" (Zech 3:4; cf. 13:4). This, of course, is in proximity to Zech 8:16 (used in Eph 4:25).

57. O'Brien, *Letter*, 329.

denotes a once and for all definite, concluding action."[58] He adds, "Verse 22 asserts that the end of the evil way is already at hand and experienced: a realized eschatology of evil is deployed."[59] Lincoln maintains, "This injunction is not an exhortation to believers to repeat that event but to continue to live out its significance."[60] Hoehner continues, "[B]elievers were taught that they had put on the new person when they laid aside the old person at conversion."[61] Moule adds, "with regard to your (definite) putting-off [and] the fact that the new man was put on."[62] This implies that the old person no longer continues with the new person. The new replaces the old.[63]

The second infinitive (4:23), however, is present tense. The word choice, ἀνανεοῦσθαι δὲ τῷ πνεύματι τοῦ νοὸς ὑμῶ (4:23) utilizes the present passive of ἀνανεόω. The subject is being acted upon on an ongoing basis. M. Barth says, "[T]he renewal is to be perpetual and cannot be concluded in one act."[64] The author weaves the completed picture of salvation with the ongoing expectations of inner renewal. This creation takes place, κατὰ θεὸν κτισθέντα (4:24), which, as pointed out earlier is reminiscent of Eden (Gen 1:26–27; cf. Eph 5:1–2). The "righteousness and holiness" indicates temporal and qualitative significance having to do with the creation. The focus of the new creation is the newly created community, not the old. Therefore, Eph 2:15 points toward the re-creation having already taken place because those in Christ have been made new, with 4:22 and 24 concurrently suggesting a completed, undifferentiated whole, and 4:23 depicting a progressive

58. M. Barth, *Ephesians, Chapters 4–6*, 505.

59. M. Barth continues, "Every trait of the Old Man's behaviour is putrid, crumbling, or inflated like rotting waste or cadavers, stinking, ripe for being disposed of and forgotten": Ibid., 507. M. Kitchen discusses willful ignorance, comparing Rom 1:24, 26, and 28 with Eph 4:17, 22. He cites Isa 44:12–20 remarking, "This was a general view of paganism among the Jews": *Ephesians*, 85. There is a chance that Eph 4:17b–19a was lifted from Isa 44:18–19a.

60. Lincoln, *Ephesians*, 285.

61. Hoehner, *Ephesians*, 610.

62. H. Moule, *Studies in Ephesians*, 118–19.

63. Stott indicates how seriously misleading the RSV is on this score, rendering the infinitive verbs as if they were imperatives, and representing the written instruction as fresh commands. He offers substantial reasons: in the parallel passage (Col 3:9–11) the aorist participles indicating renewal is contemporaneous with conversion; if the infinitives in Eph 4:22 and 24 are imperatives this renders Eph 2:23 nonsense; and, the Colossian parallel gives more explicit logic—"Do not lie to one another . . ."—"seeing that you have put off the old and put on the new." The basis for the commands (Col 3:5, 9) is that there has already been a fundamental reversal in the lives of the audience: Stott, *New Society*, 180. H. Moule understands Col 3:9 favoring Eph 4:22 as "a crisis past": *Studies in Ephesians*, 118.

64. M. Barth, *Ephesians, Chapters 4–6*, 505.

re-creation.⁶⁵ Also, 4:23 is couched in the passive voice, emphasizing that any practical progress toward new creation is invariably an act of God as it was in Eden.⁶⁶ Although πνεῦμα is taken as human spirit (4:23) the transformation is nevertheless facilitated pneumatologically, both initially (Eph 1:13; 2:18, 22) and progressively (Eph 1:17; 3:16; 4:3, 4, 30; 5:17).⁶⁷ In terms of the timing, Dockery writes, "These two pictures of what believers *are* and what they *should become* are not in conflict. Christians have been transferred from the old era of sin and death to the new era of righteousness and life" (emphasis in original).⁶⁸ He goes on to say that the Christian life takes place "between the polarities" of the historical achievement of redemption and its consummation.⁶⁹

New creation is the basis for conduct expected of the hearers. This fresh behavior is presented as both fact and possibility. It is closely aligned with the type of ethical living expected in the new exodus era and is compatible with present triumph. The new creation and donning motifs in Eph 4:22–24 suggest linkage with Isaiah and the other prophets. The writer proceeds to specify in 4:25—5:20 the conduct that is due.

9.4 ETHICAL ADMONITIONS DEMONSTRATING INE TRIUMPH IN EPH 4:25—5:20

The source of the ethical admonitions in 4:17—5:20 come from the OT and Jewish traditions.⁷⁰ Scholars such as Abbott and Sampley discuss these in detail.⁷¹ Some commentators are inclined to see the use of the OT but through the lens of Jewish instructional thought.⁷² Thielman observes that

---

65. "In all this teaching the divine and the human are beautifully blended ... Nobody has ever given birth to himself ... Nevertheless when God re-creates us in Christ accordingly to his own likeness, we entirely concur with what he has done": Stott, *New Society*, 182. Cf. Foulkes, *Epistle of Paul*, 131.

66. Adam assumed a passive, sleeping position as Eve was created.

67. "The metaphor of 'putting off and putting on' clothes (Col 3:8–10; Eph 4:22–24) does not simply mean promising to behave differently. Rather, it is the gracious action of God's Spirit ...": Dockery, "New Nature," 629.

68. Ibid., 629.

69. Ibid. M. Barth attempts to capture the tension: "Our translation does not exclude an imperative sense but seeks to retain the ring of a happy announcement which includes an appeal": *Ephesians, Chapters 4-6*, 506.

70. Kruse, "Virtues and Vices," 962–63.

71. This is the thrust of Sampley's useful article: "Scripture and Tradition ," 101–9. Cf. Abbott, *Critical and Exegetical*, 139.

72. Lincoln, "Use," 42–43; Lincoln, *Ephesians*, 300. The OT usages are "more incidental and less elaborate than what we have encountered so far": Moritz, *Profound Mystery*, 85. This, however, is not universally accepted. Lindemann concludes that the

Jewish ethical discourse was common in Second Temple Judaism and Jewish Christianity. He offers evidence that the author used these traditions in the compilation of his codes.[73] Tied closely is the incorporation of wisdom literature. If traditions are utilized in Eph 4 this does not diminish the author's use of the OT, but rather reinforces the notion that he did use the OT in a fashion that was in part recognized by Jewish tradition.[74] M. Barth acknowledges that 4:25f contains a "storehouse of Jewish, Hellenistic and Christian exhortation" but without contradicting Pauline ethics.[75] Although Thielman understands that there is plausibility in seeing parallels with some of the specifics of the admonitions, he observes the effects of a broader biblical context at work in the use of the OT and its contexts. This current study and the discussion that follows is in general agreement with Thielman.[76] The five most explicit of these linkages are addressed along with a general survey of other new exodus possibilities in the section.

9.4.1 Speaking Truth in Eph 4:25 and Zech 8:16

The transformative pattern that began with the new self replacing the old (Eph 4:23–24) is now expounded in a practical manner in the admonitions that follow, comprised of old life conduct replaced by new. The strong inferential conjunction διό ties the ethical admonitions to the newly created life that corresponds with the moral image of God (Eph 4:22–24).[77] This should bring about truthful speech: ἀποθέμενοι τὸ ψεῦδος λαλεῖτε ἀλήθειαν

---

use of the OT in Eph 4:25 is unplanned: *Aufhebung*, 82, 86. But this is a fringe opinion.

73. Thielman sees evidence of similarly combined admonitions in: *T. Iss.* 7:3–4 (debauchery, drunkenness, stealing, deceit); *T. Dan* 2:1, 4; 3:5–6; 4:6–7; 5:1–2, 7; 6:8 (deceit, anger). He also observes the association of the admonitions with the same OT passages: *T. Dan.* 5:2 (cf. Zech 8:16 and Eph 4:25); Herm. *Mand.* 41:2–6; 42:2 (cf. Isa. 63:10 and Eph 4:30); *T. Jud.* 14:1 (cf. Prov 23:31 LXX and Eph 5:18): "Ephesians," 825.

74. For example, concerning Zech 8:16 in Eph 4:25, Lincoln notices the mediation of Jewish ethical traditions but acknowledges, "It seems clear that the ultimate source ... is the OT": "Use," 42. Moritz asserts that the author of Ephesians had such a profound and strategic use of the OT, as demonstrated in his employment of the OT throughout Ephesians, that it is unnecessary to conclude that his use must have been mediated through Jewish parenesis: *Profound Mystery*, 88. Cf. Moritz's discussion of Gnilka's failure to understand the difference between the use of Zech 8:16 by Testament Daniel and Eph 4:25.

75. M. Barth, *Ephesians, Chapters 4–6*, 511 n. 68.

76. "Perhaps Paul used a common ethical tradition with which he had long been familiar but, aware of the roots of this tradition in the OT, also allowed the biblical context of some of the passages used in the tradition to shape his own thinking as he composed 4:17—5:20": Thielman, "Ephesians," 826.

77. Hoehner, *Ephesians*, 615; Wallace, *Exegetical Syntax*, 605.

ἕκαστος μετὰ τοῦ πλησίον αὐτοῦ (4:25).[78] The citation is from Zech 8:16 with an inconsequential alteration of the LXX text—a change of the preposition and corresponding article from πρὸς τὸν (accusative) to μετὰ τοῦ (genitive).

Yoder-Neufeld, Thielman, and O'Brien detect substantial similarities between the OT and NT contexts, whereas Gnilka and Lincoln do not.[79] Dahl and Sampley observe a pattern in the section in which the OT (or tradition) is cited, and an application to the contemporary community follows. In this sense Ephesians may have followed the mold of Zechariah. The movement from the OT theological assertion and NT community application pervades the ethical section, especially if less explicit OT permutations are in play.[80] Sampley goes on to say that that there are probably more parallels between Zech 8 and Eph 4 than his brief article is able to discuss. The most prominent of his observations is the similarity of purpose: they both set before their communities a series of charges contrasting "formerly" and "now," while grounding the injunctions in a declaration of God's actions.[81]

Zechariah has in view the conduct of Israel upon the nation's return from exile. Yahweh will restore the fortunes of Israel (Zech 8:2-8, 12-15, 18-23). God returns to Zion and dwells among his people (8:3). Nations will come as well (Zech 8:20-23). Zechariah addresses the postexilic community on behalf of Yahweh. His instructions are to speak truth to one another. He admonishes the postexilic community to speak properly in light of the coming fulfilment of the new exodus (Zech 8:1-8, 11-13, 14-15; esp. 6-8, 11). Zechariah explicitly pictures aspects of the new exodus coming about: the task is not too difficult for Yahweh (8:6), he will bring his people back (8:8a), they will be his own (8:8b), he will act as in former days (8:11), there will be an inheritance (8:12), though they are cursed among the nations they will be a blessing (8:13a), Yahweh will save them (8:13b), and they should not fear

78. Best discusses the identity of the πλησίον. In Zechariah the person is a fellow Israelite; in Ephesians he is a member of a church in Asia Minor; rather than anyone in need (Luke 10: 29-37): *Critical and Exegetical*, 447. The term τὸ ψεῦδος is specific rather than abstract, links with 4:14 and 22, and stands as the antithesis of ἀλήθεια ἐν τῷ Ἰησοῦ (4:21). The cosmic powers that cause division in the community of faith do so through false speech. Cf. M. Barth, *Ephesians, Chapters 4-6*, 511; Wood, "Ephesians," 64.

79. O'Brien, *Letter*, 337-38; Thielman, "Ephesians," 825; Yoder-Neufeld, *Put on*, 133-34. This is in contrast to Gnilka, who considers Essene writings as the source: "Traditionen," 401-3. Lincoln is uncertain whether the author has made direct use of the OT: *Ephesians*, 300.

80. Dahl, "Bibelstudie," 107. However, Lincoln and Moritz caution against drawing such a conclusion. They do not see clear evidence of a pattern in Zechariah that the author of Ephesians follows: Lincoln, *Ephesians*, 300; Moritz, *Profound Mystery*, 89.

81. Some of Sampley's remarks reflect his conversation with B. Anderson: Sampley, "Scripture and Tradition," 108, esp. n. 18.

(8:13c) nor provoke Yahweh as their fathers did (8:14). The writer uses his message to continue admonitions concerning the type of life expected in the eschatological community. Zech 8:16 is closely aligned conceptually with Ps 68 (as in Eph 4:8), and both are in the same proximity in Ephesians (Eph 4). Both envision the subjugation of enemies and the ascension of Yahweh as Warrior and King. However, it appears that the author's interest in Zechariah extends beyond the triumph motif. He sees in the passage the type of living that is expected of those who are recipients of Yahweh's largesse. He chooses the OT text to focus on the interpersonal aspect of life in the triumphant community, and thus serves his purposes in the ethical section. The phrase ὅτι ἐσμὲν ἀλλήλων μέλη (Eph 4:25) verifies that the behavior anticipated grows out of the fact that the community is interdependent, and harkens back to Eph 1:23; 2:16; and 4:4, 12, 15–16.[82] O'Brien notices commonalities in both lists (Ephesians and Zechariah): they follow immediately upon promises concerning the new age, and in both places speaking truth is first on the lists and forms a prevalent motif.[83] Added to this is the common sociological concerns in the immediate contexts; both deal with peace and harmony among God's people, and Gentiles and the nations (Zech 8:10, 16–17; Eph 4:25).[84] Another parallel is "truth and righteousness" in both Zech 8:8 and Eph 4:24–25. Yoder-Neufeld considers the usages here as "the tip of the iceberg" (his words) concerning the function of Zechariah in Ephesians.[85] The evidence seems to suggest that the correspondence is pervasive. Kitchen writes, "The verse in Zechariah occurs within the context of a passage which is concerned about the rebuilding of the temple—this accords well with the Temple imagery earlier in the epistle—which also was an image of organic unity and growth."[86] This linkage between Eph 4:25 and Zech 8:16 lends credence to the purpose of this present work that the triumphal eschatological age was a force in the composition of Ephesians.

82. "Openhearted candor within the fellowship is especially enjoined": Bruce, "Epistles," 360; Cf., Gombis, "Triumph," 2005a, 144.

83. O'Brien: "There are six references to 'truth' ('*emeth*) in the prophecy of Zechariah. Apart from the admonition to God's people in 7:9 to practice 'true justice' (lit. 'justice of truth'), all the instances of truth appear in chap. 8 (vv. 3, 8, 15, 16, and 19). In Ephesians six of the seven references to ἀλήθεια ('truth') word-group appear in the paraenesis of chaps 4–6, four of them in this chapter (vv. 15, 21, 24, 25; cf. 5:9; 6:14)": *Letter*, 274 n. 274. Jerusalem will be called πόλις ἡ ἀληθινὴ (Zech 8:3).

84. M. Barth submits that the motivation for speaking truth in Zechariah is starkly theological rather than sociological: "For all these are things that I hate" (Zech 8:17): *Ephesians, Chapters 4–6*, 512. However, the admonition in Zechariah applies to spurious accusations in court, revealing clear sociological tones.

85. Yoder-Neufeld, *Put on*, 133–34.

86. Kitchen, *Ephesians*, 87.

Manifestations of Present INE Triumph in Ethical Renewal 195

There are clearly parallels concerning triumph and the ethical expectations of God's restored people. O'Brien remarks, "The salvation-historical and typological connections between the two communities, and thus the accompanying practical exhortations, are patent."[87]

Is the triumph of Zechariah one that comports with Isaiah's new exodus? In chapter 2 of this current work it was found that Zechariah presents the new exodus theme in keeping with Isaiah (Zech 10:10–12). Ninow has shown that the new exodus was a prominent feature in Zechariah.[88] This postexilic prophet adopted the new exodus, but in terms that included a new age that had not been realized in the remnant community. After the return from exile Zechariah anticipated a still future new exodus. The use of Zechariah's vision adds further new exodus associations to the epistle.

Finally, is the Zechariah quotation understood as present victory? Inasmuch as Eph 4:25 and Zech 8:16 correspond to the other present triumphal uses of the OT in Ephesians, it does. The writer asserts the arrival of Zechariah's anticipated eschatological age and considers it from the standpoint of the type of speech expected. It is incumbent on the hearers to adopt speech that corresponds to that age. In light of an unrealized eschatology, the "already, not yet" tension the letter expects the living out of the triumph in the ethics of speech that have not been accomplished in its entirety. Once again this is the eschatological tension of overlapping ages in the Pauline Corpus. Its full actualization has not occurred, but the overall thrust of Ephesians as emphasizing the present triumphal aspect remains; the author using Zechariah as "now" and "not yet" points in this direction.

9.4.2 Anger Without Sin in Eph 4:26–27 and Ps 4:4

The second admonition in this section utilizes Ps 4:4a (LXX 4:5a) and, to a lesser degree, Deut 24:15, in Eph 4:26.[89] The recipients are to be angry but not sin,[90] and are not to allow the day to end with anger. It appears that the

---

87. O'Brien, *Letter*, 338.

88. Ninow comments on Zech 10:6–12: "It appears as if certain elements that are characteristic of the first coming out from Egypt form a paradigm for the new eschatological exodus": *Indicators*, 234.

89. The phrase in Ps 4:4 and Eph 4:26 is exactly the same. Abbott assumes the use of the OT as do most commentators: *Critical and Exegetical*, 139; Caird, *Letters from Prison*, 82. Lincoln, O'Brien, Best, and others note similar phrases in Hellenistic and Qumran sources: Best, *Critical and Exegetical*, 448–49; Lincoln, *Ephesians*, 301–2; O'Brien, *Letter*, 340.

90. Cf. Stählin, "Ὀργή," V:421. The present passive imperative of ὀργίζεσθε should probably not be read as an imperative, but in a concessive sense that allows for the hypothetical: McKay, *Syntax of the Verb*, 81. Agreeing: Best, *Critical and Exegetical*, 448; Lincoln, *Ephesians*, 301. Cf. M. Barth, *Ephesians, Chapters 4–6*, 513–15; Hoehner,

author of the epistle has the wider context of the psalm in mind since the OT writer addresses God as righteous (Ps 4:1), forbids deception (Ps 4:2), bids his hearers contemplate Yahweh at the close of the day (Ps 4:4b), and calls upon his audience to consider the peace and security Yahweh brings (Ps 4:8).[91] Moritz recognizes the author of Ephesians using the experience of the psalmist.[92] The hymn writer's feelings of agitation are brought upon him by the deception of his enemies (Ps 4:2); thus, he receives warning not to sin (Ps 4:5), and receives God's peace (4:7–8).[93] The verbiage of Deut 24:15 may or may not be an intentional usage by the writer of the epistle but some parallels exist.[94]

To succumb to the temptation of uncontrolled anger would be a grave tactical error in the ongoing battle with the devil (Eph 4:27).[95] This would provide him an opportunity to exploit anger in the eschatological community. Such behavior is not in keeping with putting off the old life (Eph 4:22) and living as the newly created corporate man (Eph 2:16).

Ps 4 and Deut 24 do not exhibit the new exodus. However, the two passages do clearly coincide with the overall thrust of Ephesians noted thus

---

Ephesians, 618–23; Schnackenburg, *Ephesians*, 207. O'Brien discusses the possibility that ὀργίζεσθε means righteous anger, while the anger of 4:31 is sinful. This is possible and seems to comport more accurately with contexts in Ps 4:4a and Deut 24:15 (cf. n. 94): *Letter*, 339–40. Wallace takes the phrase as an obligation to become angry in church discipline situations, considering the usage of Eph 4:26 in Pol. *Phil.* 12.1. But this possibility seems to lack palpable evidence: Wallace, "Command or Condition?" 353–72. Regardless of whether the anger is righteous or sinful there is reason for limitation. The Hebrew counterpart, רָגַז usually speaks of agitation growing out of a deep emotion. It comports well with the passive, ὀργίζεσθε. Perhaps there is a distant allusion to Gen 4:7 and Cain's anger, "sin is lurking at the door; its desire is for you." VanGemeren discusses this possibility: "Psalms," 80–86. Cf. Dahood, *Psalms I: 1–50*, 22–27.

91. Moritz, *Profound Mystery*, 90; Thielman, "Ephesians," 825. Craigie's careful analysis of the psalm is noteworthy: Craigie, *Psalms 1–50*, 77–83.

92. Moritz, *Profound Mystery*, 91.

93. H. Moule opens the possibility that the occasion of Ps 4 was the temptation on the part of David's followers to level wrath upon Absalom and his retinue (2 Sam 19:22): *Studies in Ephesians*, 122. To a lesser degree the same might be said of the urging on the part of David's men to take revenge on Saul in a cave (1 Sam 24:4), or later as Saul is bivouacked in the wilderness (1 Sam 26:6–12).

94. The common phrase in Deut 24:15, οὐκ ἐπιδύσεται ὁ ἥλιος ἐπ᾽ αὐτῷ appears to have confluence with Eph 4:25: an agitated heart meditating upon God at the end of the day (Ps 4:4a), and an angry laborer who has not received proper recompense at the close of the workday (Deut 24:15). The worker in Deuteronomy is potentially and rightfully angry. Similarly, in his nighttime vigil the psalmist is distressed over those who deceive and mock.

95. Gombis, "Triumph," 2005a, 144. According to Arnold, providing the devil an opportunity was a concept familiar to Judaism, linked to anger and falsehood, and led to God's withdrawal. He cites *T. Dan* 4:7: *Power and Magic*, 65.

far, including the present triumphal possibilities in the epistle. A feature of triumph is overcoming the devil who seeks an opportunity (Eph 4:26–27). The "not yet" victory is stipulated upon the community members who take action in the inner man (4:16) through the divine power granted in the Holy Spirit (4:16). The old life that was laid aside at conversion (Eph 4:20–21) must be actualized. This person has been freed from the corruption and deceitfulness of the futile mind (4:14, 17–24) and has put on the moral image of God likened to truth and righteousness; but this becomes an experience as he chooses not to sin through uncontrolled anger. The cosmic battle anticipates the extended warfare metaphor in Eph 6:10–17, notifying the reader that the battlefield with the forces is primarily in the mind.[96] Managing the mundane affairs of anger in the church community is a critical area of the cosmic battle.[97] Best summarizes: "However 'realised' AE's [author of Ephesians] theology may be, he is too wise to ignore the imperfections of believers, and in this he differs in no way from the remainder of the NT despite the peculiarity of his views in 2:5f."[98]

9.4.3 Grieving the Holy Spirit in Eph 4:30 and Isa 63:10

After admonitions to speak truth (Eph 4:25), control anger (Eph 4:26–27), labor rather than steal (Eph 4:28),[99] and allow no unwholesome speech but speak in grace-giving ways (Eph 4:29), the writer calls upon the audience to refrain from grieving the Holy Spirit (Eph 4:30). Stott suggests that the apparently inopportune inclusion of the Spirit may reflect the author's conception of powers and personalities behind human action. Just as the devil seeks for opportunity (Eph 4:27) the Spirit does as well, but in an altogether sacred and "holy" sense.[100] The language echoes Isa 63:10, but is an alteration of the Hebrew (וְעִצְּבוּ אֶת־רוּחַ קָדְשׁוֹ, "they grieved his Holy Spirit") or LXX (παρώξυναν τὸ πνεῦμα τὸ ἅγιον αὐτοῦ, "they provoked his Holy Spirit") renderings.

Paul's similar but expanded recounting of Israel's provocation of God's jealousy in the wilderness is found in 1 Cor 10:1–22. There he uses exodus events to warn the NT people of God to refrain from similar conduct.[101]

---

96. The mind as the *locus* of the spiritual battle was foreseen as well in Eph 1:17; 2:3; 3:10, 16; and 4:13, 17–19, 23.

97. Cf. Page, *Powers of Evil*, 188–89.

98. Best, *Critical and Exegetical*, 451.

99. Also, stealing may draw from the Decalogue (Exod 20:15; cf. Eph 6:2–3).

100. Stott, *New Society*, 189.

101. Enns, "Moveable Well," 23–38; Howard, "Christ Our Passover," 97–108; Thielman, "Ephesians," 826.

However, the passage in Ephesians is less explicit or expansive, and the immediate OT grounding for Ephesians is found in Isaiah rather than Exodus and Numbers. However, Fishbane observes the new exodus motif in Isa 63 that has clear parallels with Exod 33:12–14.[102] Isaiah 63 portrays messianic judgment and victory (Isa 63:1–6), followed by the prophet's intercession on behalf of Israel. He recalls Yahweh's past faithfulness during the exodus period, including how he dealt with them in lovingkindness (Isa 63:7), chose them (Isa 63:8), became their savior (Isa 63:8), and redeemed them (Isa 63:9). The chapter repeatedly emphasizes the role of the Spirit as evidence of God's presence during this turbulent period of the nation's history (Isa 63:10, 11, 14; with the appellative קָדְשׁוֹ in 10 and 11). The Spirit was among his people but they grieved him.[103]

The work of the Spirit was already established in Ephesians, as the one who seals (1:13); provides access to the Father (2:18); reveals the mystery (3:5); provides inner strengthening (3:16); models unity (4:3–4); and later, the one who controls (5:18), utilizes the word (6:17); and facilitates prayer (6:18).[104] In the present passage the ministry of the Spirit may be thwarted or grieved (λυπέω).[105] The basic meaning of the verb is to cause grief, pain, sadness, sorrow, or distress. It is used often in the LXX.[106] The admonition echoes Eph 1:13 where the Spirit seals for the day of redemption,[107] which should now provide motivation not to act in ways incompatible with his wishes.[108] The warning is to refrain from living in a manner that opposes

---

102. Fishbane, "Motif," 138–40.

103. Fee, "Reflections," 131–34.

104. Ridderbos properly refers to the Spirit as "pre-eminently the eschatological gift," but not every occurrence of the Spirit in the NT signals the Parousia: *Paul*, 87. Vos speaks along similar lines: *Pauline Eschatology*, 160–71; esp. 170.

105. This in contrast to quenching the Spirit, as in stifling the gift of prophecy (1 Thess 5:19; cf. 4:8): Bruce, "Epistles," 363. However, the admonitions concerning the Spirit and man's sin is generally in keeping with resisting the Spirit in Acts (Acts 7:51) and tangentially to the blasphemy of the Spirit (Matt 12:41; Mark 3:29; Luke 12:10). For a detailed analysis of λύπη: Bultmann, "Λύπη Κτλ," IV:314–25; Louw and Nida, *Lexicon*, 25.75.

106. Esp. 2 Sam 13:21, where David did not grieve the spirit of Amnon, οὐκ ἐλύπησεν τὸ πνεῦμα.

107. "Sealing" (σφραγίζω) connotes ownership: Dunn, *Theology of Paul*, 330, 453. Cf. Kennedy, "Spirit as a Pledge," 276–79. Best sees the use of "day of redemption" rather than "day of the Lord" emphasizing the deliverance of Christians rather than judgment on unbelievers: *Critical and Exegetical*, 459. Cf. Kreitzer, *Jesus and God*, 112–13, 128–29.

108. The coordinating conjunction καί (Eph 4:30) suggests that the passage does not begin a new section but is added to the last injunction: Abbott, *Critical and Exegetical*, 143; Hoehner, *Ephesians*, 631; Lincoln, *Ephesians*, 307; Robinson, *Paul's*

the desires of the Spirit who seeks to bring unity and harmony in the divine household, and who guarantees ultimate salvation.[109] The ethical problems not only violate the wishes of the Holy Spirit, they are also not in keeping with God's purposes in uniting and causing the proper functioning of the church body (Eph 4:1–16; esp. 4:3). The violation of the inclinations of the Spirit and ethical failures leads to the breakdown of communal life in the eschatological community and forms impediments contrary to divine will.[110]

Does this particular admonition indicate that the triumphal aspect of the INE has arrived? As noted previously by Fishbane, Isa 63:10 is clearly new exodus, and the context there has parallels to Eph 4. O'Brien notes that within Eph 4:30 "grieve" is juxtaposed with "redemption" and as such should recall the Israelites who were redeemed the night of the exodus but who quickly grieved Yahweh in the wilderness.[111] In Isaiah's new exodus the ethical misconduct toward the Spirit by the wilderness wanderers is the basis for proper conduct in the new exodus. Inasmuch as the new exodus is present, the conduct expected is part of the current triumph of God.

In summary, by listing the ethical admonitions the author of the letter puts forth the type of conduct that corresponds to life in the divine household. The present eschatological age is assumed, but the ethical admonitions reveal that short term victories depend on the choices and actions of the eschatological people of God. Inasmuch as the behaviors expected of the new community would be incumbent upon Israel in Isaiah and Zechariah, they are also in view among the Christians in Western Asia Minor. Generally speaking, the writer places the ethical requirements expected of new exodus Israel upon the church, with the added emphasis of present triumph.

The ethical admonitions from Isaiah, Zechariah, and the psalmist are brought to bear in the final age that is presently experienced by the audience. This is similar to the ethical admonitions in 1 Cor 10 where Israel and the exodus are used explicitly. God's people were to practice proper ethical

---

Epistle, 113. However, the caution against grieving the Spirit has central importance to the entire paragraph, 4:25—5:2, not just wholesome speech expected in 4:29: M. Barth, *Ephesians, Chapters 4–6*, 547–49; O'Brien, *Letter*, 345–46; Schnackenburg, *Ephesians*, 209. Best notices the difference in this admonition that sets it apart from the rest because it contains only the prohibition, while M. Barth takes the occasion to discuss the position that the section is made of collected and re-edited Pauline materials: M. Barth, *Ephesians, Chapters 4–6*, 548; Best, *Critical and Exegetical*, 457.

109. The Spirit is, "the Author of every human virtue": Hendriksen, *Ephesians*, 221.

110. Gombis, "Triumph," 2005a, 145.

111. O'Brien is forthright in seeing the new exodus in this portion of Ephesians, indicating that there are "salvation-historical and, ultimately, theological connections between this New Testament text and its Old Testament antecedents." The indicative: Israel grieved; becomes an imperative in the realized age: do not grieve: *Letter*, 346–49.

conduct seeing that they were those "on whom the ends of the ages have come" (1 Cor 10:11). In Ephesians the author has a similar typical-historical perspective concerning Israel in the wilderness. The terminus of the ages had been heaped upon the church; however, rather than Paul rebuking his audience, as was the case with the combative Corinthians, the author of the epistle inspires them.[112]

9.4.4 Light Over Darkness in Eph 4:31—5:14 and Isa 26:19; 60:1

The heart of the ethical section continues but now with an emphasis on the eschatological destinies of the old and new humanities (Eph 5:3–6) and the contrasts between spiritual light and darkness (Eph 5:7–14). This segment contains common themes with the previous portions of the epistle, and demonstrates the integrated nature of the letter.[113] The audience is called to further avoid grieving the Holy Spirit by putting away bitterness and clamor, and by practicing tender-hearted living after the pattern of Christ (Eph 4:31–32). The positive actions are tantamount to imitating the God after whom they are created (Eph 4:24) and loving others following the model of Christ who sacrificed all for them (Eph 5:1–2).[114] Several warnings follow against sexual vices (Eph 5:3–4) along with judgment upon such lifestyles and kingdom disinheritance (Eph 5:4–6). An elongated light-darkness schema contrasts life under the wrath of God with that which is pleasing to the Lord (Eph 5:7–14). This corresponds to the previous contrasts that marked the section since 4:22.

Throughout this current segment there are several OT verbal parallels and concepts. The primary OT new exodus allusions are Messiah the paschal sacrifice (5:2), ethical sexual conduct in the eschatological community (5:3–4), disinheritance and judgment upon those who practice such behavior (5:5–6), and the light-darkness metaphor throughout the OT (5:7–13). The allusion to Christ's paschal sacrifice in Eph 5:1–2 is strengthened by the previous mentions (Eph 1:7; 2:13, 16). As discussed earlier in these passages

---

112. "But even if believers already sit with Christ in the heavenlies (2:6) they are still engaged in a struggle with sin and the powers of evil . . . It cannot be denied that the letter contains an unresolved eschatological tension; to insist that the deliverance is fully accomplished is to ignore one side of this tension": Best, *Critical and Exegetical*, 459.

113. Past emphases in the epistle continue in this section: living out the likeness of God (4:24 with 5:1–2); walking in love (5:2 with 4:2, 15, 16); proper speech (5:3–4, 12 with 4:15, 25, 29, 31); inheritance (5:5 with 1:11, 14, 18); wrath (5:5 with 2:3); righteousness and truth (5:9 with 4:15, 21); learning (5:10 with 4:14–15, 20–21); and the Spirit (5:18 with 1:13; 2:18; 3:5, 16; 4:3, 4, 30).

114. Eph 5:1–2 sums up the immediate previous admonitions with the introductory οὖν, mining out the effects of choosing new life ethical living (4:25–32): O'Brien, *Letter*, 352.

in Ephesians (ch. 5.3 of this present work), the paschal sacrifice of Christ is rooted in the exodus and prominent in the new exodus. Specific to "fragrant aroma" (Eph 5:2) is Gen 8:21, and Exod 29:18, 25, 41. In Ephesians the wafting aroma of Christ's sacrificial death becomes a benchmark for Christian discipleship. However, the most prominent OT motif in this section is light-darkness. There are important reasons for considering aspects of Isaiah's new exodus in this metaphor in Eph 5:13–14.

The light-darkness metaphor in Eph 4:31—5:14[115] is a baffling passage, both in terms of source material[116] and those who are addressed. These questions have bearing upon whether the triumphant new exodus is in view.[117] Some see the focus to be upon those outside the church who remain in darkness (this is the "evangelistic" interpretation), while others identify them as Christians who are grappling with the dark temptations of the past.[118] Engberg-Pederson takes the latter position, asserting that the exposure of sin (Eph 5:11, 14) is on behalf of those within the church, not outside.[119] Similarly, Moritz considers those referred to in 5:14a as being Christians who are to remain exposed to Christ's light.[120] There is merit to this posi-

115. Within the light-darkness metaphor is fruit-unfruitful imagery (Eph 5:9, 11). Light-darkness is a common picture used in the OT, other portions of the NT, Qumran, and elsewhere. Notably it is found in Isa 9:2; 10:17; 42:6, 16; 49:6; 60:1; where it portrays life and salvation: O'Brien, *Letter*, 366–67, 366 n. 28, 366 n. 29.

116. The source of the call to the sleeper (Eph 5:14) has been the subject of much debate. The introductory formula διὸ λέγει (also seen in Eph 4:8 using Ps 68:18) has been taken to introduce OT material. Some consider it an early Christian hymnic fragment used as a baptismal formula, seeing that it is comparable to Hebrew poetry: Bruce, *Epistles*, 376–77; Lincoln, *Ephesians*, 331; C. Moule, *Idiom Book*, 199. But this is without clear evidence: Wedderburn, *Baptism and Resurrection*, 52–54, 80–82. Others see it as a reference to Gnostic awakening: Bultmann, *Theology*, 174–75. But this is unlikely. Edersheim suspects something akin to temple liturgy during the Feast of Trumpets: *Temple*, 262.

117. Whatever the source of the passage, it may be safely maintained that the concepts find their ultimate origination in the OT. The source of the OT text (even via a traditional baptismal formula) may account for the use of the introductory formula preceding an OT usage (rather than extra-biblical material): Kitchen, *Ephesians*, 92; H. Moule, *Studies in Ephesians*, 133; Wood, "Ephesians," 71. More discussion of the OT-Isaianic influence on Eph 5:14 will follow.

118. Darkness was already introduced in the epistle (Eph 4:18), speaking of the pre-Christian life marked by ignorance, futility, and separation from God. On the other hand, light was seen as truth and understanding in regard to the things of God (Eph 1:18). Additionally, light reveals the nature and degree of Christian transformation (Eph 5:8). Upon conversion the audience was transformed *into* light from their previous dark state (Eph 5:8). Christ, too, is seen *as* light, not merely shining a light (Eph 5:14).

119. Engberg-Pederson, "Conversion in the New Testament," 89–110.

120. Of Moritz's position Lunde and Dunne remark, "This reading suffers from having to interpret γάρ consecutively rather than causally, so that the logical connection

tion and versions of it are promulgated by reputable exegetes.[121] Reasons for this interpretation include the explicit prohibitions directed to Christians in 5:3–7, 12.[122] Also, the likelihood of an evangelistic message within a passage on ethical life in the church seems remote (Eph 5:14). In consideration of the passage, Schnackenburg sees Eph 5:14 to be directed to Christians, and he views Eph 5:13–14 as a parenthesis that explains and reiterates the transformation that took place in their lives (Eph 5:8). Schnackenburg does not see non-Christians in view, while several others follow similar lines of reasoning.[123]

On the other hand, O'Brien and Gombis maintain that the passage explains how those in the church expose sin for the benefit of non-Christians. In Eph 5:13–14 the unbeliever is in view, called to awaken out of a spiritual stupor.[124] Six reasons may be put forth in favor of adopting this position. First, it is acknowledged that the children of light are warned; but when the entire passage is considered (esp. 11, 13, 14) the primary benefit eventually falls to those in darkness, not those who are warned nor those exposing the sin.[125] The section builds to its conclusion in 5:14 and should not be judged without due weight given to the last two verses.[126] Second, the terms σκότος (5:8, 11) and νεκρός (5:14) in the near (4:18) and broad (2:1) contexts clearly designate the state of those without God. It is hard to envision 5:14–15 referring to Christians in darkness and death,[127] especially

---

between verses 13 and 14a is broken. It also struggles to cohere with the Isaianic background on which Paul is manifestly drawing": "Isaiah in Ephesians 5:14," 103 n. 74; Moritz, *Profound Mystery*, 113–15.

121. Best, *Critical and Exegetical*, 52, 493–94; Hoehner, *Ephesians*, 681–85.

122. Clearly church members were still tempted by past lifestyles (1 Cor 6:9–11); for it would seem that the inclusion of the list in Ephesians assumes an ongoing threat. Some were being deceived as to the outcome of immoral living (Eph 5:5–6, cf. 4:14) which necessitated warning (Eph 5:7–8). The question, however, is if Christians in the church are the sole focus of the passage through Eph 5:17.

123. Schnackenburg, *Ephesians*, 227.

124. Gombis, "Triumph," 2005a, 147–49; O'Brien, *Letter*, 371.

125. Gombis writes, "The logic of the passage seems to initiate from the believers and move out toward those in darkness, and the exposure of the shameful deeds has in view the manifestation for the sake of those who are 'darkness'": "Triumph," 2005a, 147–49.

126. O'Brien understands the conjunction διό (Eph 5:14) as relating back to γάρ (Eph 5:18) to form an *inclusio*. He maintains that διό is causal, introducing what light brings upon darkness. This reflects the progress of the passage from darkness to light: *Letter*, 376, and n. 76.

127. The deeds of darkness are marked by a living bondage (Eph 2:1–3), exclusion from the life of God (Eph 4:17–19), the process of decay (Eph 4:22), and the wrath of God (Eph 2:3; 5:6).

after seeing that such a life is alien to those who are actually referred to as light (2:1–3; 4:17–24).[128] Third, in the broad context there is an ongoing contrast between those who possess new life and those who remain in a corrupt state. The contrast continues into the present section with the same comparisons. The audience has been told that they are no longer in the previously described darkened condition. To now say that some of them are in this situation would apparently contradict the repeated affirmations to the contrary (4:21–24). The reader is told that a transformation (φανερούμενον, 5:14) from the dead and out of darkness is in the works (5:13–14), but this has already taken place for those in the light (2:1; 4:22–24). O'Brien admits that the language of 5:13–14 is compressed but acknowledges that the logic allows the transformation of darkness. Fourth, the reasoning of 5:13–14 follows that of 2 Cor 4:6 where Christ is the light in Christians that transforms darkness: "For it is the God who said, 'Let light shine out of darkness,' who has shone in our hearts to give the light of the knowledge of the glory of God in the face of Jesus Christ." This passage clearly speaks about what happens to Christians whose hearts were once veiled (2 Cor 4:3) but who have come out of spiritual blindness and unbelief (2 Cor 4:4; cf. Luke 1:78–79, Act 26:18). It is analogous to Eph 5:11–14, where Christ's light shines in unbelievers and darkness is overcome. The term ἐλέγχω in Eph 5:11 and 13 is used in two ways. In Eph 5:11 it is a part of an injunction to the Christian community to reveal the moral bankruptcy of those in darkness. They should be made to realize the ultimate end of their pursuits and the need for spiritual light. In the second usage (Eph 5:13) the term is used descriptively of light bringing visibility to the nature and destiny of the old life. When the light of God's truth shines on those in moral darkness, deceptions are revealed for what they really are. By revealing the nature of dark deeds the person in question may be transformed. The latter usage of ἐλέγχω seems to indicate the prevailing dominance of light over darkness. Fifth, Rom 13:11 may be put forth as a parallel passage calling for Christians to awaken and put off the deeds of darkness. The exhortation is in an ethical context following a catalog of sins. But the awakening in Rom 13 seems to center on grasping the urgency of walking properly in view of the rapidly approaching eschaton. The "deeds of darkness" are to be laid aside, but the audience is not said to be in darkness or in a state of spiritual death (νεκρός is used in reference to Christians as a former state in Rom 6:13). The awakening in Rom 13:11 is from ethical apathy and lethargy. The passage in Romans 13 also lacks the lengthy contextual buildup found in Ephesians that contrasts the old life with the new. Finally, assigning Eph 5:13–14 to non-Christians

---

128. Bruce, *Epistles*, 145; Stott, *New Society*, 199.

has better correspondence with the cosmic warfare motif in the epistle as well as the triumphal new exodus. Lunde and Dunne see that this reading best comports with the eschatological horizon of Isaiah 60 and the universal claim of the transformative nature of Yahweh's light.[129] The verses suggest that the forces of light are exposing and overtaking the forces of darkness who find themselves under the spell of such darkness. This reflects back to the absolute triumph of Christ and his church seen in Eph 1:20–23.[130] Eph 5:13–14 also anticipates the panoply section (Eph 6:17–21) but goes beyond it in demonstrating light advancing over darkness. In Eph 6 the Christian warrior fights to hold his ground, but in Eph 5:13–14 light prevails. Existentially speaking, this prevailing light is not an absolute guarantee of triumph at every given opportunity, but it reflects the church corporate as newly created life—exposing and overcoming the old life. How this fully actualizes remains a question, but the passage likely served to motivate the ancient audience not only to avoid the listed sins but to gain confidence in exposing and overcoming the deceitfulness of sin and the ploys of the devil. This ministry of exposure was one that included the church as a whole practicing righteous living, especially in regard to speech and sexuality.[131] The focus of Eph 5:13–14 is not so much on the victories of individual Christians as upon how the church in its entirety affects triumph in the world. Dahl supports this conclusion. He summarizes with special focus upon Eph 5:11:

> The exhortation could possibly refer to mutual correction among Christians, but the context makes it more natural to think of the shameful things that Gentiles do in secret: if their evil deeds are exposed by the light, Gentiles may awake from the sleep of death, so that Christ will shine upon them as the light of a new day upon those who awake in the morning . . . It is not any special action but the existence of the church as the one body . . . which makes the manifold wisdom of God known to the principalities and powers who, apparently, had assumed that they were forever to rule over various parts of a fragmented world. (Eph 3:10)[132]

129. Lunde and Dunne, "Isaiah in Ephesians 5:14," 103 n. 74.

130. Christ is seen to be the source of the light that shines into the darkness. Exposing the darkness is not a secular or religious moral crusade—true ethical change is centered upon the shining Christ. Once again the Christological focus in the epistle is apparent. Cf. Eph 1:1, 2, 3, 4, 5, 9, 11, 12, 15, 17, 20; 2:5, 6, 7, 10, 12, 13, 20; 3:1, 4, 6, 8, 11, 17, 19, 21; 4:7, 12, 13, 15, 20, 21, 32; 5:2, 5, 14, 20, 21, 23, 24, 25, 29, 32; 6:5, 6, 23, 24.

131. Porsch's treatment of ἐλέγχω shows that exposing darkness does not focus on those who engage in such activities but upon the deeds themselves and their final end: "Ἐλέγχω," 1:428.

132. Dahl et al., *Studies*, 444.

Still further, however, in the end, Lunde and Dunne consider the possibility that the "sleeper" in Eph 5:14 may not be restricted to either Christian or nonbeliever, but to both.[133] They suppose that the summons is a valid call to both parties in need of eschewing the darkness of sin. However, given the chasm heretofore developed between spiritual light and darkness it is difficult to imagine the author thinking in such atomistic terms.

Is there a strong connection between Eph 5:13–14 and Isaiah's new exodus?[134] To various degrees Moritz, O'Brien, Hodge, Hendriksen, and Lunde and Dunne demonstrate that Isa 26:19–21; 51:9–17; 52:1, and 60:1–5 are amalgamated into the thrust of Eph 5.[135] They believe there are good reasons to see the author of the epistle intentionally incorporating aspects of these passages to further his line of reasoning. If this is true, then a stronger argument is made for the influence of Isaiah in Ephesians when the previous uses of Isaiah (including Psalms and Zechariah) in the epistle are considered.[136] Although there is no explicit correspondence with the Isaiah texts, Moritz traces structural, linguistic, and contextual parallels. Isaiah 26:19 shows common rhythmic patterns and verbal usages as in Eph 5:14b. Key terms, ἔγειρε, ἀνάστα, and οἱ νεκροί are in both texts,[137] while the two texts picture the dead awakening (cf. Isa 26:14, 17–18).[138] Both give attention to ethical matters and judgment (Eph 5:3–6; Isa 26:6, 9–10, 16, 20–21). Although the Isaiah text supports the narrative with indicative verbs while Ephesians utilizes imperatives presents no problem.[139] In Eph 5:14 the text

---

133. Lunde and Dunne, "Isaiah in Ephesians 5:14," 105 n. 81.

134. Some like Noack see no specific OT connection in Eph 5:13–14: "Zitat," 52–64.

135. Hendriksen, *Ephesians*, 234; Hodge, *Commentary*, 176; Moritz, *Profound Mystery*, 100–105; O'Brien, *Letter*, 374–77; Lunde and Dunne, "Isaiah in Ephesians 5:14," 87–110. Hendriksen: "The more I study Isa. 60:1 in the light of its own context the more I begin to see certain resemblances": *Ephesians*, 234. O'Brien acknowledges his indebtedness to Moritz. Lunde and Dunne conclude that of Isa 26:19 and 60:1 it is 60:1–2 that is more heavily weighted in the Ephesians text especially given the common ethical contexts (105). Cf. Qualls and J. Watts, "Isaiah in Ephesians," 254–55.

136. Isa 27:19 in Eph 2:13, 17; Isa 63:10 in Eph 4:30; Isa 59:17 (11:4–5; 49:2; 52:7) in Eph 6:14, 15, and 17. Perhaps Isa 61:10–11 in Eph 5:24.

137. M. Barth notes that οἱ ἐν τοῖς μνημείοις (Isa 26:19) is used euphemistically for death: *Ephesians, Chapters 4–6*, 575 n. 85.

138. Other passages in Isaiah demonstrate a call to awaken: 51:9, 17; 52:1. Cf. 48:1, 12; 49:1; 51:1, 4; 55:1. This may account for the textual differences between Isaiah and Eph 5:14 because the author may have adopted a baptismal hymn, or his own amalgamation of several verses from Isaiah.

139. It is customary for NT authors to alter texts in this fashion for their own purposes. This was already seen in the use of the OT in Eph 1:20–23; 2:11, 17; 4:8, 25, 26, and 30; and shall be in Eph 5:22—6:9 and 6:10–17.

modifies the Isaiah passage for exhortatory purposes.[140] Oswalt recognizes that the light-darkness imagery marked the time of the exodus from Egypt.[141]

There are parallels as well between Isa 60:1-2 and Eph 5:13-14. In both Isaiah and Ephesians the verbs are imperatives. In Isaiah the verb is employed to command the hearers to arise. There is also the common light-darkness metaphor. The Lord's light is set in contrast to the deep darkness that is set upon the peoples of the earth (Isa 60:2). The nations will come to "your light, and kings to the brightness of your rising" (Isa 60:3); that is, the light that has arrived upon the hearers (Isa 60:1) will draw other peoples out of darkness (Isa 60:3). This leads to Israel's astonishment (φοβηθήσῃ καὶ ἐκστήσῃ τῇ καρδίᾳ, Isa 60:5). It appears that the Lord's light shines upon God's people as the rising sun upon the earth (Isa 60:2). The people of God appear to become the rising sun, to which the nations are drawn (Isa 60:3). The light seems to have a transforming effect, both in the people of God and the nations in darkness. The correspondence with Ephesians includes the overall metaphor, God shining on his people as they become his light, and the transformation of darkened peoples through the light.[142] In both cases the light of the Lord overcomes the darkness that engulfs humanity. The change from φανήσεται in Isa 60:2 to ἐπιφαύσει in Eph 5:14 may be one of intensity. The latter is used in the LXX for the shining of the sun (Job 31:26), the moon (Job 25:5), both the sun and the moon (Gen 1:15), the sun's glistening from a crocodile's sneeze (Job 41:10), and the shining of God's face (Job 41:10). The verb denotes, "the dominating, transforming, and sustaining activity of a particular source of light."[143] Moritz acknowledges that this is precisely the message of the light-darkness metaphor in Eph 5:8-14 and captures the essence of Isa 60.[144]

There is a definite note of judgment and triumph in Isa 60 as the nations who are drawn by the light pay service to Israel (Isa 60:5-15). This is in keeping with Christ and the church's victory over the cosmic powers in

---

140. However, if the MT is read, there is evidence of an imperative and the use of the light-darkness motif, which gives further correspondence with the text in Ephesians. The MT uses an imperative הָקִיצוּ for "awake" in Isa 26:19a, versus the indicative ἐγερθήσονται in the LXX. There is, therefore, further reason to see the indicative in Eph 5:14 if he had the Hebrew text in mind. Also, in terms of the light and darkness motif the MT reads טַל אוֹרֹת ("dew of the dawn," Isa 26:19b). It does not occur in the LXX.

141. Oswalt: *Isaiah, Chapters 40–66*, 155, 200, 208, 609, esp. 538.

142. There are actually three metaphors in play in Eph 5:14, all having to do with turning to God: awakening from sleep, being raised from the dead, and moving out of the darkness into the light: Foulkes, *Epistle of Paul*, 148.

143. Moritz, *Profound Mystery*, 103.

144. Ibid.

Ephesians.[145] There is also an exilic quality to the Isaiah passage that sets the historic timetable for the text. Isa 60 depicts the shining light drawing the nations, indicating that "your sons shall come from far away, and your daughters shall be carried on their nurses' arms" (Isa 60:4). The Isaiah text sees the drawing and transformation taking place during the return from Persia, which aligns with the timetable for the historical new exodus from the east, and what the writer saw arriving in Western Asia Minor.[146] This appearance of the new exodus aligns with Eph 5:14 as outsiders (and indirectly, insiders) are transformed in the eschatological age. Moritz acknowledges that Eph 5:14 focuses on the eschatological significance of the present.[147] Hoehner reminds that the "wrath" indicated in Eph 5:6 is both present and future.[148] Not only had the eschatological light arrived but also its judgment. M. Barth summarizes the import of Eph 5:14, "the transition and transformation of a man from darkness to light is as overwhelming, complete, and eschatological as is resurrection from death."[149] From the divine standpoint, the church is co-enthroned with Christ and the triumph has occurred. It is the response of the children of light and the working out of the fruits of the Spirit that remain to be fully actualized.[150]

In summary, the newly clothed humanity (Eph 4:23–24) is to exchange Gentile-like behavior for that which is fitting for the new age (Eph 4:17).

---

145. Isa 60 follows immediately upon 59:17 from which the writer unearths a major portion of the armor imagery (Eph 6:10–17). Isa 59:19 has rising sun imagery as well, picturing an expanse from west to east in which the nations fear Yahweh's glory. The now and not yet victory of the forces of God and Christ in Ephesians is the thrust of Arnold's monograph: *Power and Magic*, 167–72.

146. Hendriksen proposes that Eph 5:14 links to Isa 60:1f and the returnee motif, but expands only briefly on his suggestion: *Ephesians*, 235.

147. He finds that in two-thirds of the uses of Isa 26:19 and 60:1f in pseudepigraphal and rabbinic writings the usage is eschatological or Torah-related. That is, an awakening and coming back to life takes place in the messianic age, and the Torah is the light that brings the dead to life. Mortiz cautiously concludes, *"Christ's supremacy is beyond the reach of the 'powers'—who are in principle defeated (ch 1:21f)—and the Torah—which has been removed through the cross (ch 2.13–17)"* (emphasis in original): *Profound Mystery*, 108 n. 39; quote from 112.

148. Hoehner, *Ephesians*, 664. Cf. Rom 1:18; 2:5 where the present and future aspects are seen.

149. M. Barth, *Ephesians Chapters 4–6*, 598.

150. Dahl compares and contrasts Christian eschatological transformation with Qumran thinking: "With regard to eschatology, the problem may be defined as the differing ways that each community looks from its present to its future. For Qumran the hour of eschatological vindication is still to come; for Ephesians that hour has struck, the victory has been won, and the 'Renewal' has already taken place, although its counterpart in the human response of the believer has still to be worked out in the fruits of the spirit (Eph 5:9)": *Studies*, 118.

Three of the admonitions are buttressed by the OT: truth instead of falsehood (Eph 4:25 and Zech 8:16), anger within limits (Eph 4:26 with Ps 4:4), and thoughts and actions that do not grieve the Holy Spirit (Eph 4:30 and Isa 63:10). Additionally, an extended metaphor of light-darkness in ethical living probably undertakes Isa 26:19 and 60:1.[151] The contrast is not pictured as a standstill or stalemate. The new corporate man of the eschatological age is on the offensive, revealing and correcting the false assumptions and deceptions instigated by evil cosmic forces (Eph 5:11). As moral darkness is exposed by spiritual light a process of transformation takes place in which light overtakes darkness (Eph 5:14). In the broad context of Isaiah, chapters 26 and 60 suggest the new exodus and have general correspondence with the balance of the usages of Isaiah in the epistle. Yahweh's people are drawn by his light as they return from exile. As they do so they are irradiated, drawing the nations to Jerusalem by virtue of being charged with the light of Yahweh. The same transformative light is a mark of the eschatological community because both their speech and sexual conduct have changed. This same transformation can occur for those who are still spiritually dead. The author inspires the corporate audience to take the battle to the enemy in full confidence that the light of Christ will prevail. This sense of inevitability—God and his forces over the powers of darkness, now seen in the area of ethical living—comports with the rest of the epistle and the present triumphal INE motif. The author is careful not to say that every ethical battle will be won, but he has no reason to insist on this since he desires to leave his readers with the general certainty that Christ's light awakens and transforms those in darkness. The realized eschatology of Eph 1:20–23; 2:6; and 4:8 comes precipitously close to ethical fulfillment in Eph 5:11–14. The difference now is that the triumph is stated in progressive terms rather than in absolute ones.[152]

---

151. Lunde and Dunne affirm, "This conceptual and verbal parallelism with Isaiah can hardly be coincidental": "Isaiah in Ephesians 5:14," 99.

152. Few make a case for Prov 23:31 in Eph 5:18. It appears that if there is correspondence, it is on an unintentional verbal level. Lincoln agrees with Lindemann that the connection is incidental: Lincoln, "Use," 43; Lindemann, *Aufhebung*, 82. Nevertheless, an argument can be made (as was in Eph 2:18–22) of the Spirit's distinctive role in the INE community. But the difference between the Spirit's role in Eph 5:18 and 2:18–22 is that the Spirit assists in actualizing the new humanity (while in conjunction with communal joy and harmony) that contrasts with debauchery, rather than access to the eschatological temple. Moritz discusses the contrastive parallels of drunkenness with the Dionysus cult in Ephesus: *Profound Mystery*, 94–95. Gombis analyzes the thrust of the command, understanding it as a corporate charge accomplished by means of the five participles that follow in 5:19–21: "Fullness of God," 259–71.

9.5 CONCLUSION

The ethical section demonstrates multiple uses of the OT in Eph 4:25, 26, 30; and 5:13-14. There are also indirect conceptual parallels, such as investiture with the newly created man (Eph 4:23-24), Paschal redemption (Eph 5:2), and the contrast of light and darkness (Eph 5:7-14. Several of the OT-NT linkages fall within the purview of the new exodus (Eph 4:25 with Zech 8:16; Eph 4:30 with Isa 63:10) and suggest progressive triumph (Eph 5:13-14 with Isa 26:19; 60:1). In regard to ethics, the author does not put forth triumph in absolute terms. He sees the transformative influence of Christ and his church making progress over the forces of darkness and overtaking them. He also recognizes that the wrath of God is in play (5:6). This new state of affairs concerning the ethics and behavior of God's people was anticipated by Isaiah and comports with new exodus eschatology.

10

Present INE Triumph Exhibited in Household Codes, Eph 5:21—6:9

THE ETHICAL SECTION THAT begins at Eph 4:1 focuses on triumphant Christ (Eph 4:8) who provides the means for unity (4:1–16) and ethical living while leaving the antiquated life behind (4:17—5:12). Various instructions are given that are in keeping with the new age anticipated by the OT prophets. The section culminates with a call to the spiritual sleeper to undergo transformation, which has reason to be based upon an Isaianic death-life metaphor within the new exodus rubric (Eph 5:13–14). The ethical section gives way to the so-called "household codes"[1] that round out the tenets of everyday life in the eschatological community (Eph 5:21—6:9) and are in some respects its culmination.[2] The goal of this present investigation is to see how Isaiah's new exodus may impact this final ethical segment.

Of every family that is named (Eph 3:14–15) there are those within the eschatological temple-household (Eph 2:19–22) with responsibilities both at home and work (Eph 5:22—6:4) for which they will answer "to the Lord"

---

1. Hoehner and others discuss the possible origins of the household codes without any firm conclusions; however, recent scholarship suggests the background as Greco-Roman in nature in which the household was recognized as the basic unit of society, having a wide range of societal effects. These codes were not adopted wholesale into the NT: Best, *Critical and Exegetical*, 520–27; Hoehner, *Ephesians*, 720–29; Lincoln, *Ephesians*, 356–65; Moritz, *Profound Mystery*, 159–68; O'Brien, *Letter*, 405–8. Dunn notes some of the latest scholarship: *Theology of Paul*, 666–67.

2. The general ethical admonitions now center on the *locus* of Christian discipleship and the new humanity within the church, identified as the Christian family: Barclay, "Family as the Bearer of Religion, 76–77; Sampley, *"And the Two,"* 149. Cf. R. Longenecker, "Paul's Vision," 73–88.

(Eph 5:22; 6:1, 4, 5). Gombis contrasts the Ephesian household codes with the accepted *Haustafel* or *oikonomia* traditions of the first century.³ Instead of being driven merely by contemporary Greco-Roman moral standards, the stability of the community, or domination over households (such as *patria potestas*), Gombis argues that the epistle epitomizes the triumph of God over the cosmic forces in the sphere of home and work. While the powers of evil seek to disrupt and dehumanize fundamental relationships in society, the new humanity demonstrates liberation from these forces and puts in place a new orderliness and kindness that comes by way of the Lordship of Christ. Gombis's argument is persuasive because it does not treat the codes as disconnected from the rest of the epistle. There is correlation with the cosmic conflict motif and the intentions of the writer to demonstrate the triumph of God. However, Gombis does not investigate the OT citations in the section and the impact they may have on a triumphal INE interpretation.

Four possible uses of the OT are found in this section: Eph 5:26 alludes to Ezek 16:4, 9, and perhaps Ezek 36:25 and Song 4:7; Eph 5:28 and 33 allude to Lev 19:18; Eph 5:31 quotes Gen 2:24; and Eph 6:2–3 quotes Exod 20:12. The use of the Torah (Gen 2:24 in Eph 5:31; Lev 19:18 in Eph 5:28 and 33) argues against those who would consider that the law had no role in the church (Eph 2:15). The writer wanted to make clear that there was indeed continuity between the Jewish Scriptures, specifically the Torah, and its application to the household and Christian gospel (Eph 5:31).⁴ In the discussion that follows it will be found that to varying degrees the OT linkages in this section of the letter do appear to have INE inferences. Although these usages are not all drawn from explicit new exodus contexts, there are reasons to see underlying arguments for the INE.

10.1 MARRIAGE AS AN INE METAPHOR IN EPH 5:22–33

The uses of the OT fall within elongated marriage instructions to wives (Eph 5:22–24), husbands (Eph 5:25–32), and both (Eph 5:33).⁵ Husbands and wives are to follow these instructions because the marital relationship is analogous to Christ and the church.⁶ The wife submits to her husband just

---

3. Gombis, "Triumph " (2005a), 153–69.

4. Moritz, *Profound Mystery*, 95.

5. These are the longest instructions to husbands and wives in the NT, including the Colossian and Petrine parallels (Col 3:18—4:1; 1 Pet 2:18—3:7). The purpose of the length is not clear, but perhaps the threat of sexual immorality (Eph 5:3–6) and the opportunity to expound on Christ's relationship with the church warranted an extended exhortation.

6. Thielman, "Ephesians," 826.

as the church submits to Christ, and the husband loves his wife as Christ does the church.[7] Christ loves the church (Eph 5:25), cleanses her by washing (Eph 5:26), presents her as spotless (Eph 5:27), and nourishes and cherishes her (Eph 5:29). Although wives are addressed first, the emphasis is on the responsibilities of the husband.[8]

10.1.1 The Use of Gen 2:24 in Eph 5:31 as Typology

Gen 2:24 is perhaps the most central OT text on marriage.[9] It is introduced in Eph 5:31 to demonstrate the indissoluble union of husband and wife, and that of Christ and the church (Eph 5:30–31).[10] The central interpretive question has to do with whether the section is primarily about Christian marriage and secondarily about the union of Christ and the church, or vice versa. Gen 2:24 has been used to support both positions.

Moritz understands that the purpose of the section is primarily human marriage, with Christ's relationship with the church in the background.[11] In large part, his reasoning is that, despite the expanded excursus on Christ's devotion to the church (5:25–27), the commands to husbands and wives are reiterated in 24b and 28a. His argument is strengthened in noting that the Christ-church relationship takes place in subordinate clauses (23b, 24a, 25b, 27a, 29c).[12] Accordingly, this fits the thrust of the near context: the writer's focus on the ethical conduct of the new humanity (over Christological, ecclesiological, and eschatological concerns). He asserts that the use of the OT here is not irrelevant, based in part by how the Colossian parallel

---

7. Contemporaneous with Greco-Roman *patria potestas* was first-century Jewish patriarchal structure in which fathers had near absolute rule: Vaux, *Ancient Israel*, 19–20.

8. Three verses are dedicated to wives (Eph 5:22–24), eight focus on husbands (Eph 5:25–32), and one centers on both (Eph 5:33). Many have divided the section in a similar threefold fashion: Batey, "Mia Sarx," 104; O'Brien, *Letter*, 410. Others as twofold, interspersing wife and husband admonitions throughout: Sampley, "And the Two," 270.

9. Foulkes, *Epistle of Paul*, 161.

10. Others detect traces of Ps 45 in the description of idyllic marriage: M. Barth, *Ephesians, Chapters 4–6*, 673; 669 n. 248; McWhirter, *Bridegroom Messiah*, 144–45. McWhirter's monograph is useful to this present study because it discusses the OT marriage metaphor in the NT, specifically in parallels that reflect Origen's approach which is seldom considered in post-enlightenment scholarship: John 3:29 (Jer 33:10–11); John 4:4–42 (Gen 29:1–20); John 12:3 (Song 1:12); and John 20:11–18 (Song 3:1–4).

11. Key to his investigation is the function of the numerous comparative particles: ὡς , 22; ὡς , 23; ὡς , 24; καθώς, 25; οὕτως , ὡς, 28; καθώς, 29: Moritz, *Profound Mystery*, 117–77; esp. 118.

12. Ibid., 133, 138.

(Col 3:18–19) is rearranged in Ephesians in order to accommodate the fifth commandment in Eph 5:31.[13] He puts forth the possibility that the author of Ephesians was reacting to what he observed to be a serious misuse of the OT concept of marriage, paralleling the debates that Jesus had with the Pharisees.[14]

Central to Moritz's argument is his discussion of Eph 5:29b, 30 and how ἀντὶ τούτου (5:31a) is to be understood in the text.[15] Building on Coppens and in conjunction with M. Barth, he considers whether ἀντὶ τούτου is introducing the ramifications of Christ's love for the church and the church's oneness with his body (4:29–30) and allegorically applying them to marriage (5:31); or whether ἀντὶ τούτου refers to the Christ-church relationship as an antitype that fulfills the ultimate picture of marriage.[16] Although Moritz can conceive of the author using typology over allegory in the marriage metaphor, he does not see the author specifically taking Gen 2:24 typologically as a reference to Christ and the church.[17] He argues that Gen 2:24 is used allegorically by the writer to say only something relevant about the Christ-church relationship to marriage. However, there is good reason to override his argument and join other commentators to see ἀντὶ τούτου (5:31a) as typological, pointing to Christ's relationship with the church (5:29–30) as the basis for understanding Gen 2:24 and marriage (5:31b).[18] Moritz's main difficulty seems to turn on the referent, ἐγὼ δὲ λέγω (Eph 5:32b). Does the phrase refer to the author offering his opinion that the allegorical application of the Christ-church relationship to marriage is a great mystery, or is he reveling in the typological mystery, saying that the Christ-church relationship is the new basis for Christian marriage (Christ the antitype, and Adam and Eve's marriage the type)? Moritz seems to take it as the author's opinion about the mystery of marriage and the overall argument as allegorical.[19]

---

13. Ibid., 131.

14. The Pharisees wanted to debate divorce options from Deut 24:1–3 while Jesus brought them back to Gen 1:27 and 2:24 (Mark 10; Matt 19). Paul demonstrates his compatibility with Jesus's teaching on marriage in 1 Cor 7:10: "I give this command—not I but the Lord;" and his use of Gen 2:24 in 1 Cor 6:16 while dealing with prostitution.

15. Moritz, *Profound Mystery*, 138–40.

16. M. Barth, *Ephesians, Chapters 4–6*, 737; Coppens, "Mystery," 132–58.

17. Schnackenburg observes that a majority of recent commentators see the author of Ephesians taking the allegorical position—Gen 2:24 as a reference to Christ and the church: *Ephesians*, 260. But Moritz is cautious with his position: *Profound Mystery*, 144 n. 117; 145 n. 119.

18. Lincoln and Wedderburn, *Later Pauline Letters*, 123; O'Brien, *Letter*, 432–35.

19. Moritz, *Profound Mystery*, 148. Moritz mounts a substantive argument; and although he seems to discard it at the end, he appears to lean toward the allegorical.

However, the writer's handling of μυστήριον in Eph 5:32 and in other portions of the epistle suggest otherwise. In Eph 3:1–10 he presents μυστήριον without any hint that the new revelation is his opinion. Rather, he offers it as a treasured disclosure that has become an established fact. In receiving and proclaiming μυστήριον he gives no indication that his statements comprise a personal opinion as he does elsewhere in a marriage context (cf. 1 Cor 7:12, 25). The mystery-information permeates the epistle (Eph 1:9; 3:1–10; 5:32; 6:32) and is presented apostolically, without hint of opinion.[20] If this unapologetic approach to the mystery is accepted, the result is that ἐγὼ δὲ λέγω is not opinion but polemical declaration.[21] The author is responding to the revelation that the Christ-church relationship is a novelty and the new basis for marriage. This is not just μυστήριον but μυστήριον τοῦτο μέγα (Eph 5:32; cf. 1 Tim 3:16).[22] The writer marvels at the greatness of this typological mystery.

Eph 5:25 could be a new foundation for marriage that coincides with Gen 2:24, and ventures beyond it. If this is the case, then the author reads his Christology and ecclesiology back into Gen 2:24 in a typological-historical fashion. The Christ-church imagery illustrates, or better, forms the terminal antitype to Genesis marriage.[23] This means that the imagery utilized is not merely a model. The advent of Christ interprets idyllic marriage introduced with Adam and Eve in Gen 2:24.[24] Eph 5:29–32 uses this key marriage text while incorporating Christ-church typology to bring further weight to the argument concerning husbands. The typology should be understood along salvific-historical lines, which includes a definitive fulfillment element. Many reputable exegetes agree. O'Brien writes: "Theologically, Paul's

---

20. So Stott: *New Society*, 230–31.

21. Most scholars understand the use of ἐγὼ δὲ λέγω (Eph 5:32) as polemical—the writer pressing his interpretation against competing ones. The vying positions may have been akin to Jesus's detractors who looked for marriage loopholes, Greco-Roman secularized viewpoint, Christian asceticism as per 1 Tim 4:1–3, Qumran devaluation of marriage, or a rabbinic bisexual prime man.

22. First Tim 3:16 speaks of μέγα ἐστὶν τὸ τῆς εὐσεβείας μυστήριον, in reference to Christ's work as the secret to Christian piety. This passage and Eph 5:32 are the only two in the Bible with μυστήριον-μέγα. If a comparison is possible, the writer ranks the typological-historical relationship of Christ-church and marriage with his description of how Christ's incarnation and modeled obedience affects Christian sanctification.

23. Moritz rightfully stops short of endorsing Miletic's proposal that Jewish Adam speculation governs the passage vis-à-vis Gen 2:24. Although Adamic typology is present in Ps 8 (Eph 1:20–23) the same cannot be entertained in Eph 5:31: Miletic, *"One Flesh,"* 18–20. Bruce discusses Qumran exegesis as a parallel to the interpretive method seen in Eph 5:31–32: *Epistles*, 394–95.

24. This is not inconceivable if the author was aware of Jesus's use of Gen 1:27 and 2:24 in teaching on marriage (Mark 10:6–9). Cf. 1 Cor 6:16.

argument does not move from human marriage to Christ and his church; rather, Christ and the church in a loving relationship is the paradigm for the Christian husband and wife."[25] Kitchen understands the passage to reflect a sense of Christ-church imagery supplanting Adam-Eve imagery.[26] Lincoln asserts that the passage presents Christ and his bride, the church as the prototype of human marriage.[27] Dahl summarizes: "I don't think that the author is using the code of household duties as a device for proclaiming some new teaching about Christ and the church. I think the movement of thought is in quite the opposite direction. He is using one of the highest mysteries in order to enforce the ordinary duties of husband and wife, in order to mobilize the highest motivation."[28] Knight points out that the writer saw that God first had Christ and his church in mind, and then designed marriage after them.[29]

Therefore, ὁ μυστήριον τοῦτο μέγα ἐστίν (Eph 5:32) is the author's anticipation of the readers' possible incredulity, and forms the explanation for this new and staggering typology.[30] The mystery element indicates that the writer places his new understanding of Christian marriage within the broader framework of the μυστήριον that arrived upon the advent of Christ (Eph 3:1-10). The novelty is not that Christian marriage is a new concept or that Christ-church typology is rooted in Yahweh's marriage to Israel; rather, it has to do with the understanding that marriage is properly explained by way of the Christ-church type. Just as the μυστήριον of Christ has an impact on racial matters between Gentile and Jewish Christians (Eph 3:1-9), it defines marriage responsibilities. The extended explanation may be due to the audience's unpreparedness to understand the relationship of

25. O'Brien follows Ortlund and Bockmuehl: Bockmuehl, *Revelation and Mystery*, 204; O'Brien, *Letter*, 433; Ortlund, *Unfaithful Wife*, 156.

26. Kitchen, *Ephesians*, 106.

27. Lincoln and Wedderburn, *Later Pauline Letters*, 99.

28. Dahl et al., *Studies*, 422; 469; quote from 469. Similarly Lincoln: "even that use of Gen 2:24 depended for its force on the ultimate reference the writer believed it had to the archetypal union between Christ and the church": *Ephesians*, 381.

29. Knight, "Husbands and Wives," 176. On the other hand, Best does not see enough evidence for a typological understanding in the section. He writes that it is "probably better not to attempt to fit what AE is saying into some hermeneutical method or some predetermined dogmatic pattern:" *Critical and Exegetical*, 556–57; 559–60. But Best discusses Miletic's Adam typology without due consideration to divine marriage. Similarly, Hendicksen, who follows Roberston in seeing only a comparison between Christ-church and marriage, and Moule: Hendriksen, *Ephesians*, 257; H. Moule, *Studies in Ephesians*, 143; Robertson, *Word Pictures*, IV:547.

30. Coppens calls the writer's venture, "bold and daring exegesis;" Moritz labels it, "daring and original theology;" and Ortlund exults, "a breathtaking juxtaposition": Coppens, "Mystery," 147; Moritz, *Profound Mystery*, 146; Ortlund, *Unfaithful Wife*, 156.

Christ to his church as the basis for comprehending Gen 2:24; or perhaps they found it difficult to accept the exalted correspondence between Christ and his church as the basis for the mundane responsibilities of marriage; or simply, the immensity of the typological correspondence could not be briefly explained.

If Eph 5:31 and Gen 2:24 linkage is merely borrowed OT imagery, as Mortiz seems to maintain, the argument for OT influence in Eph 5 that follows is not substantially weakened; but if the use is typological-historical fulfillment of Gen 2:24, then it reinforces a pattern in the epistle in which the author seems to see the church falling in line with Isaiah's vision. That is, Eph 5:31 and Gen 2:24 are another display of Paul's typological-historical hermeneutic that he often employs in his handling of the OT in Ephesians. This lends credence to Paul's understanding that the coming of Christ functioned as the antitype to OT concepts and events, including perhaps Isaiah's new exodus, finding termination in Christ and the Torah-bound behavior of Christian households.

10.1.2 OT Betrothal-Marriage Metaphor as Realized Triumph

The betrothal-marriage metaphor finds its origins in the marriage of Yahweh and his people during the exodus period. Ortlund asserts that the OT is one vast network of foreshadowings of Christ and his kingdom including marriage imagery.[31] The metaphor that began in the OT is adopted in the NT with Christ acting as Yahweh's new covenant agent.[32] Jesus applied the metaphor to himself as the eschatological bridegroom (Mark 2:18–20; John 3:29). The OT divine marriage metaphor is reconfigured with Christ taking the role of Yahweh, and the function of the nation is assumed (in large part) by the church.[33] McWhirter adds to the scholarship by analyzing John's use of joyful marriage imagery in Song of Songs; Jer 33:10–11; and Gen 29:1–20 through the messianic lens of Ps 45.[34] Her proposals have not convinced all,[35] but the use of the imagery is perhaps broader and more subtle than previously understood. The marriage of Yahweh and Israel became corrupted and led to exile, but arrived anew upon the advent of Christ.

---

31. Ortlund, *Unfaithful Wife*, 151.

32. Helpful studies include: Batey, *Nuptial Imagery*, 12–37, 59–69; Chavasse, *Bride of Christ*, 19–98; Minear, *Images of the Church*, 52–53; Muirhead, "Bride of Christ," 175–97.

33. Bruce, *Epistles*, 386; Kitchen, *Ephesians*, 109; O'Brien, *Letter*, 420; Stott, *New Society*, 227.

34. McWhirter, *Bridegroom Messiah*, 144–45.

35. Foster, "Bridegroom Messiah," 564–65; Winter, "The Bridegroom Messiah and the People of God," 68–69.

O'Brien observes that Paul's typological use of marriage is in keeping with use of the betrothal-marriage metaphor in the OT,[36] and builds naturally from the adaptations introduced by Jesus, the Evangelists, John, and other writers of the NT. Paul's employment of marriage typology is grounded in the OT, not only in Gen 2:24 but the prophets as well.[37] In Paul, the OT picture of Yahweh and his bride is figurative for what eventually becomes known as its antitype in the NT: Christ and his bride, the church.[38] This observation seems unmistakable in 2 Cor 11:2-3[39] where Paul speaks as the friend of the bride.[40] He is jealous for the purity of the church, and is portrayed as a betrothed virgin. She is engaged to Christ but has, like Eve, been deceived (cf. 1 Cor 6:16-17). The usage is clearly from Hos 2:2-20 with support from Gen 3. The OT expression of the Yahweh-bride metaphor is realized eschatologically and idyllically in Christ and the church. Gal 4:22—5:1 is similar, but portrays the church as Isaac, the child of Rebekah (Gal 4:28, 31). The quotation Paul uses in Gal 4:22—5:1 is from Isa 54:1, the context of which has reference to Yahweh and his bride (Isa 54:1-7). The "husband" in Gal 4:27 refers back to Isa 54:1, where Yahweh is identified as the husband (Isa 54:5). The Galatian text has allegorical features, but, as Keesmaat recognizes, the passage is both typological-historical and a retelling of the exodus narrative.[41] The prefiguration is not specifically Isaac but Yahweh as husband, who brings forth a legitimate heir through Israel. The correspondence links Yahweh the husband and Israel his wife with their legitimate heir, the church. Through Isaiah, the reader of Galatians understands that a typological-historical fulfillment of husband-wife imagery has taken place in Christ and his church (Gal 5:1). These two uses of marriage imagery (2 Cor 11:2-3; Gal 4:22—5:1) make a case that Paul understood Christ and the church to be the typological-historical fulfillment of Yahweh the husband and Israel his bride.

36. O'Brien, *Letter*, 435.

37. The Pauline use of the prophets' marriage metaphor and the restoration of Yahweh's marriage are seen in eschatological aspects of the metaphor in 2 Cor 11:2 and Eph 5:26, with allusions to Ezek 16:4, 9.

38. Obviously there are discontinuities between the OT and NT uses of the metaphor: M. Barth, *Ephesians, Chapters 4-6*, 670-72.

39. The use of the marriage metaphor emerges out of an entire matrix of similar thought adopted from the OT, specifically the prophets. For example, 1 Cor 6:11, 16-17; 11:3 shadow the OT texts cited previously.

40. M. Barth has an extensive discussion of ancient Jewish wedding customs as they relate to Eph 5:27: *Ephesians, Chapters 4-6*, 678-84.

41. Keesmaat, "Tradition in Galatians," 155-88; esp. 188. Keesmaat interacts substantially with and builds upon: J. Scott, *Adoption as Sons*, 121-86. Cf. Keesmaat, "Function of the Exodus,"189-215.

However, in Eph 5 the metaphor is developed in a unique way among the Pauline writings. As previously seen, 2 Cor 11:1–6 uses the metaphor to picture the church as a chaste virgin. The church was beguiled and led astray, and then warned. It is a message of caution not triumph. Galatians 4:22—5:1 draws upon the metaphor to contrast salvation by means of law with that of grace. There the imagery is soteriological in nature. Romans 9:25–29 interprets the metaphor vis-à-vis Hosea. Paul undertakes the motif to defend God's faithfulness to Israel through the preservation of a remnant. The Gentiles have not dislodged Israel or Yahweh's marriage to her. Finally, Rom 7:1–6, strictly speaking, does not develop the metaphor. None of these usages explicitly represent the marriage metaphor as present triumph, as does the application in Eph 5:22–33. These usages support the argument in terms of the use of the metaphor but do not shape it as the writer does in Ephesians. Lincoln maintains that the imagery in Eph 5 is adopted from the marriage of Yahweh and Israel and is presented in the epistle not as a future marriage but as one in which the church is already Christ's bride.[42] He remarks on this aspect of Eph 5, "Here, in line with this writer's more realized eschatology, glory and holiness are seen as present attributes of the Church, and Christ's activity of endowing the Church with these qualities is a present and continuing one."[43] Smolarz considers that the NT, including Paul, consistently presents the metaphor in a realized aspect.[44] He maintains that "there is nothing in the letter to the Ephesians itself suggesting a future marriage of Christ."[45] This declaration should be balanced with the fact that the imagery in Revelation views the futuristic eschatological terminus of the metaphor (Rev 19:7; 21:2, 9; 22:17).

The timing of the three purpose clauses also suggests present triumph. They lay out the goals of Christ's self-sacrificing love for the church: "to make her holy" (Eph 5:26), "to present the church to himself in splendor" (Eph 5:27a), and "that she may be holy and without blemish" (Eph 5:27b). Some consider the first clause depicting a process,[46] but it is better taken as a definitive event in keeping with a corporate and holistic picture of salvation.[47] The sanctification of the church along with her cleansing and

42. Lincoln and Wedderburn, *Later Pauline Letters*, 99.

43. Lincoln, *Ephesians*, 377.

44. Smolarz, "Divine Marriage," ii.

45. Ibid., 266.

46. Hoehner, *Ephesians*, 752; Salmond, "Epistle to the Ephesians," 368; Stott, *New Society*, 227–28.

47. Best, *Critical and Exegetical*, 542–43; O'Brien, *Letter*, 421–22. Peterson argues for sanctification as a definitive event in the NT citing as keys, 1 Cor 1:2 and 6:11: *Possessed by God*, 53.

washing (ἵνα αὐτὴν ἁγιάσῃ καθαρίσας τῷ λουτρῷ τοῦ ὕδατος, Eph 5:26)[48] are contemporaneous with one another.[49] This lends support to the idea that the marriage is already accomplished. Concerning the second and third clauses, commentators are divided on whether to take Eph 5:27 as present or future,[50] depending on how the aorists are taken. If it is future, then the blending of present and future triumph is close to seamless (cf. Eph 4:8, 22–24, 30; 5:14).[51] But this does not damage the argument for the present aspect because that is established in the first clause. Also, the phrase ἁγίους καὶ ἀμώμους ("holy and blameless" or "without a spot or wrinkle") occurs in Eph 1:4 and 5:27, with the former emphasizing realized eschatology. Ephesians 5:27 should be taken in the same way. After discussing the atemporal nature of the aorist forms in these two passages, Dahl concludes, "God is not to be praised because he continually blesses his children, but he is praised for the once-for-all blessing that he gave in and with Christ, which was imparted to those who have come to faith."[52] Best articulates the position of those who see that all three clauses demonstrate the realized aspect, "But much that AE writes elsewhere suggests that he would have no difficulty in thinking of an existing marriage of Christ and the church as glorious and without fault; already the believers sit in the heavenlies with Christ (2:6) and God's glory is seen in them (1:12; cf 1:4; 3:18f)."[53] It is certain that the first clause speaks of the present aspect of the purified church, and based on the consensus of scholarship the second and third clauses may be taken either way.[54]

48. In recent scholarship many are moving away from taking this section as a reference to baptism because of the paucity of evidence. One reference to baptism is unexceptional because it falls within a list of aspects of unified faith (Eph 5:5). The so-called baptism liturgies are inconclusive on the matter (Eph 1:20–23; 5:13–14): Hoehner, *Ephesians*, 756–57. This is not to discount the new exodus and corporate possibilities connected with baptism: Holland, *Contours*, 153–54.

49. Cf. O'Brien's discussion and his citation of Porter's comments on aorist participles following the main verb in the Pauline Corpus (Eph 5:26), O'Brien, *Letter*, 422 n. 249; Porter, *Verbal Aspect*, 1:384.

50. Bruce, *Epistles*, 389–90; Hoehner, *Ephesians*, 761; O'Brien, *Letter*, 424.

51. Dunn observes Paul as "curiously ambiguous" in Rom 14:10; 2 Cor 11:2; Col 1:22, 28; Eph 5:27 (Eph 1:4): *Theology of Paul*, 309, n. 73. This is not to say that the occasion of the church's presentation (παρίστημι … παριστάνω) is entirely indefinite in Eph 5:27.

52. Dahl, *Studies*, 424. Agreeing is H. Moule: *Studies in Ephesians*, 140. However, "holy and blameless" in Eph 1:4 and Col 1:22 include the future Parousia; and both the second and third clauses of Eph 5:27 coincide with the imagery of Rev 21:9–11.

53. Best, *Critical and Exegetical*, 545.

54. The occasion of the marriage and cleansing is debatable. Suggestions are the crucifixion of Christ (Eph 5:25), the time of personal faith (Eph 2:8–9), or in eternity

Ortlund considers the prophets anticipating a Savior wedded to his people in a great restoration of the divine marriage in the final age. The failures of Israel are transcended by Christ and his bride, the church. The NT brings the story of the restored marriage in Christ to consummation. The marriage imagery in Eph 5 recognizes a movement toward this restoration: "The fulfillment is coming increasingly into view."[55]

Certainly a beloved and beautified church is in view, married or awaiting marriage, either now or in the Parousia, with the evidence in favor of a presently glorified bride. It seems that a common thread among the cited passages is a presentation before God and his subsequent judgment of the moral quality of those before him. This judgment of moral quality could coincide with Deut 24:1, where a provision is given for a new husband if he were to find uncleanness in his bride. This opens the possibility of Christ scrutinizing his new bride and finding her glorious. In Eph 5:27 there is no doubt as to the outcome, and this passage may be a way of stating Eph 2:7 in current terms.

10.1.3 Nuptial Imagery in Isaiah, Ezekiel, and Leviticus

Along these lines, Smolarz observes that the NT marriage imagery, including the Pauline usages, function within the parameters of the new exodus paradigm.[56] As stated previously, Keesmaat detects the new exodus in the related Galatian marriage texts. Yahweh who saves his people from Egypt has taken Israel as his bride.[57] Bridal imagery finds its origins in Egypt and the exodus period. However, from the very start the marriage was tested due to the nation's disobedience.[58] Because of Israel's harlotries, the relationship suffered estrangement leading to exile.[59] But just as the prophets viewed the downfall of the marriage, they predicted the restoration of the relationship

---

past at the point of sovereign election (Eph 1:3–4); but most likely not personal baptism. Best suggests the crucifixion, but rejects baptism seeing that it would necessitate a timeline of baptisms: *Critical and Exegetical*, 545–46. Dahl, Bruce, and others make a case for baptism: Bruce, *Epistles*, 388–89; Dahl et al., *Studies*, 420–21; Hodge, *Commentary*, 187–88; Ridderbos, *Paul*, 397–98.

55. Ortlund, *Unfaithful Wife*, 136; 151–56; quote from 152. Cf. Stienstra benefits the NT analysis of divine marriage by exploring the OT metaphor of Yahweh and Israel: *Husband of His People*, 170–86. The writer of Ephesians understandably bypasses the sexual realm. His focus is upon the care and delight of Christ toward the church and the astonishing mystery manifested in the union: M. Barth, *Ephesians, Chapters 4–6*, 629.

56. Smolarz, "Divine Marriage," 267.

57. Exod 34:14–16; Lev 17:7; Deut 31:16; Judg 2:17; 8:27, 33; Hos 2:14–15; Jer 2:1–3, 32; 31:1–3; 31–32; Ezek 23:1–4, 8.

58. Exod 32:1–10; 34:15–16.

59. Hos 2:2–7a; Jer 3:1–14a, 20–25; 9:2; Ezek 16:15–58; 23:9–49.

in the eschatological age.⁶⁰ The renewal of the marriage would be within the new exodus construct.⁶¹

The uses of the marriage metaphor in Isaiah are quite extensive and are interwoven in new exodus contexts: Isa 49:18–22; 50:1–2; 54:1–8; 61:10; and 62:3–5. The marriage of Yahweh and Israel originated early on in the historical exodus (Exod 19:5–6; Jer 31:32) and would be restored in the new exodus (Hos 2:14). This is seen prominently in Isaiah as Yahweh bedecks his bride with jewels and miraculously restores children to a bereaved mother (Isa 49:18–22); he asks rhetorically if his hand is so short that it cannot save his previously estranged wife (Isa 50:1–2); the barren woman will bear children and her widowhood will be remembered no more (Isa 54:1–8); Yahweh clothes Israel as a bridegroom and bride (Isa 61:10); and Zion will no longer be forsaken but God will rejoice over her as a bride. All of these occurrences of the marriage metaphor are used in a positive manner of rescue and restoration. They speak of Yahweh's disciplinary but unconditional love for Israel. The pictures present Yahweh as enthusiastic about his remnant-wife in whom he delights (Isa 62:4–5). The occurrences are also used in conjunction with the new exodus motif. They occur directly or near new exodus passages. Isa 50:1–2 provides an example of both motifs in close proximity:

> Thus says the Lord: Where is your mother's bill of divorce with which I put her away? Or which of my creditors is it to whom I have sold you? No, because of your sins you were sold, and for your transgressions your mother was put away. Why was no one there when I came? Why did no one answer when I called? Is my hand shortened, that it cannot redeem? Or have I no power to deliver? By my rebuke I dry up the sea, I make the rivers a desert; their fish stink for lack of water, and die of thirst.

Both the marriage metaphor and the new exodus align well together in Isaiah because both lend themselves to the encouraging message of restoration. The prevailing idea of restoration with the two motifs suggests triumph. It appears that the author of Ephesians utilizes this triumphant aspect of the metaphors in Isaiah, and imports the imagery. This understanding of the close linkage between these two motifs, along with the multiplicity of uses of both in the Pauline Corpus, suggests that together they had a presence in the writing of Ephesians. Although the new exodus is not explicit in Eph

---

60. Hos 2:14–20; Jer 3:14b–19; 31:31–34; Ezek 16:9–14; 36:24–30; with indirect application in Mal 2:14–16: God will not deal treacherously with the wife of his youth.

61. The marriage metaphor in Isaiah aligns with Ninow's and Fishbane's new exodus citations in Isaiah: Fishbane, "Motif," 121–40; Ninow, *Indicators*, 157–241.

5:22–33, it appears to remain close to the author's thinking. It is understandable that the marriage imagery was preferred given the current subject matter.

In Eph 5:26 the possible reference to Ezek 16:4, 9 (and perhaps Ezek 36:25 and Song 4:7) seems to be more than shared language.[62] A study of Ezek 16 reveals that the Yahweh-bride descriptions are strongly associated with Hosea bride imagery, and in keeping with the exiled nation that looks forward to restoration. The allusion from Ezek 16:9 in Eph 5:26 pictures Yahweh's preparation of his new bride: ἔλουσά σε ἐν ὕδατι καὶ ἀπέπλυνα. In Eph 5:26 it is descriptive of salvation as a whole. Many commentators see an allusion to the prenuptial bridal baths common in ritual Jewish marriage practices.[63] In Ezek 16:8–14 Yahweh has entered into a marriage covenant with Israel, carefully preparing her by bathing her, anointing her with oil, clothing her with royal garments, and recognizing the fame of her beauty and splendor.[64] Ezekiel's use of the marriage metaphor is similar to Isaiah. The differences lie in more of a postexilic understanding, but the restorative, triumphant features remain. In addition, the new exodus was seen as present in Ezekiel in chapter 2 of this current work (Ezek 20; 36:24–26). The new exodus in these contexts imparts restoration. In Ezek 36:24–26 and 36:33 the exodus motif and the concept of washing coalesce: "I will take you from the nations, and gather you from all the countries, and bring you into your own land. I will sprinkle clean water upon you, and you shall be clean from all your uncleannesses, and from all your idols I will cleanse you . . . Thus says the Lord God: On the day that I cleanse you from all your iniquities, I will cause the towns to be inhabited, and the waste places shall be rebuilt."

As in Isaiah, marriage imagery and the new exodus motif find association and are used to speak of restoration in the eschatological age. The washing is similar to Ezek 16:9 and its possible usage in Eph 5:26. O'Brien recognizes a conscious incorporation of the Ezekiel passage, relating the use to sanctification, which "is precisely what one does in marriage, and thus fits the imagery of Ezek 16."[65] Smolarz understands Eph 5:26–27 as a reflec-

---

62. O'Brien, *Letter*, 420–21; Snodgrass, *Ephesians*, 297–98. According to Dahl it is likely that the author also had Song 4:7 in view, but the realized eschatological implications are minimal: *Studies*, 422.

63. Abbott, *Critical and Exegetical*, 168–69; M. Barth, *Ephesians, Chapters 4–6*, 691–99; Bruce, *Epistles*, 387–89; Hoehner, *Ephesians*, 753–54; Kitchen, *Ephesians*, 103; Lincoln, *Ephesians*, 375; O'Brien, *Letter*, 422–23. As Foulkes makes clear, the breakdown in the metaphor is that Christ is the one who prepares and makes glorious his church, rather than a bride making herself beautiful: *Epistle of Paul*, 159.

64. Ortlund, *Unfaithful Wife*, 101–7.

65. O'Brien, *Letter*, 421 n. 245.

tion of Ezek 16:10–14 and the church as a royal wife, ceremonially pure and entering into covenant union with Christ.[66] The ceremonial washing is in preparation for marriage (Ezek 16:8). The church is cleansed, complete, and acceptable to Christ, the Husband. Christ's bride is presently benefiting from his care and attention (Eph 5:29). The picture that emerges in Ephesians is Christ as presently engaged and married (both images may be in play) to the church and acting as the ideal husband toward her.[67]

The use of Lev 19:18 in Eph 5:28, 33 follows closely upon the Ezekiel allusion in Eph 5:25. Leviticus 19:18 is undertaken in Eph 5 to finish out the section in Eph 5:33. The common factor between the OT and the NT use of Lev 19:18 is its employment as a benchmark for loving others in accordance with assumptive self-love.[68] In Eph 5:28, 33 such love measures the degree to which wives and fellow members of the body of Christ are to be loved. Sampley discusses the notion of "neighbor" as wife; that is, both one's neighbor and one's wife are to be loved as oneself.[69] Leviticus 19:18 was an important OT passage to the author of the missive, undergirding arguments for interpersonal Christian piety especially regarding the closest human relationship. It connects the author firmly with the Torah and Jesus's understanding of the OT passage. Given the shared language offered by the author of Ephesians, and its utilization in two verses in close proximity (5:28, 33), it seems that the usage is conscious and is imported to reflect that behavior in the new eschatological household aligns with fundamental interpersonal expectations of the Torah.

66. Smolarz, "Divine Marriage," 418.

67. Ibid., 266. Too much can be made of attempting to distinguish betrothal and restored marriage in the metaphor. Smolarz rightly observes that both aspects of the metaphor may refer to covenant renewal at the eschaton. It does not appear that either the OT or Paul is overly concerned with precisely distinguishing betrothal and marriage. This could be due to betrothal viewed as near-marriage (in distinction to modern notions of engagement): M. Barth, *Ephesians, Chapters 4–6*, 669. Schlier sees the author depicting marriage in Eph 5:23–24, betrothal in 25–27, and once again marriage in 28–31, but this may be an over categorization: *Christus*, 278–80. M. Barth observes marriage in Jer 2:2 and Ezek 16:6–14, and everlasting betrothal in Hos 2:9–20: *Ephesians, Chapters 4–6*, 626 n. 53.

68. Of course, those in the audience with an awareness of the OT would know that the phraseology is from the Torah. Jesus's use of this passage as part of his summary of the law anticipates its importance in the early church, including Paul in Romans and Galatians where the text is formally put forth. Both Pauline usages have explicit prologues and appear in ethical sections (Matt 5:43; 7:12; 19:19; Mark 12:31, 33; Luke 10:27; Rom 13:8–10; Gal 5:14; Jas 2:8). Moritz unjustly criticizes Sampley on this point: *Profund Mystery*, 149–50. Hoehner and Lincoln dismiss the use of Lev 19:18 prematurely: Hoehner, *Ephesians*, 765; Lincoln, *Ephesians*, 379.

69. Sampley analyzes loving one's wife as oneself in Jewish literature: "And the Two," 30–34. Bruce detects the idea throughout Song of Solomon: *Epistles*, 391.

In summary, it appears that Eph 5:22–33 reflects a typological-historical fulfilment of eschatological marriage imagery.[70] The OT husband-wife metaphor is adopted by the writer in typological-historical fashion and finds its ultimate terminus in Christ and the church. Just as Yahweh took Israel as his bride, Christ has taken the church, and so typologically-historically fulfilled what failed to take place in the OT, specifically during the exilic period. In the Pauline Corpus, Ephesians uses the metaphor in a distinctive fashion. The betrothal-marriage is a triumphant one. Husband-Christ acts as a delighted and loving partner, meticulously caring for his bride. There are no discordant issues with a metaphorical couple as in other uses of the imagery in Paul (2 Cor 11; cf. Gal 4–5). In Ephesians the engagement and marriage are largely complete. This finds correspondence with the functioning of the metaphor in Isaiah and Ezekiel. In Isaiah the emphasis is on rescuing the estranged wife and restoring her dignity and childbearing. In Ezekiel the focus is washing away uncleanness in preparation for royal presentation. A joyful restored marriage in the eschatological age is in view. In addition, the new exodus is in the near OT usages. Given the number and quality of correspondences between Ephesians and the OT, and specifically Isaiah and Ezekiel, the marriage metaphor serves as an indication that the new exodus motif may underlie the epistle.

10.2 CHILDREN, PARENTS, AND SLAVERY IN INE SOCIETY IN EPH 6:1–9 AND EXOD 20:12

The final segment of the ethical section involving children, parents, and slaves incorporates one OT citation, Exod 20:12 in Eph 6:2–3.[71] The question is whether this occurrence and other OT concepts in the section speak of present INE triumph.

---

70. It appears that scholarship increasingly realizes that the marriage imagery of the NT stems from the OT over ancient marriage customs. The association is typological-historical, indicating more than simple corresponding imagery. The typological-historical hermeneutic understands not only the use of OT figures but the certainty of historical antitype fulfillment.

71. The use of the OT in the household codes is a vivid illustration of the differences between Colossians and Ephesians. If Ephesians was rewritten from Colossians, then the author was compelled to insert the OT citations. He added Gen 2:24 in Eph 5:31; Ezek 16:9 in Eph 5:26; Lev 19:18 in Eph 5:28 and 33; and Exod 20:12 in Eph 6:2–3. However, as Bruce notes contra Mitton, "Attempts to establish dependence of the Ephesian passage on its counterpart in Colossians, or *vice versa*, are totally inconclusive." Bruce, *Epistles*, 397; Mitton, *Epistle*, 70–71.

10.2.1 The Longevity of Children in the Eschatological Community in Eph 6:1–4 and Exod 20:12

The use of Exod 20:12 in Eph 6:2–3 has puzzled scholars.[72] Two outstanding issues are involved, "first commandment with promise," and the source and alteration of the OT text. Thielman analyzes the first and concludes with Lincoln that the promise to children is first among all the commandments that are linked to promises. Others wrestle with this first problem and arrive at further conclusions, but these conclusions are not critical to this present study. The second problem is the subject of the discussion that follows.

The source of the OT usage in Eph 6:2–3 was once considered by scholarship to have come from Deut 5:16, but analysis demonstrates that it stems from Exod 20:12 (LXX).[73] The important change from the Septuagintal reading involves the promise of long life. The writer replaces the specific location of the long life, "the land that the Lord your God is giving you," with the more comprehensive, "on the earth." There is clearly a motif in Deuteronomy that builds off the Decalogue, tying together teaching and obeying the Torah with longevity in the land. The author of the epistle is clearly within the Pentateuchal tradition as well as the OT in general,[74] but the parallel passages in Deuteronomy all refer to longevity in the land, not the earth.[75] Several possibilities are put forth to explain the change from the

---

72. Best, *Critical and Exegetical*, 565–68; Lincoln, "Use," 38; Moritz, *Profound Mystery*, 172–74; Thielman, "Ephesians," 830.

73. Best, *Critical and Exegetical*, 566; Bruce, *Epistles*, 397–98; Hoehner, *Ephesians*, 788; Lincoln, "Use" 37–38; Moritz, *Profound Mystery*, 154–55.

74. Mortiz compares the writings of Philo, Josephus, *4 Maccabees*, and the rabbis: *Profound Mystery*, 159–63. He also indicates that the reward for allowing a mother bird to go free while taking her baby birds (Deut 22:7) has the same reward as honoring parents in Exod 20:12. This reflects the fact that the reward of a long life corresponds generally to an obedient life in matters of little and large consequence. Of course, the difference lies in punishment for disobedience and practical societal implications (157–58). O'Brien notes that punishment for recalcitrant children was on par with treason and idolatry (Exod 21:15, 17; Lev 19:3; 20:9; Deut 21:18–21; 27:16): *Letter*, 442 n. 13.

75. Cf. Deut 4:26 that incorporates disobedience and longevity in the land: "I call heaven and earth to witness against you today that you will soon utterly perish from the land that you are crossing the Jordan to occupy; you will not live long on it, but will be utterly destroyed." Deut 4:40 links obedience and longevity: "Keep his statutes and his commandments, which I am commanding you today for your own well-being and that of your descendants after you, so that you may long remain in the land that the Lord your God is giving you for all time." Deut 31:12–13 ties together teaching children and obedience, with land dwelling: "Assemble the people—men, women, and children, as well as the aliens residing in your towns—so that they may hear and learn to fear the Lord your God and to observe diligently all the words of this law, and so that their children, who have not known it, may hear and learn to fear the Lord your God, as long as you live in the land that you are crossing over the Jordan to possess."

LXX to the text in Ephesians. Hoehner, Hodge, and others see the wide-ranging principle that obedient children[76] generally live longer than disobedient ones.[77] The replacement of "land" with "earth" merely recognizes that the church does not replace the geographical nation of Israel.[78] Others, such as Lincoln, hold a similar position asserting that the change is in response to dimming hopes for the Parousia.[79] Best understands the change to address the weakening ethic of those who once believed in the imminency of Christ's return.[80] Comparatively, the use of Gen 2:24 five verses earlier warranted elaboration, but the use of Exod 20:12 without commentary was sufficient for the author. It could be that the commandment with an accompanying promise was in itself enough elaboration for the understanding of the audience. The issues with Gen 2:24 in Eph 5:31 are more complex.

Gombis proposes that the *oikonomia* is an attempt by the author to establish a constitution for the new humanity. Those in the eschatological community who live up to the standards set forth epitomize the triumph of God in Christ.[81] The battleground with the cosmic forces includes marriage, home, and work. These offer an ideal setting in which the new creation concretely demonstrates itself.[82] The triumph is seen in part by the radical differences between the secular *Haustafel* and the admonitions in the epistle. This is demonstrated not only with the lengthy guidelines to husbands to love as Christ loves but directives to parents to understand, respect, and accommodate their children.[83] Thielman's position is similar, proposing that the change in the text may be in conjunction with the new creation theme in the epistle (Eph 2:15; 3:9; 4:13, 24). He writes, "Paul may be saying that children whose obedience to their parents arises from their commitment to 'the Lord' (6:1) will live eternally not on a particular land with national boundaries such as ancient Israel, but rather on an earth without boundar-

---

76. Τέκνα refers to children young and old, but in terms of relevance those still under parental care are most likely in view. Relationships, more than age, seem to be the focus: Lincoln, *Ephesians*, 403; Moritz, *Profound Mystery*, 68–70; 69 n. 58. Stott highlights the "radical change from the callous cruelty which prevailed upon the Roman Empire" in regard to children, and that which was commanded by Jesus (Matt 18:5; Mark 10:14) and expanded upon by Paul: *New Society*, 237–38. Stott also addresses the unconditionality of the command to obey (241–42).

77. Hendriksen, *Ephesians*, 260–61; Hodge, *Commentary*, 203; Hoehner, *Ephesians*, 793.

78. Hoehner, *Ephesians*, 793.

79. Lincoln, *Ephesians*, 406.

80. Best, *Critical and Exegetical*, 568.

81. Gombis, "Triumph," (2005a), 155.

82. Gombis utilizes Elliott's, *Sociological Exegesis*, 219.

83. Gombis, "Triumph," (2005a), 165–67.

ies, as God created it to be."[84] This corresponds with the idea that God is breaking down national barriers (Eph 2:14–16). Thielman admits that there is no explicit evidence for this proposal; however, it is a noteworthy attempt to reconcile the Septuagintal change in accordance with a key underlying theme in the letter.[85] Gombis's proposal faces the same challenge, but its virtue lies in arguing from the standpoint of the entire epistle and the intentions of the author.

Building on Gombis and Thielman, a case may be made for the present aspect of the eschatological age in the ethical section, and specifically the use of the OT and the Septuagintal change at Eph 6:2–3. According to earlier passages it seems that the writer has sought to emphasize the arrival of Isaiah's new exodus vision. The use of γῆ relates to gathering up all things on the earth (Eph 1:10), every family on earth taking its name from God (Eph 3:15), and Christ descending to the earth and leaving in triumph (Eph 4:9). The author may have in mind an idea related to the first and third usages: the consummation and demonstration of God's triumph *on the earth*. In addition, he uses γῆ eschatologically concerning Gentile inclusion while utilizing OT texts (Rom 9:17 with Exod 9:1; Rom 9:28 with Isa 10:23; Rom 10:18 with Ps 19:4). In these passages the use of γῆ goes beyond the national boundaries of Israel to include the eschatological earth in which God will judge and inculcate believing Gentiles. The employment of γῆ in Colossians involves its use with "heaven" in reconciling all things through the cross (Col 1:16, 20).[86] This is also the purview in Phil 2:10.[87] Several of these passages, especially those in Romans that use γῆ standing alone without heaven, may be relevant to Eph 6:3. They speak of an eschatological earth, envisioned in the OT, in which God's rule extends throughout the entire planet. This is in keeping with the futuristic new heavens and new earth in Rev 21:1. If this is similar in Eph 6:3, the writer may be using γῆ in a way in which the OT anticipated the earth coming under the rule of God. A few verses later in Eph 6:8, slaves are told that upon their good behavior they "will receive the same again from the Lord." This promise points to some indefinite time in the future, and perhaps to the judgment seat of Christ,[88]

---

84. Thielman, "Ephesians," 830.

85. Ibid.

86. In Col 3:2, 5 the earthly and heavenly are set in contrast while emphasizing godly living.

87. Other Pauline uses of γῆ are found in 1 Cor 8:5; 10:26; and 15:47.

88. 2 Cor 5:10; Rom 14:10: Hoehner, *Ephesians*, 812. In the Colossian parallel, ἀνταπόδοσιν τῆς κληρονομίας (Col 3:24), the term κληρονομέω aligns with Eph 5:5 where it is used of ultimate reward in God's kingdom (cf. Matt 16:27; Rom 2:6). Barth observes the "eschatological foundation" of this section in Ephesians, noting two references to

or ultimately the period of the new heavens and earth, which may align with "long life on earth" in Eph 6:3. In addition to the NT texts concerning γῆ is the use of the word in Isaiah. In Isa 66:22 γῆ carries the idea of a new earth and longevity: "For as the new heavens and the new earth, which I will make, shall remain before me, says the LORD; so shall your descendants and your name remain." The term, γῆ occurs 190 times in Isaiah in reference to judgment and restoration. It is found quite often in the other prophets.[89]

The argument for long life on the eschatological earth stems primarily from the use of γῆ in Ephesians and other portions of the Pauline Corpus. Isaiah and the other prophets are supportive but not conclusive. The preceding discussion is a cautious attempt to explain the change from the LXX, and link the OT usage with the eschatological horizon of Ephesians. It is not put forth in a dogmatic fashion; however, it is compatible with the summing up of all things in heaven and upon earth (Eph 1:10), and the filling of all things (Eph 4:10), including the physical planet.[90]

10.2.2 Slavery in the Renewed Society in Eph 6:5–9

It is tempting to see correlations between slavery in Eph 6 and the exodus and new exodus periods. Certainly the slavery of the Hebrews while in Egypt played an essential role leading up to the exodus. Isaiah and the prophets have much to say about slavery as well; namely, Israel was once a slave but in the restoration will turn the tables and rule over others (Isa 14:2). Additionally, there is reason to believe that Lev 25:43 is echoed in Eph 6:9, freighted with exodus connotations: "For they are my servants, whom I brought out of the land of Egypt; they shall not be sold as slaves are sold. You shall not rule over them with harshness, but shall fear your God."[91] O'Brien has noted parallels to μετὰ φόβου καὶ τρόμου (Eph 6:5) in Exod 15:16; Isa 19:16; Ps 2:11; and remotely to Gen 9:2. They refer to the exodus (Exod 15:16), a future judgment upon the Egyptians (Isa 19:16), and the proper response of the nations to the Lord's Son installed upon Zion (Ps 2:11).

---

the last judgment in Eph 6:8–9: *Ephesians, Chapters 4–6*, 756.

89. Cf. the number of times γῆ is found in Psalms and the other prophets: Psalms (200); Jeremiah/Lamentations (260); Ezekiel (194); Daniel (83); Hosea (26); Joel (14); Amos (33); Obadiah (2); Jonah (2); Micah (15); Nahum (3); Habakkuk (10); Zephaniah (11); Haggai (6); Zechariah (44); Malachi (3).

90. O'Brien argues that the expression μακροχρόνιος ἐπὶ τῆς γῆς (Eph 6:3) does not depict immortality, but rather denotes "a long life on earth": *Letter*, 444 n. 20. He cites Arndt et al., *Greek-English Lexicon*, 488; Louw and Nida, *Lexicon*, 67.89. The argument takes into consideration the biblical-theological use of μακροχρόνιος, not merely a narrow lexical rendering.

91. Moritz, *Profound Mystery*, 153.

The terms refer to "fear of humans in the presence of God and his mighty acts."[92] However, beyond these possibilities there is no explicit evidence in Eph 6:5–9 to suggest that the author had the exodus or new exodus slavery in mind. The closest correspondence could be that the OT basis for the fair treatment of slaves was that the Hebrews were mistreated as slaves (Deut. 5:15),[93] but in Christ this is taken to an entirely new level. In the NT, the proper conduct of slaves and slave masters comes into focus in living a life worthy of Christ (Eph 4:1; cf. Philemon).[94]

Gombis asserts that the proper conduct of slaves and slave management as part of the eschatological focus of the new humanity is in stark contrast to the way slaves and slavery were practiced in the first century.[95] O'Brien agrees in seeing the new shocking expectations required of the Christian community in their handling of slave relationships.[96] In this sense the admonitions to slaves and their masters have application to this present study. The reason that this new astonishing conduct should proceed is the triumph of Christ and his church (Eph 1:20–23; 2:6; 4:8). The cosmic foes have suffered defeat in their cause to unsettle relationships in the eschatological household (Eph 2:20–22). As with former racial animosities (Eph 2:12), Christian slaves and slave owners are reconciled through the cross (Eph 2:16) and ultimately answer to Christ (Eph 6:5–9).[97] This comports with Paul's approach to slavery in Philemon and 1 Cor 7:20–24. There is some hint that Colossians adds an eschatological perspective: "In that renewal there is no longer . . . slave and free" (Col 3:11). In this rare case Colossians would preserve more of the realized aspect than does Ephesians. However, the renewal cited in Col 3:11 is not specifically referring to the eschaton (as in Col 3:4, 6) but rather the renewal that takes place through

---

92. O'Brien, *Letter*, 41. He adds details in O'Brien, *Epistle to the Philippians*, 282–84.

93. Daube, *Exodus Pattern*, 41–46.

94. This exhortation was not a call for emancipation (Philemon), although many believe that Paul set the stage for what would later lead to a wide call for manumission.

95. Gombis, "Triumph," (2005a), 67–68. For a study of slavery in the Roman Empire: Bradley, *Slaves and Masters*; Wiedemann, *Greek and Roman Slavery*. Hoehner offers a valuable extended excursus on the topic including differences between first-century slavery and slavery in the early history of the United States: *Ephesians*, 800–804. Cf. Best, *Critical and Exegetical*, 572–77; Lincoln, *Ephesians*, 415–20.

96. O'Brien, *Letter*, 454; Ridderbos, *Paul*, 317–19.

97. In this short passage (Eph 6:5–9) Χριστός occurs in 6:5, 6; κύριος in 6:7, 8; and ὁ κύριός in 6:9. A reference to Christ (or "Lord-Master") is found in every verse. This reflects an extraordinary level of external accountability. In the current eschatological age the author envisions Christ adopting the role of heavenly slave master, assuming jurisdiction equally over both slaves and their masters (Eph 6:9).

Christian growth previewed in the immediate previous context (Col 3:1–3, 5, 7–10).

10.3 CONCLUSION

There are reasons to think that the husband and wife section of the epistle grew out of the Yahweh-Israel marriage metaphor. The use of Ezek 16:9 (in Eph 5:26) has to do with the restorative aspects of the divine marriage. Yahweh meticulously washes his bride for royal presentation. Isaiah and Ezekiel anticipated the restoration and consummation of Yahweh's marriage within the new exodus. The writer appears to understand that the prophets' nuptial vision is in large part fulfilled. The marriage of Christ and the church is generally portrayed as a present triumph (Eph 5:26–27). The new exodus motif appears to underlie and correspond with the marriage picture in a present realized aspect.

There is a degree of consensus that the use of Gen 2:24 in Eph 5:31 is a typological-historical reinterpretation of marriage. Christ and the church serve as the antitype that idyllically explain the original union of husband and wife (Eph 5:32). This reflects an eschatological facet of the μυστήριον that lies alongside the revelation of ethnic solidarity in the church (Eph 2:11—3:10).

The behavior of Christian spouses, children, parents, slaves, and slave masters point toward the triumph of the new community in the household codes. It is maintained that in discussing the new state of affairs regarding these relationships the letter further demonstrates present, but not entirely complete, ethical triumph.

11

Reflections of INE Triumph in the Panoply Metaphor, Eph 6:10–24

IT IS PROPOSED IN this current study that the author of Ephesians desires that his readers fully realize the INE triumph that they presently share. Ancillary to this fundamental idea is the epistle's emphasis on actualizing triumph in the church community and in the daily affairs of life in Western Asia Minor. Eph 6:10–20 anchors this actualizing aspect of the letter.[1] Just as Eph 1:20–23 establishes the epistle upon present triumph, 6:10–20 serves to climax the application or ethical section, and in a sense the entire epistle.[2] Calling on the central concepts of the letter[3] the writer paints a warfare metaphor in graphic terms while utilizing several passages from Isaiah. In doing so the author brings his missive to a dramatic

---

1. As seen in the first chapter of this present work, commentators attempt to reconstruct the setting based on Gentile animosity toward Jews (Käsemann, Schmithals), a post-apostolic leadership crisis (Schnackenburg, Merklein), and Gnostic controversies (Pokorný, Martin). On the other hand Mortiz has high regard for more plausible approaches such as Arnold's and Lona's who see a situation of conflict either with spiritual powers (Arnold), or social environment (Lona): Arnold, *Powers of Darkness*, 226–27; Lona, *Eschatologie*, 439; Martin, "Life-Setting," 299–301; Moritz, *Profound Mystery*, 179.

2. Many see the section as the culmination of the letter: Arnold, *Powers of Darkness*, 284; Lincoln, *Ephesians*, 432; Mitton, *Epistle*, 218; Moritz, *Profound Mystery*, 181; O'Brien, *Letter*, 457–60; Sampley, "And the Two," 9; Yoder-Neufeld, *Put On*, 110–11.

3. Moritz considers Eph 1:13 as the focus of most of the "flashbacks" found in 6:10f: ἀλήθεια, λόγος-ῥῆμα, σωτηρία, πίστις, and πνεῦμα. The implication is that 1:13 anticipates the triumphal aspect of the gospel and the work of the Spirit in the struggles of Christian soldiers: *Profound Mystery*, 182.

and heart-pounding finale.[4] This aligns with the employment of Isaiah in other portions of the letter and, as noted earlier, may form an *inclusio* that hearkens back to the use of Isa 11:2 in Eph 1:8 and 17. The wisdom and insight possessed presently and sought after progressively (1:8, 17) should find demonstration on the Christian battlefield. In the present passage (Eph 6:10–20) the author seeks to motivate the audience to live out the "already" aspect of the triumph. He reminds them that triumph has arrived but with the added notion that what is true "far above" (1:21; 4:10) still requires completion in the "evil age" (4:27; 5:16; esp. 6:13, 16). From the heavenly perspective aspects of the final age have arrived; but this has not been fully realized by the saints, which is why the writer has placed an extraordinary emphasis on his audience's recognition and comprehension of present triumph (Eph 1:17–18; 3:14–19).[5] The two prayers in the epistle are major sections that seek to link the consciousness of the readers to the truths of present triumph. The short-sightedness of the audience concerning the variegated features of the μυστήριον may cause them to fall short of fully experiencing victory (Eph 3:3, 10). More than any other work in the Pauline Corpus, the epistle emphasizes the present triumph of God. But this letter does not leave the readers in a state of disconnected abstraction. The existential threats must be fully addressed before the close of the letter.

The church is to engage the enemy with full confidence that triumph is secure.[6] The battle focuses on the devil and his malevolent minions (Eph 6:11–13, 16). The audience was already warned of the devil's desire to exploit the household of faith in areas of ethical conduct (Eph 4:27). The entire age is marked by his effects (Eph 5:16) and manifested among the wrath-ridden sons of disobedience (Eph 2:2–3; 5:6). In the end God and his people prevail in a fierce cosmic battle. The question of whether Christian soldiers stand

---

4. Scholars recognize the author's use of the peroration, or war speech, used to rouse emotions in a call to battle (cf. Josh 1). Added to this tone is the change of posture from repeated calls to "walk" to "standing": Hoehner, *Ephesians*, 817; Kittredge, *Community and Authority*, 144–45; Lincoln, "Stand Therefore," 99–114; Snodgrass, *Ephesians*, 335. But O'Brien places limits on peroration: *Letter*, 459–60.

5. This is in contrast to the assertion that Paul had already been granted σύνεσις from God concerning the μυστήριον (Eph 3:4).

6. Hoehner and Best maintain that there is primarily an individual emphasis; but this section is in keeping with the rest of the epistle in stressing the corporate nature of blessings and commands. Kitchen makes an extended argument for a corporate understanding. Those that opt for an individual focus do not adequately place Eph 6:10–17 within the framework of the entire epistle: Cf. Best, *Critical and Exegetical*, 586; Hoehner, *Ephesians*, 818–19, 818 n. 6; Kitchen, *Ephesians*, 112, 116–126.

their ground or attack is still an open one. The argument revolves in part around ἵστημι (Eph 6:11, 13), πάλη (Eph 6:12), and ἀνθίστημι (Eph 6:13). Dahl, Arnold, Lincoln, Mitton, and others see both defensive and offensive weapons in the panoply. Best, Thielman, Hoehner, Kitchen, Foulkes, and Moule propose that the church presently shares Christ's triumph, and are to keep the ground already won until the final Parousia. In this sense there is no need to attack. This fits better with the argument of this current work, but the evidence is not firm nor is the point crucial. The letter may be alluding to an aggressive fight against the spiritual powers, especially within the church (Eph 5:11; 6:12), but more of a passive stand against governmental authorities and society in general (Eph 3:13; 6:20; cf. 1 Cor 2:8).[7] Another aspect of this controversy surrounds the understanding of the πάλη reference (Eph 6:12). Probably it is a technical term that is not specifically pointing to the sport of ancient wrestling. With this understanding, a soldier "wrestled" against the enemy in a sense synonymous with "struggled."[8] In the end, whether the Christian soldier takes a stand or attacks, the devil is forced to concede—in a sense now (Eph 1:21; 3:10), and certainly in the future (Eph 2:7). Although triumphant, the soldier must be aware that the devil remains a virulent opportunist who seeks to upend the mutually truthful and peaceful relationships that are to mark the community (Eph 4:25–27).

There is little doubt that several passages from Isaiah are directly utilized in the panoply section.[9] Although Isaiah is the primary influence upon Eph 6:14–17, Lincoln maintains that it is most likely that the Roman soldier is in view.[10] The theological backdrop is Isaiah, but fighter images that illustrate the picture are likely contemporary soldiers. It appears that the OT view of Yahweh the Divine Warrior conflates into the author's Roman images (of course, there was no standing Jewish army in Paul's day).

---

7. Arnold, *Power and Magic*, 121; Best, *Critical and Exegetical*, 597; W. Carr, *Angels and Principalities*, 197; Dahl et al., *Studies*, 444; Foulkes, *Epistle of Paul*, 171; Hoehner, *Ephesians*, 818; Kitchen, *Ephesians*, 114; Lincoln, *Ephesians*, 451; Mitton, *Epistle*, 227; Moritz, *Profound Mystery*, 199–201; H. Moule, *Studies in Ephesians*, 151; Schnackenburg, *Ephesians*, 278; Thielman, "Ephesians," 832–33.

8. Gordon, "Belt-Wrestling," 131–36; Levine, "Wrestling-Belt Legacy," 560–64. Arnold contends that πάλη is envisioned as a sport in Eph 6:12, while Barth leaves both options open, arguing for a conflation of sport and warfare: Arnold, *Power and Magic*, 115–18; M. Barth, *Ephesians, Chapters 4–6*, 763–64. Besides the lexical ambiguities, an interpreter who opts for a clearly athletic meaning must contend with a mixed metaphor within close contextual quarters.

9. For studies that consider the Divine Warrior motif and its interplay with war passages in the NT including Ephesians 6: Longman and Reid, "Defeat of Principalities," 136–64; Yoder-Neufeld, *Put on*, 94–153.

10. Lincoln, *Ephesians*, 436.

But Moritz and others are skeptical, observing differences between Josephus and Polybius's depictions of Roman soldiers and that of Paul.[11] However, these differences are not significant enough to make a case against Roman imagery in favor of another tradition. It was not the writer's intention to present an exhaustive picture of Roman soldiery. Rather, as stated previously, the author may have used contemporary Greco-Roman images, but these are veneer molded upon Isaiah. Other texts may provide shared language but do not play a direct role in the author's formation of Eph 6:14–17.[12]

It is possible that Ephesians draws on a third party apart from Isaiah: Qumran, Wisdom, or other Second Temple traditions have been suggested.[13] Lindemann understands the pseudonymous author relying on Jewish Wisdom literature, without direct association with Isaiah.[14] Similarly, Gnilka views the usage to be indirect by way of tradition.[15] On the other hand, Schlier and Caird see conscious usage of the Isaiah citations.[16] Lincoln maintains conscious allusion or inexact recollection.[17] Certainly Ephesians shares the common theme of holy war with the Qumran literature; however, Moritz notes that the contrasts are stark.[18] Qumran fully expected physical war with God's enemies whereas Ephesians and other works in the Pauline Corpus clearly identify a spiritual battle: "For our struggle is not against enemies of blood and flesh" (Eph 6:12); and, "for the weapons of our warfare are not merely human, but they have divine power to destroy strongholds. We destroy arguments" (2 Cor 10:4). While it is possible that Ephesians drew upon Qumran tradition, it is safe to say that both Ephesians and Qumran separately accessed Isaiah for their respective purposes. Qumran envis-

---

11. Moritz cites Josephus, *De Bello Judaico*, 3.93 and Polybius, 6.23: *Profound Mystery*, 184 n. 19; 186–87; 189 n. 40; 206–7.

12. As a sampling of warfare imagery, Isa 27:1 has Yahweh with a sword: "On that day the Lord with his cruel and great and strong sword will punish Leviathan the fleeing serpent." In Isa 40:10 God is described as a warrior. In the following verse (Isa 40:11) he is portrayed as a pastoral shepherd. The two images are juxtaposed. "Stand" is found in Exod 13:14 and may parallel Eph 6:11, 13, and 14. Several other passages in Isaiah contribute to the battle metaphor. Cf. Zenger, "God of Exodus," 29.

13. Moritz makes mention of the concept of warfare found in *T. Ab.* 7:3; Dan 7; 10:13, 20; Rev 9:11 and 19:11f., but the differences between Ephesians and Qumran apply to these as well: *Profound Mystery*, 186–87; 187 n. 33.

14. Lindemann, *Aufhebung*, 64–65; 89.

15. Gnilka, *Epheserbrief: Auslegung*, 28, 310.

16. Caird, *Letters from Prison*, 93; Schlier, *Brief*, 294–97.

17. Lincoln, *Ephesians*, 436. Similarly, Mitton, *Epistle*, 224; Schnackenburg, *Ephesians*, 283.

18. Moritz, *Profound Mystery*, 186. Cf. Braun, *Qumran*, 269; Fischer, *Tendenz*, 167–69; Kuhn, "Epistle," 115–31; Mussner, "Contributions," 159–78.

ages a looming eschatological battle with the Romans, whereas the author's eschatological battle views armies of good and evil engaged in spiritual warfare. Thielman makes specific comparisons between the Wisdom of Solomon and the direct use of the OT in Eph 6, and sees the evidence slightly in favor of the OT.[19] If the writer of the epistle did use extra-biblical sources, he found the sources' ultimate origination in the OT. Certainly the Qumranites revered Isaiah with the same respect that Paul and others afforded the prophet.[20] Wild asserts that if the OT is mediated through Wisdom it may account for one word, πανοπλία (in Eph 6:11, 13), otherwise it is entirely Isaiah.[21] Lincoln does not believe that dependency on Wisdom of Solomon can be established.[22] Some like Kuhn disagree, claiming that Eph 6 should be read against the backdrop of 1QS. But it appears that Moritz is closer to the mark: "the actual points of contact between Qumran and Ephesians which do not overlap with Isaiah are minimal."[23] This is reinforced further when consideration is given to Paul's choice of the use of Isaiah in other places, particularly Ephesians, rather than reverting to Qumran as a source.

At first glance the Isaiah linkages in Eph 6:14–17 do not seem to be used in expressly the same way as in Isaiah. Questions remain concerning the nature of the use of Isaiah and what aspects of the new exodus might be present. O'Brien, Moritz, and M. Barth make a case for understanding the wider context of Isaiah in order to explain the usages.[24] M. Barth considers the author's direct use of Isa 11:4, 5 and 59:17 in Eph 6:14, 17, but alludes to Isa 52:7 in Eph 6:15.[25] Others lie between, such as Lincoln who maintains that the pseudonymous author appropriated genuine Paul at 1 Thess 5:8: "put on the breastplate of faith and love, and for a helmet the hope of salvation."[26] Hoehner views Paul using the Isaiah text but without deliberately importing the Isaiah contexts.[27] Wild acknowledges the use of Isaiah but does not consider the OT extractions to be adequate for understanding Eph 6.

19. Thielman, "Ephesians," 832.
20. Arnold, *Power and Magic*, 110.
21. Wild, "Warrior," 286 n. 6.
22. Lincoln, "Use," 43.
23. Kuhn, "Epistle," 115–31; Moritz, *Profound Mystery*, 186.
24. M. Barth, *Ephesians, Chapters 4–6*, 767–71; 775–76; Moritz, *Profound Mystery*, 178–212; O'Brien, *Letter*, 473–74; 477–79.
25. M. Barth, "Conversion," 3–24; M. Barth, *Ephesians, Chapters 4–6*, 788 n. 175.
26. Lincoln, "Use," 43; Yoder-Neufeld, *Put on*, 96–97; 102–3; 105; 117–18; 125.
27. Hoehner, *Ephesians*, 822–23; 839–41; 843–44; 850.

An argument can be made that Eph 6 utilizes the new exodus aspect of Isaiah. It will be shown that the writer intentionally developed the Isaiah texts from their broad contexts in ways that contribute to the argument of the epistle. It appears that the author does not merely share the language of Isaiah.[28] Five primary imagery linkages having to do with Eph 6 and Isa 11, 49, 52 and 59 appear.[29] They are: (1) belt of truth: Eph 6:14a with Isa 11:5; (2) breastplate of righteousness: Eph 6:14b with Isa 59:17a; (3) prepared feet: Eph 6:15 (cf. 2:17) with Isa 52:7 (cf. 40:9); (4) helmet of salvation: Eph 6:17a and Isa 59:17b; and, (5) sword of the Spirit: Eph 6:17b with Isa 49:2 (cf. 11:4b).[30] These will be considered from the standpoint of Isaiah and how the new exodus is incorporated in Eph 6.[31]

11.1 BELT OF TRUTH IN EPH 6:14A AND ISA 11:5

J. Watts sees an "arch structure" in Isa 10:24—12:6 with 11:3b-4 serving as the apogee.[32] Ninow relates how in Isa 11:10-16 God will gather the exiles in a new exodus from the corners of the earth and reunite Judah and Ephraim.[33] To do so, God will act within the Mosaic tradition, interceding a "second time" (שֵׁנִית) by drying up the River:

> On that day the Lord will extend his hand yet a second time to recover the remnant that is left of his people, from Assyria, from Egypt, from Pathros, from Ethiopia, from Elam, from Shinar, from Hamath, and from the coastlands of the sea . . . And the

---

28. Thielman states that both Isaiah and Ephesians demonstrate sin, judgment, and restoration. However, this pattern is observed in other places in the Bible, such as the book of Judges and the prophets. The pattern does not point out any exclusive features between Isaiah and Ephesians: Thielman, "Ephesians," 831.

29. The overall section may be divided into three: Eph 6:10-13 is the admonition to be strong in the Lord; 14-17 focuses on the imperative to stand firm along with being equipped with various pieces of armor; and 18-20 is a call to prayer for vigilance. It is the second division that utilizes Isaiah.

30. The "shield of faith" (Eph 6:16) is not found in Isaiah but in many other places in the OT (Gen 15:1; Pss 5:2; 18:2, 30, 35; 28:7; 33:20; 35:2; 59:11; 91:4; 115:9-11; 144:1). The fact that a similar shield is not found in Isaiah is not significant to the present argument other than to demonstrate the writer's creative use of the OT. The writer merely expanded Isaiah's imagery by adding a shield. It is likely that Isaiah saw no need for Yahweh and his servant to employ a defensive piece of armor.

31. Both Isaiah and Ephesians adopt clothing imagery. The metaphor is mentioned two times in Isa 11:5 and four times in Isa 59:17. Eph 4:23, 24, 25 and 6:11-17 are the investiture counterparts. Cf. Rom 13:12, 14; Col 3:8, 12; 1 Thess 5:8.

32. J. Watts, *Isaiah 1-33*, 154, 169. Ackroyd maintains that Isa 12 is the culmination of Isa 1-11 and notably exodus in nature: "Isaiah 1-12, " 35.

33. Ninow, *Indicators*, 158.

> Lord will utterly destroy the tongue of the sea of Egypt; and will wave his hand over the River with his scorching wind; and will split it into seven channels, and make a way to cross on foot; so there shall be a highway from Assyria for the remnant that is left of his people, as there was for Israel when they came up from the land of Egypt. (Isa 11:11, 15–16)

Key terms such as "hand" (יָד)[34] and "recover" (קָנָה)[35] are common in the Pentateuchal and Isaiah accounts. The chapter is also messianic in nature, identifying the "shoot" (Isa 11:1) and "root" (Isa 11:10) of David as the one who will execute the new exodus. Fishbane and Motyer recognize the new exodus imagery and the stem of Jesse's role in the reenactment of the escape from Egypt.[36] Motyer writes that in Isa 11:1 and 10–16 "the promised Davidic king becomes the magnet of a new exodus."[37] The imagery in Isa 11 is both militaristic and royal. The larger context (Isa 2–12) indicates that Israel has been judged, but now in chapter 11 the Messiah will replay the exodus by redeeming God's people.[38] The messianic "Branch" was anticipated as far back as Isa 4:2–6 where just as in the exodus, "the LORD will create over the whole site of Mount Zion and over its places of assembly a cloud by day and smoke and the shining of a flaming fire by night" (Isa 4:5). The section also has the nations in view. They will be drawn to the Messiah as a beacon of hope: "as a signal to the peoples; the nations shall inquire of him" (Isa 11:10), and "He will raise a signal for the nations" (Isa 11:12). J. Watts not only sees Isa 11:3b–4 as the pinnacle of chapters 10–13, but understands that in the close context God is acting "in a way parallel to the Exodus" and is recreating a people for himself.[39] Ninow remarks, "The future deliverance—the new Exodus—is clearly phrased and formed in terms of the historical exodus."[40] Fishbane observes that the similarities between Isa 11 and Exod 14 and 15 are striking, including analogous combat imagery.[41] In Exodus and Isaiah, Fishbane finds Yahweh muting the cosmological forces. However, this new exodus, which includes the Messiah and the nations, will outshine the original and is destined for the remote future.[42] The "second

---

34. Isa 11:11; Exod 3:19–20; 6:1; 13:3; Deut 6:21.
35. Isa 11:11; Exod 15:16; Deut 32:6.
36. Cf. Fishbane, "Motif," 133–35; Motyer, *Prophecy of Isaiah*, 121–28.
37. Motyer, *Prophecy of Isaiah*, 50.
38. Hill, "Reading Isaiah," 59.
39. J. Watts, *Isaiah 1–33*, 154; 169–78; quotation from 178.
40. Ninow, *Indicators*, 160.
41. Exod 14:16; 15:3, 6, and 8. Fishbane, "Motif," 127–28.
42. Ninow, *Indicators*, 161. Cf. Hasel, *Remnant*, 348.

time" (עֵת) motif identifies a future, decisive deliverance. It is just prior to this promise of new exodus where Isa 11:5 is situated. There the root of Jesse, with the Spirit of God resting upon him, is presented as the Divine Warrior who dons righteousness about his loins and truth about his sides (Isa 11:5). He is the one who metes out justice upon the unrighteous of Judah who have abused the poor and afflicted (Isa 11:4). Deadly animals are transformed (Isa 11:6–8), and the nations look to the root of Jesse on the holy mountain (Isa 11:9–10).

The belt of truth imagery in Eph 6:14a shares verbal and conceptual correspondence with Isa 11:5. The phrase, περιζωσάμενοι τὴν ὀσφὺν ὑμῶν ἐν ἀληθείᾳ (Eph 6:14a), is similar to ἔσται δικαιοσύνῃ ἐζωσμένος τὴν ὀσφὺν αὐτοῦ καὶ ἀληθείᾳ εἰλημένος τὰς πλευράς (Isa 11:5; cf. Isa 11:4 and δικαιοσύνη there). Both share the same verb stem, ζωννύω, to gird or tie; as well as ἀλήθεια in reference to truth or faithfulness. There is a slight change in that the text in Ephesians does not have δικαιοσύνη as Isaiah; only ἀλήθεια. But δικαιοσύνη makes its appearance in the last half of the verse (Eph 6:14b) in reference to the breastplate.[43] Once again the writer shows versatility in his use of the OT, seeing ἀλήθεια and δικαιοσύνη as Isaiah does within the same cluster of terms and concepts that describe Yahweh and his servant.[44] Isaiah 45:19 reflects this: ἀλήθεια and δικαιοσύνη are used parallel to one another and attributed to the Lord: εἰμι κύριος λαλῶν δικαιοσύνην καὶ ἀναγγέλλων ἀλήθειαν.[45] The use of ἀλήθεια and δικαιοσύνη indicates that Yahweh's truthfulness (or faithfulness) and righteousness are closely aligned.[46] Yahweh

43. B. Webb views God's righteousness in Isaiah as his faithfulness to covenant promises seen in his saving acts, such as justice for the oppressed. In the use of δικαιοσύνη in Ephesians the focus is upon ethical living, although some take it as positional righteousness. Bruce, Lincoln, O'Brien, and others opt for the former: Bruce, *Epistles*, 407–8; Lincoln, *Ephesians*, 448; O'Brien, *Letter*, 474; B. Webb, *Message of Isaiah*, 229. The difference between Yahweh's righteous covenantal acts and the Christian soldier's ethical conduct may be indiscernible in the mind of the author of the epistle.

44. Kreitzer observes that in Pauline eschatology there is fluctuation between God and Jesus Christ when it comes to "him who delivers" (Col 1:13 [Father]; Gal 1:4 and 1 Thess 1:10 [Christ]). This reflects the same interchangeableness seen between Yahweh and his servant in saving contexts in Isaiah: Kreitzer, *Jesus and God*, 126.

45. Cf. Isa 65:16: "Then whoever invokes a blessing in the land shall bless by the God of faithfulness [ἀληθινός], and whoever takes an oath in the land shall swear by the God of faithfulness [ἀληθινός]; because the former troubles are forgotten and are hidden from my sight."

46. The term ἀλήθεια occurs thirteen times in LXX Isaiah: 10:20; 11:5; 16:5; 26:2, 3, 10; 37:18; 38:3; 42:3; 45:19; 48:1; 59:14; 59:15. The word depicts Yahweh's faithfulness toward the returning remnant (10:20); Yahweh's belt (11:5); a just judge (16:5); the faithful and righteous (26:2); those who are faithful in trust (26:3); the wicked are unrighteous and not truthful (26:10); perhaps Yahweh (37:18); Hezekiah's faithfulness (38:3); the servant faithfully bringing forth justice (42:3); Yahweh announcing

is faithful to his covenant promises by acting righteously and justly. This idea of truthfulness-faithfulness can be seen in Ephesians. The term ἀλήθεια occurs seven times (Eph 1:13; 4:15, 21, 24, 25; 5:9; 6:14). It refers to the gospel (1:13), speaking with doctrinal accuracy (4:15), ethical living that is rooted in original teaching (4:21), the newly created self (4:24), speaking truth versus lying (4:25), and the fruit of the light (5:9). Similar to Isaiah, Eph 4:24–25; 5:9; and 6:4 present ἀλήθεια and δικαιοσύνη together. It appears that with the exception of ἀλήθεια as the gospel (Eph 1:13) the term is used in Ephesians in close proximity to ethical living.[47] In Eph 6:14 the belt of truth probably has to do with the Isaianic idea of Yahweh's covenantal faithfulness toward upholding righteousness.

If this is the case, then the Christian soldier is a co-combatant allied with Yahweh, donning Yahweh's armor, and faithfully upholding ethical living against the inimical powers that seek to promote ethnic animosity (Eph 2:11–16), doctrinal instability (Eph 4:14–15), sexual impurity (Eph 4:17–22; 5:3–7), and interpersonal tensions (Eph 4:25–32).[48] Although righteousness is included in the Isaianic belt imagery, it is faithfulness in the Ephesian text that is emphasized. Among the various parts of the panoply, faithfulness to ethical living is put forth first in the execution of the battle. By introducing ἀλήθεια in the panoply metaphor the writer sweeps through the entirety of his letter to picture climactically the faithful enforcement of righteousness on the part of the people of God. This comports with Yahweh's behavior in the INE.

Conceptually, Isa 11:5 and Eph 6:14a both depict military conflict. The forces of righteousness are arrayed against ethical wrongdoing in both; however, there are differences. In Isaiah the root of Jesse battles against the unrighteous in Judah. In Ephesians, rather than God battling his own people, it is his people that have donned Yahweh's armor and battle the cosmic forces. When it comes to fighting enemies, the differences between Christ battling and his people battling are indistinguishable in the epistle. The audience is repeatedly told that they are ἐν Χριστῷ (Eph 1:1) and are

---

righteousness and truth (45:19); Jacob who does not invoke God in righteousness and truth (48:1); justice, righteousness and truth are stymied (59:14); truth is lacking (59:15). This survey reveals that ἀλήθεια in Isaiah is often associated with righteousness and justice. These are lacking in preexilic and exilic Judah and find resolution in Yahweh and his servant's faithful actions.

47. The reference to ἀληθείᾳ as doctrinal accuracy in Eph 4:15 probably has much to do with the prohibition toward walking as the Gentiles (Eph 4:17f). It could be that some form of libertine philosophy was afoot. This is also seen in the reaffirmation of ethical portions of the Torah (Eph 5:31—6:4).

48. M. Barth remarks: "At the same time an act of democratization and knighting takes place. God's victory is passed down to all the saints": *Ephesians, Chapters 4–6*, 775.

co-resurrected and co-enthroned with Christ (Eph 1:20–23; 2:6).[49] They are a part of a household in which God dwells, where Christ is the cornerstone, and to which access is granted through God's Spirit (Eph 2:18, 20–21). The Spirit is said to be at work in their inner being (Eph 3:17) and is filling them with the fullness of God (Eph 3:19). In addition, the recipients are told, "clothe yourselves with the new self, created according to the likeness of God in true righteousness and holiness" (Eph 4:24). Related to this is the command to imitate God and Christ ethically (Eph 5:1–2), mirroring a kingdom that is both Christ's and God's (Eph 5:5), and specifically in the way marriages are conducted (Eph 5:24–25) and in the fashion after which children are nurtured and slaves are regarded (Eph 6:1–9). If the audience is ἐν Χριστῷ, clothed with the likeness of God after δικαιοσύνη, and is completely identified with the Father, Son, and Spirit, then both God and the Christian hearers are battling against evil in an interchangeable fashion. In the writer's mind, what the root of Jesse accomplishes against evildoers in Judah the church as a combatant undertakes against the cosmic forces in Western Asia Minor.[50] In Isaiah, Yahweh as Warrior and his servant-warrior are functionally equivalent (Isa 42:1–4; 50:10). Also, Israel is oftentimes referred to as the servant (Isa 41:8–9; 44:1–2). The author's view of the interchangeableness of God, Christ, and his people follows Isaiah's view of Yahweh, his servant, and Israel. This is attributed to assumptions concerning corporate solidarity. But the battle is not one in which external forces are taken to task by church members; rather, a picture emerges in which the ethereal forces seek to upend the church in terms of moral conduct, unity, and doctrinal orthodoxy. The focus of the battle is against these threats that seek to manifest themselves within the eschatological household.

In summary, the belt of truth or faithfulness finds origination in Isa 11:5. The faithfulness that the stem of Jesse dons (Isa 11:1–5) to execute new exodus righteousness and justice (Isa 11:11–16) is assumed by the church. In the author's composition of Ephesians the new and greater exodus anticipated by Isaiah has arrived and has serious ethical implications in the eschatological community. The church takes on Yahweh's armor in their

---

49. The phrase ἐν Χριστῷ occurs in eighty-nine verses in the Pauline Corpus; thirteen times in Ephesians (1:1, 3, 10, 12, 20; 2:6, 7, 10, 13; 3:6, 11, 21; 4:32): Moritz, *Profound Mystery*, 192.

50. Ephesians 4:24; 5:9; and 6:14 all emphasize ἀλήθεια and δικαιοσύνη and may all reflect Isa 11:5. In the same vicinity is Isa 11:2 (πνεῦμα σοφίας καὶ συνέσεως, πνεῦμα βουλῆς καὶ ἰσχύος, πνεῦμα γνώσεως καὶ εὐσεβείας), which is shared in Eph 1:8, 17 (σοφίᾳ καὶ φρονήσει and πνεῦμα σοφίας καὶ ἀποκαλύψεως). Just as the church is to take on the servant's armor, it is to adopt his sagacity in battle.

new exodus battle. Isaiah's triumphant new exodus has arrived, but aspects of the battle are still in play.

11.2 BREASTPLATE OF RIGHTEOUSNESS IN EPH 6:14B AND ISA 59:17A

Although Isa 59 has no explicit associations with the exodus, it is clearly eschatological[51] and fits within the INE motif.[52] In addition to Isaiah and the prophets in general, flanking Isa 59 are explicit new exodus texts: Isa 51:1—52:15; 55:12; and Isa 63:7–19.[53] Chapter 59 focuses on the sins that have hidden God's face from his people (Isa 59:2). The primary offense has to do with actions taken toward the innocent (Isa 59:7, 13, 15). In addition, there is crookedness in justice (Isa 59:8–9, 11, 14, 15), and an absence of righteousness (δικαιοσύνη). The servant-warrior is righteous in that he acts to correct injustice toward the oppressed. The term δικαιοσύνη occurs fifty-two times in Isaiah, twice more than any other prophet.[54] Often the contexts of δικαιοσύνη in Isaiah reveal righteousness on behalf of the oppressed as it does in Isa 59. Because no one comes to the aid of the innocent, Yahweh dons the soldier's panoply (Isa 59:16–17) and levies wrath upon the guilty (Isa 59:18). Isaiah 59:16 reveals this: "He saw that there was no one, and was appalled that there was no one to intervene; so his own arm brought him victory." This section of Isaiah focuses on Israel's glorious future (Isa 60–66), but before this takes place the prophet confesses the wickedness of the nation (Isa 59:9–15a) and Yahweh strikes out in vengeance to punish the egregious sins of his people. He acts as the Divine Warrior donning himself with the breastplate of righteousness to repay all according to their deeds (Isa 59:18).[55] Yahweh the Redeemer will come to Zion to redeem those who turn from their transgression (Isa 59:20).

---

51. Kreitzer notes that Paul uses Isa 59:20 in Rom 11:26 to describe God's final judgment of the world, which includes the first advent of Christ and proceeding forward: *Jesus and God*, 127. In a slightly different fashion his use of Isa 59:20 in 1 Thess 5:8 is for preservation and protection in the calamitous Day of the Lord. This is similar to the citations in Eph 6:14 and 17. In all three uses of Isa 59 Isaiah's eschatological timeline is in view.

52. B. Anderson looks at Second Isaiah and sees the new exodus as a sweeping motif: "Exodus Typology," 177–95.

53. Fishbane, "Motif," 135, 138–39.

54. The use of the term in other books: Jeremiah (7); Ezekiel (22); Daniel (12); Hosea (3); Joel (1); Amos (3); Micah (2); Zephaniah (1); Zecharaiah (1); Malachai (3).

55. As examined earlier, from this same section of Isaiah the writer most likely uses Isa 60:1 in Eph 5:14.

In Ephesians the readers are told to put on the breastplate of righteousness (ἐνδυσάμενοι τὸν θώρακα τῆς δικαιοσύνης, Eph 6:14b). This line has verbal and conceptual correspondence with Isa 59:17a, ἐνεδύσατο δικαιοσύνην ὡς θώρακα. All three words are shared: ἐνδύω, θώραξ, and δικαιοσύνη. It was found that the belt of truth in Isaiah has strong associations with righteousness. The two virtues are observed in Yahweh and are to be realized in his people. Ethical conduct is in mind, especially in terms of societal justice. As with the belt of truth, the breastplate is Yahweh's but now is the possession of the church. The emphasis in Isaiah is on the severe vengeance that Yahweh pours out on Judah and the nations. This retribution is now turned upon the cosmic powers as the church adopts Yahweh's battle.[56] There is, as in Isaiah, a glorious future, but wickedness is first to be confronted and punished.

To review, the adoption of the breastplate of righteousness from Isaiah reinforces the new exodus battle that is taken up by the church. The challenge for the community of faith is ethical living marked by δικαιοσύνη.[57] Just as the conflict in Isaiah coincided with the new exodus, the battle in Ephesians has arrived with the new age. To say that conflict is incompatible with the triumphal new exodus would be to deny both Isaiah's and Paul's view of the final age. They see both aspects present in the buildup to the final Parousia. There is, of sorts, an age within an age. Isaiah's final epoch has arrived, and within that era is the conflict predicted by prophet. Just as the author of the epistle viewed ultimate futuristic peace in the Parousia as the terminus antitype of Isaiah's vision, he also saw the conflicts in Isaiah as the typological-historical battles in the new exodus age leading to the Parousia. Both are present and triumphal in the writer's mind: Isaiah's peace and conflict—with the latter in its last gasps.[58] It appears that the author understood that the triumphal conflicts of Isaiah's new exodus are propheticly, certainly, and typologically pointing to final victory and peace.

---

56. Following Isa 59:17 is, "According to their deeds, so will he repay; wrath to his adversaries, requital to his enemies" (Isa 59:18). Paul utilizes this text in Rom 2:6 in reference to the hardened and unbelieving. Romans shares similar uses of Isaiah that are found in Eph 6: Isa 59:20 with Rom 11:25; Isa 52:5–7 with Rom 2:24; 10:15. Cf. Wagner, "Isaiah," 117–29.

57. The term δικαιοσύνη (6:14) is taken ethically rather than forensically, based primarily on the general use in Isaiah, Eph 4:24, and the recurring ethical admonitions found in Eph 4:14—6:9.

58. Fee recognizes in the epistle that the victory is not fully realized, hence the need for Christians to be equipped for the ongoing battle: *Spirit*, 724.

11.3 PREPARED FEET IN EPH 6:15 (2:17) AND ISA 52:7

Arnold understands that the primary contact point between Isa 52 and Eph 6 is the new exodus, especially at Isa 52:6: "Therefore my people shall know my name; therefore in that day they shall know that it is I who speak; here am I."[59] Also, Isa 51:9–10 reveals another, more explicit exodus passage: "Was it not you who cut Rahab in pieces, who pierced the dragon? Was it not you who dried up the sea, the waters of the great deep; who made the depths of the sea a way for the redeemed to cross over?" Rahab is an epithet for Egypt (Isa 30:7; Ps 87:4), while the dried up sea speaks of the exodus crossing. "Redeemed" (גָּאַל, Isa 51:10; 52:3) refers to the paschal redemption inaugurated upon the first Passover in Egypt; a transaction without cost to the beneficiaries (Isa 52:3).[60] In addition, Isa 51 views the desert transformed into an Eden-like setting (Isa 51:3).[61] This is performed by the "arm of the Lord" (Isa 51:5, 9), an image reminiscent of the exodus.[62] All of these passages contribute to the context of Isa 52:7 and its usage in Eph 6:17.

Isa 52 opens with a call to Jerusalem to clothe itself in priest-like garments.[63] From the onset of the nation it was Yahweh's intention for Israel to be a nation of priests (Exod 19:6). In Isa 52:4 both the Egyptian and Assyrian oppressions are brought into view. The Lord himself ("Here I am," Isa 52:6) accompanies his people (Isa 52:12), as in the departure from Egypt. But in the original exodus the cloud and fire went before (Exod 13:21–22), and then moved behind at the sea crossing (Exod 14:19). It is never said that the cloud and fire went both before and after simultaneously in the original exodus, but in the new exodus God himself goes both before and after (Isa 52:12), personally accompanying his people. Yahweh's redemption is cause for the grand announcement of good news (Isa 52:7): "How beautiful upon the mountains are the feet of the messenger who announces peace, who brings good news, who announces salvation, who says to Zion, 'Your God reigns.'" The emancipation of God's people and the gathering of the nations have arrived.[64] Both Jerusalem (Isa 52:9) and the peoples (Isa 52:10)

---

59. Arnold, *Power and Magic*, 109.

60. On גָּאַל, Motyer, *Prophecy of Isaiah*, 418–19.

61. Fishbane argues that the new exodus functions as a prismatic window to the transhistorical; pointing out that in the OT the new exodus exceeds the influence of the Eden motif: "Motif," 121–40.

62. Exod 6:6; 15:16; Deut 4:34; 5:15; 7:19; 9:29; 11:2; 26:8.

63. Exod 28:2; Ninow, *Indicators*, 189.

64. Do the nations come believing or to pay homage? There may not be a great deal of difference because Yahweh's justice has destroyed the wicked. It seems that those left, both Jew and Gentile, are the believing remnant. Motyer understands the nations observing Yahweh's works (Isa 52:10) and joining in his salvation: *Prophecy of Isaiah*, 420.

will hear of Yahweh's towering triumph. The point of the exodus-departure from the land of exile is highlighted (Isa 52:11–12). It is not primarily for purposes of liberation, but for the proper reinstitution of the priesthood in Jerusalem. "Depart, depart, go out from there! Touch no unclean thing" is directed to the priests and has strong ethical overtones (Isa 52:11). In contrast to the first exodus, the second will not take place in haste (Isa 52:12).[65] There is a noted difference between fleeing (בָּרַח, Exod 14:5) and departing (סוּר, Isa 52:11). Motyer observes that there will be no panic or pressure in the idyllic new exodus.[66]

"Prepared feet" has verbal and conceptual correspondence with Isa 52:7.[67] Ephesians 6:15 reads, καὶ ὑποδησάμενοι τοὺς πόδας ἐν ἑτοιμασίᾳ τοῦ εὐαγγελίου τῆς εἰρήνης; and the relevant portion of Isa 52:7 is ὡς πόδες εὐαγγελιζομένου ἀκοὴν εἰρήνης, ὡς εὐαγγελιζόμενος ἀγαθά. Common terms are πούς, εὐαγγέλιον, and εἰρήνη. Both passages have a warfare setting, but significantly, they are transformed into places of peace.[68] In Ephesians prepared feet describe podiatric equipment without mentioning shoes per se, aligning with the OT text where feet are emphasized over footwear.[69] The stress is on what the prepared soldier declares rather than on the precise equipment on his feet. In Isaiah the feet refer to those who glide upon the mountaintops to proclaim Yahweh's military conquest. The usages in Isaiah and Ephesians are quite similar, both expressing a picture of the announcement of victorious news. In Ephesians it is the message of the gospel of Christ, reconciliation of racial acrimony, and the μυστήριον (Eph 1:13; 2:17; 3:6–7; 6:15, 19). In Isaiah the news is of Yahweh's eschatological victory, perhaps manifested historically in Cyrus's actions. Israel had experienced deliverance and would once again in the future. She encountered Yahweh's judgment in exile, but a repentant and believing remnant would be restored. Yahweh arrives at Mount Zion to establish his place over his people and the

---

65. Exod 12:11; Deut 16:3.

66. Motyer, *Prophecy of Isaiah*, 422.

67. Paul uses Isa 52:7 in Rom 10:15. The meaning in Romans is the bringing of the gospel; in Eph 6:15 the author adds the idea of readiness (ἐν ἑτοιμασίᾳ), which is disputed. Lincoln takes it as readiness or preparation, highlighting the subject to be prayed upon in Eph 6:18: *Ephesians*, 448–49. Yoder-Neufeld proposes that ἑτοιμασίᾳ reflects "eschatological reserve" until peace is fully realized, but this is unconvincing: *Put on*, 137. The term seems best understood as reflecting an attitude of urgency and alertness that is incumbent upon soldiers in a lethally charged atmosphere (Eph 6:18).

68. M. Barth notes the sudden transition from war to peace in Isa 11:4–9, citing Harnack's observation of a "lofty paradox": M. Barth, *Ephesians, Chapters 4–6*, 770–71; Harnack, *Militia Christi*, 13. The contrast is also seen in the immediate context: Isa 52:7 has the announcement of peace and Isa 52:10 presents the Lord baring his arm.

69. Lincoln, *Ephesians*, 448.

nations pay homage. His eternal kingdom is now in place along with those of his people who honor him. In Eph 6:15 the church propagates a similar message in the battle against the cosmic forces. The fact that Paul cites Isa 52:7 in Rom 10:15 and Isa 52:15 in Rom 15:21 in ministry contexts, strongly suggests that Isa 52 and its environs shape his own calling and ministry.[70] Paul's self-conceptualization as seen through the lens of Isaiah may have been imported into Eph 6:15, with application to the church as a gospel-sending military unit.

The arrival of Yahweh's kingdom in Isaiah may be classified as a "nearly yet" in Eph 6. This is strongly reminiscent of Eph 2:17: "So he came and proclaimed peace to you who were far off and peace to those who were near." There the dissolution of the differences between Jewish and Gentile believers is an established fact. If the Isaiah concept of "proclaimed peace" (Isa 52:7) is seen as the background of the first usage, it is most likely similarly established in the second usage in Eph 6:15. Only in Eph 6:15 is the proclamation a part of the church's armor and therefore maintains a potential sense not completely actualized. However, as stated previously, the conflict and peace anticipated by Isaiah in the new exodus is naturally assumed by the writer and is reflected in Ephesians. Although this may cause difficulty to the linearity of the modern mind, it poses no difficulty to the author's understanding of Isaiah. The present triumphal new exodus is still intact as the church battles the cosmic forces.

11.4 HELMET OF SALVATION IN EPH 6:17A AND ISA 59:17B

As seen previously, Isa 59 has no immediate new exodus associations but does fall within the contours of the INE. Yahweh's punishment of Israel and Judah, as well as all the nations, is in view. At Isa 59:17b Yahweh is motivated to act; he is astonished that no one intercedes on behalf of the oppressed (Isa 59:14–16). As a consequence he puts on the breastplate of righteousness, places on his head the helmet of salvation, and clothes himself with garments of vengeance and zeal. The helmet of salvation does not reflect vengeance only. Actually σωτήριον anticipates Isa 59:20, "And he will come to Zion as Redeemer, to those in Jacob who turn from transgression, says the Lord." The punishment of wickedness is in view, but σωτήριον is the central referent. Yahweh's helmet is therefore most likely one of regal glory and victory rather than one that provides protection.[71] This would cor-

---

70. Wagner, "Isaiah," 123–24.

71. J. Watts assigns the helmet and other accoutrements to Persian royal action on behalf of Israel. The uniform is "dressing for war in qualities required for victory": *Isaiah 1–33*, 287.

respond with, as noted previously, the conspicuous absence of a shield for Yahweh. Protection by shield and helmet, though vital for human soldiers, is unnecessary for the Divine Warrior.

The helmet of salvation finds correspondence between Isaiah and Ephesians. The phrase τὴν περικεφαλαίαν τοῦ σωτηρίου δέξασθε (Eph 6:17a) links with Isa 59:17, περιέθετο περικεφαλαίαν σωτηρίου ἐπὶ τῆς κεφαλῆς. The common terms are σωτήριον and περικεφαλαία. The different verbs, δέχομαι ("to receive, accept") and περιτίθημι ("to put around") emphasize in Ephesians that the helmet is received from God and Christ.[72] In both Isa 59 and Eph 6 the helmet of salvation emphasizes God rescuing his repentant people. In both contexts salvation is accompanied by deep inner ethical renewal ("those in Jacob who turn from transgression," Isa 59:20), the conversion of multiethnic peoples, and eventually the summation of history ("So those in the west shall fear the name of the LORD, and those in the east, his glory; for he will come like a pent-up stream that the wind of the LORD drives on," Isa 59:19 [cf. Isa 60:3–5, 10–14; 16, 18–20; 66:18–23]). M. Barth and others consider the warrior's helmet in Isa 59:17 to be most likely regal or ornate in nature rather than strictly a helmet for battle. The regal or ornate helmet in Eph 6:17 would have been used in the sense of the certainty of a battle won, with σωτήριον synonymous with victory. M. Barth has good reason to suggest the same usage in Eph 6:17.[73]

O'Brien notices that the salvation language in connection with the helmet is the same that was used to describe salvation already accomplished (Eph 1:20–23; 2:5, 6): "The present aspect of salvation is emphatically stressed."[74] In this sense Arnold is accurate in commenting that, "Ephesians unquestionably emphasizes the present aspect of 'salvation' to a greater degree than any of the other epistles attributed to Paul. The Ephesian author's use of 'salvation' in 6:17 is no exception."[75] His point has added validity if 1 Thess 4:8 is contrasted. There the helmet of salvation is for the "hope" of salvation, indicating a futuristic eschatology with an emphasis on events to come. Similarly in Rom 5:9–10, salvation is coterminus with the Day of

---

72. Ultimately the rest of the armor is obtained from God as well. Receiving and putting on the helmet may signal the final preparations before engaging the enemy since the helmet and the sword take the least amount of time to put on. An assistant or fellow soldier hands over the final touches of battle gear. In Ephesians, God dons the church in the final fearful moments as the battle begins.

73. M. Barth, *Ephesians, Chapters 4–6*, 775.

74. O'Brien, *Letter*, 481 n. 182. O'Brien notes that although present triumphal eschatology is unquestionably stressed it is not fully realized.

75. Arnold summarizes: This, however, outruns the evidence if "salvation" is taken as ultimate salvation. But Arnold seems to use it as a spiritual position, sitting in the heavenlies with Christ: *Power and Magic*, 111.

Judgment rather than preceding it.[76] Both Best and Lincoln recognize this present aspect, indicating that the author of Ephesians is satisfied to describe salvation in 6:17 within the present or realized eschatological sphere.[77] Kitchen adds, "Eph 6:10–20 is therefore also a fitting conclusion to the entire epistle, since it portrays an image of the perfected church, reconciled and renewed, over which Christ rules as Lord; this is the 'summing up' of all things."[78] M. Barth is uncertain of the timing of salvation in 6:17, citing the "evil day" ahead (Eph 6:13).[79] But, once again, the entire concept of the presence of evil is not incompatible with the writer's understanding of the arrival of new exodus salvation in Ephesians (Eph 4:27; 5:16). This is in keeping with the expectations of the new exodus in Isaiah.

11.5 SWORD OF THE SPIRIT IN EPH 6:17B AND ISA 49:2 (11:4B)

Isaiah 49 pictures the release of prisoners in a new exodus and their return to their homeland (Isa 49:9). Those who are freed will travel without the normal discomforts of the desert (Isa 49:10). As an improvement upon the first exodus, there will be neither hunger nor thirst, and the sun will not oppress (Isa 49:8, 10). Yahweh himself will lead (Isa 49:10). The mountains are transformed into roads and no longer form an impediment to travel (Isa 49:11). Those returning from the vast reaches of the world do not include pilgrims from the east (Isa 49:12); perhaps to indicate that something more than the historical new exodus from Persia is described, or that the easterners have already returned.[80] In this new and greater exodus, Isa 49 views the commissioning of the servant (Isa 49:1–6) who will not only restore Israel but will become a light to the nations (Isa 49:6; cf. Isa 48:20).[81] Ninow maintains that chapters 47 and 48 focus on Israel's liberation from Persia, but that the following chapter (49) takes on a strong international tone. The drawing of the nations overshadows the deliverance of Israel. The highlight

---

76. M. Barth, *Ephesians, Chapters 4–6*, 776.

77. "AE's stress here on the present nature of salvation is in line with his normal understanding of it": Best, *Critical and Exegetical*, 602–3; quote from 603; Lincoln, *Ephesians*, 450. Best notes Paul's approving use of Isa 49:8 in 2 Cor 6:2 in a realized eschatological sense.

78. Kitchen, *Ephesians*, 127.

79. M. Barth, *Ephesians, Chapters 4–6*, 776.

80. Motyer, *Prophecy of Isaiah*, 392.

81. Melugin, *Isaiah 40–55*, 69–71. Cf. Muilenburg, *Isaiah*, 567; Whybray, *Isaiah 40–66*, 137; Young, *Isaiah*, 3:269.

is Gentiles who come to recognize Yahweh's sovereignty: "Kings shall see and stand up, princes, and they shall prostrate themselves" (Isa 49:7).[82]

There is also a tie with Isa 11:4b where the root of Jesse is in battle array. He strikes the earth with the rod of his mouth, and with the breath of his lips he kills the wicked. The common theme is military might displayed in terms of divine orality. This is within a new exodus section (Isa 11:15–16) and is part of Yahweh's smiting of the nations (Rev 19:15).

Once again, as with the previous armor linkages, there are verbal and conceptual correspondences. Eph 6:17b, τὴν μάχαιραν τοῦ πνεύματος, ὅ ἐστιν ῥῆμα θεοῦ, ties with Isa 49:2, ἔθηκεν τὸ στόμα μου ὡσεὶ μάχαιραν ὀξεῖαν, and Isa 11:4b, πατάξει γῆν τῷ λόγῳ τοῦ στόματος αὐτοῦ καὶ ἐν πνεύματι διὰ χειλέων ἀνελεῖ ἀσεβῆ. The common terms and concepts shared by Isa 49:2 and Eph 6:17 are μάχαιρα ("sword," Isa, Eph) and στόμα ("mouth," Isa)/ ῥῆμα ("word," Eph). The mutual imagery is God the Warrior communicating with a sharp sword, either from his mouth or with words. Ephesians adds τοῦ πνεύματος, but πνεῦμα is found in Isaiah. A close parallel is Isa 61:1 in which the spirit is presented in conjunction with the communication of the gospel: "The spirit of the Lord GOD is upon me, because the LORD has anointed me; he has sent me to bring good news to the oppressed." The common terms with Isa 11:4b are στόμα and πνεῦμα, while λόγος in Isaiah relates with ῥῆμα in Ephesians. Once again the imagery is God's servant dressed for battle (Isa 11:5); but rather than emphasizing the communicative ministry of the servant as in Isa 49:2, the point has more to do with bringing equity to the earth.

In Isa 49 the servant speaks, wondering if he has toiled in vain (Isa 49:4). He gains courage as he recounts that Yahweh provided for his ministry by calling him from the womb and making his mouth a sharp sword (Isa 49:2). He is placed in the shadow of God's hand and is chosen to restore Israel (Isa 49:6). Yahweh and his servant liberate the prisoners and lead them across a desert to their homeland (Isa 49:9–13). This is a cause for rejoicing (Isa 49:13). In Isa 11 the root of Jesse acts with the rod of his mouth and the breath of his lips to restore the remnant of his people.

Just as the servant of Isa 49 finds reassurance in his prophetic ministry, the Christian warrior finds confidence in his communication of the gospel message in the face of cosmic powers. The sharp sword of God's word emphasizes the good news portion of Isaiah's message rather than that of judgment.[83] No doubt judgment is a part of the gospel message (Eph 5:5; Rom

---

82. Ninow, *Indicators*, 183.
83. Lincoln, *Ephesians*, 450.

3:23; 6:23) but the emphasis is on the victory of God and his people.[84] The metaphorical sword of the Spirit aligns with feet prepared with the gospel. Both function communicatively; however, the sword speaks of the message originating and finding resource in the Spirit. As with the other soldiery accoutrements the new exodus is present.

In summary, because the writer has incorporated Isaiah to form the eschatology of Ephesians it is not surprising that he uses the prophet once again to close the letter in Eph 6:14–17. The Isaiah passages are in new exodus passages or their contexts. Also, the Isaiah passages announce or predict triumph over the enemies of God and the restoration of God's people. The author uses the passages for the ongoing conflict that the church faces with the cosmic powers that seek to disrupt life in the new exodus community.

11.6 BOLDNESS OF SPEECH IN EPH 3:12; 6:19, 20

It is noteworthy that Wild sees Lev 26:13 in close alignment with Eph 3:12 and 6:19, 20.[85] The common term is παρρησία, or boldness of speech.[86] Leviticus 26:13 reads, "I am the Lord your God, the one leading you from out of the land of Egypt, where you were slaves. And I broke the bond of your yoke, and led you out in an open manner." The last phrase, καὶ ἤγαγον ὑμᾶς μετὰ παρρησίας, links with the depiction of Paul desiring to speak with freedom and openness concerning the mystery and the gospel.[87] He is an ambassador in chains with no ability to travel (Eph 6:20; cf. 2 Cor 5:20). It could be that with the use of παρρησία earlier in the letter (Eph 3:12), and conscripted twice more at the close (Eph 6:19, 20), the term forms a co-theme to Paul's circumstances in the epistle. The writer may be revealing Paul's desire for existential triumph that mirrors what the Hebrews longed for in Egypt. The line of thought is that the apostle yearns for his own exodus in order to freely and boldly proclaim the gospel. Arnold picks up on this idea, offering that both Paul and Israel found themselves in bondage with the hope of freedom.[88] This is not maintained with certainty, but if it is the case then the letter closes with an allusion to the exodus and its personal application to Paul's circumstances.

---

84. Aulén surmises that the peace in Eph 2:13, 15, and 16 between the warring factions of humanity is brought about by a bloodied cross that may remotely correspond to a bloody sword (cf. Eph 5:2); but this is christocentric speculation: *Victor*, 20–23.

85. Wild, "Warrior," 290–93.

86. Fredrickson, "Παρρησία," 163–83; Marrow, "Parrhesia," 431–36.

87. The term is also used in Prov 1:20; 10:10; 13:5; and Job 27:10.

88. Arnold, *Powers of Darkness*, 235. Cf. Moritz, *Profound Mystery*, 194 n. 59.

One other note may be added. The "opening" of Paul's mouth (and the previous panoply context having to do with the communication of the gospel, 6:15, 17) shares close associations with Isa 59:21: "And as for me, this is my covenant with them, says the Lord: my spirit that is upon you, and my words that I have put in your mouth, shall not depart out of your mouth, or out of the mouths of your children, or out of the mouths of your children's children, says the Lord, from now on and forever." Common terms with Eph 6 include πνεῦμα (6:17), ῥῆμα (6:17), and στόμα (6:19). It could be that the earlier usage of Isa 59 in Eph 6:14 and 17 resonates here as well. The idea put forth in Isaiah is that Yahweh's Spirit will forever place his words in the mouths of his people.[89] This may be an expression of Paul's sentiment in terms of actualizing in his own ministry his desire to communicate God's message (Eph 3:8). This may also point to his defense before the imperial court.[90] It was possible for the new exodus community to stifle the Spirit through improper speech (4:29–31; 5:3–4); however and conversely, God's people may access the Spirit for bold proclamation of the μυστήριον (6:15, 17, 19–20).

11.7 CONCLUSION

While some of the armor imagery in Pauline works is found in wisdom sources, it is most likely that the metaphor stems from Isaiah. As in the rest of Ephesians, the author continues Isaiah's message and adapts it for his own purposes. In Isaiah the battle metaphor takes place within the new exodus era. The return of God's people from exile is facilitated through Yahweh and his servant's military exploits. The still-future new exodus is undertaken similarly. In Eph 6, Yahweh and his servant's panoply is adopted by the church. Because they are ἐν Χριστῷ (Eph 1:1), κατὰ θεὸν κτισθέντα (Eph 4:24), and told to μιμηταὶ τοῦ θεοῦ (Eph 5:1), the interchangeableness of Yahweh's armor and that of Christians is virtually seamless. Just as there is identification between Yahweh, the servant, and Israel; there is a similar one with Yahweh, the servant, Israel, and Christ and the church. The picture of the church that emerges in Eph 6 lends itself to one of invincibility since the armor employed is that of Yahweh himself.[91] Isaiah and the writer's view of the corporate nature of God's people seem to be integral as well. The military accoutrements translate into psychological traits of the Christian warrior rather than into physical manifestations. The various appeals for

---

89. Ezek 3:27; 29:21; and 33:22 speak similarly with an emphasis on God enabling the speaker and supplying the message.

90. Lenski, *Interpretation*, 678–79; Wood, "Ephesians," 89–90.

91. Wild, "Warrior," 287.

inspired insight in the epistle (1:8, 17–19; 3:3–4, 10, 18–19; 4:13, 18, 21; 5:15, 17; 6:4, 8–9) are bundled in the panoply metaphor and its environs in one last climatic plea, akin to a general sending forth his troops.

It may be maintained that the author of the epistle had in view Isaiah's prediction of an eschatological new exodus that was fulfilled upon the triumphant ministry of Christ (Eph 1:20–23; 4:8–11), and has come about for the church. In addition, the eschatological experience of the new exodus military metaphor in Isaiah would be shared by the Christians in Western Asia Minor. As in Isaiah the new exodus warfare would include iterative, progressive aspects. This is certainly the case in Eph 6; but the progress must be viewed within the contextual triumph represented in the letter. There are no grounds to insist that the progressive element of the "not yet" in the panoply section overshadows or negates present triumph. To do so would impose a foreign linearity upon Isaiah and the author, and would negate what has already been firmly established in the epistle. Both the prophet and the author of the missive understood the new exodus as Moses's historical exodus—an era of both conflict and triumph. In the case of the writer, Isaiah's predictions of a new exodus had arrived triumphantly in Christ, and the new age has come about despite ongoing hostilities with the ethereal forces. This is not entirely understood by the audience (for whom the author must repeatedly pray). But the lack of comprehension is not whether the new exodus has come but rather a deficiency in understanding its power (Eph 1:17–19). For the writer this appears to be the proper understanding of Isaiah. Rather than trying to convince his audience that Isaiah was right and that the prophet's predictions applied to them (as seen in the Gospels), he assumes the triumph to be so and proceeds to make an appeal for its psychological application.

12

Conclusion

THIS INVESTIGATION ARGUES THAT the composition of Ephesians was influenced by the present triumphal aspect of Isaiah's new exodus. When the frequent use of Isaiah is viewed in Pauline Corpus, there is reason to believe that the prophet was a central source of thought in the works attributed to Paul. In addition, there is evidence that the Pauline letters generally demonstrate a typological-historical hermeneutic by showing that Isaiah's new exodus arrived upon the advent of Christ. This may be the case with the utilization of direct and contextual new exodus passages from Isaiah, Psalms, the Pentateuch, and postexilic prophets in Ephesians—but with the added emphasis of the present triumphal aspect of the INE. It appears that the employment of Isaiah and other portions of the OT in Ephesians sets the epistle apart from other letters in the Pauline Corpus, specifically Colossians, Romans, and 1 Corinthians.

In Ephesians, Isaiah is used by quotation, allusion, and echo. The quotations are explicit; the allusions share a common word or two; and the echoes have conceptual rather than verbal correspondence. It would be shortsighted to consider the echoes to be less influential than the explicit citations. The author of Ephesians and the other Pauline works show evidence of an immersion in the OT, and use of the Hebrew Scriptures both formally and informally. Less formality leading up to an OT usage may show more rather than less treatment. Also, since the OT and Isaiah are used prominently in Ephesians and other places it is likely that there are less explicit echoes in the epistle; however, it is difficult to determine with confidence if the author consciously employed them.

The following points summarize the findings of this work as to whether the present triumphal aspect of the INE guided the composition of the letter.

12.1 THE BROAD USE OF ISAIAH IN EPHESIANS

The two following tables illustrate how the use of Isaiah in Ephesians is distributed in Isaiah, and how the occurrences of Isaiah are placed in Ephesians.

Table 12.1			
Ephesians Use of Isaiah Distributed in Isaiah*			
	Quotations	Allusions	Echoes
Isa 1–39	Eph 6:14a (11:5) Eph 6:17b (11:4)	Eph 1:8, 17 (11:2) Eph 2:20 (28:16)	Eph 1:4, 5, 9, 11 (14:1; 41:8–9; 43:10, 14; 44:1–2; 49:7) Eph 2:5 (26:14, 19)
Isa 40–55	Eph 6:17b (49:2) Eph 6:15 (52:7)		Eph 1:7, 13, 14; 2:13, 16; 4:30; 5:2, 25–27 (44:22; 48:20; 50:2)
Isa 56–66	Eph 2:13, 17 (57:19; 52:7) Eph 6:14b (59:17a) Eph 6:17a (59:17b) Eph 4:30 (63:10)	Eph 5:14 (60:1; 26:19)	Eph 6:19 (59:21) Eph 4:22, 24 (61:10) Eph 5:23–27 (61:10)
* For purposes of clarity, some of the Isaianic usages in Ephesians are kept within the section of Isaiah in which they first appear.			

Table 12.2			
Ephesians Use of Isaiah Distributed in Ephesians*			
	Quotations	Allusions	Echoes
Eph 1		Isa 11:2 (1:8, 17)	Isa 14:1; 41:8–9; 43:10; 44:1–2; 49:7 (1:4, 5, 9, 11) Isa 44:22; 48:20; 50:2 (1:7, 14; 2:13, 16; 5:25–27)
Eph 2	Isa 57:19; 52:7 (2:13, 17)	Isa 28:16 (2:20)	Isa 26:14, 19 (2:5)
Eph 3			

Eph 4	Isa 63:10 (4:30)		Isa 61:10 (4:22, 24; 6:10–17)
Eph 5		Isa 60:1; 26:19 (5:14)	Isa 61:10 (5:23–27)
Eph 6	Isa 11:4, 5; 49:2; 52:7; 59:17 (6:14, 15, 17)		Isa 59:21 (6:19)
* For purposes of clarity some of the Isaianic usages in Ephesians are kept within the section of Ephesians in which they first appear.			

Table 12.1 depicts how Isaiah appears to exhibit usage in the epistle by quotation, allusion, and echo. In table 12.2 the analysis shows that the letter seems to demonstrate a broad representation of the prophet. The sections of Isaiah are represented in nearly every sector of Ephesians.

12.1.1 Isaianic Quotations

An Isaiah quotation comes into play in the reconciliation of Jews and Gentiles in the new community. Former enemies experience the eschatological peace predicted by Isaiah. This applies to Jews and their association with the nations (Eph 2:13, 17 with Isa 57:19; and 52:7).

The ethical section of the letter is reinforced by a quotation from Isaiah. The people of Isaiah's day were capable of grieving the Holy Spirit. The author warns against living contrary to the Spirit in matters of speech (Eph 4:30 with Isa 63:10).

The closing section is built upon explicit Isaiah quotation imagery. Yahweh and his servant's panoply is adopted by the church (Eph 6:14, 15, 17 with Isa 11:4–5; 49:2; 52:7; 59:17).

12.1.2 Isaianic Allusions

Allusions from Isaiah speak of the special acumen that Yahweh and his servant possess in order to rule in the new age. God and his servant would have an unusual capacity of wisdom and understanding. It is possible for the recipients of the letter to experience wisdom and understanding as well; to both rule with Christ and understand the mystery elements of the final age (Eph 1:8, 17 with Isa 11:2). The use of Isa 11:2 is in close proximity to two panoply citations (Eph 6:14a with Isa 11:5; Eph 6:17b with Isa 11:4), which fortifies the certainty of the allusion.

The traditional walls of the temple courts that separated gender and races are eliminated in the new age. The temple is replaced by the household of God; founded upon church leaders, erected with saints who are the building materials, and precisely set in place with Christ as the cornerstone (Eph 2:20 with an allusion to Isa 28:16).

A final allusion is the death-new life metaphor. In Ephesians it is used to emphasize the transformation of the spiritually and ethically dead (Eph 5:14 with Isa 60:1; 26:19).

12.1.3 Isaianic Echoes

The echoes of divine choice (Eph 1:4, 5, 9, and 11) and paschal redemption (Eph 1:7, 14; 2:13, 16; 5:25–27) are found in the letter. Both are rooted in the historical exodus and undertaken in Isaiah (Isa 14:1; 41:8–9; 43:10; 44:1–2; 49:7 [choosing]; Isa 44:22; 48:20; 50:2 [paschal redemption]). The emphasis in Isaiah is Yahweh choosing and blessing his people, forgiving their sins, and acting as their kinsman redeemer.

As with the allusion in Eph 5:14 (with Isa 26:19), there is another possible use of Isaiah's death-new life motif in Eph 2:5, this time as an echo. Remnant corpses are brought to life in contrast to the wicked that neither rise nor are remembered. In Eph 2:5 the Isaiah imagery represents how redemption is applied to the death-like state of the audience before its members came to salvation (Eph 2:5 with Isa 26:14, 19). The repeated use of the death-life motif in Ephesians strengthens the echo.

Another possible use is the employment of Yahweh and his servant's clothing. In Ephesians, Christians are clothed with new life (Eph 4:22, 24 with Isa 61:10). Seeing that the investiture motif is used by way of citation in Eph 6:14–15, 17 the argument for the echo is reinforced. In addition, Isa 61:10 may coincide with Eph 5:23–27 regarding Israel being Yahweh's ornamented bride carried forward in the church as the NT antitype.

An Isaiah echo may contribute to the author's closing remarks about restrictions forced upon Paul's ministry. Isaiah predicts that the words Yahweh places in the mouth of his people will never depart (Eph 6:19 with Isa 59:21). This is supported by the immediate previous quotations where the audience is told to be ready to communicate the gospel of peace (Eph 6:15, 17 with Isa 11:4; 49:2).

In summary, it has been found that a broad representation of Isaiah was utilized in Ephesians and contributes to the major topics of the epistle: extraordinary insight, divine choice and paschal redemption, death and new creation life, racial reconciliation, the eschatological household, holy investiture and ethics, light overcoming darkness, and Christian warfare.

12.2 ISAIAH'S NEW EXODUS CONTEXTS IN THE EPISTLE

A significant number of the Isaiah quotations, allusions, and echoes found in Ephesians come from new exodus texts or contexts. The following table demonstrates the distribution of new exodus Isaiah occurrences in Ephesians.[1]

	Table 12.3		
	New Exodus Distribution in Isaiah as Found in Ephesians*		
	Isa 1–39	40–55	56–66
New Exodus in Isaiah	4:2–6 11:10–16 12:1–6 19:19–25 24:23 35:1–10	40:3–11 41:17–20 42:14–17 43:1–7 43:16–21 44:1–5, 27 48:20–21 49:8–12 50:2–3 51:1—52:15 55:12	63:7–19 64:1
Quotations of Isaiah in Ephesians	Eph 6:14a (11:5) Eph 6:17b (11:4)	Eph 6:17b (49:2) Eph 6:15 (52:7)	Eph 2:13, 17 (57:19; 52:7) Eph 4:30 (63:10) Eph 6:14b (59:17a) Eph 6:17a (59:17b)
Allusions of Isaiah in Ephesians	Eph 1:8, 17 (11:2) Eph 2:20 (28:16)		Eph 5:14 (60:1; 26:19)

---

1. The Isaianic new exodus texts cited in this diagram are a compilation of the author and Ninow, Fishbane, Stuhlmueller, and R. Watts: Fishbane, "Motif," 121–40; Ninow, *Indicators*, 157–95; Stuhlmueller, *Creative Redemption*, 59–98; R. Watts, *New Exodus in Mark*, 367–88.

Echoes of Isaiah in Ephesians	Eph 1:4, 5, 9, 11 (14:1; 41:8–9; 43:10, 14; 44:1–2; 49:7) Eph 2:5 (26:14, 19)	Eph 1:7, 13, 14; 2:13, 16; 4:30; 5:2, 25; 6:17 (44:22; 48:20; 50:2)	Eph 6:19 (59:21) Eph 4:22, 24 (61:10) Eph 5:23–27 (61:10) Eph 6:10–17 (61:10)
* For purposes of clarity some of the Isaianic usages in Ephesians are kept within the section of Isaiah in which they first appear.			

There is a representation of Isaiah's new exodus occurrences in Ephesians. The two quotations in Isa 1–39 do not fall precisely in new exodus passages, but they do occur within the INE context (both are in the same chapter and proximity of Isaiah): Eph 6:14a, 17b in Isa 11:4–5—preceding the explicit new exodus passage by five verses. In addition, Eph 6:14a and 17b are panoply passages that have a cluster of other new exodus text usages in Ephesians nearby. Of the two quotations from Isa 40–55, Ephesians 6:17b (with Isa 49:2) occurs within the same chapter as the INE passage (Isa 49:8–12), and the second (Eph 6:15 with Isa 52:7) falls precisely in a new exodus section. Of five quotation passages in Ephesians that are associated with the final section of Isaiah (Eph 2:13, 17; 4:30; 6:14b, 17a with Isa 56–66 [and Isa 40–55]), two fall precisely in INE passages (Eph 2:17; 4:30). The other three land in somewhat remote areas (Isa 57 and 59).

In terms of the allusions, in Isa 1–39 Eph 1:8 falls in close proximity to the INE passage (Eph 1:8, 17 with Isa 11:2 compared to the INE Isa 11:10–16). Eph 2:20 appears to find correspondence from Isa 28:16, which is somewhat remote from INE sections. There are no allusions represented in Isa 40–55, and in the final section (Isa 56–66) Eph 5:14 with Isa 60:1 (and possibly Isa 26:19) is distant from the nearest INE occurrence (Isa 63:7–19).

Of the twelve Isaiah passages that appear to be utilized as echoes in Ephesians, three demonstrate origins precisely in INE passages (Isa 44:1–2; 48:20; 50:2), and four appear to draw from the same chapter as INE occurrences (Isa 41:8–9; 43:10; 49:7; 44:22). Five of the twelve do not have close correspondence (Isa 14:1; Isa 26:14, 19; 59:21; 61:10).

The following diagrammatical summary indicates the use of Isaiah in Ephesians in terms of how closely the usages align with INE passages in Isaiah.

	Table 12.4		
	The Use of INE Passages in Ephesians		
	Quotations	Allusions	Echoes
Precisely from INE Passages	Eph 2:13, 17 (57:19; 52:7) Eph 6:15 (52:7)		Eph 1:4, 5, 9, 11 (44:1–2) Eph 1:7, 13, 14; 2:13, 16; 4:30; 5:2, 25–27 (48:20; 50:2)
In Close Proximity to INE Passages	Eph 6:14a (11:5) Eph 6:17b (11:4) Eph 6:17b (49:2)	Eph 1:8, 17 (11:2)	Eph 1:4, 5, 9, 11 (41:8–9; 43:10, 14; 49:7) Eph 1:7, 14; 2:13, 16 (44:22)
Remote Association to INE Passages	Eph 4:30 (63:10) Eph 6:14b (59:17a) Eph 6:17a (59:17b)	Eph 2:20 (28:16) Eph 5:14 (60:1; 26:19)	Eph 1:4, 5, 9, 11 (14:1) Eph 2:5 (26:14, 19) Eph 6:19 (59:21) Eph 4:22, 24 (61:10) Eph 5:23–27 (61:10) Eph 6:10–17 (61:10)

There is correspondence between Isaianic quotations, allusions, and echoes in the epistle with INE occurrences and contexts in Isaiah. Several INE usages in Ephesians either precisely land in INE passages or in close proximity (such as the same context or chapter), while others are outside the INE orbit. Admittedly, all the Isaiah usages do not come from precise INE passages, but if those usages from exact passages are combined with those in proximity there is a significant amount of evidence under consideration. Of all the central topics in Ephesians that are supported by Isaiah (as noted in the preceding), those most directly maintained by Isaianic new exodus quotations are extraordinary insight, divine choice, paschal redemption, ethics, and warfare. However, to constrict INE influence in Ephesians to these five topics would be an inaccurate representation of Isaiah in the letter. The allusions and echoes in Ephesians, and those places utilized in Isaiah that fall outside strictly new exodus sections, should be deliberated upon as well. For example, the drawing of the nations to Zion comports with the new exodus and is used by the author at a crucial stage of the letter (Eph 2:13, 17 with Isa 57:19; 52:7), but it does not fall within a strictly new exodus section of Isaiah. The same can be said of the death to life motif, eschatological household, investiture, light overcoming darkness, and divine marriage. All of these are aspects of the new exodus in Isaiah. Because of the pervasiveness of the new exodus in Isaiah, and the multiple uses of Isaiah in the epistle; quotations, echoes, and allusions, both in and ouside of exodus portions of Isaiah should be given due weight.

12.3 THE TRIUMPHAL ASPECT OF ISAIAH'S NEW EXODUS REFERENCES

The Isaiah usages that come from new exodus contexts speak of the triumph of Yahweh and his remnant. The author of the epistle adjusts these references and offers them as if triumph has arrived. What was prophesied by Isaiah as future is presented as having appeared.

Among the quotations, Isa 57:19 and 52:7 (in Eph 2:13, 17) are triumphant. Peace and reconciliation have been accomplished. Isaiah 63:10 anticipates the new age and the author adopts the passage for present ethical conduct in Eph 4:30. The panoply section draws from Isa 11:4, 5; 49:2; 52:7; 59:17 (in Eph 6:14, 15, 17), predicting the vengeance of the Divine Warrior. His triumph is prophesied as in process or the object of celebration.

The allusions, Isa 11:2 (in Eph 1:8, 17); 28:16 (in Eph 2:20); and Isa 60:1; 26:19 (in Eph 5:14) display the triumph of the new age. The victory depicted in Isa 11 coincides with the citations concerning the panoply in Eph 6. Isa 28:16 is the oft-used cornerstone passage; and it is explicitly used in the NT for Christ, and refers to the arrival of the new age. Christ as the cornerstone of the eschatological temple signals warrior victory (Eph 2:20). Isa 60:1 announces that the glory of Yahweh has risen, and 26:19 anticipates the remnant dead rising. The author interprets these as having occurred (Eph 5:14, cf. 2:4–6).

If the echoes are accepted, they too display triumph. There is a present aspect to divine choosing (Eph 1:4, 5, 9, 11 with Isa 41:8–9; 43:10; 44:1–2; 49:7) and paschal redemption (Eph 1:7, 14; 2:13, 16 with Isa 44:22; 48:20; and 50:2). Isa 26:14, 19 (in Eph 2:5) show death-new life imagery. Isaiah 61:10 (in Eph 4:22, 24) repeats (Eph 6:14, 15, 17) the clothing motif. In Isa 61:10 renewed Israel is bedecked as a bridegroom and bride. A marriage in Isaiah is anticipated, which envisions triumph; in Ephesians the imagery is betrothal, marriage, or both—presented in glorious terms. The final echo from Isa 59:21 (with Eph 6:19) is a solemn vow from Yahweh that his words will never depart from Israel in the eschatological age. The message reflects the permanent bond between Yahweh and his people. The scene is idyllic and everlasting. This may have been on the author's mind as he considered his prospects for communicating the gospel while he was in prison.

Ephesians harbors passages from Isaiah that are new exodus in nature and which picture victory for remnant Israel and the believing nations. Isaiah anticipates these events occurring in the new exodus.

12.4 OTHER OT USAGES IN EPHESIANS SUPPLEMENTAL TO ISAIAH

The non-Isaiah OT usages in the next table are listed by distribution in Ephesians (listed with previously considered Isaiah passages).

	Table 12.5		
	Non-Isaiah Usages Distributed in Ephesians with Comparison to Isaiah		
	Quotations	Allusions	Echoes
Eph 1	Pss 110:1; 8:6 (1:20–22)	Isa 11:2 (1:8, 17)	Isa 14:1; 41:8–9; 43:10, 14; 44:1–2; 49:7 (1:4, 5, 9, 11) Isa 44:22; 48:20; 50:2 (1:7, 13, 14; 2:13, 16; 4:30; 5:2, 25–27)
Eph 2	Isa 57:19; 52:7 (2:13, 17)	Isa 28:16 (2:20) Ezek 37:19, 22 (2:14)	Isa 26:14, 19 (2:5)
Eph 3		Dan 7:15; 28; 8:1, 15, 27; 9:2; 10:2, 7; 12:5 (3:3, 4, 9; cf. 1:9; 5:32; 6:19)	Ps 103 (3:18)
Eph 4	Ps 68:18 (4:8) Zech 8:16 (4:25) Ps 4:4 (4:26) Isa 63:10 (4:30)		Isa 61:10 (4:22, 24) Ezek 11:19–20 (Eph 4:24)

Eph 5	Gen 2:24 (5:31)	Isa 60:1; 26:19 (5:14) Ezek 16:4, 9; 36:25; Song 4:7 (5:26) Lev 19:18 (5:28, 33)	Gen 8:21; Exod 29:18, 25, 41 (5:2) Isa 61:10 (5:23–27)
Eph 6	Exod 20:12 (6:2–3) Isa 11:4, 5; 49:2; 52:7; 59:17 (6:14, 15, 17)		Lev 25:43 (6:9) Isa 59:21 (6:19)

12.4.1 Non-Isaiah Quotations

Among the citations, the opening of the epistle is anchored by the present triumphal use of Pss 110 and 8. Christ and his church are currently enthroned in the heavens above all powers (Eph 1:20–23 with Pss 110:1; 8:6).

The parenetic section of the epistle is secured by the use of another psalm, equally suggestive of present victory, but in regard to gifting God's people with resources to live out triumph (Eph 4:8 with Ps 68:18).

The ethical section is supported with the use of Zechariah (Eph 4:25 with Zech 8:16). Zechariah admonishes the postexilic community to speak properly in light of the coming new age (Zech 8:1–8, 11–13, 14–15; esp. 6–8, 11). Zechariah explicitly pictures aspects of the new exodus coming about. The author of Ephesians uses Zechariah's wording to continue admonitions concerning the type of life expected in the eschatological community. Closely following is Ps 4:4 in Eph 4:26 with a command concerning anger. This fits the eschatological context of Ephesians in that it describes the type of life expected in the final age.

In the household codes, the commands given to husbands and wives include Gen 2:24 (Eph 5:31). The author's use of the passage reflects a transformative view of Christian marriage and Yahweh's marriage to Israel. The relationship between Christ and his church becomes the ultimate outworking of Yahweh and his wife Israel, as well as human marriage. Also, Christ's betrothal and marriage to the church in Eph 5:22–33 is fulfilled and celebrated.

The final quotation is the use of the Decalogue in regard to children and parents (Eph 6:2–3 with Exod 20:12). The Exodus passage is utilized as a guide to conduct in the eschatological household. As with Zech 8:16

and Ps 4:4 the emphasis is on demeanor within the triumphal eschatological community. Speaking properly, managing anger, and honoring parents reflect the outworking of the triumph of Christ and his church, and the subjugation of the ethereal powers.

12.4.2 Non-Isaiah Allusions

Ezekiel provides significant correspondence in the epistle by way of allusion. There appears to be verbal, structural, and thematic parallels between Ezek 37 and Eph 2. The new exodus is a prevailing theme in Ezek 37 as well. The preparative marriage imagery of Ezek 16:4, 9 in Eph 5:26 introduces another prominent new exodus motif. Yahweh's marriage to Israel harkens back to the origination of the covenant during the historical exodus. The marriage covenant was subsequently broken by Israel's disobedience. The imagery in Ezekiel is that of the restored relationship between Yahweh and Israel. This corresponds to the many images in Isaiah of Yahweh's restored marriage. In Ephesians this conjoins with the general description of the present, celebrative, betrothal-marriage of Christ and the church. With the preponderance of the marriage metaphor in the exodus and prophetic traditions, it is not difficult to imagine the author of Ephesians incorporating this imagery in Eph 5. His purpose for doing so is to indicate that Christ and the church are the idyllic antitype, both of human marriage and of Israel and Yahweh's troubled marriage.

Another non-Isaiah allusion of note is the repeated use of μυστήριον, which may find its pattern in Daniel (Eph 1:9; 3:3, 4, 9; 5:32; 6:10). The employment of the motif appears to signal a Pauline self-understanding in terms of the apostle's eschatological role. It is likely that the author incorporates μυστήριον to demonstrate personal triumph (despite Paul's circumstances) that corresponds with the OT victory theme and that pervades the epistle. Explicit triumph resumes in Eph 3:10.

A further allusion is found stemming from Lev 19:18 and is used in Eph 5:28 and 33. The application is the degree to which a husband is to love his wife. Similar to Zech 8:16, Ps 4:4, and Gen 2:24, the focus is behavior in the eschatological age.

12.4.3 Non-Isaiah Echoes

The author may have had Ps 103 in mind in the composition of Eph 3:18 and its context. Psalm 103 has striking similarities to Eph 3 as well as to explicit exodus thought and language. The tone is God's mercy and triumph. Although it is difficult to say whether the writer intentionally had the psalm in mind during the composition, the conspicuous resemblances appear to favor some degree of correspondence.

Another non-Isaiah echo is in Eph 5:2 (Gen 8:21; Exod 29:18, 25, 41). Christians are to follow Christ's example of sacrifice. His death is a model for saints to follow. Earlier in the epistle (Eph 1:7, 14; 2:13, 16) Christ's paschal death is utilized, which reinforces and strengthens the likelihood of a conscious echo in Eph 5:2. Christ's death is now an exemplar for eschewing sin and living after God's likeness. The paschal motif is rooted in Israel's exodus experience and finds fresh expression in the new exodus.

In summary, two of the citations from Psalms (110; 68) explicitly declare present triumph. In Ephesians one anchors the opening eulogy, the other grounds the ethical section. Ps 68 clearly demonstrates exodus imagery, and in both psalms the OT is used to declare the Messiah conquering Yahweh's foes and the arrival of the Messianic age. However, in comparison to the influence of these psalms in the epistle, the utilization of Isaiah has proven to be more prominent. When the quotations and allusions are taken into account, Isaiah is pervasive in nearly the entire letter. Also, as discussed previously, a significant number of the passages from Isaiah originate in precise new exodus passage or in close contexts. Pss 110 and 68 play significant but supplemental roles. The other non-Isaiah quotations (Zech 8:16; Ps 4:4; Gen 2:24; Lev 19:18; Exod 20:12) promote ethical life in the new age and are supplemental as well. Ps 8 pictures man recapturing his place of glory, and Ezek 16:4 and 9 support the realized betrothal-marriage of Christ and his church alongside Isaiah. The non-Isaiah allusions, though not explicit, provide a measure of support for the themes of the non-Isaiah quotations, especially in terms of the images of the cleansing of Yahweh's bride in terms of the church and Christian husbands (Ezek 16:4, 9 in Eph 5:26), and the assumptive self-love expected of husbands toward their wives (Lev 19:18 in Eph 5:28, 33). Among the echoes it is difficult to eliminate the possibility of the use of Ps 103 in Eph 3:18 and its environs.

12.5 SPATIALITY AND UNFOLDING LINEARITY IN ISAIAH AND PAUL

Ephesians reflects Isaiah's understanding of spatiality and linearity. Reality includes above and below, now and future. It is because of this multidimensional view of the Christian life that the author can speak of triumph above and not fully below, now and not fully yet, all without difficulty. These aspects of God's activities with his people are existentially real to the author. It appears there is no ontological duality in the writer's mind. It is one reality with diverse expressions.

The author appears to view the new exodus from Isaiah's perspective. Isaiah and others in the OT adopted the historical exodus as a template for the future work of God. It is explained as an era, not a one-time event. The apparent discordance between realized and unrealized eschatology in Ephesians is resolved by understanding the simultaneous present and progressive aspects of the new exodus. The writer of Ephesians appears to follow Isaiah by recognizing the new exodus as both triumph and conflict. In Isaiah the arrival of the new exodus is marked by a period of judgment that leads to restoration. Both the writer of Ephesians and the book of Isaiah consider the new exodus to be an era that includes struggle and triumph leading to the final Parousia. Zechariah seems to have this same understanding in mind (Zech 8:16 in Eph 4:25), while demonstrating the importance of ethics while experiencingthe new exodus.

12.6 EPHESIANS DISTINGUISHED FROM ROMANS, 1 CORINTHIANS, AND COLOSSIANS

Many commentators clearly distinguish the verbal, structural, and thematic characteristics of Ephesians from the generally accepted Paulines. There is little question as to the unique qualities of the letter. In addition, this current work has pointed out the distinguishing presence of the INE in Ephesians as compared with the balance of the Pauline Corpus.[2] This has been reinforced by scholars.[3]

But a legitimate question may remain as to whether Ephesians is to be differentiated in regard to the present triumphal aspect of the INE. This query is particularly relevant when directed to the Pauline Corpus, and especially Romans, 1 Corinthians, and Colossians. In response, it may be said that the INE is not exclusive to Ephesians, or its present triumphal aspect. Certainly the INE and its present triumphal manifestations have been recognized to some extent throughout much of the NT and Paul in particular. What stands out in Ephesians is the prominence of the INE when compared to the other Pauline letters, not its exclusivity. Brief comments on Romans, 1 Corinthians, and Colossians are in order.

Romans demonstrates many similarities to Ephesians in the use of the OT, and in particular the present triumph of the INE. However, in Romans

---

2. See section 2.3 in distinguishing the Pauline Corpus from Ephesians, and the full body of this present work for the distinction of Isaiah in Ephesians from the Pauline Corpus.

3. Perhaps the most sweeping demonstration of these differences may be seen by contrasting the use of the OT in Romans, 1 Corinthians, and Colossians with that of Ephesians in Beale, *Commentary*, 607–752, 841–70.

the use of the OT involves an apologetic, defending God's actions regarding Gentile inclusion. The OT explains and defends God's actions and reaffirms his faithfulness to Israel. The OT is also used to trumpet the soteriological and eschatological aspects of what has taken place with the salvation of the Gentiles. In Ephesians the use of the OT is primarily harnessed to depict the present triumph of the INE. The OT is also used prominently in Ephesians to give ethical instruction concerning conduct in that age. Romans speaks of the INE, including triumph and ethical conduct, but the cumulative force of the OT is God's salvific faithfulness in regard to his elect and Israel. For example, in Rom 7:24-25 Paul announces liberation from the old nature which comes about through Christ. In Rom 8:35-39 the reader is told that Christians cannot be separated from the love of God in Christ. Romans 11:33-36 is a crescendo of praise that rounds out Rom 9-11 announcing the marvel of God's wisdom in providing salvation. In each instance the focus is upon the present soteriological aspects of salvation; specifically, God's justification for including Gentile salvation in his plan for Israel. The use of Isaiah and the OT is quite extensive in Romans, as is the present triumph and the new exodus, but the focus is soteriological and eschatological concerning the elect and Israel. The church's present triumph over cosmic powers is not the focus of Romans.

In addition, 1 Corinthians has many similarities to Ephesians. There is the repeated use of the OT, and specifically the imagery of the exodus. Similar to Ephesians, the exodus in 1 Corinthians is adopted to promote ethical conduct. Among other things, exodus imagery is undertaken to dissuade the Corinthians from the misconduct of the wilderness. However, this imagery is conceptualized as a warning rather than an announcement of Isaianic triumph. Additionally, a major use of the OT is brought to bear in the contrast between human and divine wisdom. Present victory is not as emphasized in 1 Corinthians as it is in Ephesians. First Corinthians 15 has to do with questions pertaining to future resurrection, not present triumph.

In contrast to Colossians, differences are seen in Ephesians as to how the OT is used; as well as the discussion of power and knowledge. Regarding the OT, it was shown that the Hebrew Scriptures are used more pervasively and explicitly in Ephesians, specifically to emphasize the present triumph of the INE. The usages of the OT in Colossians are more subtle and supplemental, whereas in Ephesians they are integral and formative. If one holds to the direct dependence of Ephesians upon Colossians, an argument may be made that a major difference is precisely the use of the OT. In addition, both letters focus on power but in different ways. Colossians mentions power twice for purposes of highlighting inner spiritual development and ministrial labor (Col 1:11, 29). However, Ephesians speaks of power seven times, four times referring to inner spiritual strength (Eph 1:19; 3:7, 16, 20), and three times related to cosmic powers (Eph 1:22; 2:2; 6:12). The focus on powers suggests that Ephesians is more intent upon strength leading to triumph, not simply inner spiritual vigor. The contrasting use of knowledge is another example of the differences between Ephesians and Colossians. Knowledge is referred to three times in Ephesians (Eph 1:17; 3:19; 4:13), having to do with inner spiritual insight and maturity. On the other hand, Colossians speaks of knowledge five times in reference to insight and maturity (Col 1:9, 10; 2:2, 3; 3:10). The difference lies in the degrees of emphasis. Ephesians has more to do with power and triumph while Colossians places a greater stress on knowledge. Ephesians emphasizes power in connection with present and future triumph; whereas Colossians focuses on the accumulation of divine knowledge. The use of the OT and the themes of power and knowledge are in both letters, but significant differences remain. The OT appears in Colossians, including allusions to the INE, but what is lacking in comparison to Ephesians is the cumulative force of the present triumphal INE.

The Pauline Corpus, and particularly Romans, 1 Corinthians, and Colossians share commonalities with Ephesians. All three use the OT and undertake the INE to varying degrees. However, there are distinct differences between these three letters and the use of the OT and INE in comparison to Ephesians. Romans focuses on issues of salvation in regard to the Gentiles and Israel; 1 Corinthians emphasizes divine wisdom over human wisdom and how these apply to conduct; and Colossians is concerned with divine knowledge.

12.7 CONCLUSION

Since the present triumphal new exodus is a weighty motif in Isaiah, and Isaiah is used repeatedly in Ephesians, it stands to reason that the new exodus should appear in the epistle. Ephesians does not contain particularly obvious images of Isaiah's new exodus, such as miraculous water crossing and desert travel. However, these are seldom found in the use of the new exodus in the NT. Usually a NT author highlighted certain aspects of the exodus while assuming that his audience understood the subtleties.

The author of Ephesians employs Isaiah more than any other OT source, including Psalms, the Pentateuch, and the remaining prophets. Isaiah's quotations, allusions, and echoes are found nearly throughout the letter. Many originate from Isaiah passages and contexts that to a considerable degree speak of the triumph of the new exodus. There are other metaphors undertaken in Isaiah such as paschal redemption, inheritance, new creation, temple building, marriage, investiture, and warfare; with virtually all the images contributing to a triumphal form of Isaiah's new exodus.

The inclusion of non-Isaiah quotations, allusions, and echoes in the letter reinforce the possibility of the present triumphal aspect of the new exodus, as well as INE ethical implications. The church in Western Asia Minor is called to direct their ethical conduct, household behavior, and slave and slave master relations in accordance with what was expected of those in the new exodus era.

The author of Ephesians appears to follow Isaiah in seeing the new period as a time in which triumph is mingled with difficulty. The writer couches the use of Isaiah and non-Isaiah texts in a way that assumes the arrival of the new exodus, yet this era includes struggles that lead to the summing up of all things. Although the new exodus has begun, the author is passionate that his audience fully comprehend and embrace the new era while anticipating its culmination in the age to come. The epistle suggests the arrival of the present triumphal aspect of the new age, and perhaps specifically the INE, in a way that distinguishes it from the balance of the Pauline Corpus.

Bibliography

Aageson, James W. "Written Also for Our Sake: Paul's Use of Scripture in the Four Major Epistles, with a Study of 1 Corinthians 10." In *Hearing the Old Testament in the New Testament*, edited by Stanley E. Porter, 152–81. Grand Rapids: Eerdmans, 2006.

Abasciano, Brian J. "Diamonds in the Rough: A Reply to Christopher Stanley Concerning the Reader Competency of Paul's Original Audiences." *Novum Testamentum* 49, 2 (2007) 153–83.

———. *Paul's Use of the Old Testament in Romans 9.1–9: An Intertextual and Theological Exegesis*. London: T & T Clark, 2005.

Abbott, Thomas K. *A Critical and Exegetical Commentary on the Epistles to the Ephesians and to the Colossians*. New York: Scribner's Sons, 1897.

Aberbach, Moses, and Leivy Smolar. "Aaron, Jeroboam, and the Golden Calves." *Journal of Biblical Literature* 86, 2 Je (1967) 129–40.

Achtemeier, Paul J. "An Apocalyptic Shift in Early Christian Tradition: Reflections on Some Canonical Evidence." *Catholic Biblical Quarterly* 45, 2 Ap (1983) 231–48.

Ackroyd, Peter R. "Isaiah 1–12: Presentation of a Prophet." Leiden, NL: Brill, 1978.

Albright, William Foxwell. "A Catalogue of Early Hebrew Lyric Poems (Psalm 68)." Hebrew *Union College Annual* 23, 1950–1951 Part 1 (1951) 1–39.

———. *Notes on Psalms 68 and 134*. Oslo: Universitetforlaget, 1955, 1–12.

Alexander, Joseph A. *Commentary on the Prophecies of Isaiah*. Grand Rapids: Zondervan, 1953 [orig. pub. 1846–47 in two vols.].

Alford, Henry. *The Greek Testament; With a Critically Revised Text; a Digest of Various Readings, Marginal References to Verbal and Idiomatic Usage, Prolegomena, and a Critical and Exegetical Commentary*. London: Rivingtons, 1871.

Allan, John A. "The 'In Christ' Formula in Ephesians." *New Testament Studies* 5, 1 O (1958) 54–62.

Allison, Dale C. *The New Moses: A Matthean Typology*. Minneapolis: Fortress, 1993.

Amsler, Samuel. *L'ancien Testament Dans L'église: Essai D'herméneutique Chrétienne*. Neuchâtel: Delachaux & Niestlé, 1960.

Anderson, Bernhard W. "Exodus and Covenant in Second Isaiah and Prophetic Tradition." In *Magnalia Dei*, 339–60. Garden City: Doubleday, 1976.

———. "Exodus Typology in the Second Isaiah." In *Israel's Prophetic Heritage; Essays in Honor of James Muilenburg*, edited by Bernhard W. Anderson and Walter J. Harrelson, 177–95. New York: Harper, 1962.

———. *From Creation to New Creation: Old Testament Perspectives*. Minneapolis: Fortress, 1994.

Anderson, David R. *The King-Priest of Psalm 110 in Hebrews*. New York: Lang, 2000.
Andrew, M. E. "Esther, Exodus and Peoples." *Australian Biblical Review* 23 (1975) 25–28.
Arndt, William, et al. *A Greek-English Lexicon of the New Testament and Other Early Christian Literature*. Chicago: University of Chicago Press, 1979.
Arnold, C. E. *The Colossian Syncretism: The Interface between Christianity and Folk Belief at Colossae*. Tübingen, DE: Mohr, 1995.
———. "Ephesians." In *Dictionary of Paul and His Letters*, edited by Gerald F. Hawthorne et al., 238–49. Downers Grove, IL: InterVarsity, 1993.
———. *Ephesians: Power and Magic: The Concept of Power in Ephesians in Light of Its Historical Setting*. Grand Rapids: Baker, 1992.
———. *Powers of Darkness: Principalities & Powers in Paul's Letters*. Downers Grove, IL: InterVarsity, 1992.
Asumang, Annang. "Vehicles of Divine Mystery: Paul's Danielic Self Understanding in Ephesians 3." *Conspectus* 7, March (2009) 1–26.
Aulén, Gustaf. *Christus Victor: An Historical Study of the Three Main Types of the Idea of Atonement*. Translated by A. G. Hebert. New York: Macmillan, 1951.
Aune, David Edward. *Revelation 6–16*. Nashville: Nelson, 1998.
Aus, Roger David. "Comfort in Judgment: The Use of the Day of the Lord and Theophany Traditions in Second Thessalonians 1." PhD diss., Yale University, 1971.
———. *Matthew 1–2 and the Virginal Conception: In Light of Palestinian and Hellenistic Judaic Traditions on the Birth of Israel's First Redeemer, Moses*. Oxford: University Press of America, 2004.
———. "Relevance of Isaiah 66:7 to Revelation 12 and 2 Thessalonians 1." *Zeitschrift für die neutestamentliche Wissenschaft und die Kunde der älteren Kirche* 67, 3–4 (1976) 252–68.
Baker, David L. "Typology and the Christian Use of the Old Testament." In *The Right Doctrine from the Wrong Texts? Essays on the Use of the Old Testament in the New*, edited by G. K. Beale, 313–30. Grand Rapids: Baker, 1994.
Baker, Nathan L. "Living the Dream: Ethics in Ephesians." *Southwestern Journal of Theology* 22, 1 Fall (1979) 39–55.
Balentine, George L. "Death of Jesus as a New Exodus." *Review & Expositor* 59, 1 (1962) 27–41.
Balz, Horst Robert, and Gerhard Schneider. *Exegetical Dictionary of the New Testament*. Grand Rapids: Eerdmans, 1990.
Barclay, John M. G. "The Family as the Bearer of Religion in Judaism and Early Christianity." In *Constructing Early Christian Families: Family as Social Reality and Metaphor*, edited by Halvor Moxnes, 66–80. London: Routledge, 1997.
———. "Paul's Story: Theology as Testimony." In *Narrative Dynamics in Paul: A Critical Assessment*, edited by Bruce W. Longenecker, 113–56. Louisville, KY: Westminster John Knox, 2002.
Barr, James. "Invitation to the Septuagint." *Review of Biblical Literature* 4 (2002) 7–32.
Barrett, C. K. *From First Adam to Last: A Study in Pauline Theology*. London: Adam & Charles Black, 1962.
Barstad, Hans M. *A Way in the Wilderness: The "Second Exodus." In the Message of 2 Isaiah*. Manchester: University of Manchester Press, 1989.
Barth, Christoph, and Geoffrey William Bromiley. *God with Us: A Theological Introduction to the Old Testament*. Grand Rapids: Eerdmans, 1991.

Barth, Markus. "Conversion and Conversation: Israel and the Church in Paul's Epistle to the Ephesians." *Interpretation* 17, no. 1 Ja (1963) 3-24.

———. *Ephesians, Introduction, Translation and Commentary, Chapters 1-3*. Garden City, NY: Doubleday, 1974.

———. *Ephesians, Introduction, Translation and Commentary, Chapters 4-6*. Garden City, NY: Doubleday, 1974.

Bateman, Herbert W. I. V. "Psalm 110:1 and the New Testament." *Bibliotheca Sacra* 149, 596 O-D (1992) 438-53.

Batey, Richard A. "The Mia Sarx Union of Christ and the Church." *New Testament Studies* 13, 3 Ap (1967) 270-81.

———. *New Testament: Nuptial Imagery*. Leiden, NL: Brill, 1971.

Baur, Ferdinand Christian. *Paul the Apostle of Jesus Christ: His Life and Works, His Epistles and Teachings*. Peabody, MA: Hendrickson, 2003.

Beale, G. K. *1-2 Thessalonians*. Downers Grove, IL: InterVarsity, 2003.

———. *The Book of Revelation: A Commentary on the Greek Text*. Grand Rapids: Eerdmans, 1999.

———. "Colossians." In *Commentary on the New Testament Use of the Old Testament*, edited by G. K. Beale and D. A. Carson, 841-70. Grand Rapids: Baker Academic, 2007.

———. "The Danielic Background for Revelation 13-18 and 17:9." *Tyndale Bulletin* 31 (1980) 163-70.

———. "An Exegetical and Theological Consideration of the Hardening of Pharaoh's Heart in Exodus 4-14 and Romans 9." *Trinity Journal* 5, 2 Aut (1984) 129-54.

———. *John's Use of the Old Testament in Revelation*. Sheffield: Sheffield Academic, 1998.

———. "The Old Testament Background of Paul's Reference to 'the Fruit of the Spirit' in Galatians 5:22." *Bulletin for Biblical Research* 15, 1 (2005) 1-38.

———. "Peace and Mercy Upon the Israel of God: The Old Testament Background of Galatians 6:16b." *Biblica* 80, 2 (1999) 204-23.

———. *The Temple and the Church's Mission: A Biblical Theology of the Dwelling Place of God*. Downers Grove, IL: InterVarsity, 2004.

Beale, G. K., and D. A. Carson, eds. *Commentary on the New Testament Use of the Old Testament*. Grand Rapids: Baker Academic, 2007.

———. "Philemon." In *Commentary on the New Testament Use of the Old Testament*. Grand Rapids: Baker Academic, 2007, 918.

Beetham, C. A. "The Scriptures of Israel in the Letter of Paul to the Colossians." PhD diss., Wheaton College Graduate School, 2005.

Beker, Johan Christiaan. *Heirs of Paul: Paul's Legacy in the New Testament and in the Church Today*. Minneapolis: Fortress, 1991.

———. *Paul's Apocalyptic Gospel: The Coming Triumph of God*. Philadelphia: Fortress, 1982.

———. *Paul the Apostle: The Triumph of God in Life and Thought*. Philadelphia: Fortress, 1980.

———. "Recasting Pauline Theology: The Coherence-Contingency Scheme as an Interpretive Model." In *Pauline Theology. Volume 1, Thessalonians, Philippians, Galatians, Philemon*, edited by Jouette M. Bassler, 15-24. Minneapolis: Fortress, 1994.

———. "The Triumph of God." In *Paul the Apostle: The Triumph of God in Life and Thought*, 351–67. Philadelphia: Fortress, 1980.
Belleville, Linda L. *Reflections of Glory: Paul's Polemical Use of the Moses-Doxa Tradition in 2 Corinthians 3:1–18*. Sheffield: Journal for the Study of the Old Testament, 1991.
———. "Tradition or Creation? Paul's Use of the Exodus 34 Tradition in 2 Corinthians 3:7–18." In *Paul and the Scriptures of Israel*, 165–86. Sheffield: Academic, 1993.
Bellis, Alice Ogden. "The New Exodus in Jeremiah 50:33–38." In *Imagery and Imagination in Biblical Literature*, 157–68. Washington, DC: Catholic Biblical Association of America, 2001.
Bergren, Theodore A. "The Tradition History of the Exodus-Review in 5 Ezra 1." In *Of Scribes and Sages Volume 2, Later Versions and Traditions*, 34–50. New York: T & T Clark, 2004.
Bernard, J. H. *The Pastoral Epistles: With Introduction and Notes*. Cambridge: University Press, 1899.
Best, Ernest. *A Critical and Exegetical Commentary on Ephesians*. Edinburgh: T & T Clark, 1998.
Biguzzi, Giancarlo. "Efesini: La Misteriosa Del Muro Abbattuto." *Estudios Biblicos* 58, 3 (2000) 347–64.
Bjerkelund, Carl Johan. *Parakalô Form, Funktion Und Sinn Der Parakalô-Sätze in Den Paulinischen Briefen*. Oslo: Scandinavian University Press, 1967.
Blass, Friedrich, et al., *A Greek Grammar of the New Testament and Other Early Christian Literature*. Chicago: University of Chicago Press, 1961.
Bloch, Ariel A., and Chana Bloch. *The Song of Songs: A New Translation with an Introduction and Commentary*. New York: Random House, 1995.
Blomberg, Craig. "Matthew." In *Commentary on the New Testament Use of the Old Testament*, edited by G. K. Beale and D. A. Carson, 1–109. Grand Rapids: Baker Academic, 2007.
Bock, Darrell L. *Acts*. Grand Rapids: Baker Academic, 2007.
Bockmuehl, Markus. *The Epistle to the Philippians*. Peabody, MA: Hendrickson, 1998.
———. *Revelation and Mystery in Ancient Judaism and Pauline Christianity*. Tübingen, DE: Mohr, 1990.
Bonsirven, J. *Exegese Rabbinique Et Exegese Paulinienne*. Paris: Beauchesne, 1939.
Bornkamm, Günther. "Μυστήριον." In *Theological Dictionary of the New Testament*, edited by Gerhard Kittel et al. 4:802–28. Grand Rapids: Eerdmans, 1964–c1976.
———. *Paul*. Translated by D. M. G. Stalker. London: Hodder and Stoughton, 1971.
Bowman, John. *The Gospel of Mark: The New Christian Jewish Passover Haggadah*. Leiden, NL: E. J. Brill, 1965.
Bradley, K. R. *Slaves and Masters in the Roman Empire: A Study in Social Control*. New York: Oxford University Press, 1987.
Braun, Herbert. *Qumran Und Das Neue Testament 1*. Tübingen, DE: Mohr, 1966.
Breeze, Mary. "Hortatory Discourse in Ephesians." *Journal of Translation and Textlinguistics* 5, 4 (1992) 313–47.
Brown, Raymond E. *The Churches the Apostles Left Behind*. New York: Paulist, 1984.
———. *An Introduction to the New Testament*. New York: Doubleday, 1997.
———. *The Semitic Background of the Term "Mystery" In the New Testament*. Philadelphia: Fortress, 1968.

Brown, Stephen G. "The Intertextuality of Isaiah 66:17 and 2 Thessalonians 2:7: The Solution to the 'Restrainer' Problem." In *Paul and the Scriptures of Israel*, edited by Craig A. Evans and James A. Sanders, 254–75. Sheffield: Journal for the Study of the Old Testament, 1993.

Bruce, F. F. *The Epistles to the Colossians, to Philemon, and to the Ephesians*. Grand Rapids: Eerdmans, 1984.

———. "Eschatology." In *Evangelical Dictionary of Theology*, edited by Walter A. Elwell, 362–65. Grand Rapids: Baker, 1984.

———. *The New Testament Development of Old Testament Themes*. Grand Rapids: Eerdmans, 1968.

———. *Paul, Apostle of the Heart Set Free*. Grand Rapids: Eerdmans, 1977.

———. "The Victory of God." In *The New Testament Development of Old Testament Themes*, 40–50. Grand Rapids: Eerdmans, 1969.

Brueggemann, Walter. "'Exodus' in the Plural (Amos 9:7)." In *Many Voices, One God*, 15–34. Louisville, KY: Westminster John Knox, 1998.

———. *Hope within History*. Atlanta: Knox, 1987.

———. "Righteousness as Power for Life." In *Hope within History*, 27–48. Atlanta: Knox, 1987.

———. *Theology of the Old Testament: Testimony, Dispute, Advocacy*. Minneapolis: Fortress, 1997.

Brunson, Andrew C. *Psalm 118 in the Gospel of John: An Intertextual Study on the New Exodus Pattern in the Theology of John*. Tübingen, DE: Mohr, 2003.

Büchsel, F. "Λύω, Κτλ." In *Theological Dictionary of the New Testament*, edited by Gerhard Kittel et al., IV:351–56. Grand Rapids: Eerdmans, 1964.

Bultmann, Rudolf. *The Gospel of John; a Commentary*. Translated by G. R. Beasley-Murray. Philadelphia: Westminster, 1971.

———. "Λύπη Κτλ." In *Theological Dictionary of the New Testament*, edited by Gerhard Kittel et al., IV:313–24. Grand Rapids: Eerdmans, 1964.

———. *Theology of the New Testament*. New York: Scribner, 1951.

Burke, Trevor J. *Adopted into God's Family: Exploring a Pauline Metaphor*. Downers Grove, IL: InterVarsity, 2006.

Burns, Rita. "The Book of Exodus." In *Exodus, a Lasting Paradigm*, edited by Bastiaan M. F. van Iersel et al., 11–15. Edinburgh: T & T Clark, 1987.

Cadbury, Henry J. "The Key to Ephesians." *Journal of the American Academy of Religion* 20, no. 3 (1952) 210–12.

Caird, G. B. *The Apostolic Age*. London: Duckworth, 1955.

———. "The Descent of Christ in Ephesians 4:7–11." *Studia Evangelica* II (1964) 535–45.

———. *Paul's Letters from Prison: Ephesians, Philippians, Colossians, Philemon*. Oxford: Oxford University Press, 1976.

Campbell, William S. "Colossians Remixed: Subverting the Empire." *Modern Believing* 48, 2 Ap (2007) 68–69.

———. *Paul and the Creation of Christian Identity*. London: T & T Clark, 2006.

———. *Paul's Gospel in an Intercultural Context: Jew and Gentile in the Letter to the Romans*. Frankfurt: Lang, 1992.

———. "Unity and Diversity in the Church: Transformed Identities and the Peace of Christ in Ephesians." *Transformation* 25, 1 (2008) 15–31.

Caragounis, Chrys C. *The Ephesian Mysterion: Meaning and Content*. Lund, SE: Gleerup, 1977.

Cargal, Timothy B. "Seated in the Heavenlies: Cosmic Mediators in the Mysteries of Mithras and the Letter to the Ephesians." *Society of Biblical Literature Seminar Papers* 33 (1994) 804–21.

Carr, David McLain. "Light in the Darkness: Rediscovering Advent Hope in the Lectionary Texts from Isaiah." *Quarterly Review* 15, 3 Fall (1995) 295–320.

Carr, Wesley. *Angels and Principalities: The Background, Meaning, and Development of the Pauline Phrase Hai Archai Kai Hai Exousiai*. Cambridge: Cambridge University Press, 1981.

Carras, G. P. "Jewish Ethics and Gentile Converts: Remarks on 1 Thess 4:3–8." In *The Thessalonian Correspondence*, edited by Raymond F. Collins, 306–15. Leuven: Leuven University Press, 1990.

Carrez, Maurice. "The Pauline Hermeneutics of the Resurrection." In *Resurrection and Modern Biblical Thought*, 30–48. New York: Corpus, 1970.

Carson, D. A., and Douglas J. Moo. *An Introduction to the New Testament*. 2nd ed. Grand Rapids: Zondervan, 2005.

Casey, Jay. "The Exodus Theme in the Book of Revelation against the Background of the New Testament." In *Exodus, a Lasting Paradigm*, edited by Bastiaan M. F. van Iersel et al., 34–46. Edinburgh: T & T Clark, 1987.

Casey, Maurice. *Son of Man: The Interpretation and Influence of Daniel 7*. London: SPCK, 1979.

Cassidy, Richard J. *Paul in Chains: Roman Imprisonment and the Letters of St. Paul*. New York: Crossroad, 2001.

Cassuto, Umberto. *A Commentary on the Book of Exodus*. Jerusalem: Magnes, 1997.

Castellino, G. "La Dossologia Della Lettera Agli Efesini (1, 3–14)." *Salesianum* 8 (1946) 147–67.

Ceresko, Anthony R. "Psalm 149: Poetry, Themes (Exodus and Conquest), and Social Function." *Biblica* 67, 2 (1986) 177–94.

———. "The Rhetorical Strategy of the Fourth Servant Song (Isaiah 52:13–53:12): Poetry and the Exodus-New Exodus." *Catholic Biblical Quarterly* 56, 1 Ja (1994) 42–55.

Chadwick, Henry. "Die Absicht Des Epheserbriefes." *The Zeitschrift für die Neutestamentliche Wissenschaft* 51, 3/4 (1960), 145–53.

Charlesworth, James H. "Bashan, Symbology, Haplography, and Theology in Psalm 68." In *David and Zion: Biblical Studies in Honor of J. J. M. Roberts*, edited by Bernard Frank Batto et al., 351–72. Winona Lake, IN: Eisenbrauns, 2004.

Chavasse, Claude. *The Bride of Christ: An Enquiry into the Nuptial Element in Early Christianity*. London: Religious Book Club, 1940.

Cheon, Samuel. *The Exodus Story in the Wisdom of Solomon: A Study in Biblical Interpretation*. Sheffield: Sheffield Academic, 1997.

Childs, Brevard S. *Biblical Theology of the Old and New Testaments: Theological Reflection on the Christian Bible*. Minneapolis: Fortress, 1993.

———. *The Book of Exodus; a Critical, Theological Commentary*. Philadelphia: Westminster, 1974.

———. *Introduction to the Old Testament as Scripture*. Philadelphia: Fortress, 1979.

———. *Isaiah*. Louisville, KY: Westminster John Knox, 2001.

———. *Old Testament Theology in a Canonical Context*. Philadelphia: Fortress, 1986.

———. "Psalm 8 in the Context of the Christian Canon." *Interpretation* 23, 1 Ja (1969) 20–31.
Ciampa, Roy. *The Presence and Function of Scripture in Galatians 1 and 2*. Tübingen, DE: Mohr, 1998.
Ciampa, Roy, and Brian S. Rosner. "1 Corinthians." In *Commentary on the New Testament Use of the Old Testament*, edited by G. K. Beale and D. A. Carson, 695–752. Grand Rapids: Baker Academic, 2007.
Coleridge, Samuel Taylor, and Henry Nelson Coleridge. *Specimens of the Table Talk of the Late Samuel Taylor Coleridge*. London: Murray, 1835.
Collins, Raymond F. *1 & 2 Timothy and Titus: A Commentary*. London: Westminster John Knox, 2002.
———. "The Function of Paraenesis in 1 Thess 4:1–12; 5:12–22." *Ephemerides Theologicae Lovanienses* 74, 4 D (1998) 398–414.
Conzelmann, Hans. "Die Briefe an Die Epheser." In *Die Briefe An Die Galater, Epheser, Philipper, Kolosser, Thessalonicher Und Philemon*, edited by Jürgen Becker et al., 86–124. Göttingen, DE: Vandenhoeck & Ruprecht, 1985.
Coppens, Joseph. "'Mystery' in the Theology of Saint Paul and Its Parallels at Qumran." In *Paul and Qumran: Studies in New Testament Exegesis*, edited by J. Murphy-O'Connor, 132–58. Chicago: Priory, 1968.
Corell, Alf. *Consummatum Est: Eschatology and Church in the Gospel of St. John*. New York: Macmillan, 1958.
Cozart, Richard M. "The Theological Use of Isaiah in Ephesians 1." MTh thesis, University of Wales, 2007.
Craigie, Peter C. *Psalms 1–50*. Waco: Word, 1983.
Croatto, J. Severino. "Jesus, Prophet Like Elijah, and Prophet-Teacher Like Moses in Luke-Acts." *Journal of Biblical Literature* 124, no. 3 Fall (2005) 451–65.
Cullmann, Oscar. *Christ and Time: The Primitive Christian Concept of Time and History*. Philadelphia: Westminster, 1950.
Dahl, Niles Alstrup. "Bibelstudie Über Den Epheserbrief." In *Kurze Auslegung Des Epheserbriefes*, 7–83. Göttingen, DE: Vandenhoeck & Ruprecht, 1965.
———. "The Neglected Factor in New Testament Theology." In *Jesus the Christ: The Historical Origins of Christological Doctrine*, edited by Donald H. Juel, 153–63. Minneapolis: Fortress, 1991.
Dahl, Nils Alstrup, et al. "Cosmic Dimensions and Religious Knowledge (Eph 3:18)." In *Studies in Ephesians: Introductory Questions, Text- & Edition-Critical Issues, Interpretation of Texts and Themes*, 366–88. Tübingen, DE: Mohr, 2000.
———. *Studies in Ephesians: Introductory Questions, Text & Edition Critical Issues, Interpretation of Texts and Themes*. Tübingen, DE: Mohr, 2000.
Dahood, Mitchell J. *Psalms I: 1–50*. London: Yale University Press, 2007.
———. *Psalms II: 51–100*. London: Yale University Press, 2007.
Danell, G. A. "The Idea of God's People in the Bible." In *The Root of the Vine; Essays in Biblical Theology*, edited by Anton Fridrichsen, 23–36. New York: Philosophical Library, 1953.
Darko, Daniel K. *No Longer Living as the Gentiles: Differentiation and Shared Ethical Values in Ephesians 4:17–6:9*. London: T & T Clark, 2008.
Das, A. Andrew. *Paul, the Law, and the Covenant*. Peabody, MA: Hendrickson, 2001.
Daube, David. "Earliest Structure of the Gospels." *New Testament Studies* 5, 3 (1959) 174–87.

———. *The Exodus Pattern in the Bible*. London: Faber and Faber, 1963.
David, Barry C. "Is Psalm 110 a Messianic Psalm?" *Bibliotheca Sacra* 157, 626 Ap-Je (2000) 160–73.
Davids, P. H. "Adoption." In *Evangelical Dictionary of Theology*, edited by Walter A. Elwell, 25–26. Grand Rapids: Baker, 1984.
Davies, William David. *Paul and Rabbinic Judaism: Some Rabbinic Elements in Pauline Theology*. London: SPCK, 1948.
Davis, Barry Craig. "A Contextual Analysis of Psalms 107–118." PhD diss., Trinity Evangelical Divinity School, 1996.
Denny, David Roy. "The Significance of Isaiah in the Writings of Paul." PhD diss., New Orleans Baptist Theological Seminary, 1985.
Denton, David R. "Inheritance in Paul and Ephesians." *Evangelical Quarterly* 54, Jl-S (1982) 157–62.
Deterding, Paul E. "Exodus Motifs in First Peter." *Concordia Journal* 7, 2 (1981) 58–65.
Dexinger, F. "Samaritan Eschatology." In *The Samaritans*, edited by Alan David Crown, 266–92. Tübingen, DE: Mohr, 1989.
Dijkstra, M. "'I am neither a prophet nor a prophet's pupil:' Amos 7:9–17 as the Presentation of a Prophet Like Moses." In *Elusive Prophet*, edited by Johannes C. de Moor, 105–28. Boston: Brill, 2001.
Dillard, Raymond B. "Intrabiblical Exegesis and the Effusion of the Spirit in Joel." In *Creator, Redeemer, Consummator: A Festschrift for Meredith G. Kline*, edited by Howard Griffith and John R. Muether, 87–94. Greenville, SC: Reformed Academic, 2000.
Dockery, David S. "New Nature and Old Nature." In *Dictionary of Paul and His Letters*, edited by Gerald F. Hawthorne et al., 628–29. Downers Grove, IL: InterVarsity, 1993.
Dodd, C. H. *According to the Scriptures; the Sub-Structure of New Testament Theology*. New York: Scribner, 1953.
———. *Ephesians*. New York: Abingdon, 1929.
Donfried, Karl P. *Paul, Thessalonica, and Early Christianity*. Grand Rapids: Eerdmans, 2002.
Duff, Paul Brooks. "Metaphor, Motif, and Meaning: The Rhetorical Strategy Behind the Image 'Led in Triumph' in 2 Corinthians 2:14." *Catholic Biblical Quarterly* 53, 1 Ja (1991) 79–92.
Dumbrell, William J. "Paul's Use of Exodus 34 in 2 Corinthians 3." In *God Who Is Rich in Mercy*, 179–94. Homebush, NSW: Lancer Books, 1986.
Dunn, James D. G. *The Partings of the Ways: Between Christianity and Judaism and Their Significance for the Character of Christianity*. London: SCM, 1991.
———. "Spirit Speech: Reflections on Romans 8:12–27." In *Romans and the People of God: Essays in Honor of Gordon D. Fee on the Occasion of His 65th Birthday*, edited by Gordon D. Fee et al., 82–91. Grand Rapids: Eerdmans, 1999.
———. *The Theology of Paul the Apostle*. Grand Rapids: Eerdmans, 1998.
Dupont, Jacques. *Gnosis, La Connaissance Religieuse Dans L'épitres De Saint Paul*. Louvain, BE: Nauwelaerts, 1949.
Durham, John I. "Isaiah 40–55: A New Creation, a New Exodus, a New Messiah." In *The Yahweh/Baal Confrontation and Other Studies in Biblical Literature and Archaeology: Essays in Honour of Emmett Willard Hamrick: When Religions*

Collide, edited by Emmett Willard Hamrick et al., 47–56. Lewiston, NY: Mellen, 1995.

Dyrness, William A. *Themes in Old Testament Theology*. Downers Grove, IL: InterVarsity, 1977.

Eadie, John. *A Commentary on the Greek Text of the Epistle of Paul to the Ephesians*. Grand Rapids: Baker, 1979.

Edersheim, Alfred. *The Temple: Its Ministry and Services*. Peabody, MA: Hendrickson, 1994.

Egan, Rory B. "Lexical Evidence on Two Pauline Passages." *Novum Testamentum* 19, 1 Ja (1977) 34–62.

Eichrodt, Walther. *Theology of the Old Testament*. Philadelphia: Westminster, 1961.

Ellicott, C. J. *A Commentary, Critical and Grammatical, on St. Paul's Epistle to the Ephesians*. 2nd ed. Andover, MA: Draper, 1862.

Elliott, John Hall. *A Home for the Homeless: A Sociological Exegesis of 1 Peter, Its Situation and Strategy*. Philadelphia: Fortress, 1981.

Ellis, E. Earle. *Paul and His Recent Interpreters*. Grand Rapids: Eerdmans, 1961.

———. *Paul's Use of the Old Testament*. Edinburgh: Oliver and Boyd, 1957.

Emerton, John A. "The 'Mountain of God' in Psalm 68:16." In *History and Traditions of Early Israel*. Leiden, NL: Brill, 1993, 24–37.

Endo, Masanobu. *Creation and Christology: A Study on the Johannine Prologue in the Light of Early Jewish Creation Accounts*. Tübingen, DE: Mohr, 2002.

Engberg-Pedersen, Troels. "Ephesians 5:12–13: Ἐλέγειν and Conversion in the New Testament." *Zeitschrift für die Neutestamentliche Wissenschaft und die Kunde der älteren Kirche* 80, 1–2 (1989) 89–110.

Enns, Peter. "The Interpretation of Psalm 95 in Hebrews 3:1—4:13." In *Early Christian Interpretation of the Scriptures of Israel: Investigations and Proposals*, edited by Craig A. Evans and James A. Sanders, 352–63. Sheffield: Sheffield Academic, 1997.

———. "The 'Moveable Well' in 1 Cor 10:4: An Extrabiblical Tradition in an Apostolic Text." *Bulletin for Biblical Research* 6 (1996) 23–38.

Enz, Jacob J. "The Book of Exodus as a Literary Type for the Gospel of John." *Journal of Biblical Literature* 76, 3 (1957) 208–15.

Evans, C. A. "Ascending and Descending with a Shout: Psalm 47:6 and 1 Thessalonians 4:16." In *Paul and the Scriptures of Israel*, edited by Craig A. Evans and James A. Sanders, 238–53. Sheffield: Journal for the Study of the Old Testament, 1993.

———. "New Testament Use of the Old Testament." In *New Dictionary of Biblical Theology*, edited by T. Desmond Alexander and Brian S. Rosner, 72–80. Downers Grove, IL: InterVarsity, 2000.

Evans, Craig A., and James A. Sanders, eds. *Early Christian Interpretation of the Scriptures of Israel: Investigations and Proposals*. Sheffield: Sheffield Academic, 1997.

———. *Paul and the Scriptures of Israel*. Sheffield: Journal for the Study of the Old Testament, 1993.

Evans, Craig A., and William Richard Stegner. *The Gospels and the Scriptures of Israel*. Sheffield: Sheffield Academic, 1994.

Evans, John Frederick. "'You Shall Know That I Am Yahweh,' Ezekiel's Recognition Formula as a Marker of the Prophecy's Intertextual Relation to Exodus." Doctoral diss., Covenant Theological Seminary, 1995.

Fairbairn, Patrick. *The Typology of Scripture*. Philadelphia: Daniels & Smith, 1852.

Fanning, Buist M. *Verbal Aspect in New Testament Greek.* Oxford: Clarendon, 1990.
Farrer, Austin Marsden. *The Glass of Vision.* Westminster: Dacre, 1948.
Fay, Greg. "Paul, the Empowered Prisoner: Eph 3:1–13 in the Epistolary and Rhetorical Structure of Ephesians." PhD diss., Marquette University, 1994.
Fee, Gordon D. *The First and Second Letters to the Thessalonians.* Grand Rapids: Eerdmans, 2009.
———. *God's Empowering Presence: The Holy Spirit in the Letters of Paul.* Peabody: Hendrickson, 1994.
———. "Old Testament Intertextuality in Colossians: Reflections on Pauline Christology and Gentile Inclusion in God's Story." In *History and Exegesis: New Testament Essays in Honor of Dr. E. Earle Ellis for His 80th Birthday,* edited by E. Earle Ellis and Sang-Won Son, 201–21. New York: T & T Clark, 2006.
———. *Paul's Letter to the Philippians.* Grand Rapids: Eerdmans, 1995.
———. *Paul, the Spirit, and the People of God.* Peabody, MA: Hendrickson, 1996.
———. "Some Exegetical and Theological Reflections on Ephesians 4:30 and Pauline Pneumatology." In *Spirit and Renewal: Essays in Honor of J. Rodman Williams,* edited by J. Rodman Williams, 131–34. Sheffield: Sheffield Academic, 1994.
Ferch, Arthur J. *The Son of Man in Daniel Seven.* Berrien Springs, MI: Andrews University Press, 1983.
Fischer, Karl Martin. *Tendenz Und Absicht Des Epheserbriefes.* Göttingen, DE: Vandenhoeck und Ruprecht, 1973.
Fishbane, Michael A. *Biblical Interpretation in Ancient Israel.* Oxford: Oxford University Press, 1985.
———. "The 'Exodus' Motif/The Paradigm of Historical Renewal." In *Biblical Text and Texture: A Literary Reading of Selected Texts.* Oxford: Oneworld, 1998, 121–40.
Fitzmyer, Joseph A. *First Corinthians: A New Translation with Introduction and Commentary.* New Haven, CT: Yale University Press, 2008.
———. *The Letter to Philemon: A New Translation with Introduction and Commentary.* New York: Doubleday, 2000.
Flaming, James. "The New Testament Use of Isaiah." *Southwest Journal of Theology,* 11 (1968) 89–103.
Foerster, Werner, and Georg Fohrer. "Σῴζω, Κτλ." In T*heological Dictionary of the New Testament,* Gerhard Kittel et al., 3:199–200. Grand Rapids: Eerdmans, 1971.
Fontenrose, Joseph Eddy. *Python; a Study of Delphic Myth and Its Origins.* Berkeley: University of California Press, 1959.
Forman, Mark. "The Politics of Promise: Echoes of Isaiah 54 in Romans 4:19–21." *Journal for the Study of the New Testament* 31, March (2009) 301–24.
Foster, Paul. "The Bridegroom Messiah and the People of God: Marriage in the Fourth Gospel." *Expository Times* 118, 11 Ag (2007) 564–65.
Foulkes, Francis. *The Acts of God: A Study of the Basis of Typology in the Old Testament.* London: Tyndale, 1958.
———. *The Epistle of Paul to the Ephesians, an Introduction and Commentary.* Grand Rapids: Eerdmans, 1963.
France, R. T. "The Formula-Quotations of Matthew 2 and the Problem of Communication." *New Testament Studies* 27, 2 (1981) 243–44.
———. *Jesus and the Old Testament; His Application of Old Testament Passages to Himself and His Mission.* Downers Grove, IL: InterVarsity, 1971.

Fredrickson, David E. "Παρρησία in the Pauline Epistles." In *Friendship, Flattery, and Frankness of Speech: Studies on Friendship in the New Testament World*, edited by John T. Fitzgerald, 163–83. Leiden, NL: E. J. Brill, 1996.

Fredriksen, P. "Judaism, Circumcision and Apocalyptic Hope." In *The Galatians Debate: Contemporary Issues in Rhetorical and Historical Interpretation*, edited by Mark D. Nanos, 235–60. Peabody: Hendrickson, 2002.

Frisch, Amos. "The Exodus Motif in 1 Kings 1–14." *Journal for the Study of the Old Testament* 87, Mr (2000) 3–21.

Fuller, Reginald H. "The Kingdom of God in the Proclamation of Jesus." In *The Historical Jesus*, edited by Craig A. Evans, ed. 156–79. London: Routledge, 2004.

Gaiser, Frederick J. "'Your Sins Are Forgiven . . . Stand up and Walk': A Theological Reading of Mark 2:1–12 in the Light of Psalm 103." *Ex Auditu* 21 (2005) 71–87.

Galdon, Joseph A. *Typology and Seventeenth-Century Literature*. The Hague: Mouton, 1975.

Gallus, Laslo. "The Exodus Motif in Revelation 15–16." *Andrews University Seminary Studies*, 1 (2008) 21–43.

Gamer, David. "Adoption in Christ." ThD diss., Westminster Theological Seminary, 2002.

Gärtner, Bertil E. *John 6 and the Jewish Passover.* In Coniectanea Neotestamentica; 17. Lund, SE: C. W. K. Gleerup, 1959.

———. *The Temple and the Community in Qumran and the New Testament: A Comparative Study in the Temple Symbolism of the Qumran Texts and the New Testament.* Cambridge: Cambridge University Press, 1965.

Gaventa, Beverly Roberts. "Galatians 1 and 2: Autobiography as Paradigm." *Novum Testamentum* 28 (1986) 309–26.

Gempf, Conrad H. "The Imagery of Birth Pangs in the New Testament." *Tyndale Bulletin* 45, 1 (1994) 119–35.

Getty, Mary Ann. "The Theology of Philemon." *Society of Biblical Literature Seminar Papers* 26 (1987) 503–8.

Gladd, Benjamin L. *Revealing the Mysterion: The Use of Mystery in Daniel and Second Temple Judaism with Its Bearing on First Corinthians.* Berlin: Gruyter, 2009.

Glasson, T. F. *Moses in the Fourth Gospel.* Naperville, IL: Allenson, 1963.

Gnilka, Joachim. *Der Epheserbrief: Auslegung.* 3rd ed. Freiburg: Herder, 1971.

———. "Paränetische Traditionen Im Epheserbrief." In *Melanges Bibliques En Hommage Au R. P. B. Rigaux*, edited by A. Descamps and A. de Halleux, 397–410. Duculot, FR: Gembloux, 1970.

Goldingay, John. "Chronicler as a Theologian." *Biblical Theology Bulletin* 5, Je (1975) 99–126.

———. *Israel's Faith.* Downers Grove, IL: InterVarsity, 2006.

———. *Israel's Gospel.* Downers Grove, IL: InterVarsity, 2003.

Goldsworthy, G. "Relationship of Old Testament and New Testament." In *New Dictionary of Biblical Theology*, edited by T. Desmond Alexander and Brian S. Rosner, 81–88. Downers Grove, IL: InterVarsity, 2000.

Gombis, Timothy G. "Being the Fullness of God in Christ by the Spirit: Ephesians 5:18 in Its Epistolary Setting." *Tyndale Bulletin* 53, 2 (2002) 259–71.

———. "Ephesians 3:2–13: Pointless Digression, or Epitome of the Triumph of God in Christ?" *Westminster Theological Journal* 66, 2 Fall (2004) 313–23.

———. "Power Demonstrated in Weakness." *Act 3 Review* 15, 1 (2006) 81–101.

———. "The Triumph of God in Christ: Divine Warfare in the Argument of Ephesians." PhD diss., University of St. Andrews, 2005a.

———. "The Triumph of God in Christ: Divine Warfare in the Argument of Ephesians." In *Tyndale Bulletin* 56, 2 (2005b) 157–60.

Goodspeed, Edgar J. *The Key to Ephesians*. Chicago: University of Chicago, 1956.

———. *The Meaning of Ephesians*. Chicago: University of Chicago Press, 1933.

Goppelt, Leonhard. *Typos, the Typological Interpretation of the Old Testament in the New*. Grand Rapids: Eerdmans, 1982.

Gordon, Cyrus Herzl. "Belt-Wrestling in the Bible World." *Hebrew Union College Annual* 23, 1 (1951) 131–36.

Gourgues, Michel. *A La Droite De Dieu: Résurrection De Jésus Et Actualisation Du Psaume 110, 1 Dans Le Nouveau Testament*. Paris: Gabalda, 1978.

Grabbe, Lester L. *Judaic Religion in the Second Temple Period: Belief and Practice from the Exile to Yavneh*. London: Routledge, 2000.

Gray, John. "Desert Sojourn of the Hebrews and the Sinai-Horeb Tradition." *Vetus Testamentum* 4, 2 (1954) 148–54.

Gregory, Bradley C. "The Legal Background of the Metaphor for Forgiveness in Psalm CIII 12." In *Vetus Testamentum* 56, 4 (2006) 549–51.

Guignebert, Charles. *The Jewish World in the Time of Jesus*. New York: University Books, 1959.

Gundry, Robert Horton. "Style and Substance in 'the Myth of God Incarnate' According to Philippians 2:6–7." In *Crossing the Boundaries: Essays in Biblical Interpretation in Honour of Michael D. Goulder*, edited by M. D. Goulder et al., 271–94. Leiden, NL: Brill, 1994.

———. *The Use of the Old Testament in St. Matthew's Gospel: With Special Reference to the Messianic Hope*. Leiden, NL: Brill, 1967.

Gunkel, Hermann, and Joachim Begrich. *Introduction to Psalms: The Genres of the Religious Lyric of Israel*. Macon, GA: Mercer University Press, 1998.

Guthrie, Donald. *The Pastoral Epistles: An Introduction and Commentary*. Grand Rapids: Eerdmans, 1988.

Hafemann, Scott J. "Paul and His Interpreters." In *Dictionary of Paul and His Letters*, edited by Gerald Hawthorne and Ralph P. Martin, 666–70. Downers Grove, IL: InterVarsity, 1993.

———. *Paul, Moses, and the History of Israel: The Letter/Spirit Contrast and the Argument from Scripture in 2 Corinthians 3*. Tübingen, DE: Mohr, 1995.

Hannah, Darrell D. "Isaiah within Judaism of the Second Temple Period." In *Isaiah in the New Testament*, edited by Steve Moyise and M. J. J. Menken, 7–33. London: T & T Clark, 2005.

Hanson, Anthony T. "John 1:14–18 and Exodus 34." *New Testament Studies* 23, 1 O (1976) 97–109.

———. "The Use of the Old Testament in the Pastoral Epistles." *Irish Biblical Studies* 3 (1981) 203–19.

Hanson, Paul D. *The Dawn of Apocalyptic: The Historical and Sociological Roots of Jewish Apocalyptic Eschatology*. Philadelphia: Fortress, 1979.

Harder, Günther. *Paulus Und Das Gebet*. Gütersloh, DE: Bertelsmann, 1936.

Harman, Allan M. "Aspects of Paul's Use of the Psalms." *Westminster Theological Journal* 32 (1969) 1–23.

Harnack, Adolf von. *Militia Christi: The Christian Religion and the Military in the First Three Centuries*. Philadelphia: Fortress, 1981.
Harris, M. J. "Philemon." In *New Dictionary of Biblical Theology*, edited by T. Desmond Alexander and Brian S. Rosner, 336–37. Downers Grove, IL: InterVarsity, 2000.
Harris, W. Hall. *The Descent of Christ: Ephesians 4:7–11 and Traditional Hebrew Imagery*. Grand Rapids: Baker, 1998.
Hasel, Gerhard F. *The Remnant: The History and Theology of the Remnant Idea from Genesis to Isaiah*. Berrien Springs, MI: Andrews University Press, 1972.
Hatina, Thomas R. In *Search of a Context: The Function of Scripture in Mark's Narrative*. London: Sheffield Academic, 2002.
Hattori, Yoshiaki. "Divine Dilemma in Ezekiel's View of the Exodus: An Exegetical Study of Ezekiel 20:5–29." In *Law and the Prophets*, edited by Oswald T. Allis et al., 413–24. Nutley: Presbyterian and Reformed, 1974.
Hauser, Alan J. "Two Songs of Victory: A Comparison of Exodus 15 and Judges 5." In *Directions in Biblical Hebrew Poetry*, 265–84. Sheffield: Journal for the Study of the Old Testament, 1987.
Hay, David M. *Glory at the Right Hand: Psalm 110 in Early Christianity*. Nashville: Abingdon, 1973.
Hayes, Christine Elizabeth. "Golden Calf Stories: The Relationship of Exodus 32 and Deuteronomy 9–10." In *Idea of Biblical Interpretation*, 45–93. Boston: Brill, 2004.
Hays, Richard B. *The Conversion of the Imagination: Paul as Interpreter of Israel's Scripture*. Grand Rapids: Eerdmans, 2005.
———. *Echoes of Scripture in the Letters of Paul*. New Haven, CT: Yale University Press, 1989.
———. "'Who Has Believed Our Message?' Paul's Reading of Isaiah." In *The Conversion of the Imagination: Paul as Interpreter of Israel's Scripture*, 25–49. Grand Rapids: Eerdmans, 2005.
Heil, John Paul. *Ephesians: Empowerment to Walk in Love for the Unity of All in Christ*. Atlanta: Society of Biblical Literature, 2007.
Henderson, Suzanne Watts. "Colossians Remixed: Subverting the Empire." In *Interpretation* 60, 1 Ja (2006) 108–10.
Hendriksen, William. *Ephesians*. London: Banner of Truth Trust, 1972.
Hengel, Martin. *Studies in Early Christology*. Edinburgh: T & T Clark, 1995.
———. *The Zealots: Investigations into the Jewish Freedom Movement in the Period from Herod I until 70 A.D.* Edinburgh: T & T Clark, 1989.
Heriban, J. *Retto Phronein E Kenosis: Studio Esegetico Su Fil 2:1–5, 6–11*. Rome: Libr Ateneo Salesiano, 1983.
Hickling, C. J. A. "Paul's Reading of Isaiah." In *Studia Biblica*, 215–23. Sheffield: Journal for the Study of the Old Testament, 1980.
Hieke, Thomas. "Der Exodus in Psalm 80: Geschichtstopik in Den Psalmen." In *Studies in the Book of Exodus*, 551–58. Louvain, BE: Leuven University Press, 1996.
Hiers, Richard H. "Day of the Lord." In *Anchor Bible Dictionary*, edited by David Noel Freedman, 2:82–83. New York: Doubleday, 1992.
Hill, Linzy H. "Reading Isaiah as a Theological Unity Based on an Exegetical Investigation of the Exodus Motif." PhD diss., Southwestern Baptist Theological Seminary, 1993.
Hodge, Charles. *A Commentary on the Epistle to the Ephesians*. Grand Rapids: Eerdmans, 1950.

Hodgson, Robert. "1 Thess 4:1-12 and the Holiness Tradition." *Society of Biblical Literature Seminar Papers* 21 (1982) 199–215.
Hoehner, Harold W. *Ephesians: An Exegetical Commentary.* Grand Rapids: Baker Academic, 2002.
Hoffman, Yair. *The Doctrine of the Exodus in the Bible.* Tel Aviv: Tel Aviv University Press, 1983.
———. "A North Israelite Typological Myth and a Judaean Historical Tradition: The Exodus in Hosea and Amos." *Vetus Testamentum* 39, 2 (1989) 169–82.
Holland, Tom. *Contours of Pauline Theology: A Radical New Survey of the Influences on Paul's Biblical Writings.* Fearn, UK: Mentor, 2004.
Holm-Nielsen, Svend. "The Exodus Traditions in Psalm 105." In *Annual of the Swedish Theological Institute, XI,* 22–30. Leiden, NL: Brill, 1978.
Holtzmann, Heinrich Julius. *Kritik Der Epheser-Und Kolosserbriefe: Auf Grund Einer Analyse Ihres Verwandtschaftsverhältnisses.* Leipzig: Wilhelm Engelmann, 1872.
The Holy Bible: Containing the Old and New Testaments with the Apocryphal/ Deuterocanonical Books: New Revised Standard Version. Nashville: Thomas Nelson, 1989.
Hooker, Morna Dorothy. "Adam Redivivus: Philippians 2 Once Again." In *The Old Testament in the New Testament: Essays in Honour of J. L. North,* edited by Steve Moyise and J. L. North, 220–34. Sheffield: Sheffield Academic, 2000.
Horbury, William. *Jewish Messianism and the Cult of Christ.* London: SCM, 1998.
Horsley, Richard A., and John S. Hanson. *Bandits, Prophets, and Messiahs: Popular Movements in the Time of Jesus.* San Francisco: Harper & Row, 1988.
Houlden, J. L. *Paul's Letters from Prison: Philippians, Colossians, Philemon, and Ephesians.* Philadelphia: Westminster, 1977.
Houwelingen, P. H. R. van. "The Great Reunion: The Meaning and Significance of The 'Word of the Lord' in 1 Thessalonians 4:13–28." *Calvin Theological Journal* 42, 2 N (2007) 308–24.
Howard, J. K. "Christ Our Passover: A Study of the Passover-Exodus Theme in 1 Corinthians." *Evangelical Quarterly* 41, Ap-Je (1969) 97–108.
Hubbard, Moyer V. *New Creation of Paul's Letters and Thought.* New York: Cambridge University Press, 2002.
Hübner, Hans. "New Testament Interpretation of the Old Testament." In *Hebrew Bible, Old Testament: The History of Its Interpretation,* edited by Magne Sæbø, 332–72. Göttingen, DE: Vandenhoeck & Ruprecht, 1996.
Hugenberger, G. P. "Introductory Notes on Typology." In *The Right Doctrine from the Wrong Texts? Essays on the Use of the Old Testament in the New,* edited by G. K. Beale, 331–41. Grand Rapids: Baker, 1994.
Huie-Jolly, Mary R. "Threats Answered by Enthronement: Death/Resurrection and the Divine Warrior Myth in John 5:7–29, Psalm 2 and Daniel 7." In *Early Christian Interpretation of the Scriptures of Israel: Investigations and Proposals,* edited by Craig A. Evans and James A. Sanders, 191–217. Sheffield: Sheffield Academic, 1997.
Hummel, Charles E. "The Old Testament Basis of Typological Interpretation." *Biblical Research,* 9 (1964) 38–50.
Hunter, Alastair G. "Jonah from the Whale: Exodus Motifs in Jonah 2." In *Elusive Prophet,* edited by Johannes C. de Moor, 142–58. Boston: Brill, 2001.

Husbands, Mark, and Daniel J. Treier. *Justification: What's at Stake in the Current Debates*. Downers Grove, IL: InterVarsity, 2004.
Iersel, Bastiaan M. F. van, et al. *Exodus, a Lasting Paradigm*. Edinburgh: T & T Clark, 1987.
Isbell, Barbara Ann. *The Exodus Motif in John's Apocalypse*. MA Th. thesis, Southwestern Baptist Theological Seminary, 2004.
Isbell, Charles D. *The Function of Exodus Motifs in Biblical Narratives: Theological Didactic Drama*. Lewiston, NY: Mellen, 2002.
Janzen, J. Gerald. "Resurrection and Hermeneutics: On Exodus 3:6 in Mark 12:26." *Journal for the Study of the New Testament* 23, F (1985) 43–58.
Jeal, Roy R. *Integrating Theology and Ethics in Ephesians: The Ethos of Communication*. Lewiston, NY: Mellen, 2000.
Jeremias, Joachim. *The Eucharistic Words of Jesus*. Philadelphia: Fortress, 1977.
———. "Κεφαλὴ Γωνίας-Ἀκρογωνιαῖος." *The Zeitschrift für die Neutestamentliche Wissenschaft* 29, 3/4 (1930) 264–80.
———. *Theological Dictionary of the New Testament*, edited by Gerhard Kittel, IV, 864. Grand Rapids: Eerdmans, 1985.
Jeremias, Joachim, and Hermann Strathmann. *Die Briefe an Timotheus Und Titus*. Göttingen, DE: Vandenhoeck & Ruprecht, 1981.
Jewett, Robert. *Paul's Anthropological Terms: A Study of Their Use in Conflict Settings*. Leiden, NLBrill, 1971.
Jobes, Karen H. "Jerusalem, Our Mother: Metalepsis and Intertextuality in Galatians 4:21–31." *Westminster Theological Journal* 55, 2 Fall (1993) 299–320.
Jobes, Karen H., and Moisés Silva. *Invitation to the Septuagint*. Grand Rapids: Baker Academic, 2000.
Johnstone, William. "Looking at the Gateway: Chronicles in Itself and in Its Relation to the Pentateuch." In *Chronicles and Exodus: An Analogy and Its Application*. Sheffield: Sheffield Academic, 1998.
Jonge, Marinus de. *Outside the Old Testament*. Cambridge: Cambridge University, 1985.
Josephus, Flavius. *The Works of Josephus*, Vol. III. Translated by William Whiston. Grand Rapids: Baker, 1974.
Juel, Donald. *Messianic Exegesis: Christological Interpretation of the Old Testament in Early Christianity*. Philadelphia: Fortress, 1987.
Kaiser, Walter C. *The Messiah in the Old Testament*. Grand Rapids: Zondervan, 1995.
———. *Toward an Old Testament Theology*. Grand Rapids: Zondervan, 1978.
Käsemann, Ernst. "Ephesians and Acts." In *Studies in Luke-Acts*, edited by Leander E. Keck et al., 288–97. Philadelphia: Fortress, 1980.
———. "Justification and Salvation-History in the Epistle to the Romans." In *Perspectives on Paul*, 60–78. Philadelphia: Fortress, 1971.
———. *New Testament Questions of Today*. Philadelphia: Fortress, 1979.
———. *Perspectives on Paul*. Philadelphia: Fortress, 1971.
Kautzsch, E. *De Veteris Testamenti Locis a Paulo Apostolo Allegatis*. Leipzig: Metzger & Wittig, 1869.
Keesmaat, Sylvia C. "Creation, Exodus and Tradition in Romans 8:18–39." In *Paul and His Story*, 97–135. Sheffield: Sheffield Academic, 1999.
———. "Exodus and the Intertextual Transformation of Tradition in Romans 8:14–30." *Journal for the Study of the New Testament* 54, Je (1994) 29–56.

———. "Exodus and Tradition in Galatians." In *Paul and His Story*, 155–88. Sheffield: Sheffield Academic, 1999.

———. "In the Face of the Empire: Paul's Use of Scripture in the Shorter Epistles." In *Hearing the Old Testament in the New Testament*, edited by Stanley E. Porter, 182–212. Grand Rapids: Eerdmans, 2006.

———. "The Function of the Exodus Tradition in Galatians." In *Paul and His Story*, 189–215. Sheffield: Sheffield Academic, 1999.

———. *Paul and His Story*. Sheffield: Sheffield Academic, 1999.

———. "Paul and His Story: Exodus and Tradition in Galatians." In *Early Christian Interpretation of the Scriptures of Israel: Investigations and Proposals*, edited by Craig A. Evans and James A. Sanders, 300–33. Sheffield: Sheffield Academic, 1997.

Keil, Carl Friedrich, and Franz Delitzsch. *Isaiah. Commentary on the Old Testament in Ten Volumes*. Grand Rapids: Eerdmans, 1900.

Kennedy, H. A. A. *St. Paul and the Mystery Religions*. London: Hodder and Stoughton, 1913.

———. "St. Paul's Conception of the Spirit as a Pledge." *Expositor* 4, October (1901) 276–79.

Kidner, Derek. *Psalms 1–72: An Introduction and Commentary*. Nottingham: InterVarsity, 2008.

Kim, Jinkyu. "Message of Psalm 110 in Context: An Eschatological Interpretation." ThD diss., Westminster Theological Seminary, 2003.

Kim, Seyoon. *The Origin of Paul's Gospel*. Tübingen, DE: Mohr, 1981.

———. *Paul and the New Perspective: Second Thoughts on the Origin of Paul's Gospel*. Grand Rapids: Eerdmans, 2002.

Kim, Sungsoo. "A Study of the Exodus Motif in Isaiah." PhD diss., Calvin Theological Seminary, 1982.

King, Greg A. "The Day of the Lord in Zephaniah." *Bibliotheca Sacra* 152, 605 Ja-Mr (1995) 16–32.

Kirby, John C. *Ephesians, Baptism and Pentecost; an Inquiry into the Structure and Purpose of the Epistle to the Ephesians*. Montreal: McGill University, 1968.

Kitchen, K. A. "The Exodus." In *Anchor Bible Dictionary*, edited by David Noel Freedman II, 2:700–708. New York: Doubleday, 1992.

Kitchen, Martin. *Ephesians*. London: Routledge, 1994.

Kittredge, Cynthia Briggs. *Community and Authority: The Rhetoric of Obedience in the Pauline Tradition*. Harrisburg, PA: Trinity, 1998.

Klausner, Joseph. *From Jesus to Paul*. Translated by William F. Stinespring. New York: Macmillan, 1943.

———. *The Messianic Idea in Israel, from Its Beginning to the Completion of the Mishnah*. New York: Macmillan, 1955.

Klein, Ralph W. *1 Samuel*. Waco, TX: Word, 1983.

Klijn, Albertus Frederik Johannes. "The Aramaic Origins of the Four Gospels." *Nederlands Theologisch Tijdschrift* 34, no. 3 Jl (1980) 250–51.

———. "First Thessalonians 4:13–18 and Its Background in Apocalyptic Literature." In *Paul and Paulinism*. London: SPCK, 1982, 67–73.

Knight, George W. "Husbands and Wives." In *Recovering Biblical Manhood and Womanhood: A Response to Evangelical Feminism*, edited by John Piper and Wayne A. Grudem, 165–78, Wheaton, IL: Crossway, 1991.

———. *The Pastoral Epistles: A Commentary on the Greek Text*. Grand Rapids: Eerdmans, 1992.

Knox, John. *Philemon Among the Letters of Paul: A New View of Its Place and Importance*. Rev. ed. New York: Abingdon, 1959.

Knox, Wilfred Lawrence. *The Acts of the Apostles*. Cambridge: Cambridge University Press, 1948.

Koch, Dietrich-Alex. *Die Schrift Als Zeuge Des Evangeliums: Untersuchungen Zur Verwendung Und Zum Verständnis Der Schrift Bei Paulus*. Tübingen, DE: Mohr, 1986.

Koester, Helmut. "Ephesos in Early Christian Literature." In *Ephesos Metropolis of Asia: An Interdisciplinary Approach to Its Archaeology, Religion, and Culture*, edited by Helmut Koester, 119–40. Valley Forge, PA: Trinity, 1995.

Köstenberger, Andreas J. "Hearing the Old Testament in the New: A Response." In *Hearing the Old Testament in the New Testament*, edited by Stanley E. Porter, 255–94. Grand Rapids: Eerdmans, 2006.

Köster, Helmut. *Introduction to the New Testament History. Volume 2. History and Literature of Early Christianity*. Philadelphia: Fortress Press., 1982.

Kotansky, Roy D. "Demonology." In *Dictionary of New Testament Background*, edited by Craig A. Evans and Stanley E. Porter, 269–73. Downers Grove, IL: InterVarsity, 2000.

Kraus, Hans-Joachim. *Geschichte Der Historisch-Kritischen Erforschung Des Alten Testaments Von Der Reformation Bis Zur Gegenwart*. Neukirchen Kreis Moers, DE: Verlag der Buchhandlung des Erziehungsvereins, 1956.

Kraus, Hans-Joachim, and Keith R. Crim. "The Enemy Powers." In *Theology of the Psalms*, 125–36. Minneapolis: Augsburg, 1986.

Kreitzer, L. Joseph. "'Crude Language' and 'Shameful Things Done in Secret' (Ephesians 5.4, 12): Allusions to the Cult of Demeter/Cybele in Hierapolis?" *Journal for the Study of the New Testament* 71, S (1998) 51–77.

———. *The Epistle to the Ephesians*. London: Epworth, 1997.

———. "Eschatology." In *Dictionary of Paul and His Letters*, edited by Gerald F. Hawthorne et al., 253–69. Downers Grove, IL: InterVarsity, 1993.

———. *Hierapolis in the Heavens: Studies in the Letter to the Ephesians*. London: T & T Clark, 2007.

———. *Jesus and God in Paul's Eschatology*. Sheffield: Journal for the Study of the Old Testament, 1987.

———. "Living in the Lycus Valley: Earthquake Imagery in Colossians, Philemon and Ephesians." In *Hierapolis in the Heavens: Studies in the Letter to the Ephesians*, 93–106. London: T & T Clark, 2007.

Kruse, C. G. "Virtues and Vices." In *Dictionary of Paul and His Letters*, eidted by Gerald F. Hawthorne et al., 962–63. Downers Grove, IL: InterVarsity, 1993.

Kselman, John S. "Psalm 77 and the Book of Exodus." *Journal of the Ancient Near Eastern Society* 15 (1983) 51–58.

Kuhn, Karl G. "The Epistle to the Ephesians in the Light of the Qumran Texts." In *Paul and Qumran: Studies in New Testament Exegesis*, edited by J. Murphy-O'Connor, 115–31. Chicago: Priory, 1968.

Lampe, G. W. H., and K. J. Woollcombe. *Essays on Typology*. Napierville, Canada: Allenson, 1957.

Lang, Martin. "Amos Und Exodus: Einige Überlegungen Zu Am 3–6." *Biblische Notizen*, 119–120 (2003) 27–29.

Lapide, Pinchas. "Exodus in the Jewish Tradition." In *Exodus: A Lasting Paradigm*, edited by Bastiaan M. F. van Iersel et al., 47–55. Edinburgh: T & T Clark, 1987.

Larkin, William J. *Ephesians: A Handbook on the Greek Text*. Waco: Baylor University Press, 2009.

Lee, Won W. "The Concept of Wilderness in the Pentateuch." In *Israel in the Wilderness: Interpretations of the Biblical Narratives in Jewish and Christian Tradition*, edited by Kenneth Pomykala, 1–16. Leiden, NL: Brill, 2008.

Lenski, R. C. H. *The Interpretation of St. Paul's Epistles to the Galatians, to the Ephesians and to the Philippians*. Columbus, OH: Wartburg, 1946.

Levine, Étan. "The Wrestling-Belt Legacy in the New Testament." In *New Testament Studies* 28, 4 O (1982) 560–64.

Lichtenberger, Hermann. "Spirits and Demons in the Dead Sea Scrolls." In *The Holy Spirit and Christian Origins: Essays in Honor of James D. G. Dunn*, edited by James D. G. Dunn et al., 14–21. Grand Rapids: Eerdmans, 2004.

Lightfoot, J. B. *Notes on the Epistles of St. Paul: I and II Thessalonians, I Corinthians 1–7, Romans 1–7, Ephesians 1:1–14*. Winona Lake, IN: Alpha, 1978.

Lincoln, Andrew T. *Ephesians*. Dallas: Word, 1990.

———. "Ephesians and Heavenly Life in the Church at Worship." In *Paradise Now and Not Yet: Studies in the Role of the Heavenly Dimension in Paul's Thought with Special Reference to His Eschatology*. Cambridge: Cambridge University Press, 1981, 135–68.

———. "The Household Code and Wisdom Mode of Colossians." *Journal for the Study of the New Testament* 74, Je (1999) 93–112.

———. "Re-Examination of 'the Heavenlies' in Ephesians." *New Testament Studies* 19, 4 Jl (1973) 468–83.

———. "'Stand Therefore . . .': Ephesians 6:10–20 as Peroratio." *Biblical Interpretation* 3, 1 Mr (1995) 99–114.

———. "The Use of the OT in Ephesians." *Journal for the Study of the New Testament* 14 February (1982) 16–57.

Lincoln, Andrew T., and A. J. M. Wedderburn. *The Theology of the Later Pauline Letters*. Cambridge: Cambridge University Press, 1993.

Lind, Millard. *Yahweh Is a Warrior: The Theology of Warfare in Ancient Israel*. Scottdale, PA: Herald, 1980.

Lindars, Barnabas. *New Testament Apologetic: The Doctrinal Significance of the Old Testament Quotations*. London: SCM, 1961.

Lindars, Barnabas, et al. *It Is Written: Scripture Citing Scripture: Essays in Honour of Barnabas Lindars*. Cambridge: Cambridge University Press, 1988.

Lindemann, Andreas. "Bemerkungen Zu Den Adressaten Und Zum Anlab Des Epheserbriefes." *The Zeitschrift für die Neutestamentliche Wissenschaft* 67, 3/4 (1976) 235–51.

———. *Der Epheserbrief*. Zürich: Theologischer Verlag, 1985.

———. *Die Aufhebung der Zeit: Geschichtsverständnis u. Eschatologie im Epheserbrief*. Gütersloh, DE: Gütersloher Verlagshaus Mohn, 1975.

Lindeskog, Gösta. "The Theology of Creation in the Old and New Testaments." In *The Root of the Vine; Essays in Biblical Theology*, edited by Anton Fridrichsen, 1–22. New York: Philosophical Library, 1953.

Litwak, Kenneth D. *Echoes of Scripture in Luke-Acts: Telling the History of God's People Intertextually.* London: T & T Clark, 2005.

Loader, William R. G. "Christ at the Right Hand: Ps 110:1 in the New Testament." *New Testament Studies* 24, 2 Ja (1978) 199–217.

Lock, Walter. *The Epistle to the Ephesians.* London: Methuen, 1929.

Loewenstamm, Samuel E. *The Evolution of the Exodus Tradition.* Jerusalem: Magnes, 1992.

Lona, Horacio E. *Die Eschatologie Im Kolosser-Und Epheserbrief.* Würzburg, DE: Echter Verlag, 1984.

Longenecker, Bruce W. *The Triumph of Abraham's God: The Transformation of Identity in Galatians.* Nashville: Abingdon, 1998.

Longenecker, Richard N. *Biblical Exegesis in the Apostolic Period.* Grand Rapids: Eerdmans, 1974.

———. "Paul's Vision of the Church and Community Formation in His Major Missionary Letters." In *Community Formation in the Early Church and the Church Today*, edited by Richard N. Longenecker, 73–88. Peabody, MA: Hendrickson, 2002.

Longman, Tremper, and Raymond B. Dillard. *An Introduction to the Old Testament.* 2nd ed. Grand Rapids: Zondervan, 2006.

Longman, Tremper, and Daniel G. Reid. *God Is a Warrior.* Grand Rapids: Zondervan, 1995.

———. "Paul: The Warrior's Defeat of Principalities and Other Powers." In *God is a Warrior*, 136–64. Grand Rapids: Zondervan, 1995.

Lorek, Piotr. "The Motif of Exile in the Hebrew Bible; an Analysis of a Basic Literary and Theologicial Pattern." PhD diss., University of Wales, 2005.

Loretz, Oswald. "Exodus, Dekalog Und Ausschliessllichkeit Jahwes Im Amos Und Hosea Buch in Der Perspektive Ugaritischer Poesie." *Ugarit-Forschungen*, 24 (1993) 217–48.

———. "Konflikt Zwischen Neujahrsfest Und Exodus in Psalm 81." In *Mythos Im Alten Testament Und Seiner Umwelt*, 127–43. Berlin: Gruyter, 1999.

Louw, J. P., and Eugene Albert Nida. *Greek-English Lexicon of the New Testament: Based on Semantic Domains.* New York: United Bible Societies, 1989.

Lund, Øystein. *Way Metaphors and Way Topics in Isaiah 40–55.* Tübingen, DE: Mohr, 2007.

Lunde, Jonathan M., and John A. Dunne. "Paul's Creative and Contextual Use of Isaiah in Ephesians 5:14." *Journal of the Evangelical Theological Society* 55/1, (2012) 87–110.

———. "Paul's Creative and Contextual Use of Psalm 68 in Ephesians 4:8." *Westminster Theological Journal* 74, (2012) 99–117.

Lust, Johan. "Exodus 6:2–8 and Ezekiel." In *Studies in the Book of Exodus*, edited by M. Vervenne, 209–24. Louvain, BE: Leuven University Press, 1996.

Luz, U. "Überlegungen Zum Epheserbrief Und Seiner Paränese." In *Neues Testament Und Ethik: Für R. Schnackenburg*, edited by H. Merklein, ed. 376–96. Freiburg: Herder, 1989.

Lyons, George. "Pauline Autobiography: Toward a New Understanding." PhD diss., Emory University, 1982.

Macdonald, John. *The Theology of the Samaritans.* Philadelphia: Westminster, 1964.

MacDonald, Margaret Y. "Citizens of Heaven and Earth: Asceticism and Social Integration in Colossians and Ephesians." In *Asceticism and the New Testament*, edited by Leif E. Vaage and Vincent L. Wimbush, 269-98. New York: Routledge, 1999.

MacDonald, Margaret Y., and Daniel J. Harrington. *Colossians and Ephesians*. Collegeville, PA: Liturgical, 2000.

Macintosh, A. A. "Christian Exodus: An Analysis of Psalm 114." *Theology* 72, 589, Jl (1969) 317-19.

Mánek, Jindrich. "New Exodus (of Jesus) in the Books of Luke." *Novum Testamentum* 2, 1 Ja (1957) 8-23.

Marcus, Joel. *The Mystery of the Kingdom of God*. Atlanta: Scholars, 1986.

Marrow, Stanley B. "Parrhesia and the New Testament." *Catholic Biblical Quarterly* 44, 3 Jl (1982) 431-46.

Marsh, John. *The Fulness of Time*. New York: Harper, 1952.

Marshall, I. Howard. "Ephesians." In *New Testament Theology: Many Witnesses, One Gospel*, 379-96. Downers Grove, IL: InterVarsity, 2004.

Marshall, Molly Truman. "The Fullness of Incarnation: God's New Humanity in the Body of Christ." *Review & Expositor* 93, 2 (1996) 187-201.

Martin, Ralph P. *Ephesians, Colossians, and Philemon*. Louisville, KY: John Knox, 1991.

———. "An Epistle in Search of a Life-Setting." *Expository Times* 79, 10 Jl (1968) 296-302.

———. *Reconciliation: A Study of Paul's Theology*. Atlanta: John Knox, 1981.

Martyn, J. Louis. "Apocalyptic Antinomies in the Letter to the Galatians." *New Testament Studies*, 31 (1985) 410-24.

———. *Galatians: A New Translation with Introduction and Commentary*. New York: Doubleday, 1997.

Mathewson, David. "New Exodus as a Background for 'the Sea Was No More' in Revelation 21:1c." *Trinity Journal*, 2 (2003) 243-58.

Mauerhofer, Erich. "Der Brief an Die Epheser. 35. Teil: Kap. 3,20.20." *Fundamentum* 19, 4 (1998) 15-20.

Maurer, Christian. "Der Hymnus Von Epheser I Als Schlussel Zum Ganzen Briefe." *Evangelische Theologie* 11 (1951) 151-72.

Mbuvi, Andrew Mutua. *Temple, Exile, and Identity in 1 Peter*. London: T & T Clark, 2007.

McDaniel, Chip. "The Temple and the Church's Mission: A Biblical Theology of the Dwelling Place of God." *Journal of the Evangelical Theological Society* 49, 1 Mr (2006) 187-88.

McDonald, Lee Martin. "Ephesus." In *Dictionary of New Testament Background*, edited by Craig A. Evans et al., 318-21. Downer Grove, IL: InterVarsity, 2000.

McDonald, Lee Martin, and Stanley E. Porter. *Early Christianity and Its Sacred Literature*. Peabody: Hendrickson, 2000.

McKay, K. L. *A New Syntax of the Verb in New Testament Greek: An Aspectual Approach*. New York: Lang, 1994.

McKelvey, R. J. "Christ the Cornerstone." *New Testament Studies* 8, 4 Jl (1962) 352-59.

———. *The New Temple: The Church in the New Testament*. London: Oxford University Press, 1969.

McKenzie, Cameron S. "Echoes of Time and Space: The Ark and the Exodus in 1 Samuel 4-6." *Didaskalia* 12, 2 Spr (2001) 59-80.

McKenzie, Steve. "Exodus Typology in Hosea." *Restoration Quarterly* 22, 1–2 (1979) 100–108.
McMahan, Craig T. "The Wall Is Gone." *Review & Expositor* 93, 2 Spr (1996) 261–66.
McWhirter, Jocelyn. *The Bridegroom Messiah and the People of God: Marriage in the Fourth Gospel.* Cambridge: Cambridge University Press, 2006.
Meade, David G. *Pseudonymity and Canon: An Investigation into the Relationship of Authorship and Authority in Jewish and Earliest Christian Tradition.* Grand Rapids: Eerdmans, 1987.
Meeks, Wayne A. *The First Urban Christians: The Social World of the Apostle Paul.* New Haven, CT: Yale University Press, 1983.
Melugin, Roy F. "The Book of Isaiah and the Construction of Meaning." In *Writing and Reading the Scroll of Isaiah: Studies of an Interpretive Tradition 1*, edited by Craig C. Broyles, 39–55. Leiden, NL: Brill, 1997.
———. *The Formation of Isaiah 40–55.* Berlin: Gruyter, 1976.
Merklein, H. "Paulinische Theologie Im Der Rezeption Des Kolosser Und Epheserbriefes." In *Paulus Im Den Neutestamentlichen Spätschriften: Zur Paulusrezeption Im Neuen Testament*, edited by Karl Kertelge and Gerhard Lohfink, 25–69. Freiburg: Herder, 1981.
Metzger, Bruce Manning. "The Meaning of Christ's Ascension." In *Search the Scriptures, New Testament Studies in Honor of Raymond T. Stamm*, edited by Raymond T. Stamm et al., 118–28. Leiden, NL: Brill, 1969.
Meyer, Heinrich A. W., et al. *Critical and Exegetical Handbook to the Epistle to the Ephesians and the Epistle to Philemon.* Translated from the fourth edition by Maurice J. Evans. Translated revised and edited by William P. Dickson. Edinburgh: T & T Clark, 1880.
Michel, Otto. "Κατοικέω." In *Theological Dictionary of the New Testament*, Gerhard Kittel et al., V:153. Grand Rapids: Eerdmans, 1967.
———. *Paulus Und Seine Bibel.* Darmstadt: Wissenschaftliche Buchgesellschaft, 1972, original 1929.
Miletic, Stephen Francis. *"One Flesh"-Eph. 5:22–24, 5:31: Marriage and the New Creation.* Rome: Editrice Pontificio Istituto Biblico, 1988.
Milik, J. T. *Ten Years of Discovery in the Wilderness of Judea.* London: SCM, 1959.
Millar, J. G. "Victory." In *New Dictionary of Biblical Theology*, edited by T. Desmond Alexander and Brian S. Rosner, 830–32. Downers Grove, IL: InterVarsity, 2000.
Miller, Patrick D. *The Divine Warrior in Early Israel.* Cambridge: Harvard University Press, 1973.
———. *They Cried to the Lord: The Form and Theology of Biblical Prayer.* Minneapolis: Fortress, 1994.
Milne, Pamela J. "Psalm 23: Echoes of the Exodus." *Studies in Religion/Sciences Religieuses* 4, 3 (1975) 237–47.
Minear, Paul S. *Images of the Church in the New Testament.* Philadelphia: Westminster, 1960.
Mitton, C. Leslie. *The Epistle to the Ephesians: Its Authorship, Origin, and Purpose.* Oxford: Clarendon, 1951.
Moo, Douglas J. *The Epistle to the Romans.* Grand Rapids: Eerdmans, 1996.
Moore, George Foot. *Judaism in the First Centuries of the Christian Era: The Age of the Tannaim.* 3 vols. Cambridge: Harvard University, 1944.

Moritz, Thorsten. "Ephesians." In *New Dictionary of Biblical Theology*, edited by T. Desmond Alexander and Brian S. Rosner, 315-19. Downers Grove, IL: InterVarsity, 2000.

———. *A Profound Mystery: The Use of the Old Testament in Ephesians*. Leiden, NL: Brill, 1996.

———. "The Psalms in Ephesians and Colossians." In *The Psalms in the New Testament*, edited by Steve Moyise and Maarten J. J. Menken, 181-96. London: T & T Clark, 2004.

———. "'Summing up of All Things': Religious Pluralism and Universalism in Ephesians." In *One God, One Lord: Christianity in a World of Religious Pluralism*, edited by Andrew D. Clarke and Bruce W. Winter, 88-111. Grand Rapids: Baker, 1992.

Morris, Leon. "Redemption." In *Dictionary of Paul and His Letters*, edited by Gerald F. Hawthorne et al., 384-85. Downers Grove, IL: InterVarsity, 1993.

Mott, Stephen C. "Ethics." In *Dictionary of Paul and His Letters*, edited by Gerald F. Hawthorne et al., 269-75. Downers Grove, IL: InterVarsity, 1993.

Motyer, J. A. *The Prophecy of Isaiah: An Introduction & Commentary*. Downers Grove, IL: InterVarsity, 1993.

Moule, Charles F. D. *An Idiom Book of New Testament Greek*. 2nd ed. Cambridge: Cambridge University Press, 1959.

———. "Reflections on So-Called Triumphalism." In *The Glory of Christ in the New Testament: Studies in Christology in Memory of George Bradford Caird*, edited by L. D. Hurst et al., 219-28. Oxford: Oxford University Press, 1987.

Moule, H. G. C. *Studies in Ephesians*. Grand Rapids: Kregel, 1977.

Mouton, Elna. *Reading a New Testament Document Ethically*. Atlanta: Society of Biblical Literature, 2002.

Mowvley, Henry. "John 1:14-18 in the Light of Exodus 33:7—34:35." *Expository Times* 95, 5 (1984) 135-7.

Moyise, Steve. "The Old Testament in Paul." In *The Old Testament in the New: An Introduction*, 75-97. New York: Continuum, 2001.

———. *The Old Testament in the Book of Revelation*. Sheffield: Sheffield Academic, 1995.

Moyise, Steve, and M. J. J. Menken. *Isaiah in the New Testament*. New York: T & T Clark, 2005.

Muddiman, John. *The Epistle to the Ephesians*. Peabody, PA: Hendrickson, 2004.

Muilenburg, James. *The Book of Isaiah*. In *The Interpreter's Bible*, edited by George Arthur Buttrick. Nashville: Abingdon, 1956.

Muirhead, I. A. "Bride of Christ." *Scottish Journal of Theology* 5, 2 (1952) 175-87.

Muller, Earl C. "Returning Home: New Covenant and Second Exodus as the Context for 2 Corinthians 6:14-7:1." *Catholic Biblical Quarterly* 57, 1 (1995) 199-200.

Mullins, Terence Y. "Petition as a Literary Form." *Novum Testamentum* 5, 1 Ja (1962) 46-54.

Munck, Johannes. *Paul and the Salvation of Mankind*. Richmond: John Knox, 1959.

Mundle, Wilhelm, et al. "Redemption, Loose, Ransom, Deliverance, Release, Salvation, Savior (Λύω, Λύτρον, Ῥύομαι, Σώζω, Σωτήρ)." In *The New International Dictionary of New Testament Theology*, edited by Colin Brown, 3:205-23. Grand Rapids: Zondervan, 1975.

Murray, John. *Principles of Conduct: Aspects of Biblical Ethics.* Grand Rapids: Eerdmans, 1957.
Mussner, Franz. "Contributions Made by Qumran to the Understanding of the Epistle to the Ephesians." In *Paul and Qumran: Studies in New Testament Exegesis,* edited by J. Murphy-O'Connor, 159–78. Chicago: Priory, 1968.
Myers, Ched. *Binding the Strong Man: A Political Reading of Mark's Story of Jesus.* Maryknoll, HI: Orbis, 1988.
Newman, Carey C. "Election and Predestination in Ephesians 1:4–6a: An Exegetical-Theological Study of the Historical, Christological Realization of God's Purpose." *Review & Expositor* 93, 2 Spr (1996) 237–47.
Newton, John. "Analysis of Programmatic Texts of Exodus Movements." In *Exodus, a Lasting Paradigm,* edited by Bastiaan M. F. van Iersel et al., 56–62. Edinburgh: T & T Clark, 1987.
Nicholl, Colin R. *From Hope to Despair in Thessalonica: Situating 1 and 2 Thessalonians.* New York: Cambridge University Press, 2004.
Nielsen, Charles M. "Scripture in the Pastoral Epistles." *Perspectives in Religious Studies* 7, 1 Spr (1980) 4–23.
Ninow, Friedbert. *Indicators of Typology within the Old Testament: The Exodus Motif.* Frankfurt: Lang, 2001.
Nixon, Robin Ernest. *The Exodus in the New Testament.* London: Tyndale, 1963.
Noack, Bent. "Das Zitat in Ephes 5:14." *Studia Theologica* 5, 1 (1952) 52–64.
Noh, Jae Young. "Returning Home: New Covenant and Second Exodus as the Context for 2 Corinthians 6:14—7:1." *Journal of the Evangelical Theological Society* 39, 4 (1996) 669–70.
Noort, Edward. "Joshua and Amalek: Exodus 17:8–16." In *Interpretation of Exodus,* 155–70. Dudley, MA: Peeters, 2006.
Norden, Eduard. *Agnostos Theos; Untersuchungen Zur Formengeschichte Religiöser Rede.* Leipzig: Teubner, 1913.
Oblath, Michael D. "Of Pharaohs and Kings-Whence the Exodus." *Journal for the Study of the Old Testament* 87, Mr (2000) 23–42.
O'Brien, Peter T. "Ephesians 1: An Unusual Introduction to a New Testament Letter." *New Testament Studies* 25, 4 Jl (1979) 504–16.
———. *The Epistle to the Philippians: A Commentary on the Greek Text.* Grand Rapids: Eerdmans, 1991.
———. *The Letter to the Ephesians.* Grand Rapids: Eerdmans, 1999.
———. "The Summing up of All Things (Ephesians 1:10)." In *The New Testament in Its First Century Setting: Essays on Context and Background in Honour of B.W. Winter on His 65th Birthday,* edited by Bruce W. Winter and P. J. Williams, 206–19. Grand Rapids: Eerdmans, 2004.
Ochs, Carol. "Exodus: A Warrant for Political Transformation." *Religion and Intellectual Life* 6, 3–4 Spr-Sum (1989) 125–33.
Oropeza, B. J. "Echoes of Isaiah in the Rhetoric of Paul: New Exodus, Wisdom, and the Humility of the Cross in Utopian-Apocalyptic Expectations." *Intertexture of Apocalyptic Discourse in the New Testament.* Atlanta: Society of Biblical Literature, 2002, 87–112.
Ortlund, Raymond C. *Whoredom: God's Unfaithful Wife in Biblical Theology.* Grand Rapids: Eerdmans, 1996.

Osborne, Grant R. "Type, Typology." In *Evangelical Dictionary of Theology*, edited by Walter A. Elwell, 1118. Grand Rapids: Baker, 1984.

Oswalt, John. *The Book of Isaiah, Chapters 1–39*. Grand Rapids: Eerdmans, 1986.

———. *The Book of Isaiah, Chapters 40–66*. Grand Rapids: Eerdmans, 1998.

Overfield, P. Derek. "Pleroma: A Study in Content and Context." *New Testament Studies* 25, 3 Ap (1979) 384–96.

Page, Sydney H. T. *Powers of Evil: A Biblical Study of Satan and Demons*. Grand Rapids: Baker, 1995.

Pao, David W. *Acts and the Isaianic New Exodus*. Tübingen, DE: Mohr, 2000.

Park, Hyung Dae. *Finding Herem?: A Study of Luke-Acts in the Light of Herem*. London: T & T Clark, 2007.

Parry, Marilyn. "Isaiah 49:1–7, I Corinthians 1:1–9, John 1:29–42." *Expository Times* 119, 3 D (2007) 126–27.

Parsons, Michael. "The New Creation." *Expository Times* 99, 1 O (1987) 3–4.

Pate, C. Marvin. *The Reverse of the Curse: Paul, Wisdom and the Law*. Tübingen, DE: Mohr, 2000.

Pate, C. Marvin, et al. "Paul: The Reverse of the Curse." In *The Story of Israel: A Biblical Theology*, 206–31. Downers Grove, IL: InterVarsity, 2004.

———. "The Prophets: Sin, Exile and Restoration." In *The Story of Israel: A Biblical Theology*, 88–104. Downers Grove, IL: InterVarsity, 2004.

———. *The Story of Israel: A Biblical Theology*. Downers Grove, IL: InterVarsity, 2004.

Patton, Corrine L. "'I Myself Gave Them Laws That Were Not Good': Ezekiel 20 and the Exodus Traditions." *Journal for the Study of the Old Testament*, 69 (1996) 73–90.

Patzia, Arthur G. *Ephesians, Colossians, Philemon*. Peabody, MA: Hendrickson, 1990.

———. *The Making of the New Testament: Origin, Collection, Text and Canon*. Downers Grove, IL: InterVarsity, 1995.

Penna, Romano. "The Apostle's Suffering: Anthropology and Eschatology in 2 Corinthians 4:7–5:10." In *Paul the Apostle: A Theological and Exegetical Study*, 232–58. Collegeville, PA: Liturgical, 1996.

Penner, Erwin. "The Enthronement of Christ in Ephesians." *Direction* 12, 3 Jl (1983) 12–19.

———. "The Enthronement Motif in Ephesians." PhD diss., Fuller Theological Seminary, 1983.

Percy, Ernst. *Die Probleme Der Kolosser-Und Epheserbriefe*. Lund, SE: Gleerup, 1946.

Perkins, Pheme. *Ephesians*. Nashville: Abingdon, 1997.

Peterson, David. *Possessed by God: A New Testament Theology of Sanctification and Holiness*. Grand Rapids: Eerdmans, 1995.

Pfitzner, Victor C. *Paul and the Agon Motif: Traditional Athletic Imagery in the Pauline Literature*. Leiden: Brill, 1967.

Piper, John. "Prolegomena to Understanding Romans 9:14–15: An Interpretation of Exodus 33:19." *Journal of the Evangelical Theological Society* 22, no. 3 S (1979) 203–16.

Piper, Otto Alfred. "Unchanging Promises: Exodus in the New Testament." *Interpretation* 11, 1 Ja (1957) 3–22.

Pokorný, Petr. *Der Brief Des Paulus an Die Epheser*. Berlin: Evangelische Verlagsanstalt, 1992.

———. *Der Epheserbrief Und Die Gnosis: Die Bedeutung Des Haupt-Glieder-Gedankens in Der Entstehenden Kirche*. Berlin: Evangelische Verlagsanstalt, 1965.

———. "Epheserbrief Und Gnostische Mysterien." *Zeitschrift für die neutestamentliche Wissenschaft und die Kunde der älteren Kirche* 53, 3-4 (1962) 160-94.
Pomykala, Kenneth, ed. *Israel in the Wilderness: Interpretations of the Biblical Narratives in Jewish and Christian Traditions*. Leiden, NL: Brill, 2008.
Porsch, F. "Ἐλέγχω." In *Exegetical Dictionary of the New Testament*, edited by Horst Robert Balz and Gerhard Schneider, 1:428. Grand Rapids: Eerdmans, 1990.
Porter, Stanley E. *Verbal Aspect in the Greek of the New Testament: With Reference to Tense and Mood*. Vol. 1. New York: Lang, 1989.
Qualls, Paula F., and John D. W. Watts. "Isaiah in Ephesians." *Review & Expositor* 93, 2 Spr (1996) 249-59.
Quinn, Jerome D., and William C. Wacker. *The First and Second Letters to Timothy: A New Translation with Notes and Commentary*. Grand Rapids: Eerdmans, 2000.
Rad, Gerhard von. *Old Testament Theology*. Louisville, KY: Westminster John Knox, 2001.
———. "Typological Interpretation of the Old Testament." In *Essays on Old Testament Hermeneutics*, edited by Claus Westermann, 17-39. London: SCM, 1963.
Rahlfs, Alfred, et al., *Göttingen Septuagint*. Göttingen, DE: Vandenhoeck & Ruprecht, 2008.
Rahlfs, Alfred, and Robert Hanhart. *Septuaginta*. Stuttgart: Deutsche Bibelgesellschaft, 2006.
Rapske, Brian M. "Prison, Prisoner." In *Dictionary of New Testament Background*, edited by Craig A. Evans and Stanley E. Porter, 827-30. Downers Grove, IL: InterVarsity, 2000.
Reid, Daniel G. "The Christus Victor Motif in Paul's Theology." PhD diss., Fuller Theological Seminary, 1982.
———. "Triumph." In *Dictionary of Paul and His Letters*, edited by Gerald F. Hawthorne et al., 946-54. Downers Grove, IL: InterVarsity, 1993.
Rice, Gene. "An Exposition of Psalm 103," *Journal of Religious Thought* 39, 1 Spr-Sum (1982) 57-58.
Richard, Earl, and Daniel J. Harrington. *First and Second Thessalonians*. Collegeville, PA: Liturgical, 1995.
Ridderbos, Herman N. *Paul: An Outline of His Theology*. Grand Rapids: Eerdmans, 1975.
Roberts, J. H. "The Enigma of Ephesians: Rethinking Some Positions on the Basis of Schnackenburg and Arnold." *Neotestamentica* 27 (1993) 93-106.
———. *The Letter to the Ephesians*. Cape Town: Lux Verbi, 1991.
———. "Pauline Transitions to the Letter Body." In *L'apôtre Paul: Personnalité, Style Et Conception Du Ministère*, edited by Albert Vanhoye, 93-99. Leuven: Leuven University, 1986.
Robertson, Archibald T. *A Grammar of the Greek New Testament in the Light of Historical Research*. Nashville: Broadman, 1923.
———. *Word Pictures in the New Testament*. Nashville: Broadman, 1930.
Robinson, J. Armitage. *St. Paul's Epistle to the Ephesians*. 2nd ed. London: Macmillan, 1904.
Rochberg-Halton, Francesca. "Elements of the Babylonian Contribution to Hellenistic Astrology." *Journal of the American Oriental Society* 108, 1 Ja-Mr (1988) 51-62.
Roepe, Georgius. *De Veteris Testamenti Locorum in Apostolorum Libris Allegatione Commentatio*. Halle, DE: Friderici Ruff, 1827.

Roloff, Jürgen. *Apostolat, Verkündigung, Kirche*. Gütersloh, DE: Mohn, 1965.
Roon, A. van. *The Authenticity of Ephesians*. Leiden, NL: Brill, 1974.
———. "The Ephesian Mysterion." *Nederlands Theologisch Tijdschrift* 33, 2 Ap (1979) 143–44.
Rosner, Brian S. "Seven Questions for Paul's Ethics: 1 Thessalonians 4:1–12 as a Case Study." In *Understanding Paul's Ethics: Twentieth Century Approaches*, edited by Brian S. Rosner, 351–60. Grand Rapids: Eerdmans, 1995.
Ross, Allan P. "Psalms." In *The Bible Knowledge Commentary Old Testament*, edited by Roy B. Zuck, John F. Walvoord, 779–899. Wheaton, IL: Victor, 1989.
Rossell, William H. "New Testament Adoption, Graeco-Roman or Semitic." *Journal of Biblical Literature* 71, 3 D (1952) 233–34.
Rowlett, Lori L. *Joshua and the Rhetoric of Violence: A New Historicist Analysis*. Sheffield: Sheffield Academic, 1996.
Rowley, H. H. *The Biblical Doctrine of Election*. London: Lutterworth, 1950.
Sahlin, Harald. "The New Exodus of Salvation According to St. Paul." In *The Root of the Vine; Essays in Biblical Theology*, edited by Anton Fridrichsen, 81–95. New York: Philosophical Library, 1953.
Salmond, Steward D. F. "The Epistle of Paul to the Ephesians." In *Expositor's Greek Testament*. Vol. 3. London: Hodder and Stoughton, 1903.
Sampley, J. Paul. *"And the Two Shall Become One Flesh": A Study of Traditions in Ephesians 5:21–33*. New York: Cambridge University Press, 1971.
———. "Scripture and Tradition in the Community as Seen in Ephesians 4:25ff." *Studia Theologica* 26, 2 (1972) 101–9.
Sanborn, Scott F. "The New Exodus in the Risen Lamb." *Kerux*, 1 (1999) 18–24.
Sanders, James A. "Isaiah in Luke." In *Interpreting the Prophets*, edited by James Luther Mays and Paul J. Achtemeier. Philadelphia: Fortress, 1987.
Sandmel, Samuel. "Parallelomania." *Journal of Biblical Literature* 81, 1 Mr (1962) 1–13.
Scharlemann, Martin H. "Exodus Ethics: Part One-1 Peter 1:13–16." *Concordia Journal* 2, 4 (1976) 165–70.
Schille, Gottfried. "Der Autor Des Epheserbriefes." *Theologische Literaturzeitung* 82 (1957) 325–34.
———. *Frühchristliche Hymnen*. Berlin: Evangelische Verlagsanstalt, 1965.
———. "Liturgisches Gut Im Epheserbrief." Diss., University of Göttingen, 1953.
Schlier, Heinrich. *Christus Und Die Kirche Im Epheserbrief*. Tübingen, DE: Mohr, 1930.
———. *Der Brief an Die Epheser: Ein Kommentar*. Düsseldorf: Patmos, 1958.
Schmid, J. *Der Epheserbrief des Apostels Paulus. Seine Adresse, Sprache Und Literarischen Beziehungen Untersucht*. Edited by J. Gottsberger and J. Sickenberger. Freiburg: Herder, 1928.
Schmithals, Walter. "The Corpus Paulinum and Gnosis." In *The New Testament and Gnosis: Essays in Honour of Robert McL. Wilson*, edited by R. McL. Wilson et al., 107–24. Edinburgh: T & T Clark, 1983.
Schnackenburg, Rudolf. *Ephesians: A Commentary*. Edinburgh: T&T Clark, 1991.
Schoeps, Hans Joachim. *Paul; the Theology of the Apostle in the Light of Jewish Religious History*. Philadelphia: Westminster, 1961.
Schrenk, Gottlob "Ἐκλογή." In *Theological Dictionary of the New Testament*, edited by Gerhard Kittel et al., 4:186–92. Grand Rapids: Eerdmans, 1964–c1976.
Schürer, Emil. *A History of the Jewish People in the Time of Jesus Christ*. Peabody, MA: Hendrickson, 1994.

Schweitzer, Albert. *The Mysticism of Paul the Apostle.* Translated by William Montgomery. New York: Macmillan, 1956.

Schweitzer, Steven James. "Reading Utopia in Chronicles." PhD diss., University of Notre Dame, 2009.

Scott, Ernest Findlay. *The Epistles of Paul to the Colossians, to Philemon and to the Ephesians.* New York: Harper & Row, 1930.

Scott, James M. *Adoption as Sons of God: An Exegetical Investigation into the Background of Yiothesia in the Pauline Corpus.* Wissenschaftliche Untersuchungen Zum Neuen Testament 48. Tübingen, DE: Mohr, 1992.

———. "Adoption, Sonship." In *Dictionary of Paul and His Letters,* edited by Gerald F. Hawthorne et al., 15–18. Downers Grove, IL: InterVarsity, 1993.

———. *Exile: Old Testament, Jewish, and Christian Conceptions.* Leiden, NL: Brill, 1997.

———. "'For as Many as Are of Works of the Law Are under a Curse' (Galatians 3:10)." In *Paul and the Scriptures of Israel,* edited by Craig A. Evans and James A. Sanders, 187–221. Sheffield: Journal for the Study of the Old Testament, 1993.

———. "Restoration of Israel." In *Dictionary of Paul and His Letters,* edited by Gerald F. Hawthorne et al., 796–805. Downers Grove, IL: InterVarsity, 1993.

———. *Restoration: Old Testament, Jewish, and Christian Perspectives.* Leiden, NL: Brill, 2001.

Seifrid, Mark A. "Romans." In *Commentary on the New Testament Use of the Old Testament,* edited by G. K. Beale and D. A. Carson, 607–94. Grand Rapids: Baker Academic, 2007.

Shauf, Scott. *Theology as History, History as Theology: Paul in Ephesus in Acts 19.* Berlin: Gruyter, 2005.

Shea, William H. "Literary and Theological Parallels between Revelation 14–15 and Exodus 19–24." *Journal of the Adventist Theological Society,* 2 (2001) 164–79.

Shin, Bong Chur "New Exodus Motif in the Letter to the Hebrews." PhD diss., University of Wales, 2007.

Shkul, Minna. *Reading Ephesians: Exploring Social Entrepreneurship in the Text.* London: T & T Clark, 2009.

Silva, Moisés. "Galatians." In *Commentary on the New Testament Use of the Old Testament,* edited by G. K. Beale and D. A. Carson, 785–812. Grand Rapids: Baker Academic, 2007.

———. "Old Testament in Paul." In *Dictionary of Paul and His Letters,* edited by Gerald F. Hawthorne et al., 630–42. Downers Grove, IL: InterVarsity, 1993.

———. "Philippians." In *Commentary on the New Testament Use of the Old Testament,* edited by G. K. Beale and D. A. Carson, 835–39. Grand Rapids: Baker Academic, 2007.

Smalley, Stephen S. "Eschatology of Ephesians." *Evangelical Quarterly* 28, 3 Jl-S (1956) 152–57.

Smith, Derwood C. "The Ephesian Heresy." *American Academy of Religion* (1974, 45–54.

———. "Ephesian Heresy and the Origin of the Epistle to the Ephesians." *Ohio Journal of Religious Studies* 5, no. 2 O (1977) 78–103.

Smith, Gary V. "Paul's Use of Psalm 68:18 in Ephesians 4:8." *Journal of the Evangelical Theological Society* 18, 3 Sum (1975) 181–89.

Smith, Robert Houston. "Exodus Typology in the Fourth Gospel." *Journal of Biblical Literature* 81, 4 D (1962) 329–42.

Smolarz, Sebastian. "Covenant and the Metaphor of Divine Marriage in Biblical Thought with Special Reference to the Book of Revelation." PhD diss., University of Wales, 2005.

Snaith, Norman H. *Notes on the Hebrew Text of Isaiah, Chapters XXVIII-XXXII*. London: Epworth, 1945.

Snodgrass, Klyne. *Ephesians*. Grand Rapids: Zondervan, 1996.

———. "The Use of the Old Testament in the New." In *Interpreting the New Testament: Essays on Methods and Issues*, edited by David Alan Black and David S. Dockery, 209–29. Nashville: Broadman & Holman, 2001.

Stählin, G. "Οργή." In *Theological Dictionary of the New Testament*, edited by Gerhard Kittel et al., V:421. Grand Rapids: Eerdmans, 1964.

Stanley, Christopher D. *Paul and the Language of Scripture: Citation Technique in the Pauline Epistles and Contemporary Literature*. Cambridge: Cambridge University, 1992.

———. "'Pearls before Swine': Did Paul's Audiences Understand His Biblical Quotations?" *Novum Testamentum* 41, 2 Ap (1999) 124–44.

———. "'The Redeemer Will Come ἘΚ Σιών': Romans 11.26–27 Revisited." In *Paul and the Scriptures of Israel*, edited by Craig A. Evans and James A. Sanders, 118–42. Sheffield: Journal for the Study of the Old Testament, 1993.

Steck, Odil Hannes. "Das Problem Theologischer Strömungen in Nachexilischer Zeit." *Evangelische Theologie* 28, 9 S (1968) 445–58.

———. *Israel Und Das Gewaltsame Geschick Der Propheten*. Neukirchen-Vluyn: Neukirchener, 1967.

Stendahl, Krister. "The Called and the Chosen." In *The Root of the Vine; Essays in Biblical Theology*, edited by Anton Fridrichsen, 63–80. New York: Philosophical Library, 1953.

———. *Paul among Jews and Gentiles, and Other Essays*. Philadelphia: Fortress, 1976.

———. *The School of St. Matthew, and Its Use of the Old Testament*. Uppsala, SE: Gleerup, Lund, 1954.

Stevenson, Gregory M. "Communal Imagery and the Individual Lament: Exodus Typology in Psalm 77." *Restoration Quarterly* 39, 4 (1997) 215–29.

Stienstra, Nelly. *YHWH Is the Husband of His People: Analysis of a Biblical Metaphor with Special Reference to Translation*. Kampen, NL: Pharos, 1993.

Stockhausen, Carol Kern. *Moses' Veil and the Glory of the New Covenant: The Exegetical Substructure of 2 Cor. 3:1–4, 6*. Rome: Pontificio Instituto Biblico, 1989.

Stott, John R. W. *God's New Society: The Message of Ephesians*. Downers Grove, IL: InterVarsity, 1979.

Strack, Hermann Leberecht, and Paul Billerbeck. *Kommentar Zum Neuen Testament Aus Talmud Und Midrasch*. Munich: Beck, 1922.

Strauss, Mark L. *The Davidic Messiah in Luke-Acts: The Promise and Its Fulfillment in Lukan Christology*. Sheffield: Sheffield Academic, 1995.

Strelan, Rick. *Paul, Artemis, and the Jews in Ephesus*. New York: Gruyter, 1996.

Stuhlmueller, Carroll. *Creative Redemption in Deutero-Isaiah*. Rome: Biblical Institute, 1970.

Suh, Robert H. "The Use of Ezekiel 37 in Ephesians 2." *Journal of the Evangelical Theological Society* 50, 4 D (2007) 715–33.

Surburg, Raymond F. *Introduction to the Intertestamental Period*. St. Louis: Concordia, 1975.
Swancutt, Dianna M. "Hungers Assuaged by the Bread from Heaven: 'Eating Jesus' as Isaian Call to Belief: The Confluence of Isaiah 55 and Psalm 78(77) in John 6:22–71." In *Early Christian Interpretation of the Scriptures of Israel: Investigations and Proposals*, edited by Craig A. Evans and James A. Sanders, 218–51. Sheffield: Sheffield Academic, 1997.
Swartley, Willard M. *Israel's Scripture Traditions and the Synoptic Gospels: Story Shaping Story*. Peabody, MA: Hendrickson, 1994.
Swete, Henry Barclay. *An Introduction to the Old Testament in Greek*. Cambridge: Cambridge University Press, 1902.
Tachau, Peter. *"Einst" Und "Jetzt" Im Neuen Testament; Beobachtungen Zu Einem Urchristlichen Predigtschema Im Der Neutestamentlichen Briefliteratur Und Zu Seiner Vorgeschichte*. Göttingen, DE: Vandenhoeck & Ruprecht, 1972.
Tan, Kim Huat. "The Shema and Early Christianity." *Tyndale Bulletin* 59 (2008) 181–206.
Tasker, R. V. G. *The Old Testament in the New Testament*. Philadelphia: Westminster, 1947.
Taylor, Nicholas H. "Paul's Apostolic Legitimacy: Autobiographical Reconstruction in Gal 1:11–2:14." *Journal of Theology for Southern Africa* 83, Je (1993) 65–77.
Teeple, Howard Merle. "The Mosaic Eschatological Prophet." Diss., University of Chicago, 1957.
Terrien, Samuel L. *The Psalms: Strophic Structure and Theological Commentary*. Grand Rapids: Eerdmans, 2003.
Theron, Daniel J. "'Adoption' in the Pauline Corpus." *Evangelical Quarterly* 28, Ja-Mr (1956) 6–14.
Thielman, Frank. "Ephesians." In *Commentary on the New Testament Use of the Old Testament*, edited by G. K. Beale and D. A. Carson, 813–33. Grand Rapids: Baker Academic, 2007.
———. *Ephesians*. Grand Rapids: Baker Academic, 2010.
Thiessen, Matthew. "Hebrews and the End of the Exodus." *Novum Testamentum* 49, 4 (2007) 353–69.
Thompson, James W. "1 and 2 Thessalonians: A Socio-Rhetorical Commentary." *Restoration Quarterly* 50, 2 (2008) 128–29.
Thompson, Michael. *Clothed with Christ: The Example and Teaching of Jesus in Romans 12:1—15:13*. Sheffield: Journal for the Study of the Old Testament, 1991.
Tov, Emanuel. *The Text-Critical Use of the Septuagint in Biblical Research*. 2nd ed. Jerusalem: Simor, 1997.
Towner, Philip H. *1–2 Timothy and Titus*. Downers Grove, IL: InterVarsity, 1994.
———. "1–2 Timothy and Titus." In *Commentary on the New Testament Use of the Old Testament*, edited by G. K. Beale and D. A. Carson, 891–918. Grand Rapids: Baker Academic, 2007.
———. "Household and Household Codes." In *Dictionary of Paul and His Letters*, edited by Gerald F. Hawthorne et al., 417–19. Downers Grove, IL: InterVarsity, 1993.
———. "The Pastoral Epistles." In *New Dictionary of Biblical Theology*, edited by T. Desmond Alexander and Brian S. Rosner, 330–36. Downers Grove, IL: InterVarsity, 2000.

Trebilco, Paul R. *Jewish Communities in Asia Minor*. Cambridge: Cambridge University Press, 1991.
Tuckett, C. M. *The Scriptures in the Gospels*. Louvain, BE: Leuven University, 1997.
Turner, Max. "Mission and Meaning in Terms of 'Unity' in Ephesians." In *Mission and Meaning: Essays Presented to Peter Cotterell*, edited by A. Billington et al., 138–66. Carlisle, UK: Paternoster, 1995.
Turpie, David McCalman. *The Old Testament in the New: A Contribution to Biblical Criticism and Interpretation*. London: Williams & Norgate, 1868.
Unnik, Willem Cornelis van. *Tarsus or Jerusalem, the City of Paul's Youth*. London: Epworth, 1962.
Urbach, Efraim Elimelech. *The Sages, Their Concepts and Beliefs*. Cambridge: Harvard University, 1987.
Usami, K. *Somatic Comprehension of Unity: The Church in Ephesus*. Rome: Biblical Institute.
VanderKam, James C. *The Book of Jubilees*. Sheffield: Sheffield Academic, 2001.
VanGemeren, Willem A. "Psalms." In *The Expositor's Bible Commentary*, edited by Frank Ely Gaebelein and Dick Polcyn, 1–880. Grand Rapids: Zondervan, 1991.
Vaux, Roland de. *Ancient Israel: Its Life and Institutions*. Grand Rapids: Eerdmans, 1997.
Viviano, Benedict. "Peter as Jesus' Mouth: Matthew 16:13–20 in the Light of Exodus 4:10–17 and Other Models." *Society of Biblical Literature Seminar Papers* 37 (1998) 226–52.
Vollmer, Hans. *Die Alttestamentlichen Citate Bei Paulus Textkritisch Und Biblisch-Theologisch Gewürdigt: Nebst Einem Anhang Ueber Das Verhältnis Des Apostels Zu Philo*. Tübingen, DE: Mohr, 1895.
Vos, Geerhardus. *The Pauline Eschatology*. Grand Rapids: Eerdmans, 1952.
Wagner, J. Ross. *Heralds of the Good News: Isaiah and Paul "In Concert" In the Letter to the Romans*. Boston: Brill, 2002.
———. "Isaiah in Romans and Galatians." In *Isaiah in the New Testament*, edited by Steve Moyise and M. J. J. Menken, 117–32. London: T & T Clark, 2005.
———. "Moses and Isaiah in Concert: Paul's Reading of Isaiah and Deuteronomy in the Letter to the Romans." In *"As Those Who Are Taught": The Interpretation of Isaiah from the LXX to the SBL*, edited by Claire Mathews McGinnis and Patricia K. Tull, 87–106. Atlanta: Society of Biblical Literature, 2006.
Wal, A. J. O. van der. "Themes from Exodus in Jeremiah 30–31." In *Studies in the Book of Exodus*, edited by M. Verve, 559–66. Louvain, BE: Leuven University Press, 1996.
Wallace, Daniel B. *Greek Grammar Beyond the Basics: An Exegetical Syntax of the New Testament with Scripture, Subject, and Greek Word Indexes*. Grand Rapids: Zondervan, 1996.
———. "Οργίζεσθε in Ephesians 4:26: Command or Condition?" *Criswell Theological Review* 3, Spr (1989) 353–72.
Walsh, Brian J., and Sylvia C. Keesmaat. *Colossians Remixed: Subverting the Empire*. Downers Grove, IL: InterVarsity, 2004.
Waltke, Bruce K., and Charles Yu. *An Old Testament Theology: An Exegetical, Canonical and Thematic Approach*. Grand Rapids: Zondervan, 2007.
Waltzer, Michael. *Exodus and Revolution*. New York: Basic, 1985.
Wanamaker, Charles A. *The Epistles to the Thessalonians: A Commentary on the Greek Text*. Grand Rapids: Eerdmans, 1990.

Watson, Francis. *Paul, Judaism, and the Gentiles: Beyond the New Perspective.* Revised and expanded edition. Grand Rapids: Eerdmans, 2007.
Watts, John D. W. *Isaiah 1–33.* Waco, TX: Word Books, 1985.
———. "The Song of the Sea-Ex. XV." *Vetus Testamentum* 7 (1957) 371–80.
Watts, Rikki E. "Consolation or Confrontation: Isaiah 40–55 and the Delay of the New Exodus." *Tyndale Bulletin* 41, 1 (1990) 31–59.
———. "Exodus." In *New Dictionary of Biblical Theology*, edited by T. Desmond Alexander and Brian S. Rosner, 478–87. Downers Grove, IL: InterVarsity, 2000.
———. *Isaiah's New Exodus in Mark.* Grand Rapids: Baker, 2000.
Webb, Barry G. *The Message of Isaiah: On Eagles' Wings.* Leicester, UK: InterVarsity, 1996.
Webb, Robert L. *John the Baptizer and Prophet: A Socio-Historical Study.* Sheffield: Journal for the Study of the Old Testament, 1991.
Webb, William J. *Returning Home: New Covenant and Second Exodus as the Context for 2 Corinthians 6:14–7:1.* Sheffield: Academic, 1993.
Wedderburn, A. J. M. *Baptism and Resurrection: Studies in Pauline Theology against Its Graeco-Roman Background.* Tübingen, DE: Mohr, 1987.
Weiler, Anton. "The Experience of Communities of Religious Refugees." In *Exodus, a Lasting Paradigm*, edited by Bastiaan M. F. van Iersel et al., 63–71. Edinburgh: T & T Clark, 1987.
Weima, Jeffrey A. D. "1–2 Thessalonians." In *Commentary on the New Testament Use of the Old Testament*, edited by G. K. Beale and D. A. Carson, 871–89. Grand Rapids: Baker Academic, 2007.
Weiser, Artur. *The Psalms, a Commentary.* Philadelphia: Westminster, 1962.
Whiteley, D. E. H. *The Theology of St. Paul.* Philadelphia: Fortress, 1964.
Whybray, R. N. *Isaiah 40–66.* Grand Rapids: Eerdmans, 1981.
Wiedemann, Thomas E. J. *Greek and Roman Slavery.* Baltimore: Johns Hopkins University Press, 1981.
Wild, R. A. "'Be Imitators of God': Discipleship in the Letter to the Ephesians. In *Discipleship in the New Testament*, edited by Fernando F. Segovia, 127–43. Philadelphia: Fortress, 1985.
———. "The Warrior and the Prisoner: Some Reflections on Ephesians 6:10–20." *Catholic Biblical Quarterly* 46, 2 Ap (1984) 284–98.
Wilder, William N. *Echoes of the Exodus Narrative in the Context and Background of Galatians 5:18.* New York: Lang, 2001.
Wiles, Gordon P. *Paul's Intercessory Prayers: The Significance of the Intercessory Prayer Passages in the Letters of St. Paul.* New York: Cambridge University Press, 1974.
Wilk, Florian. *Die Bedeutung Des Jesajabuches Für Paulus.* Göttingen, DE: Vandenhoeck & Ruprecht, 1998.
———. "Die Zitation Von Jesajaworten." In *Die Bedeutung Des Jesajabuches Für Paulus*, 16–206. Göttingen, DE: Vandenhoeck & Ruprecht, 1998.
———. "Isaiah in 1 and 2 Corinthians." In *Isaiah in the New Testament*, edited by Steve Moyise and M. J. J. Menken, 133–58. New York: T & T Clark, 2005.
Williams, H. H. Drake. *The Wisdom of the Wise: The Presence and Function of Scripture within 1 Cor 1:18–3:23.* Leiden, NL: Brill, 2001.
Williamson, H.G. M. *The Book Called Isaiah: Deutero-Isaiah's Role in Composition and Redaction.* Oxford: Clarendon, 1994.

———. "Recent Issues in the Study of Isaiah." In *Interpreting Isaiah: Issues and Approaches*, edited by David G. Firth and H. G. M. Williamson, 21–39. Downers Grove, IL: Inter-Varsity, 2009.

Wink, Walter. *Engaging the Powers: Discernment and Resistance in a World of Domination*. Minneapolis: Fortress, 1992.

———. *Naming the Powers: The Language of Power in the New Testament*. Philadelphia: Fortress, 1984.

———. *Unmasking the Powers: The Invisible Forces That Determine Human Existence*. Philadelphia: Fortress, 1986.

Winston, David. *The Wisdom of Solomon: A New Translation with Introduction and Commentary*. Garden City, NY: Doubleday, 1979.

Winter, Sean F. "The Bridegroom Messiah and the People of God: Marriage in the Fourth Gospel." *Journal for the Study of the New Testament* 30, 5 (2008) 68–69.

Wise, Michael Owen, et al. *The Dead Sea Scrolls: A New Translation*. Revised edition. San Francisco: Harper, 2005.

Witherington, Ben. *The Acts of the Apostles: A Socio-Rhetorical Commentary*. Grand Rapids: Eerdmans, 1998.

———. *1 and 2 Thessalonians: A Socio-Rhetorical Commentary*. Grand Rapids: Eerdmans, 2006.

———. *The Letters to Philemon, the Colossians, and the Ephesians: A Socio-Rhetorical Commentary on the Captivity Epistles*. Grand Rapids: Eerdmans, 2007.

Witte, Markus. "From Exodus to David: History and Historiography in Psalm 78." In *History and Identity*, 21–42. New York: Gruyter, 2006.

Wolfe, Benjamin Paul. "The Place and Use of Scripture in the Pastoral Epistles." PhD diss., University of Aberdeen, 1990.

Wood, A. Skevington. "Ephesians." In *The Expositor's Bible Commentary*. Frank Ely Gaebelein and J. D. Douglas, eds. Grand Rapids: Zondervan, 1978, 3–92.

Wright, N. T. *The Climax of the Covenant: Christ and the Law in Pauline Theology*. Minneapolis: Fortress, 1992.

———. "Gospel and Theology in Galatians." *Journal for the Study of the New Testament Supplement Series* 108 (1994) 222–39.

———. *Jesus and the Victory of God*. Minneapolis: Fortress, 1996.

———. "New Exodus, New Inheritance: The Narrative Substructure of Romans 3–8." In *Romans and the People of God*, 26–35. Grand Rapids: Eerdmans, 1999.

———. "The New Inheritance According to Paul: The Letter to the Romans Re-Enacts for All Peoples the Israelite Exodus from Egypt to the Promised Land-from Slavery to Freedom." *Biblical Review* 14, 3 Je (1998) 16, 47.

———. *The New Testament and the People of God*. Minneapolis: Fortress, 1992.

———. "Poetry and Theology in Colossians 1:15–20." *New Testament Studies* 36, 3 Jl (1990) 444–68.

———. *The Resurrection of the Son of God*. London: SPCK, 2003.

Yates, Gary E. "New Exodus and No Exodus in Jeremiah 26–45: Promise and Warning to the Exiles in Babylon." *Tyndale Bulletin* 57, 1 (2006) 1–22.

Yee, Tet-Lim N. *Jews, Gentiles, and Ethnic Reconciliation: Paul's Jewish Identity and Ephesians*. Cambridge: Cambridge University Press, 2005.

Yoder, John Howard. *The Politics of Jesus: Vicit Agnus Noster*. Grand Rapids: Eerdmans, 1972.

Yoder-Neufeld, Thomas R. *Ephesians*. Waterloo, Canada: Herald, 2002.

———. *Put on the Armour of God: The Divine Warrior from Isaiah to Ephesians.* Sheffield: Sheffield Academic, 1997.

Young, Edward J. *The Book of Isaiah.* Grand Rapids: Eerdmans, 1965.

Young, Frances M., and David Ford. *Meaning and Truth in 2 Corinthians.* London: SPCK, 1987.

Zakovitch, Yair. *"And You Shall Tell Your Son": The Concept of the Exodus in the Bible.* Jerusalem: Magnes, 1991.

Zenger, Erich. "The God of Exodus in the Message of the Prophets as Seen in Isaiah." In *Exodus, a Lasting Paradigm*, edited by Bastiaan M. F. van Iersel et al., 22–33. Edinburgh: T & T Clark, 1987.

Zimmerli, Walther, et al. *Ezekiel: A Commentary on the Book of the Prophet Ezekiel.* Philadelphia: Fortress, 1979.

Scripture Index

OLD TESTAMENT

Genesis

1	17, 30, 121, 236n30
1:15	28
1:26–27	206
1:27	190
1:28	59
2:24	57, 58
	76, 211, 212–16, 214, 216, 226, 230, 261, 263
8:21	201, 263
9:2	228
12:1	30
15:6	23
16–25	30
21:10	116, 123
21:14	123
29:1–20	216
31:14	116

Exodus

1:14	150n31
3:6	40
3:11–12	188
5:21	150n31
5:26	261
6:6	58, 64, 110, 129
7:11	64
7:22	64
8:7	64
8:18	64
8:19	41
9:1	227
9:11	64
9:22	41
10:12–15	42
10:12–23	41
12:1–27	76
12:41–41	31
13:9	31
13:14	31
13:21	41
13:21–22	243
14:14	81
14:19	243
14:30	129
15	23
15:3	81
15:1–18	42
15:16	228
15:20	167
16	41
16:9–27	24
17	41
17:1–10	41
19:4	42
19:5	64
19:5–25	62
19:5–6	109, 221
19:6	243
19:6–20	61
19:16–19	60
20:12	211, 224–30, 225–28, 261, 263
21	64
21:8	111
29:18	57, 201, 263

Exodus (continued)

29:25	201, 263
29:41	201, 263
29:45–46	61
31:3	58
32:13	116, 123
32:31–33	153
32:32	49
32–34	48–49
33:7 - 34:35	41
33:17–33	64
34:6	63
34:9	116, 123
36:30	42
40:34	42

Leviticus

11:44	62
19:18	76, 211, 223, 262, 263
25:43	228
25:48	111
26:13	249

Numbers

	177n61
10:35	167
13:1–38	56
23	23
24	23
24:7	63
24:8	32
24:17	63

Deuteronomy

	17, 121
4:10	64
4:37	59
4:40	225n75
5:15	229
5:16	225
7:6	64
7:8	58, 64, 110, 111, 123
9:10	64
9:26	111
10:18	167
13:5	51, 111
13:7	136
18:15	23
18:15–19	23, 32
18:16	64
18:18	23
18:20–30	23
20:15	136
23:1	54
23:15–16	66
24:1	220
24:1–3	213n14
24:15	195, 196, 196n94
25:4	21
26:15	167
26:18–19	62
26:5–9	32
27:26	54
29–32	48
30:4	60
31:12–13	225n75
31:30	64
32	49
32:8–9	116
33:12	109
33:26	167

Joshua

3:7	32–33
4:14	32–33
4:22–23	33
11:23	116, 123
24:5–7	33

Judges

2:1	33
5	81
5:12	171
6–7	152–53

1 Samuel

10:18	33
17	152
17:47	81
24:4	196n93
26:6–12	196n93

2 Samuel

7:6	34
7:23	64
7:24	53

1 Chronicles

17:21	34, 111

2 Chronicles

6:41	188, 189n56

Ezra

	44
9	34n41
9:8–9	29

Nehemiah

9	34n41
9:7	106n55
9:9–17	38
9:12	64
9:19	64
32	106n55

Esther

	38

Job

	66
25:5	206
29:14	188
31:26	206
40:10	188
41:10	206

Psalms

	1, 17, 47, 250
2:2	98
2:7	106n52
2:11	228
4	98
4:4	195–97, 208, 261, 263
5:2	236n30
6:8	98
8	76, 99, 144, 186, 263
8:6	3, 97, 137, 261
18:2	236n30
18:30	236n30
18:35	236n30
19:4	227
23	38
28:7	236n30
30:11	188
33:20	236n30
35:26	188
45	216
47:5	60
59:11	236n30
68	39, 76, 141, 147, 166–75, 194, 263
68:5	167
68:18	166, 177, 261
77	38
78	38
78:52–53	23
80	38
81	38
83:9–11	23
85	38, 41
87:4	243
91:4	236n30
93:1	188
95	41
103	147, 159, 162, 262
104:1	188
105	38, 39
106	38
106:47	60
109:1	100
109:18	188
110	39, 39n74, 76, 98, 100, 122, 144, 175, 263
110	97n10
110:1	3, 97, 98, 137, 261
114	38
114:1	236n30
114:8	23
115:9–11	236n30
116:10	52
118	38, 64
119:43	117
129:8	64
132:16	188
132:9	188, 189n56
135	38
136	38
147:2	60
149	39

Proverbs

23:31	208n152

Song of Songs

	216
4:7	211

Isaiah

	16, 17, 23, 28, 38, 66, 121, 230, 235
2:1–5	140
2:1—4:6	61
2:19	92
2:2–4	137, 148
2:3	62
4:2–6	105–6
4:5	237
4:5–6	92
4:16–19	187
5:1	109
6:1	92
6:1–13	44
6:3	92, 113
7	109
7:19	66
8:14–15	141
9	98
9:2	201n115
9:6	136
10:17	201n115
10:23	227
10:24—12:6	236
10:33—11:10	44
11	98, 248
11:1	24
11:1–5	240
11:2	58, 66, 113, 122, 144, 232, 254, 257, 259
11:2–5	116
11:3–4	236
11:4	92, 189, 235, 248, 254, 255, 259
11:4–5	77, 122, 144, 254, 257
11:5	189, 235, 236, 236–41, 254, 259
11:6–8	238
11:9	92
11:9–10	238
11:10–16	92, 105–6, 257
11:11	236–37
11:11–14	35
11:11–16	240
11:12	60
11:15–16	23, 236–37, 248
12	98
13:5	92
13:13	92
13:20	66
13:21	66
14:1	66, 104–7, 105–6, 106, 123, 255, 257
14:2	228
14:13–14	92
14:30	66
14:4	66
14:7	66
16–21	105–6, 117
19:14	64
19:16	228
19:16–25	187
19:19–25	92, 143, 148
19:20	63, 92
20	143
21	143
22	121, 143
23	143
24	143
24:21	92
24:23	143
25:1–12	143
25–26	82, 92
25:6–10	148
26:12	128
26:1–21	143
26:13	64
26:14	76, 143, 255, 257, 259
26:19	76, 126, 127, 128, 200–208, 209, 255, 257, 259
26:19–21	205
26:3	128
26:4	128
26:5	128
26:6	128
27:1	234n12
27:10	66
27:12–13	60
27:13	60
28	64

28:14–15	64	43:14–21	35–36, 105–6
28:16	64, 76, 141, 143, 144, 255, 259	43:16–21	23, 92
28:16–17	64	44:1–2	104–7, 105–6, 106, 123, 240, 255, 257, 259
29:13	59	44:3	117, 123
29:14	50	44:3–5	105–6
29:19	180n12	44:22	76, 255, 257, 259
30:7	243	44:23	121
32:14–18	54	45	56
32:16	66	45:1–25	28
32:18	66	45:3	58
34:4–5	122	45:23	56, 155n51
34:14	66	48:16	117, 123
34:17	66	48:20	255, 257, 259
35:1–10	92, 105–6, 122, 143	48:20–21	23
35:4	150n31	49	54
35:10	150n31	49:1	19
37:16	92	49:1–6	247
40	136	49:1–9	44
40:3	40, 167	49:2	77, 189, 236, 247–49, 248, 254, 255, 259
40:3–5	105–6, 122	49:4	248
40–41	93	49:5–6	135
40:10	150n31, 234n12	49:6	201n115, 248
40:12	150n31	49:7	104–7, 105–6, 106, 123, 248, 255, 257, 259
40:13	150n31	49:8	52, 247
40:17	150n31	49:8–12	92, 105–6, 117, 257
40:22	92	49:9	247
40–55	257	49:9–13	248
40:9	135	49:10	247
41:17	180n12	49:11	247
41:17–20	92, 105–6, 117	49:12	105–6, 247
41:8–9	104–7, 105–6, 106, 123, 240, 255, 257, 259	49:13	180n12, 248
42:1	117, 123	49:14	150n31
42:1–4	240	49:18–22	221
42:16	201n115	49:20	150n31
42:1–7	44	50:1–2	221
42:6	201n115	50:1–3	92
43:1	150n31	50:2	255, 257, 259
43:1–3	105–6, 117	50:4–11	44
43:1–4	28	50:10	240
43:2	92	51:1—52:15	93, 106, 117, 137, 241
43:5	150n31	51:2	58
43:5–6	105–6	51:3	23, 150n31, 243
43:6	53	51:5	243
43:10	104–7, 106, 123, 255, 257, 259	51:7	150n31
43:14	28, 76, 111, 130n35	51:9	188, 243

Isaiah (continued)

51:9–10	243
51:9–11	23
51:9–17	205
51:10	243
51:10–11	43
51:12–13	150n31
51:14	150n31
51:21–22	150n31
52:1	188, 205
52:3	111, 243
52:3–6	28
52:4	53, 243
52:5–7	242n56
52:6	243
52:7	76, 117, 126, 134–35, 135, 136, 137, 143, 189, 235, 236, 243, 243–45, 244, 245, 254, 257, 259
52:7–15	77
52:8–12	93
52:9	243
52:10	243
52:11	52, 53, 64
52:11–12	23, 52, 244
52:12	243
52:13–14	59
52:13—53:12	44, 56
52:15	245
53:3–4	24
53:12	56
54:1	54, 217
54:1–3	48
54:1–8	221
54:2–5	58
54:5	76, 217
54:11	180n12
54:13	62
55:12	241
56–58	182
56–66	257
56:1–8	136
56:3–8	137
56:6–8	148
57	136, 257
57:13	116, 123
57:14	167
57:15	66
57:18	138
57:19	76, 126, 134–35, 135, 135–36, 137, 138, 143, 254, 259
57:20	66
57:21	182
59	236, 257
59:7	241
59:8–9	241
59:11	241
59:13	241
59:14	241
59:14–16	245
59:15	241
59:16–17	241
59:17	62, 77, 189, 235, 241–42, 242, 245–47, 254, 259
59:18	242n56
59:19	207n145, 246
59:20	242n56
59:21	250, 255, 257, 259
60	204, 207n145
60:1	76, 200–208, 201n115, 209, 255, 257, 259
60:1–2	206
60:1–5	205
60:3–5	246
60:10–14	246
60:16	133, 246
60:17–18	188
60:18–20	246
60–66	81, 241
61	189
61:1	117, 123, 180n12, 248
61:3	188
61:10	188, 221, 255, 257, 259
61:10–11	188
62:1–2	188
62:3–5	221
62:10	167
62:12	62
63	198
63:1	188
63:7–10	257
63:7–19	93, 241

63:10	62, 76, 197–200, 199, 208, 209, 259	11:19–20	76
		16:4	76, 211, 222, 263
63:10–11	117, 123	16:8–14	222
64:4	50	16:9	76, 211, 222, 230, 263
64:4–5	221	16:10–14	223
64:10	54	20	37, 222
65:9	116, 123	20:34	52
65:17	130	20:34–36	23
66:1	92, 121	20:41	57
66:15	61	20:5–6	106n54
66:18–20	140	30:2–3	61
66:18–21	137	34:23–24	24
66:18–23	187, 246	36:10–11	58
66:19	133	36:24–26	37, 222
66:22	130, 228	36:25	64, 211
		36:26	52

Jeremiah

	28, 38, 128	36:26–27	117
1:5	19	36:27	62
3:16	57, 58	36:28	64
6	62	36:29	64
6:13–15	61	36:29–30	58
7:3	61	36:33	64, 222
7:7	61	37	262
8	62	37:13–14	126
8:10–12	61	37:14	62
11:15	109	37:22	126
12:7	109	37:23	64
16:14–15	23	37:27	61, 76
23:3	57, 58	37:28	126
23:5	24	37:6	62
23:7–8	23, 37	39:27	60
31:2	23	40–48	139
31:31	52		

Daniel

	37, 76, 114, 121, 153, 162, 262
2:20	153
2:21	153
2:23	153
2:28	114
2:28–30	114
2:47	114
4:8–9	153, 154
4:9	114
4:18	153, 154
5:11	153, 154
5:14	153
6:3	153

31:31–34	37
31:32	221
31:33–34	62
33:10–11	216
33:25–26	106n53
33:4–11	37
46:10	61
50–51	34n41

Ezekiel

	38, 66, 128, 230
6	117
9:4	117
11:19	52

Daniel (continued)

7:13	61, 114
7:15	153
7:18	154
7:21	154
7:22	154
7:25	154
7:27	154
7:28	153
8:1	153
8:15	153
8:17	114
8:27	153
9	34n41
9:2	153
10:2	153
10:7	153
12:2	34n41, 37
12:5	153

Hosea

	23, 76, 218
2:2–20	217
2:14–15	23
2:16–17	37
11:1	32, 40
11:1–11	37
12:9	23

Joel

	38
1:15	61
2:1	60, 61
2:11	61
2:31–32	61
15	60

Amos

5:18–20	61
5:26	24
9:7–15	37

Obadiah

15	61

Jonah

2:1–10	37

Micah

4:1–3	62
4:1–5	140
5:5	136
7:14–17	37

Nahum

1:15	37

Zephaniah

1:14–16	60
1:14–18	61

Haggai

	29
2:5–6	37
2:23	106n56

Zechariah

	29, 38, 193, 195, 199
1:17	106n57
2:10	60, 61
2:12	106n57
3:1–4	189n56
3:2	106n57
6:13	98
8	193–94
8:1–8	37
8:6–8	37
8:11–13	37
8:14–15	37
8:16	76, 192–95, 208, 209, 261, 263, 264
9:9	180n12
9:9–10	82
9:14	60
13–14	34n41
14:5	61

Malachi

	29
1:11	64
3:1	38
4:5	61

APOCRYPHA

Judith
2:11–15	44–45
5:5–13	44

Wisdom of Solomon
	235
10:17–19	43

Baruch
3:27	107n58

2 Maccabees
5:19	107n58

3 Maccabees
6.4	43

2 Esdras
3:13–17	107n58
15:10–12	43
15:60	43
16:1	43

NEW TESTAMENT

Matthew
1–3	24
2:15	40
3:3	40
12:20–21	82
19	213n14
21:16	99n17
22:44	97n10
24	29
24:15	154
24:31	60
25:31	61
26:26–29	69
26:64	97n10

Mark
	67
1	24
1:15	80
2:18–20	216
10	213n14
10:45	64
12:26	40
12:36	97n10
13:14	154
14:62	97n10

Luke
	27n1
1–3	24
1:78–79	203
4	189
11:17–22	41
11:20–23	82
20:42	97n10
20:42–43	99n23
22:69	97n10

John
1:14–18	41
2:27	62
3:29	216
6	41
6:35	41
6:45	62
7:37–38	41
8:12	41
14:3	61
18:36	84

Acts
2:17	80
2:33	118
2:34	97n10
2:34–35	99n23
3:22	24, 41
3:25–26	108
5:31	99n23
6:7	58
7:17–43	41
7:37	24
7:43	24
10	6
12:24	58
13:16–18	27n1
13:16–23	41
15:13–18	108

Acts (continued)

17:22–31	6
19	101
19:2	118
19:13–16	101n34
19:17	101n34
19–20	4
19:20	58
20:18–35	14
22:3	16
23:6	16
26:5	16
26:18	203

Romans

	70, 133n43, 250
1:13	107n59
2:6	242n56
2:24	242n56
3	48
3:23	110, 249
3:24	129
3:24–25	68
4:19–21	48
5:12–21	99n18
5:9–10	246
6:13	203
6:16–20	66
6:23	249
6:3–4	69
6:8	61
7:1–6	218
7:22	156
7:24–25	265
7:6	49
8	61, 103
8:14–30	129
8:15	129
8:17	61, 187
8:20	59
8:21	99n18
8:22	61
8:2–27	49
8:28	107n58
8:28–30	95n1, 108
8:35–39	265
8:37	84, 86
8:39	157
8:9–11	118
8:9–23	187
9	48
9–11	107
9:11	108
9:1–5	49
9:17	227
9:25–29	218
9:26	107n60
9:28	227
9:33	64
9:3–4	153
9:4	107n60
10	48
10:11–15	50
10:15	245
10:18	227
11	48
11:1	16
11:25	242n56
11:26	241n51
11:28	108
11:33–36	265
11:5	108
12:1	62
12:2	156
12:5	99n24
13:11	203
13:12	62
14:10	219n51
14:11	155n51
15	48
15:7–12	108
15:21	245
15:21–24	50
16:25–26	80
16:25b-26	18

1 Corinthians

	4, 114, 250
1:2	64
1:3–4	159
1:8	85n37
1:15–20	86
1:19	50
1:30	129
2:8	232
2:9	50

Scripture Index 313

2:12	186n40	3:3	69
3:3	85n37	4:3	203
3:17	62	4:4	59, 203
5:5	61, 85n37	4:6	203
5:7	68	4:13	52
5:17	128	4:16	156, 186n40, 187
6:5–11	50, 50–51	4:16–18	156
6:16	213n14	5:8	61
6:16–17	217	5:17	86, 187
7:10	213n14	5:17–19	84
7:14	62	5:20	249
7:20–24	229	6:2	52
7:31	86	6:6	62
9:9	21	6:7	62
10	51	6:17	52
10:1–11	113	6:18	53, 107n60
10:1–22	64, 197	7:1	62
10:1–6	25	10:3–5	62
10:3	69	10:4	233
10:6	24	11	224
10:10	56	11:1–6	218
10:11	24, 200	11:2	219n51
10:16	99n24	11:22	16
10:26	64	11:2–3	217

Galatians

10:30	64		
11:7	59		53–55
11:25	68	1:4	64
12:12	99n24	1:13–17	19
12:27	99n24	1:15–16	19
15:20	86	2:20	64
15:20–21	86	3:1–5	55
15:23	86	3:6–9	55
15:24–28	100	3:8	80
15:25–27	3	3:10	54
15:27	99n17	3:10–14	55
15:45–49	59	3:14	117, 118
15:52	60	3:16	80
15:57	86	3:26	69

2 Corinthians

		3:29	80
1:3–4	95n1, 103n42	4:1–7	55, 95n1
1:3–11	95n1	4:4	80
1:14	61, 85n37	4:5	53
1:22	118	4:5–7	118
2:14	64, 82, 83, 83n20	4:7	66
2:14—14:7	153	4:21–26	54
3	68	4:22—25:1	217, 218
3:1–18	52	4:27	54

Galatians (continued)

4:28	217
4:31	217
5:1	217
5:12	54
5:18	54
5:22	54
6:15	128, 187
6:16	54, 113

Ephesians

	248
1	183
1–2	159
1:1	153, 154, 239, 250
1:3	97, 121
1:3–7	87
1:3–14	72, 110, 158
1:4	62, 104, 107–10, 109, 176, 219, 219n51, 255, 259
1:4–14	74
1:5	104, 255, 259
1:7	76, 110, 123, 255, 259, 263
1:7–10	110–112
1:8	112, 112–16, 113, 115, 119, 144, 172, 175, 232, 250, 257, 259
1:9	76, 107–10, 114, 123, 214, 255, 259
1:9–10	87
1:10	80, 88, 102–4, 121, 158, 227
1:10–14	116–19
1:11	104, 107–10, 116, 161, 255, 259
1:12	110, 219
1:13	76, 87, 97, 117, 117–18, 118, 184, 185, 191, 198, 239, 244
1:14	76, 88, 102–4, 110, 116, 118, 123, 137, 255, 259, 263
1:15	154, 176
1:15–19	119, 119–20, 155, 158
1:15–23	74
1:16–19	123
1:17	97, 112–16, 113, 122, 144, 172, 175, 191, 232, 259, 266
1:17–18	232
1:17–19	183, 250
1:18	103, 154
1:19	123, 266
1:19–20	96
1:20	97, 97n10, 100, 121
1:20–23	95–104, 96–97, 122, 161, 172, 204, 208, 219n48, 240, 250, 261
1:20—22:6	76, 164
1:20—22:10	126
1:21	87, 88, 93, 97, 101n34, 157, 175, 232
1:21–23	122
1:22	99n17, 266
1:23	122, 158, 175, 176
2	75, 140, 142, 262
2	126
2:1	144
2:1–2	128, 152
2:1–3	96, 202n127, 203
2:1–6	87, 96, 125
2:1–10	127–33, 131, 138
2:1–22	74, 125
2:2	89, 97, 144, 175, 183, 266
2:2–3	232
2:3	128, 202n127
2:3–4	144
2:4	176
2:4–7	131
2:5	76, 128, 143, 172, 175, 255, 259
2:5–6	127, 128, 131
2:5–7	144
2:6	97, 121, 122, 128, 208, 219, 240
2:7	88, 152
2:8–10	128, 144
2:10	87, 109, 128, 186, 187, 189
2:11–16	239
2:11–17	144
2:11–18	133–38
2:12	229

Scripture Index

2:13	76, 123, 137, 143, 144, 172, 175, 254, 255, 257, 259, 263	3:10	97, 121, 122, 149, 157, 232, 250
2:13–17	152	3:11	123
2:13–22	164	3:11–12	152
2:14–15	183	3:12	149
2:14–16	135n49, 227	3:13	145, 152, 232
2:14–17	136	3:14	160
2:15	128, 144, 155n53, 174, 175, 176, 186, 187, 189, 190, 226	3:14–15	156, 210
		3:14–19	146, 147, 154–60, 159, 232
		3:14–21	165
2:16	123, 144, 229, 255, 259, 263	3:15	121, 155n53, 227
		3:16	97, 157, 191, 266
2:17	76, 135n50, 141, 143, 172, 175, 244, 245, 254, 257, 259	3:16–17	187
		3:16–19	183
		3:17	157, 176, 240
2:18	97, 137, 152, 191, 240	3:18	154, 156, 157, 176, 219, 262
2:18–21	76		
2:18–22	64, 144, 145	3:18–19	157, 250
2:19	138, 154	3:18–20	87
2:19–22	138–43, 186, 210	3:19	176, 240, 266
2:20	64, 115, 120, 143, 144, 172, 175, 255, 257, 259	3:20	161, 232, 266
		3:20–21	146, 160–162
2:20–21	240	3:21	161
2:20–22	134, 229	4	176
2:21	62, 142, 157	4–6	157
2:21–22	139	4:1	145, 164, 181, 183, 229
2:22	141, 142, 191	4:1–10	165–75
2:9	128	4:1–16	164, 178, 199
3	151, 159, 183	4:1–3	181
3:1	145, 150, 153	4:1—6:9	164
3:1–10	76, 214, 215	4:2	181
3:1–13	146, 147–51, 154, 187	4:3	191
3:1–21	145–63	4:3–4	97
3:2	150	4:4	191
3:3	120, 148, 232	4:7	173
3:3–4	250	4:7–8	166
3:3–5	114, 119	4:7–10	76
3:5	87, 97	4:8	157, 164, 166, 168, 172, 173, 208, 210, 219
3:6	148		
3:6–7	244	4:8–10	152, 175
3:6–9	149	4:8–11	250
3:7	152, 266	4:9	227
3:7–9	115	4:9–10	173n43
3:8	153, 154, 250	4:10	87, 88, 97, 121, 122, 176, 232
3:8–12	146		
3:9	155n53, 186, 187, 226	4:11–12	115
		4:11–13	120

Ephesians (continued)

4:11–16	175–77
4:12	99n24, 154, 177
4:12–13	166
4:12–16	187
4:13	158, 175, 176, 177, 226, 250, 266
4:14	157, 175, 183
4:14–15	239
4:15	176, 185, 239
4:16	176, 177
4:17	183, 207
4:17–19	184, 186, 202n127
4:17–22	239
4:17–24	203
4:17–32	164
4:17—15:20	178–209, 180, 187
4:17—16:9	182
4:18	183, 250
4:20–21	183, 197
4:21	185, 239, 250
4:22	183, 188, 190n63, 202n127, 255, 259
4:22–24	185–91, 219
4:22—25:14	183
4:22—26:9	76
4:23	190–191, 191
4:23–24	189, 192, 207
4:24	62, 188, 200, 226, 239, 240, 250, 255, 259
4:25	185, 192–95, 208, 209, 239, 261
4:25–27	232
4:25–32	239
4:25—25:20	191–208
4:26	208
4:26–27	174, 195–97
4:27	232
4:29–30	213
4:29–31	250
4:30	76, 87, 88, 97, 118, 191, 197–200, 199, 208, 209, 219, 257, 259
4:31—35:14	200–208
5	107–10
5:1	250
5:1–2	190, 200, 240
5:1–6	164
5:2	64, 176, 200, 201, 263
5:3	154
5:3–4	200, 250
5:3–6	200
5:3–14	74
5:5	88, 219n48, 240
5:5–6	200
5:6	202n127, 232
5:7–13	200
5:7–14	164, 200
5:8	89
5:9	201n115, 239
5:11	201n115, 204, 232
5:11–14	208
5:13–14	202, 206, 209, 210, 219n48
5:14	201n116, 219, 255, 257, 259
5:15	250
5:15—16:9	164
5:16	232
5:17	191, 250
5:18	97
5:21—26:9	210–230
5:22	211
5:22–24	211–12
5:22–33	76, 221–22, 224
5:22—26:9	174
5:23	99n24
5:23–27	255
5:24–25	240
5:25	176, 212, 214
5:25–27	255
5:25–32	211–12
5:26	211, 212, 218, 222, 230, 262
5:26–27	62, 222
5:27	88, 218, 219, 219n51, 220
5:28	176, 211, 262, 263
5:29	212, 213
5:29–32	214
5:30	213
5:30–31	212
5:31	170, 211, 226, 230
5:32	76, 114, 213, 214, 215
5:33	176, 211, 211–12, 223, 262

6	236	1:10	85n37
6:1	211	2:6–11	173n43
6:1–4	225–28	2:7	56
6:1–9	224–30, 240	2:9–11	56, 83
6:1–17	113	2:10	155n51, 184n27, 227
6:2–3	170, 211, 227	2:10–11	56, 103
6:4	211, 250	2:14–16	56
6:5	211	2:17	57
6:5–9	229	2:25	57, 62
6:8	88	2:30	57
6:8–9	250	3:2	56
6:9	97, 121	3:5	16
6:10–11	87	3:21	103
6:10–13	236n29	4:18	57
6:10–17	77, 86	4:19	156
6:10–20	62, 247		
6:10–24	231–51	## Colossians	
6:11	232, 235		57–59, 114, 180n11, 250
6:11–13	53, 232	1:3–14	95n1
6:12	97, 121, 122, 232, 233, 266	1:5	117
6:13	232, 235	1:6	57, 58
6:13–17	74	1:9	266
6:14	116, 122, 144, 185, 235, 236–41, 241–42, 242, 254, 257, 259	1:9–10	58, 120
		1:10	57, 266
		1:13	129
6:14–15	255	1:13–14	58
6:14–17	232, 235, 236n29, 249	1:13–17	4
6:15	235, 243–45, 244, 245, 250, 254, 255, 257, 259	1:14	110
		1:15	59
		1:15–20	135n49
6:16	232	1:16	227
6:17	76, 144, 235, 245–47, 247–49, 248, 250, 254, 255, 257, 259	1:19–20	84
		1:20	227
		1:22	62, 219n51
6:18	154	1:24	59, 152
6:18–20	236n29	1:26–27	59
6:19	76, 114, 244, 250, 255, 259	1:28	219n51
		2:2	59, 266
6:19–20	250	2:3	58, 266
6:19–21	145	2:14	129
6:20	152, 153, 232, 249	2:14–15	82
6:23	176	2:15	103
6:24	176	2:22	59
6:32	214	3	266
## Philippians		3:1	97n10
	55–57	3:1–3	230
1:6	85n37	3:5	190n63

Colossians (continued)

3:9–10	59
3:9–11	190n63
3:10	186
3:11	229
3:12	59, 62
3:18–19	213
3:18—14:1	211n5
4:3	59

1 Thessalonians

	59–63
1:4	109
1:8	64
1:9–10	60
2:14–16	60
3:13	61, 62
4:4	62
4:7	62
4:8	246
4:9	62
4:13–28	60
4:16	60
4:16–17	60, 86
4:17	61, 85
5:2	61
5:3	61, 62
5:4–5	85n37
5:8	62, 241n51

2 Thessalonians

	59–63
1:7–8	61
2:1–2	62
2:1–12	61
2:2	61, 85n37
2:8	85
2:13–15	95n1, 108

1 Timothy

	4, 63, 66
1:5	14
1:8–10	64
1:14–16	63
1:16	64
2:5	63
2:6	64, 129
2:8	62, 64
2:15	62
3:14–15	64
3:16	214
4:1	64
4:1–3	214n21
4:3–4	64
6:16	64

2 Timothy

	4, 63, 64–65, 66
1:9	62
1:10	64, 86
1:12	85n37
1:18	85n37
2:3–4	62
2:17	64
2:19	64
2:20	64
3:8	64
4:1	86
4:8	85n37
4:13	13
4:17–18	87

Titus

	64, 66
2:11–14	64
3:4–6	64

Philemon

	66–67, 229
4–7	95n1
18–19	66

Hebrews

2:6–8	99n17
2:8	100
2:17–18	100n31
3:2	24
4:1–2	41
5:6	97n10
7:1–3	25
7:17	97n10
7:26–27	100n31
9:25	100n31
13:22	148n20

1 Peter

	41
1:3–5	95n1
2:18—13:7	211n5
3:21	24
3:22	100
5:12	148n20

Revelation

	41, 114
1:13	41
2:1–7	4
5–22	24
8:7	41
8:9	60
8:12	41
9:3	41–42
11:12	61
11:15	60
11:19	41
12:14	42
15:3–4	42
15:5–8	42
16:21	41
19:7	218
19:15	248
19:16	85
21:1	227
21:1–4	42
21:2	218
21:3	61
21:9	218
21:12	42
22	42
22:17	218

QURAM, DEAD SEA SCROLLS, PSEUDEPIGRAPHA

1 Enoch

39:6–8	61
45:4	61
62:14	61
71:16	61

Dead Sea Scrolls

	72

Psalms of Solomon

	44
2	44n114
9	44n114
11	44n114
18	44n114

Qumran documents

	72

Song of the Sea

	81

Subject and Names Index

Abasciano, Brian J., 6, 7, 48
Abbott, Thomas K., 191
Abraham, 30, 107n58, 123
    being child of, 138n64
    call of, 104
    as faithful servant, 23
    inheritance and, 116
    liberation of family, and God's relationship, 28
    role of, 55
    Yahweh's covenant with, 133
Abraham and Sarah birth narrative, 48
Absalom, 196n93
Adam, 59
    first and last, 59
    reference to pre-fall, 99
adoption, 108–9
Akiba, Rabbi, 34n40
Albright, William Foxwell, 166
Alexandria, 43
Alexandrian Septuagintal (LXX-A) version, 21, 26
allusions, 47
    in Isaiah, 254–55
    non-Isaiah, 262
"already" nature, of Pauline triumphalism, 85
Amsler, Samuel, 22
Anatolian religions, 9
Anderson, Bernhard W., 36, 174
anger
    righteous, 196n90
    without sin, 195–97
anti-Semitism in Alexandria, and Wisdom of Solomon, 43
antitypes

in 1 Corinthians, 51
of Christ, Moses and Israel as, 49
in NT, 23
Apamea, 6
apocalyptic imagery, in Daniel, 37
apocalyptic view of triumph, 84
Apocrypha, 42, 43, 114n84
apostles, as foundation of temple, 140
archetype, 23
armor imagery, 62, 189, 250
Arnold, C.E., 3n22, 9, 11, 88, 90n55, 101, 101n33, 129, 176–77, 232, 243, 246, 249
Artemis
    cult of, 9
    warning against worship of, 11
ascetical mysticism, Ephesians and, 14
Asia Minor
    fear in, 101
    Jew/Gentile interaction, 6
astral religions, 9
astrological powers, 101
astrological practices, 9
Asumang, Annang, 155n51
athletic metaphors, 17
atonement, substitutionary, 66
audience, 25
Aulén, Gustaf, 84n29, 249n 84
Aus, Roger David, 61
authorship of Ephesians, 2–4, 25

Baal, 171
    prophets of, 16
Babylon, exodus comparison to Egypt, 130
Babylonia-Persia, 28

exilic periods, 34
  return from, 38
Baker, David L., 23
Balentine, George, 36, 112
Balz, Horst Robert, 114
baptism, 12, 69, 165, 219n48
Barr, James, 20n151
Bartad, Hans M., 68
Barth, Markus, 2, 11, 72, 125, 134, 135, 148n20, 180n12, 189–90, 192, 194n84, 207, 213, 235, 239n48, 246, 247
battle metaphor, 250
Baur, E.C., 8
Beale, G.K., 7, 48, 54, 57, 58, 59, 139
Beelzebul controversy, 41
Beker, John Christiaan, 56, 72, 84, 89, 117, 179–80
belt of truth, 236–41
Benjamin, 167
berakah, 95, 107, 110, 118, 158
Best, Ernest, 2, 9, 95n1, 146n5, 147, 149, 160, 175n53, 178, 179n8, 193, 197, 198n107, 199n113, 215n29, 219, 232, 247
betrothal-marriage metaphor, 216–20
Biguzzi, Giancarlo, 10
Billerbeck, Paul, 42
birth pangs, 61
blasphemy of the Spirit, 198n105
boasting, warning against, 132
Bockmuehl, Markus, 147
body of Christ, 166
  functioning of, 166
boldness of speech, 249–50
"bowing the knee," 155n51
breastplate of righteousness, 236, 241–42
bride and bridegroom imagery, 189n56
  in Hosea, 222
bride of Christ, church as, 224
"bringing near," 136
Brown, Raymond, 2
Bruce, F.F., 4, 11, 89, 119, 146n5, 158n70, 184n27
Brueggemann, Walter, 30, 188
Brunson, Andrew C., 95n1

Büchsel, F., 112
building motif, in Isaiah, 141
Bultmann, Rudolf, 8, 84n28

Caird, G.B., 2, 169, 233
Campbell, W., 134
captivity captive, 171
Carmen Christi, 56
Casey, Jay, 111
Chadwick, Henry, 10
Charlesworth, James H., 166
Cheon, 43
children
  in INE society, 224–30
  longevity in eschatological community, 225–28
  of wrath, 127n14
Childs, Brevard S., 30, 34–35, 42, 92, 99n17, 113, 136, 141, 141n80, 182, 189
Christ
  and church, 76
  church as bride, 224
  church co-enthroned with, 207
  church covenant with, 223
  coming, 60
  death of, 68
  and death of enmity, 137
  descent of, 173n43
  ethical change and, 204n130
  in form of servant, 56
  as foundation of temple, 140
  God's victory through, 122
  light of, 203
  and new covenant, 216
  as new Moses, 168–69
  paradoxical pattern of, 152
  reconciliation by, 83
  return of, 61, 85–87
  salvation through, 63
  triumph of, 174, 210
  typological interpretation of events, 24
Christ-church imagery, 214–15
Christ-church relationship, 212, 213
Christian community
  assurances for, 64
  slave relationships, 229

Christian gospel, Jewish scriptures
  continuity with, 211
Christian life, 13, 164
  multidimensional view of, 263
  practical victory in, 176
Christian warrior, 248
Christians
  between two ages, 88
  warnings to, 183
church, 122, 165
  blessings as a people of God, 108
  as bride of Christ, 224
  as chaste virgin, 218
  and Christ, 76, 161
  Christ co-enthroned with, 207
  Christ's defeat of powers provoking disharmony, 174
  Christ's victory shared with, 122
  communal acts of, 69
  covenant union with Christ, 223
  elevated position of, 96
  in Ephesians 6, 250
  Gentile inclusion in, 136–37
  as God's possession, 118
  image of perfected, 247
  as Isaac, 217
  members tempted by past lifestyles, 202n122
  practice of righteous living, 204
  relation to Christ, 88
Ciampa, Roy, 7
circular letter hypothesis, 4, 15
circumcision, participation in, 138n64
citizenship, 139n65
clothing imagery, 185n34, 188, 191n67, 236n31, 255, 259
  priest-like garments, 243
cloud and fire, 243
clouds and smoke, 60–61
Coleridge, Samuel Taylor, 8n59
Colossae, Jewish population, 5
communal acts, of church, 69
compassion, of Yahweh, 130
conflict, 184n32
conflict-victory, 142
Conzelmann, Hans, 8, 88
Coppens, Joseph, 213
Cornelius, 6

cornerstone, 141–42
corporate agaph, 14
corrupt old self, 185
cosmic powers, 165, 266
  battleground with, 226
  location of, 97
  triumph of God in Christ over competing, 15
  victory over, 150
covenant, 33, 68–69, 107n58
  church with Christ, 223
  participation in, 138n64
creation
  and election, 105n50
  language, 155n53
Cullmann, Oscar, 84
Cybele cult, 9
Cyrus, 28, 36

Dahl, Nils Alstrup, 2, 8n59, 12, 89, 108, 125n1, 157, 181, 193, 204, 207n150, 215, 219, 232
Dahood, Mitchell J., 166
Damascus road christophany, 18–19
Danell, G.A., 105n50
darkness
  deeds of, 202n127, 203
  light over, 200–208
Darko, Daniel K., 127n14, 182
Das, A., 104
Daube, David, 111, 129
David, 24, 32n29, 152
  and Goliath, 16
Davidic king, 98
Davidic Messiah, 126
day of redemption, 198n107
Day of the Lord, 61, 198n107
  Jesus on, 29
  present and future, 85–86
dead awakening, 205
dead people, types in Ephesians 2, 128
Dead Sea Scrolls, 42, 43, 72
death-life metaphor, 210
death-new life metaphor, 255, 259
death of Christ, and death of enmity, 137
Deborah and Barak's victory, 171
  over Sisera, 166–67

deeds of darkness, 203
deity, association between name and power, 101n34
Delitzsch, Franz, 113
deliverance, 28
  Pauline understanding of, 129
delivery, concept of, 87
Demeter and Cybele cult, 12
demonic powers, 11–12, 16
Denny, David Roy, 98
departing, vs. fleeing, 244
depravity of man, 49–50
descent of Christ, 173n43
desert, God's presence in, 167
Deuteronomic reforms, 32
devil, battle focus on, 232
disciples, as foundation of temple, 140
disharmony in church, Christ's defeat of powers provoking, 174
disobedience, 225n75
divination, 101
divine calling, 19
divine choice, 104–7, 259
  echoes of, 255
divine gifts, 113
divine insight, 120
divine knowledge, 266
  Paul's understanding of, 9
divine marriage, prophets' anticipation of restoration, 220
divine omnipotence, 126
divine power, 11
divine triumph, 161
  benefits provided, 164
divine warfare, 81n8, 142
Divine Warrior, 171, 241, 246, 259
divorce, 213n14
Dockery, David S., 191
Dodd, C.H., 2, 18, 46
Domitian persecution (AD 96), 13
doxology, 146, 158, 160–162
Duff, Paul Brooks, 83n20
Dunn, James D.G., 2, 79n3, 88n43, 89, 90n55, 100n24, 104, 117, 132n35, 150n28
Dunne, John A., 172, 204, 205
Dupont, Jacques, 9
dwelling motif, 61

earth, vs. land, 225–26
echoes, 47
Egypt
  exodus comparison to Babylon, 130
  liberation from, 32, 37
  Rahab and, 243
Eichrodt, Walther, 22
election
  blessings with, 108
  and creation, 105n50
Elijah, 16, 32n29
Ellicott, C.J., 15
Ellis, E. Earle, 17, 22, 25, 46, 68
enemies of God, Psalm 68 on, 170–171
Engberg-Pederson, Troels, 201
enmity, death of, Christ's death and, 137
Ephesus
  Gentile vs. mixed audience for Paul, 5–6
  Jewish community in, 5
  survey of approaches to purpose, 7–16
eschatological age
  Gentile inclusion in, 134
  restoration in, 222
eschatological battle, 235
eschatological community, longevity of children, 225–28
eschatological temple, 139–40
  Lord's return to, 142
  relationship of Christian Jews and Gentiles in, 145
eschatology
  in Ephesians, 75
  Isaiah and, 249
  Pauline, 79–85
  realized, 103, 131, 180
  vs. unrealized, 264
Essene influence, 14
ethical admonitions, in Ephesians 4:25—25:20, 191–208
ethical living, 127n12
  Ephesians on, 51
  new age and, 182–83
Evans, C. A., 46

Subject and Names Index

evil, in present, 86
exodus event, 22, 69. *See also* new exodus
   formative influence of, 27–70
   as lesson to Hebrews, 31
   reflection throughout OT, 39
exodus motif, 33
   in Ezekiel, 222
   in OT historical figures, 23
exodus typology, 23, 68
   in Second Isaiah, 36
Ezekiel the Dramatist, 45
Ezekiel the Tragedian, *Exagoge* of, 45

factionalism, in the Corinthian Church, 50
false teachers, warning of, 56
Farrer, Austin Marsden, 24
fear, in new exodus, 150n31
Fee, Gordon D., 56, 179
feet, prepared, 236, 243–45
"first and last Adam," 59
first fruits, 86
firstborn, 59, 86
Fischer, Karl Martin, 10
Fishbane, Michael A., 22, 30, 133, 198, 199, 237
fleeing, vs. departing, 244
food, forbidden, 64
Ford, David, 52
forgiveness
   new covenant of, 38
   Pauline understanding of, 129
Forman, Mark, 48
Foulkes, Francis, 22, 24, 232
France, R. T., 22
freedom, hope of, 249
fruit-unfruitful imagery, 201n115
"fruitful and multiply" motif, 58
fullness of God motif, 158, 165
future age, 87–88

Gamaliel, 16
Gamer, David, 108
Gärtner, Bertil E., 41, 142
gathering theme, in Second Temple writings, 60
Gaventa, Beverly Roberts, 18

Gentile Christians
   privilege of, 134
   unity with Jewish Christians, 10–11
Gentile God-fearers, understanding of OT, 6
Gentiles
   demonstrating uniqueness of Yahweh to, 153
   as fellow-heirs, 162
   and Holy Spirit, 117–18
   inclusion of, 115, 117, 148–49
   inculcation of, 133–38
   proclamation of Christ to, 80
   unification with Jews, 126
Gideon, 32n29, 152
gifts
   diversity of, 166
   in Ephesians 4, 176
   Psalm 68 on, 170
Gladd, Benjamin L., 114
Gnilka, Joachim, 21, 135, 193, 233
Gnosticism, 13
God. *See also* Holy Spirit; Yahweh
   ability to answer prayer, 160
   election and care for Israel, 49
   everlasting new sanctuary, 126
   faithfulness of, 106
   faithfulness to Israel, 218
   intimacy with, 62
   light of truth, 203
   moral image of, 192
   power of, 165
   provocation of jealousy in wilderness, 197
   redemptive work, OT transition to NT, 18
   response to, 130–131
   as sovereign head of creation, 155
   sovereign plan of, 117
   superior wisdom of, 149
   supremacy of, 159
Goliath, 152
Gombis, Timothy G., 15, 96–97, 101n33, 111n74, 127, 142, 149, 150n27, 152, 184n32, 202, 208n152, 226, 229
Goodspeed, Edgar J., 2, 13, 182

Goppelt, Leonhard, 22–23, 24
gospel message, 248
"gospel of your salvation," 117
Grabbe, Lester L., 42, 43
grace, 166
    triumph of, 85
Greco-Roman moral traditions, 182
grieving the Holy Spirit, 197–200, 254
    caution against, 199n113
Gunkel, Robert Horton, 172–73

Hagar, bondage of children, 54
Hagar-Ishmael narratives, 30
hailstones, 41
Hannah, Darrell D., on use of Isaiah, 44
Hanson, Paul D., 63
Harnack, Adolf von, 56
Harris, W. Hall, *The Descent of Christ*, 75
Hatina, Thoms R., 67–68
Haustafel, 211
Hays, Richard B., 7, 17–18, 22, 46, 48, 49
heart, hardness and callousness of, 184n31
Heaven, 97
heavenly places, 120–22
heavens, power of evil at work against God, 121
Hebrew Scriptures, Pauline literature and, 250
Hebrews, Yahweh's emancipation of, 129
Hellenism, influence on Paul, 17
helmet of salvation, 236, 245–47
Hendrikson, William, 205
Herbian, J., 56
Hickling, C., 46
Hierapolis, 4
Hill, Linzy H., 174n45
historical exodus, Psalm 68 images, 167
historical typology, 23–25
Hodge, Charles, 186n40, 205, 226
Hoehner, Harold W., 2, 3n22, 95n1, 112n78, 125n2, 127n14, 132, 132n35, 161, 181, 190, 207, 210n1, 226, 232, 235
holiness, 164, 185
    Paul's call to, 62
Holland, Tom, 42, 48
Holy Spirit, 97, 123
    blasphemy of, 198n105
    and Gentiles, 117–18
    grieving, 197–200, 254
    caution against, 199n113
    and holiness, 62
    indwelling of, 142
    and inheritance, in Ephesians, 116–19
    "marked with the seal" of, 117
    promise of, 117
    renewal of, 64
    role in access to heavenly reality, 97
    role in actualizing the new humanity, 208n152
    work of, Ephesians on, 198
honor, 188
hope, 103n41
    of freedom, 249
Horbury, William, 63
horoscopes, 101
household, 139n65
household codes, 210–230
    in Colossians, 120n106
Household of God, 64
Houwelingen, P. H. R. van, 60
Hubbard, Moyer V., 128, 187, 188
Huie-Jolly, Mary R., 98
human wisdom, vs. wisdom of God, 50
humility, 165
Hummel, Horace, 24
husband
    marriage instructions to, 211–12
    Yahweh as, 217
Hymenaeus, 64

ignorance, of pre-Christian era, 147
imagery in Ephesians, 236
imperatives, vs. infinitives, 190n63
inclusio, 127n12, 232
INE (Isaianic New Exodus)

cohesion between sections, 179–82
 in Ephesians, 94, 258
 Ephesians prominence, 264
 illusions in Pastoral epistles, 66
 influence of, 68–70, 78
 marriage as metaphor, 211–24
 as motif in NT, 67
 Paschal redemption, 110–112
 passages of triumph, 78–79
 Paul's understanding of, 62
 pervasiveness in NT, 67–68
 preliminary summary of Ephesians passages, 76–77
 present triumphal redemption, in Eph 2:1–10, 127–33
 in Romans vs. 1 Corinthians, 51
 works recognizing in Ephesians, 73–75
INE triumph, 104–10
 arrival of, 199
 in mystery, wisdom, and insight in Ephesians 1:8, 17, 112–16
 in new creation, 185–91
 of present or future, 89
 present vs. past, 131–32
inferred typology, vs. innate, 25
infinitives, vs. imperatives, 190n63
inheritance, 123
innate typology, vs. inferred, 25
inner man, 156
innocent, actions taken toward, 241
insight, INE triumph in, 112–16
intimacy with God, 62
Isaac, church as, 217
Isaiah in the New Testament (Moyise and Menken), 1
Isaianic motifs, 68
Isbell, Charles D., 23, 32n29
Israel
 as antitype of Christ, 49
 eschatological restoration of, 55
 God's faithfulness to, 218
 love of Yahweh for, 221
 as servant, 240
 as witness to nations, 80
 Yahweh's choice of, 76
 Yahweh's punishment of, 245

Jahweh, 31. *See also* Yahweh
Janzen, J. Gerald, 40
Jeal, Roy R., 154n48, 178
Jeremiah, 37
Jeremias, Joachim, 140n74
Jesus. *See also* Christ
 as messiah-king, 82
 as "new Moses," 40
 truth of, 184
 view of Daniel as prophet, 154
 as Yahweh-Warrior of Isaiah, 40
Jewish literature, in Second Temple period, 29
Jewish proselytism, 136
Jewish scriptures, continuity with Christian gospel, 211
Jewish synagogues, openness to Gentiles, 6
Jews, unification with Gentiles, 10–11, 126
Johnstone, William, 33n37
Jordan, crossing, 33
Josephus, 5, 42, 114n84, 233
 allusions to the new exodus, 43–44
Joshua, 32–33, 32n29
joy, 188
Jubilees, exodus event, 44
Judah, 167
 Yahweh's punishment of, 245
judgment, 76, 143, 200
 of God, 127n14
justice, crookedness in, 241

Käsemann, Ernst, 8, 15, 46, 133
Keesmaat, Sylvia C., 46, 57n196, 129, 130, 152, 217, 220
Kidner, Derek, 166
Kim, Jinkyu, 98
Kim, S., 18–19
Kirby, John C., 12
Kitchen, Martin, 95n1, 116, 145n3, 194, 215, 232, 247
Klausner, Joseph, 69
Knight, George, 4, 64, 215
knowledge, 266
Knox, Wilfred Lawrence, 13
Koch, Dietrich-Alex, 47
Köstenberger, Andreas J., 7n57

Subject and Names Index

Kraus, Hans-Joachim, 99, 171
Kreitzer, L. Joseph, 12, 127n14, 142, 167, 238n44, 241n51
Kuhn, Karl G., 14, 21, 72, 235

Lampe, G.W.H., 22
land, vs. earth, 225–26
Laodicea, 4, 10
Larkin, William J., 185n34, 186n40
law
    participation in, 138n64
    warning against excesses, 169–70
law and spirit, continuity and discontinuity of, 54
leadership, vacuum after Paul's departure, 13
Levites, 177n61
liberation from slavery, exodus story and, 129
light, 164
light-darkness metaphor, 200–208
light of Christ, 203
Lincoln, Andrew T., 2, 13, 15, 72–73, 97, 100, 100n26, 103, 112n78, 120n106, 134n49, 140n74, 147, 160, 168, 169, 179, 180, 181n18, 190, 192n74, 193, 208n152, 215, 218, 225, 226, 232, 233, 235, 247
Lind, Millard, 81n9
Lindemann, Andreas, 2, 8, 13, 14, 72, 102, 233
Lindeskog, Gösta, 105n50
linearity, 263–64
    in Ephesians, 87–90
    in Isaiah, 92–94
Litwak, Kenneth D., 67, 68
Lock, Walter, 141, 147
long life, promise of, 225
Longenecker, Bruce W., 22, 54–55
Longman, Tremper, 15, 81n8
lordship, 142
Lorek, Piotr, 34n41
love, 164, 176, 223
    prayer request for, 154–60
    of Yahweh for Israel, 221
Lund, Øystein, 67, 68
Lunde, Jonathan M., 172, 204, 205
Luz, U., 12

Lyons, George, 18

magic, 9, 101
majesty, 188
Mánek, Jindrich, 41
manna, 23
marriage, 230
    new foundation for, 214
    Paul's typological use of, 217
    prophets' anticipation of restoration of divine, 220
    of Yahweh and Israel, 221
marriage covenant, 262
marriage metaphor, 211–24, 259
    in Isaiah, Ezekiel, and Leviticus, 220–224
Marshall, Molly Truman, 136
Martin, Ralph P., 11, 126
Masoretic Text (MT), 20
Maurer, Christian, 72
McKelvey, R.J., 142
McWhirter, Jocelyn, 216
Melchizedek, 97n10, 98
Melchizedekan Priest, 100n31, 122
Menken, Maarten J.J., *Isaiah in the New Testament*, 1
Merklein, H., 88
Messiah, 44. *See also* Christ
messiah-king, Jesus as, 82
Metzger, Bruce Manning, 98
Meyer, Heinrich, 9
Michel, Otto, 46, 47
Miletus, 14
Miller, Patrick D., 171
Miriam, 167
Mitton, C, Leslie, 13, 232
modesty, 165
moral image of God, 192
Moritz, Thorsten, 4–5, 21, 98, 99, 99n18, 100, 102n40, 126, 127, 128, 130, 135, 146–47, 155n53, 173n44, 192n74, 196, 201, 205, 206, 207, 208n152, 212–13, 216, 225n74, 233, 235
    A Profound Mystery: The Use of the Old Testament in Ephesians, 74
Moses, 23, 30, 44, 69, 153, 169
    as antitype of Christ, 49

ascension at Sinai, 168
God's people under, 64
messianic typology in, 32
rebellion against, 64
use as type, 24–25
Motyer, J.A., 237, 243n64, 244
Moule, H.G.C., 190, 232
Moyise, Steve, *Isaiah in the New Testament*, 1
MT (Masoretic Text), 20
Muddiman, John, 8n59, 10, 178
Muilenburg, James, 36
Muller, Earl C., 52n174
multiracial Christian community, 137
Mussner, Franz, 14, 72
mystery, 80
    INE triumph in, 112–16
mystery-information, 214
"mystery of his will," 114
mysticism, 101
    ascetical, Ephesians and, 14

"name" of Christ, 101n34
Naphtali, 167
national barriers, God breaking down, 227
nations motif, 115n88
Near East divine warfare, 15
new age, 76
new covenant, 69
    and Christ, 216
    of forgiveness, 38
new creation motif, 76, 128, 144, 186–88
    INE triumph in, 185–91
    inner transformation and, 188
    Jewish apocalyptic matrix and, 187
    survey of theology in OT, 188
new exodus, 27–30, 38, 43, 93, 105–6, 115, 116, 117, 137, 150, 168. *See also* INE (Isaianic New Exodus)
    Ephesians and, 77, 205–6, 236
    Ezekiel and, 37
    fear in, 150n31
    in Galatians marriage texts, 220
    in Hebrews, 41
    impact on Paul's thinking, 70
    as inspiration for Ephesians 1, 123
    in Isaiah, 92n56, 198, 241
    Isaiah's prediction of eschatological, 250
    Isaiah's promise of, 109
    Isaiah's views on, 93
    in John, 41
    marriage motif and, 221
    narrative in NT, 40–42
    in New Testament, 266
    in OT, 30–42
    prisoner release in, 247
    in Second Isaiah, 36
    triumphant warrior king and, 173
    Wright and Holland focus on, 48
    in Zechariah, 193, 195
"new exodus era," 90
New Testament (NT). *See also scripture index*
    antitype in, 23
    copyists' competing options, 21
    new exodus narrative in, 40–42
    references to Psalm 110, 39n74
Nicholl, Colin R., 62
Ninow, Friedbert, 23, 38, 105–6, 137, 195, 195n88, 236, 237, 247
Nixon, Robin Ernest, 30
Noh, Jae Young, 52n174
non-Christians, 202
nonvisionary prophetic commissions, 19
Norden, Eduard, 8
"not yet," of Pauline triumphalism, 85–87
"Now," eschatological, 102–4

O'Brien, Peter T., 2, 10, 74, 102, 108, 111, 139, 141, 180n12, 193, 194, 195, 196n90, 199, 199n111, 202, 203, 205, 214–15, 217, 222, 225n74, 228, 229, 235, 246
oikonomia, 211, 226
Old Testament (OT). *See also scripture index*
    in Ephesians, 1
    exodus event reflected throughout, 39
    NT authors utilization of, 7
    prophetic commissions in, 19

receptivity of concepts in Pauline letters, 6
textual transmission, 20
Ortlund, Raymond C., 216, 220
Osborne, Grant R., 25
Oswalt, John, 206
outsider, acceptance by Jewish community, 136

panoply metaphor, 17, 231–51, 254, 257
Pao, David W., 58
parallelomania, 4n 28
parents, in INE society, 224–30
Parousia, 48, 50, 61
  future, 102
  futuristic peace in, 242
paschal emancipation, 127
paschal redemption, 123, 144, 243, 255, 259
  through servant-messiah, 138
paschal sacrifice, of Christ, 200
Passover observances, 31, 68
  Christ's death and, 111
  imagery in John, 41
Pastoral epistles, 63. See also scripture index
Pate, C. Marvin, 49, 55
Paul
  apocalyptic substratum of gospel, 179–80
  apostolic ministry of, 19
  audience knowledge of ministry, 150
  authorship of Ephesians, 2–4, 25, 72
  biographical information, 151
  Ephesians' awareness of suffering, 145
  influence after death, 13
  paradox of imprisonment and triumph, 152
  qualifications and circumstances, 146
  self-perception in tradition of prophets, 19
Pauline epistles
  central doctrines, 84
  disputed and undisputed, 2
Pauline thought
  influence of Isaiah's new exodus on, 45–67
  OT as foundation, 16–20
Pauline triumphalism
  "already" nature of, 85
  "not yet" of, 85–87
Paul's eschatology, 60
  spatial and horizontal (chronological) features, 90–91
peace, 128, 138, 245, 259
  present application of, 136
  proclamation of, 136
Penner, Erwin, 131, 170
Pentateuch, 250
  Exodus as theological center, 30–31
  exodus typology in, 23
Pentecost, influence of, 168
Percy, Ernst, 2
Perkins, Pheme, 14, 72
Persia. See also Babylonia-Persia
Pharisees, 213n14
Philetus, 64
Philistines, 33
Philo, 114n84
Piper, John, 48
"pledge of our inheritance," 118
Pokorný, Petr, 8
Polybius, 233
power
  of God, 165
  prayer request for, 154–60
power motif, 11–12
praise, 188
prayer
  for the audience, 123
  of Daniel, 153
  in Ephesians, 158, 183, 232
  God's ability to answer, 160
  for power, 158
  for power and love, 146, 154–60
  power language of, 98n12
  for present realization, 119–20
  Sirach 36:10, 43
  for understanding, 95
  for vigilance, 236n29

Subject and Names Index 331

premonarchy, 33
present triumph
   of ascended Christ, 165-75
   emphasizing, 232
   in Ephesians, 95-104
   and ethical potential, 184-85
   present, 263
priest-like garments, 243
priesthood, reinstitution of, 244
prisoners, release in new exodus, 247
proclaimed peace, Isaiah concept of, 245
"promise-fulfillment" sense, 22
promise to children, 225
promised land, 33
prophets, 250
   anticipation of new era, 38
   anticipation of restoration of divine marriage, 220
   on Day of the Lord, 85n37
   exodus theme in, 39
   postexilic, 29
proselytes, terminology, 137
prostitution, 213n14
prototype, 23
Pseudepigrapha, 42

Qedusah, 44
quadrangle conception, vertical and horizontal, 157
Qualls, Paula, 74, 147
quotations, 47

rabbinic literature
   exodus event in, 42
   references to exodus and eschatological redemption, 44
rabinnical tradition, Paul and, 17
Rad, Gerald von, 22, 31
Rahab, 243
ransom, 110
reality, 263
   Israel's understanding of, 24
realized eschatology, 103, 131, 180
reconciliation, 259
   by Christ, 83
recurring theme, and God's action in future, 22

Red Sea crossing, and Jordan crossing, 38
redeemed, 243
redemption, 112, 118, 127
   effects of, 134
   future vs. past action, 118
   glory of, 9
   non-Jews and, 133
   Pauline concept of, 111
   present realization of, 112
   and union of Jewish and Gentile believers, 138
Reid, Daniel G., 15, 81n8, 84
rescue and redemption motif, 129
resurrection, 76
return of the Lord, as Thessalonians topic, 60
Revelation, regathering of God's People, 60
rhetorical perspective, on Ephesians, 182
Ridderbos, Herman N., 9, 46, 69, 75, 80, 85, 123, 158n70, 198n104
righteous anger, 196n90
righteous living, church practice of, 204
righteousness, 185, 188
   absence of, 241
   on behalf of oppressed, 241
   forces of, 239
   transformative power of, 188
rising sun imagery, 207n145
Robinson, J. Armitage, 10
Rochberg-Halton, Francesca, 101
Roman soldiers, 233
Roon, A., 75
root of David, 237
root of Jesse, 248

Sahlin, Harald, 41, 46
saints, choosing of, 109-10
salvation, 188
   through Christ, 63
   vs. ongoing expectations of inner renewal, 190
   present aspect of, 246
   triumphal effects of, 125

Sampley, J. Paul, 72, 189n56, 191, 193, 223
Samuel, 32n29
sanctification, 222
Sanders, James A., 46
Sarah, 54
Schille, Gottfried, 12
Schlier, Heinrich, 8, 133, 233
Schmid, J., *Der Epheserbrief des Apostels Paulus*, 72
Schmithals, Walter, 8, 10
Schnackenburg, Rudolf, 3, 96, 147, 181n16, 186n37, 202
Schneider, Gerhard, 114
Schrenk, Gottlob, 108
Schürer, Emil, 5
Scott, Ernest Findlay, 10
Scott, James M., 49, 53, 54
second exodus, 130
Second Temple Judaism, 139
  ethical discourse in, 192
Second Temple period writings, 29, 42–45, 233
  on choosing of Israel, 107n58
  reversal of Diaspora, 60
second time motif, 237–38
Seifrid, Mark A., 48
self-love, 223
servant, 59
  Isaiah on, 248
  Israel as, 240
servant-messiah, Pascal redemption through, 138
servant motif, in Isaiah, 153
servant songs, 44
servant-warrior, 241
shield of faith, 236n30
Shkul, Minna, 15
shoot of David, 237
Silva, Moisés, 21, 22, 47, 56
Similitudes of Enoch, 44
sin, anger without, 195–97
Sinai, 61
  Yahweh's revelation at, 30
Sisera, Deborah and Barak's victory over, 166–67
slavery
  in Christian community, 229
  helpless condition in, 130–131
  in INE society, 224–30
  liberation from, 129
  release from, 111
  in renewed society, 228–29
Smith, Contra G., 167
Smith, Derwood C., 10
Smolarz, Sebastian, 218, 220, 222, 223n67
Smyrna, 6
Snaith, Norman H., 36
Solomon, 34
Son of Man, 37
  eschatological mystery-truth of, 114
  garments of, 41
song of trust, 128, 143
sons of disobedience, 127n14
spatiality, 263–64
  in Ephesians, 87–90
  in Isaiah, 92–94
speaking truth, 192–95
speech, boldness of, 249–50
spirit of confusion, 64
spirit of God, 248. *See also* Holy Spirit
spiritual exile, 29
spiritual powers, fight against, 232
spiritual reversal, 144
spiritual strength, 266
spiritual temple, 138–43
  multiracial composition, 175
spoils of war, 170
Stanley, Christopher D., 6, 7, 46
Steck, Odil Hannes, 29
Stendahl, Krister, 104n44
stonework, ancient, 140n75
The Story of Israel; a Biblical Theology, 75
Stott, John R.W., on RSV version, 190n63
Strack, Herman Leberecht, 42
strength, 188
Stuhlmacher, P., 135
stump of Jesse, 113, 115, 120
substitutionary atonement, 66
"suffering servant," 17n132
Suh, Robert H., 75, 126, 142, 144
supremacy of God, 159

sword of the Spirit, 236, 247–49

tabernacle, 139–40
Tachau, Peter, 88, 89n50
Tannaim, 45
targumic writings, 21, 42
"taught by God," 62
Teacher of Righteousness, 114n84
temple, 139–40, 254–55
　construction, exodus theme and, 34
　establishment in Zion, 171
　rebuilding, 194
　spiritual, 138–43
temple cult, Paul's indictment of, 61
temple eschatology, 142
tender-hearted living, 200
Terrien, Samuel L., 166
Testament of Zebulun, 129
Thielman, Frank, 1, 11, 75, 111, 135, 147, 148, 170, 192, 193, 225, 226–27, 232, 235, 236n28
"third exodus," 29
Third Sibylline Oracle, 44
time, God's consummation of, 80
Timothy, 13, 14
Torah, 207n147, 211, 223n68
　Christ as replacement, 134
Towner, Philip H., 63, 64
transformation, 203, 207
Trebilco, Paul R., 5, 6n47
triumph, 144, 161–63
　"already" nature, 232
　apocalyptic view of, 84
　of Christ, 15–16, 174, 210
　in Ephesians, 87–90
　INE passages of, 78–79
　Paul's view of, 79
　present, 263
　of ascended Christ, 165–75
　emphasizing, 232
　in Ephesians, 95–104
　and ethical potential, 184–85
　realized, 216–20
triumphant warrior imagery, 81
trumpet blast, 60
truth
　of Jesus, 184
　speaking, 192–95
truth and righteousness, 194
truthfulness-faithfulness, 239
Turpie, David McCalman, 47
typological-historical hermeneutic, 22–25
typological-historical interpretation of new exodus, 26n179
typology
　in biblical studies, 22
　innate vs. inferred, 25

unbeliever, in Ephesians 5:13–14, 202
unity, 10, 164, 165
　of Ephesians ethical section, 181
　of Isaiah, 17n132
　of Jewish and Gentile believers, 138
Ur, Abraham departure from, 30
Usami, K., 136

validation, in Paul's word choices, 19
vengeance, of Yahweh, 242
victory shout, 142
victory theme, 2
virtuous living, 186
visionary prophetic commissions, 19
Vos, Geerhardus, 29, 90n55, 103n41, 132, 156

Wagner, J. Ross, 54
　Heralds of the Good News, 48
Walsh, Brian J., 57n196
war
　physical vs. spiritual, 233
　spoils of, 170
warfare metaphor, 231–32, 234n12
warning psalms, 38
warrior king
　new exodus and, 173
　Yahweh's ascension as, 194
Watts, John D. W., 38, 59, 74, 236, 237, 245n71
Watts, Rikki E., 40, 67, 92n56, 147
Webb, William J., 52, 238n43
wickedness, punishment of, 245
Wild, R.A., 235, 249
wilderness generation, 41

wilderness journey, 92
Wilk, Florian, 47, 68
winds of doctrine, 157
wisdom, 164
   of God, vs. human wisdom, 50
   INE triumph in, 112–16
wisdom and insight, 112n78, 115
"wisdom and understanding," 119
wisdom literature, 192, 233
wives, marriage instructions to, 211–12
Wood, A. Skevington, 10, 146n5
Woollcombe, K.J., 22
"word of truth," 117
Wright, N. T., 42, 46, 48, 59, 90n55, 102n38, 110, 117, 135

Yahweh, 92, 196
   as Abraham's shield, 81
   ascension as Warrior King, 194
   close encounter with, 19
   compassion of, 130
   conflict with the enemies of, 93
   covenant with Abraham, 133
   demonstrating uniqueness to Gentiles, 153
   eternal kingdom, 245
   as exodus warrior, 172
   future cosmological victory of, 81–82
   as husband, 217
   judgment in exile, 244
   love for Israel, 221
   marriage with Israel, 221
   peace announcement, 138
   people of God with, 61
   punishment of Israel and Judah, 245
   restoration of Israel's fortunes, 193
   revelation at Sinai, 30
   sword of, 122
   vengeance of, 242
   as Warrior, 240, 241
Yahweh-Warrior of Isaiah, Jesus as, 40
Yee, Tet-Lim, 133n42
   Jews, Gentiles, and Ethnic Reconciliation, 75
Yoder, John Howard, 134
Yoder-Neufeld, Thomas R., 193, 194
   Put on the Armor of God, 75
Young, Edward J., 52

Zebulun, 167
Zechariah, 98
Zimmerli, Walther, 19, 126
Zion, 171
zodiacs, 101

www.ingramcontent.com/pod-product-compliance
Lightning Source LLC
Chambersburg PA
CBHW061845300426
44115CB00013B/2519